When Watchers Ruled the Nations

Pagan Gods at War with Israel's God and the Spiritual World of the Bible

By Brian Godawa

When Watchers Ruled the Nations: Pagan Gods at War With Israel's God and the Spiritual World of the Bible
1st Edition

Warrior Poet Publishing
www.warriorpoetpublishing.com

ISBN: 9798710862506 (hardcover)
SBN: 978-1-942858-82-9 (Paperback)
ISBN: 978-1-942858-81-2 (Ebook)

Scripture quotations taken from *The Holy Bible: English Standard Version.* Wheaton: Standard Bible Society, 2001.

This book is dedicated to Robert Cruickshank, Jr.

Fellow research nerd.

We don't agree on everything.

But what we do agree on is pretty cool.

Table of Contents

The Spiritual World of Jezebel and Elijah

The Spiritual World of Ancient China and the Bible

Introduction

This is the sequel to my best-selling book, *When Giants Were Upon the Earth*. In that book, I combined the appendices of the 8-novel series Chronicles of the Nephilim for those who wanted all the biblical research in one volume for study. It was such a hit, that I decided to do the same for my series Chronicles of the Watchers. The problem is that the appendices of the first three Watchers books grew to be so large that I had to separate them each into companion books. What you are reading here are those first three research books of the Watchers series, plus my important book, *Psalm 82*, that explains the concept of the Watchers and their biblical operations in more detail. *Psalm 82* is an introduction for the entire Watchers series.

I beg forgiveness from the reader for the few paragraphs or sections repeated in some of the books in this box set. This was because each book had its own specific context but sometimes those contexts overlapped and required the same material to be explained. If I were to delete redundant passages in this box set from one of the books to eliminate the repetition, then the flow of thought in that book would be interrupted and incomplete.

So I left them in with the hope that the reader will find them helpful as review with new application for new sections.

Some sections that are repeated are: "Host of Heaven," and "Shining Ones and Stars" in *Psalm 82* and *The Spiritual World of Moses and Egypt*. Also, the section on the "Watchers" as a summary in each of the *Spiritual World* books tailored to each novel separately. Lastly, sections on Leviathan in each of the books. But be careful, I add some new information on Leviathan in *The Spiritual World of Moses and Egypt* that is not in the other books.

That's what you get for buying a box set! :-) :-)

Brian Godawa
Author, Chronicles of the Watchers
Chronicles of the Nephilim
Chronicles of the Apocalypse

Psalm 82

The Divine Council of the Gods, the Judgment of the Watchers & the Inheritance of the Nations

By Brian Godawa

Psalm 82: The Divine Council of the Gods, The Judgment of the Watchers and the Inheritance of the Nations
5th Expanded Edition

Warrior Poet Publishing
www.warriorpoetpublishing.com

ISBN: 978-1-942858-40-9 (paperback)
ISBN: 978-1-942858-41-6 (ebook)

Scripture quotations taken from The Holy Bible: English Standard Version. Wheaton: Standard Bible Society, 2001, except where noted as the NASB:
New American Standard Bible: 1995 Update. (LaHabra, CA: The Lockman Foundation, 1995).

Get the First Novel of the Bestselling Biblical Fiction Series Chronicles of the Nephilim!

For a Limited Time Only in eBook

FREE

This is Not Your Sunday School Noah's Ark.

The first novel in the series Chronicles of the Nephilim is *Noah Primeval*. It tells of the events that lead to the Great Flood, with Noah at the very center of the storyline of God's chosen Seed. See how the Nephilim, the Sons of God and the Watchers fit into the War of the Seed. Faithful to the Scriptures. Open to Biblical imagination. Get it in eBook FREE!

Click this link to get your free book:

https://godawa.com/free-noah-book/

Chapter 1: The Divine Council of the Gods

One of the most intriguing storylines of the Bible is that of Christ's victory over the powers. When I discovered it, it changed my life. It inspired me to write a series of 14+ biblical novels—*Chronicles of the Nephilim*, *Chronicles of the Apocalypse* and *Chronicles of the Watchers*—that incarnate that story unlike anything done before.

A Definition

But what exactly is this messianic cosmic battle between Christ and the powers? And how does it affect us? It is sometimes called Christus Victor, and consists of the idea that mankind's Fall in the Garden resulted in a sinfulness of humanity that was so entrenched against God it led to universal idolatry as embodied in the tower of Babel story (Gen 11). As a result of man's incorrigible evil, God placed all of the nations and their lands under the authority of other spiritual powers, but kept one people and their land for his own: Israel. Those Gentile nations and their gods would be at war with the promised messianic seed of Israel. But in the fullness of time, Messiah would arrive, overcome those spiritual powers of the nations, and take back rule of the earth in the kingdom of God.

Gods or Men?

Psalm 82 is a doorway into the Christus Victor narrative because it summarizes the three-act structure of that messianic story of allotment, judgment and inheritance. Here is the full text of the Psalm in all its simple and concise glory:

> Psalm 82:1–8
> God has taken his place in the divine council;
>   in the midst of the gods he holds judgment:
> "How long will you judge unjustly
>   and show partiality to the wicked? *Selah*
> Give justice to the weak and the fatherless;
>   maintain the right of the afflicted and the destitute.

Rescue the weak and the needy;
    deliver them from the hand of the wicked."
They have neither knowledge nor understanding,
    they walk about in darkness;
    all the foundations of the earth are shaken.
I said, "You are gods,
    sons of the Most High, all of you;
nevertheless, like men you shall die,
    and fall like any prince."
Arise, O God, judge the earth;
    for you shall inherit all the nations!

Much scholarly debate has occurred over the identity of these "gods" of the divine council. Are they human judges who merely represent divine justice, or are they actual divine beings?

I am convinced that they are Yahweh's heavenly host of divine beings surrounding his throne, referred to by the technical term "Sons of God" or "Sons of the Most High". Here's why…

Gods, Not Men

First off, the Psalm itself uses the Hebrew word *elohim,* which is accurately translated as "gods." As much as Christians have been conditioned to believe the Bible claims no other gods exist but Yahweh, this simply is not biblical. But don't panic. Hear me out.

The most common Hebrew word translated in English as "God" or "gods" in the Bible is *elohim*. But God has many names in the text and each of them is used to describe different aspects of his person. *El*, often refers to God's powerful preeminence; *El Elyon* (God Most High) indicates God as possessor of heaven and earth; *Adonai* means God as lord or master; and *Yahweh* is the covenantal name for the God of Israel as distinguished from any other deity.

Elohim in Hebrew is a plural word. It is used of both the singular being of the One God, as well as of a plurality of other beings who are not the singular One God. That is where some confusion comes into interpretation. Our modern Western English language does not translate the ancient Hebrew conceptual world very well at all. Here is a good example: In the biblical Hebrew, angels are sometimes called *elohim* (Psa 8:5; Heb 2:7), gods or idols of pagan nations are sometimes called *elohim* (Psa 138:1), supernatural beings of the divine council are sometimes called *elohim* (Psa 82:6), departed spirits of humans are sometimes called *elohim* (1Sam 28:13), and demons are sometimes called *elohim* (Deut 32:17).[1] So what gives? How can all these different entities be called by the same word—and a word that is also used of the One God?

Scholar Michael S. Heiser has pointed out that the Hebrew word *Elohim* was more of a reference to a plane of existence than to a substance of being. In this way, Yahweh was *Elohim*, but no other *elohim* was Yahweh. Yahweh is incomparably THE *Elohim* of *elohim* (Deut. 10:17).[2] We must stop imposing our categories of modern concepts onto the Bible, and try to interpret the text within the ancient Hebrew paradigm.

A common misunderstanding of Christians is that when the Bible refers to other gods it does not mean that the gods are real beings but merely *beliefs* in real beings that do not exist. For instance, when Deuteronomy 32:43 proclaims "rejoice with him, O heavens, bow down to him, all gods," this is a poetic way of saying "what you believe are gods are not gods at all because Yahweh is the only God that exists." What seems to support this interpretation is the fact that a few verses before this (v. 39), God says, "See now, that I, even I am he, and there is no god [*elohim*] beside me."

Does this not clearly indicate that God is the only God [*elohim*] that really exists out of all the non-existent "gods" [*elohim*] that others believe in?

Not in its biblical context it doesn't.

When the text is examined in its full context of the chapter and rest of the Bible we discover a very different notion about God and gods. The phrase "I am, and there is none beside me" was an ancient Biblical slogan of incomparability of sovereignty, not exclusivity of existence. It was a way of saying that a certain authority was the most powerful *compared to* all other authorities. It did not mean that there were no other authorities that existed.

We see this sloganeering in two distinct passages, one of the ruling power of Babylon claiming proudly in her heart, "I am, and there is no one beside me" (Isa. 47:8) and the other of the city of Nineveh boasting in her heart, "I am, and there is no one else" (Zeph. 2:15). The powers of Babylon and Nineveh are obviously not saying that there are no other powers or cities that exist other than them, because they had to conquer other cities and rule over them. "No other beside me" meant "no other equal in power or authority." God is seated on his throne of authority and power and there is no one standing beside him on that throne, having equal status. All others are "below" him. In the same way, Yahweh uses that colloquial phrase, not to deny the existence of other gods, but to express his incomparable sovereignty over them.[3]

---

[1] Geoffrey W. Bromiley, "God, Names of," *The International Standard Bible Encyclopedia, Revised.* Wm. B. Eerdmans, 1988; 2002, p. 504-508.

[2] Michael S. Heiser, *The Myth That is True: Rediscovering the Cosmic Narrative of the Bible*, unpublished manuscript, 2011, p 25-29. Available online at www.michaelsheiser.com. I have read quite a few scholars on the divine council, but Michael Heiser has been the most helpful and represents the major influence on this essay.

[3] Michael S. Heiser, "Monotheism, Polytheism, Monolatry, or Henotheism? Toward an Assessment of Divine Plurality in the Hebrew Bible" (2008). Faculty Publications and Presentations. Paper 277, p. 12-15,

The Hebrew word for "gods," *elohim*, is plural but it is not polytheistic. Sometimes, it is a reference to created yet divine beings that we generically refer to as "angels." They are also biblically referred to as "holy ones" (Deut 33:2-3; Heb 2:2), "host of heaven" (1 King 22:19-23), or "Sons of God" (Job 1:6; 38:7). These Sons of God or host of heaven are called elohim, or "gods" in Psalm 82 and elsewhere in the Bible.

Psalm 89 clarifies this "assembly of gods" as being divine, not human, because it is in the heavens, not on earth.

> Psalm 89:5-7
> Let the heavens praise your wonders, O Yahweh,
> your faithfulness in the assembly of the holy ones!
> For who in the skies can be compared to Yahweh?
> Who among the gods is like Yahweh,
> a God greatly to be feared in the council of the holy ones,
> and awesome above all who are around him?

In this text, we see that there is an assembly of gods/holy ones who surround Yahweh in the heavens. These are clearly not humans on earth. And humans are not assembled in the skies. The text explicitly calls the assembly of Yahweh's holy ones "gods." But it uses the hypothetical question of incomparability with Yahweh, "who among the gods is like Yahweh?" The implied answer is none of them.

But they are still called gods (*elohim*), not "as gods," not "like gods," but gods. Here are several other passages that reiterate this idea of gods as real spiritual divine beings.

> Psalm 29:1
> Ascribe to the LORD, O gods, ascribe to the LORD glory and strength.

> Psalm 58:1-2
> Do you indeed decree what is right, you gods? Do you judge the children of man uprightly? No, in your hearts you devise wrongs; your hands deal out violence on earth.

> Deuteronomy 32:43
> "Rejoice with him, O heavens; bow down to him, all gods..."

Some may argue that these are verses that merely speak metaphorically of pagan gods bowing down to Yahweh in power because they do not actually exist. But as we have seen, the "gods" that these passages are talking about, are referring to the heavenly host, not necessarily pagan deities. These are real

---

http://digitalcommons.liberty.edu/cgi/viewcontent.cgi?article=1276&context=lts_fac_pubs&sei-redir=1#search=%22heiser+Monotheism,+Polytheism,+Monolatry,+or+Henotheism%22 accessed March 23, 2011.

gods that have some actual relational interaction with Yahweh.

Notice that Psalm 58:1-2 is a restatement of the Psalm 82 notion of the gods who fail to judge the nations righteously. That is not a metaphor either, that is real relational interaction that Yahweh is claiming. He has given these gods some kind of authority over human beings. We will see exactly what kind of authority that is in the next chapter, but for now, suffice it to say these gods are described as real beings that Yahweh is interacting with.

So, there you have it. The Bible's definition of "gods," is not the same as our modern cultural religious definition of gods. The Bible itself says that there are gods, but they are not the same kind of deity as Yahweh. They are created gods. Yahweh is uncreated and the eternal creator of all other beings. This is something that makes evangelical Christians skittish, but something one must accept if one accepts the evangelical principle of Sola Scriptura. If the Bible says it, it's true, regardless of where our preconceived biases may lean. Our fears are often expressions of our own lack of knowledge.

But there are some who argue that these "gods" are actually human judges who are called "gods" symbolically because they represent God in their identities as judges using God's Law. They argue that Moses was told that he would "be as God" to both Pharaoh and Aaron because he spoke on God's behalf (Ex 7:1; 4:16).

This cannot possibly be the case. First, there is a BIG difference between being called "gods" (*elohim*) and "being as God." The first is identity; the second is analogy.

Secondly, as Psalm 82 declares, these *elohim* (gods) are in God's divine council, which elsewhere is also described explicitly as a council of spiritual beings, not human beings (Job 1, 2; 1 King 22:19-23).

Thirdly, this assembly is "in the skies," or heaven, not on earth where human judges would be.

Fourthly, their punishment of death "like any earthly prince" is made in ironic contrast to being divine (Psalm 82:6-7). That punishment would be a meaningless tautology if the "gods" were actually human. The text does not say they would die *as* men, but that they would die *like* men. This is a statement of simile, not identity; it suggests a different ontological nature between gods and men.

The basic argument for the "gods" being human judges seeks to make the term (and its equivalent, "Sons of God") a symbolic analogy rather than an essential identity. They quote a verse like the following to justify this belief:

> 2 Chronicles 19:5-6
> He appointed judges in the land in all the fortified cities of Judah, city by city, and said to the judges, "Consider what you do, for you judge not for man but for the LORD. He is with you in giving judgment."

This view claims that because the judges are given authority by God to make legal judgments, and those judgments are "for the Lord," then judges could be considered gods in that they stand in the place of God, and he endorses their judgments. In this view, "gods" is a term of analogy, not identity.

But there are significant problems with this interpretation. The biggest one is that the text never calls those judges "gods." That is imported by the bias of the one seeking to justify the claim. It is a smuggled premise that begs the question. They are, in fact, not called gods anywhere in the text; God is "with them" in their judgments, but that is not the same as being called gods. In contrast, the beings of the divine council are explicitly called gods.

Even in today's legal system, we do the same thing as described in 2 Chronicles. When we stand in a court of law presided over by a judge and pledge to tell the truth before God, we are claiming that God resides behind the judge and court in their pursuit of justice. But we are not pledging to the judge as a "god," or even as God's representative; we are pledging to the actual God who stands transcendently behind the court. Yes, the judge has God's authority to make his judgments (Rom 13:1-2), but we do not call him a god in his representation. Our pledge is to the God who is actually and truly behind the judge, not to the judge as if he were in place of God.

The significance of the term "gods" being used of the beings in the divine council is a reference to their divine identity, not their representational authority.

Another problem with this human interpretation of "gods" is projection, or what I like to call "hermeneutical imperialism." Hermeneutics is the science and art of interpreting a text; that is, interpreters do not interpret the text within the context of the original writers and readers, but rather within their own modern context, which results in projecting their own cultural bias onto the text instead of discovering the cultural bias *within* the text.

If we want to understand how the ancient Jews understood the terms they used, we should look at how they themselves interpreted the texts. If one uses only Scripture to interpret Scripture without its cultural context, then one is not actually using Scripture to interpret Scripture, but conforming Scripture to one's own cultural bias and preconceived ideas.

When we look at the ancient Jewish understanding of Psalm 82, we see the gods as divine beings, not human.

In the Dead Sea Scrolls, an ancient Jewish document labeled 11QMelchizedek reveals that they understood the gods of Psalm 82 to be satanic spirits to whom God allotted the nations.

> 11QMelchizedek 2.10-16
> As for that which he said, How long will you judge unjustly and show partiality to the wicked? Selah (Psalms 82:2), <u>its interpretation concerns Satan and the spirits of his lot who rebelled by turning away from the precepts of God</u> to…And Melchizedek will avenge the vengeance of the judgements of God…and he will drag them from the hand of Satan and from

> the hand of all the spirits of his lot. And all the 'gods of Justice' will come to his aid to attend to the destruction of Satan.[4]

Now, there were certainly a variety of theological viewpoints in Judaism, but this text does illustrate the dominant divine interpretation of that ancient context.

Here is another text from a well-known noncanonical Jewish text that interprets the Sons of God in Deuteronomy 32:8-10 as also being angels or territorial spirits spoken of in Psalm 82.

> Jubilees 15:31-32
> [There are] many nations and many people, and they all belong to him, but over all of them he caused spirits to rule so that they might lead them astray from following him. But over Israel he did not cause any angel or spirit to rule because he alone is their ruler and he will protect them.

This passage from Jubilees is actually an interpretation of Deuteronomy 32:8-10 that I will explore in the next chapter. But the point here is that the Sons of God in Deuteronomy were considered to be the same divine spirits who ruled over and judged the nations in Psalm 82. They were decidedly *not* human judges.

But there is another ancient interpreter of Psalm 82 that settles the argument over the divine identity of the gods/Sons of God. And that exegetical expert is none other than *the* Son of God.

What Would Jesus Exegete?

My personal view is that if the Bible says it, then we should say it. I am fine with using the term "divine beings" if it makes you feel more comfortable, but the bottom line is that the Sons of God who surround Yahweh's heavenly throne as his host are divine. The Bible calls them gods.

Jesus, God in the flesh, used this very Psalm to justify his claims to deity in John 10:31-39. So if Jesus's own exegesis of Psalm 82 results in ascribing divinity to the gods, then we need to agree with the author and finisher of our faith.

First, let's look at the context. Jesus says to the Jews listening to him, "I and the Father are one" (John 10:30). He did not mean "one in purpose," but rather "one in essence or identity." We know this because the Jews respond by picking up stones to stone Jesus (v. 31). They understood him as engaging in blasphemy and accused him, "because you, being a man, make yourself God" (v. 33). So Jesus answers by appealing to Psalm 82.

---

[4] Geza Vermes, *The Dead Sea Scrolls in English, Revised and extended 4th ed.* (Sheffield: Sheffield Academic Press, 1995), 361.

> John 10:34–36
> Jesus answered them, "Is it not written in your Law, 'I said, you are gods'? If he called them gods to whom the word of God came—and Scripture cannot be broken—do you say of him whom the Father consecrated and sent into the world, 'You are blaspheming,' because I said, 'I am the Son of God'?

Some say that those "gods" in Psalm 82 are simply human judges who represent God. But Jesus is clearly claiming actual deity with his term Son of God, not mere representation. He did not claim to be a representative human judge like other Israelite judges. That would have been a denial of his deity, degrading him to the level of human judges.

That would contradict the very point he was making at the start by saying "I and the Father are one" in essence or identity. He would be claiming that he is no different from human judges who represent God and that "Son of God" is a term of representation, not identity or essence. Shame on trinitarians for even considering such a contradiction.

If Jesus had intended his reference to the sons of God to represent nothing more than mere human judges, then he would have been ascribing to his own sonship no more authority or divinity than that held by human judges. He would have been denying deity, not arguing for it. His claim to be the Son of God would be stripped of its divine essence. That would be worse than nonsense; it would be blasphemous nonsense.

I think it's clear that Jesus was claiming to be divine in this passage. He was defining Sons of God as actual divine beings, not representative human judges. And his point in quoting Psalm 82 was to prove to them that his own claim to divinity was not blasphemous because they already accepted some beings other than Yahweh as having divinity. Jesus was not merely one of those divine Sons of God, he was THE uniquely begotten Son of God, God in the flesh.

Job

This heavenly assembly of gods is not an anomaly. It shows up in many places throughout the Bible that indicate a clear context of spiritual beings who engage in council with Yahweh and carry out his judgments. A heavenly legal courtroom.

Job 1:6 and 2:1 describe an apparently regular occurrence of "Sons of God" (*bene ha elohim* in Hebrew) presenting themselves before Yahweh, along with the satan as legal adversary in that heavenly court.

> Job 1:6-7, 12
> Now there was a day when the sons of God came to present themselves before the LORD, and Satan also came among

> them. The LORD said to Satan, "From where have you come?" Satan answered the LORD and said, "From going to and fro on the earth, and from walking up and down on it"... And the LORD said to the satan, "Behold, all that [Job] has is in your hand. Only against him do not stretch out your hand." So the satan went out from the presence of the LORD.

The satan operates as a spiritual prosecutor in God's heavenly court seeking indictment of righteous Job by accusing him of self-interest in serving God. God then allows him to carry out a task in order to test Job. But it is important to note that this is not an earthly court with humans, but a heavenly court in God's presence.

These sons of God are not human judges, but God's heavenly host. And this is confirmed later in Job, lest there be any doubt. God chastises Job from the whirlwind and he asks him, "Where were you when I laid the foundation of the earth?... when the morning stars sang together and all the sons of God shouted for joy?" (Job 38:4–7).

Yahweh himself states that the Sons of God were present at the creation of the heavens and earth, shouting for joy (Job 38:7) long *before* human judges were created.

These Sons of God also show up in Psalm 82 as "Sons of the Most High."

> Psalm 82:6
> I said, "You are gods,
> sons of the Most High, all of you;

"Sons of the Most High" is a synonym for "Sons of God." "Most High" in Hebrew is *El Elyon*, another name of Yahweh. God has many names: Elohim, Yahweh, El Elyon, El Shaddai and so forth. So the gods around him have several names: gods, heavenly host, holy ones, Sons of God and Sons of the Most High. Sons of the Most High in Psalm 82 is interchangeable with Sons of God.

Sons of God/Most High is not a mere metaphor, as in "we are all children of God," but rather it is a technical term used only of this special class of being. Though some argue that Israel is called the son of God, this is simply not true. The passage they quote says, "When Israel was a child, I loved him, and out of Egypt I called my son" (Hos 11:1). Yes, in this case "son" is used of Israel as a metaphor, but it is not the term "son of God" or "sons of God". That is a very important distinction, because when Jesus claimed to be the Son of God, the Jews were offended by this as a claim of deity (John 10:36). This would not be the case if "Son(s) of God" were a mere metaphor like the word "son" that Hosea uses. There are many presidents in America, but there is only one President of the United States. The technical term "sons of God/Most High" is highly specific, not a generic metaphor like "son".

These are the same Sons of God that left their heavenly habitation and came to earth and mated with the human daughters of men.

Genesis 6:1–2
[1] When man began to multiply on the face of the land and daughters were born to them, [2] the sons of God saw that the daughters of man were attractive. And they took as their wives any they chose.

This passage is also a highly debated one. Many interpreters also argue that these Sons of God in Genesis 6 are humans from the lineage of Seth or despotic god-kings.

Space does not permit a full defense here of the supernatural nature of the Sons of God in Genesis 6 (see my book *When Giants Were Upon the Earth* for a fully developed argument). But I will make the point that both New Testament inspired authors Peter and Jude considered those Sons of God in Genesis 6 to be divine angels.

Jude 6–7 (NASB95)
And **angels** who did not keep their own domain, but abandoned their proper abode, He has kept in eternal bonds under darkness for the judgment of the great day, just as Sodom and Gomorrah and the cities around them, since they in the same way as these indulged in gross immorality and went after strange flesh…

2 Peter 2:4–5
For if God did not spare **angels** when they sinned, but cast them into hell and committed them to chains of gloomy darkness to be kept until the judgment; if he did not spare the ancient world, but preserved Noah, a herald of righteousness, with seven others, when he brought a flood upon the world of the ungodly…

Peter places this angelic sin at the time of the Flood. The only possible biblical reference to this sin is the wicked behavior of the Sons of God in Genesis 6 marrying women by force.

Genesis 6:1–10
When man began to multiply on the face of the land and daughters were born to them, the sons of God saw that the daughters of man were attractive. And they took as their wives any they chose… The LORD saw that the wickedness of man was great in the earth, and that every intention of the thoughts of his heart was only evil continually.

Some try to deny the negative connotations of the behavior of the sons of God in this passage. I deal with that more extensively in When Giants Were Upon the Earth. But for now, let me make the point that the dominant view in the ancient Jewish mindset (including the New Testament) was that the Sons of God were angels who sinfully defied the heavenly/earthly boundaries.

Both Peter and Jude speak of the sin of the angels in the same context as Sodom and Gomorrah. Jude calls them angels who "indulged in gross immorality and went after strange flesh." "Strange flesh" cannot mean homosexuality in this passage, because the Greek words are *heteros sarx* (different flesh). Homosexuality would be same flesh (*homo sarx*). The "strange flesh" here must be a difference of flesh between angels and humans. The sin of Sodom, linked to the sin of the angels in Noah's time, was not men desiring sex with men so much as it was humans desiring sex with angels (Genesis 6 all over again).

The Sodom story was not merely known in Second Temple Judaism as an example of homosexuality, but was linked with Genesis 6 as an example of humans trying to have sinful sex with angels who had a heavenly flesh different from human flesh.

> Testament of Naphtali 3:4-5
> …so that you do not become like Sodom, which departed from the order of nature. Likewise the Watchers departed from nature's order; the Lord pronounced a curse on them at the Flood.[5]

> Jubilees 10:1, 5
> The polluted demons began to lead astray the children of Noah's sons and to lead them to folly and to destroy them…
> [Noah prayed,] [6]"And Thou knowest how Thy Watchers, the fathers of these spirits, acted in my day: and as for these spirits which are living, imprison them and hold them fast in the place of condemnation."

Though The Testament of Naphtali and the book of Jubilees are not Scripture, they were highly regarded Jewish writings that expressed the dominant ancient Jewish view, which was echoed in the first century by the Jewish historian Josephus, who wrote of Genesis 6 that "many angels of God accompanied with women, and begat sons that proved unjust, and despisers of all that was good."[7]

If New Testament apostolic authority exegetes the sin of Genesis to be that of divine angelic beings, in accord with the ancient Jewish worldview, then I think we are biblically safe to agree with them.

---

[5] Charlesworth, James H. *The Old Testament Pseudepigrapha: Volume 1*. New York; London: Yale University Press, 1983, 812.

[6] James H. Charlesworth, *The Old Testament Pseudepigrapha and the New Testament: Expansions of the "Old Testament" and Legends, Wisdom, and Philosophical Literature, Prayers, Psalms and Odes, Fragments of Lost Judeo-Hellenistic Works, vol. 2* (New Haven; London: Yale University Press, 1985), 75.

[7] Flavius Josephus, *Antiquities of the Jews* 1:73.

1 Kings 22

My personal favorite Sons of God passage is the story of wicked king Ahab asking for the prophet Micaiah's advice on attacking Ramoth-Gilead. Micaiah describes a scenario so obviously supernatural and spiritual that little explanation is required. Though the beings in the council here are not described as "gods" like elsewhere, they are described as the "host of heaven," which we have already shown the Bible defines as divine beings or gods (Jer 19:13; Deut 4:19; 17:3; 29:26; 2 Chron 33:3-5; Acts 7:42-43).

> 1 Kings 22:19–23
> And Micaiah said, "Therefore hear the word of the LORD: I saw the LORD sitting on his throne, and all the host of heaven standing beside him on his right hand and on his left; and the LORD said, 'Who will entice Ahab, that he may go up and fall at Ramoth-Gilead?' And one said one thing, and another said another. Then a spirit came forward and stood before the LORD, saying, 'I will entice him.' And the LORD said to him, 'By what means?' And he said, 'I will go out, and will be a lying spirit in the mouth of all his prophets.' And he said, 'You are to entice him, and you shall succeed; go out and do so.' Now therefore behold, the LORD has put a lying spirit in the mouth of all these your prophets; the LORD has declared disaster for you."

The fascinating thing about this vision is that we get a glimpse into the actual process of counseling that God takes from his heavenly host. We see them suggest different things, and then God chooses one and empowers the spirit to accomplish his task.

It's all rather scandalous to a modern Christian mind that prefers a nice, simple and uncomplicated spiritual world where God sits on his throne and declares the end from the beginning without anyone's input. But biblical facts are the facts. God uses a bureaucracy of intermediary divine agents, called gods, Sons of God, heavenly host, or holy ones, with whom he interacts and engages counsel.

Or as the Psalm we've been looking at from the very start puts it:

> Psalm 82:1
> God has taken his place in the divine council;
> in the midst of the gods he holds judgment:

There are plenty of other passages that describe the divine council of heavenly beings around Yahweh who counsel with him and carry out his decisions with duly delegated legal responsibility (Deut 32:43 LXX; Zech 2:13-3:7; Jer 23:18-22).

And there are other passages where the divine council is not mentioned, but scholars explain that the plural grammar of the speech and activity imply the heavenly court motif of God addressing the council (Gen 1:26; 11:3, 4, 7; Isa 6:8; 40:1; 41:21-23). It is so prevalent throughout the Bible that one can only deny it to one's theological detriment.

You can read more about this theological paradigm of the Sons of God in my book *When Giants Were Upon the Earth*. And you can read a story of how this divine council plays out in history in my novel series *Chronicles of the Nephilim*, *Chronicles of the Apocalypse* and *Chronicles of the Watchers*

In the next chapter, I will explain the allotment of the nations at Babel and how it begins this storyline of the rise and fall of the Watchers and their inheritance of the nations.

Chapter 2:
The Allotment of the Nations

In Chapter 1, I defined the biblical motif of Christus Victor as Christ's victory over the spiritual powers who ruled sinful mankind. I defined the divine council biblically as an assembly of gods, called "Sons of God," "holy ones," and "heavenly host" who surround Yahweh, engage in legal counsel with him and carry out his decisions.

But the next question is, how did man come under the rule and authority of these gods, these divine beings from Yahweh's heavenly host?

I am using Psalm 82 as a portal into this fascinating storyline of the Bible. So let's take a look again at what it says.

> Psalm 82:1–8
> God has taken his place in the divine council;
> in the midst of the gods he holds judgment:
> "How long will you judge unjustly
> and show partiality to the wicked? *Selah*
> Give justice to the weak and the fatherless;
> maintain the right of the afflicted and the destitute.
> Rescue the weak and the needy;
> deliver them from the hand of the wicked."

So we see that for some reason, God has given some of these members from his divine council authority to rule over mankind on earth as their judges. Where did this come from? Why would God do such a thing? Isn't God alone the judge of all the earth? And why is he blaming failure to rule on divine beings? Does that make them fallen angels?

To answer those questions, we need to go back to the beginning. Not Genesis 1, but rather the beginning of the allotment of the nations to the gods: back to the Tower of Babel. But instead of going straight to Genesis 11, which tells the story of Babel, we need to read what Moses reveals about Babel in Deuteronomy 32.

The Deuteronomy 32 Worldview

Deuteronomy 32 is famously known as the Song of Moses. In it, Moses sings a song of the story of Israel and how she had come to be God's chosen nation. He begins by glorifying God and then telling them to "remember the days of old" (v. 7).

Deuteronomy 32:8–9
When the Most High gave to the nations their inheritance,
when he divided mankind,
he fixed the borders of the peoples
according to the number of the sons of God.
But the LORD's portion is his people,
Jacob his allotted heritage.

The context of this passage is the Tower of Babel incident in Genesis 11. It is the only "division of mankind" in the text of Genesis. Rebellious humanity sought divinity in unified rebellion, so God separated them by confusing their tongues, which divided them into the seventy nations described in Genesis 10. The incident at Babel led to the creation of nations and their ownership of those territorial lands as the "inheritance" of those peoples. Nations are essentially God's creation to protect mankind from destroying itself through idolatrous one-world global unity in wickedness.

The apostle Paul referred to this allotment of national boundaries in Acts 17:26 when he said that God "made from one man every nation of mankind to live on all the face of the earth, having determined allotted periods and the boundaries of their dwelling places." That "one man" from whom every nation was made is not Adam, but Noah, because the allotment of nations occurred at Babel, not the Garden.

But that's not all. Deuteronomy 32 says that the borders of those nations were fixed "according to the number of the Sons of God." That is, the Sons of God are in authority over these nations, both geographically and spiritually. This allotment is in contrast with Yahweh's allotment of Jacob. The seventy nations were allotted to the Sons of God, in the same way that Yahweh allotted to himself the nation of Israel, described as (the people of) "Jacob."

The Septuagint, or the Greek translation of the Old Testament from which Jesus and the apostles quoted, translates "Sons of God" in Deuteronomy 32:8 as "angels of God," thus again affirming that the ancient Jewish world understood those beings as divine, not human.

And allotment is used synonymously in the passage with inheritance and heritage. In fact, the inheritance or allotment of land is one of the major themes of the Old Testament. God promises the Land of Canaan as an inheritance to the twelve tribes of Israel.

Joshua 11:23
So Joshua took the whole land, according to all that the LORD had spoken to Moses. And Joshua gave it for an inheritance to Israel according to their tribal allotments.

Remember this important theological truth; it will come into play later: *allotment and inheritance are about land and ownership under the old covenant.*

Since Genesis 10 describes seventy nations, the number of the Sons of

God here must be seventy to match those nations. Or maybe seventy groups of Sons of God. But who are these seventy chosen divine beings? They can't be the myriad of "ten thousands" of heavenly host usually described as being around Yahweh's throne (Deut 33:2-3; Dan 7:10). They are only seventy. Yet Psalm 82 clearly states that they are part of that divine council. Then, who are they?

Are the Sons of God in Psalm 82 Evil?

Psalm 82:3-4 describes these gods as being given responsibility to administer justice over the peoples. The commands that God gives them about not showing partiality, giving justice and rescuing the weak, are all expressions found in the Law and the Prophets (Deut 1:16-17; Jer 22:3; Prov 24:11). The gods over the nations were supposed to rule according to God's justice.

Another Psalm reflects the same injustice of the ruling gods and their guilt before God's Word.

> Psalm 58:1–2
> Do you indeed decree what is right, you gods? Do you judge the children of man uprightly? No, in your hearts you devise wrongs; your hands deal out violence on earth.

Shallow readings of both Psalm 82 and 58 give one the impression that these "gods" are good spiritual powers that are entrusted with authority, since God would not impose bad rulers, would he? And then it appears that they fail to rule justly and end in darkness, which leads to their punishment in 82:7 of "dying like men," or "falling" like any other earthly ruler. So they sound like good divine beings gone bad.

But I think this is not an accurate understanding. I will argue that the Sons of God who inherited the nations at Babel (Deut 32:8-9) and ruled those nations in antiquity (Psa 82:2-3) were already fallen and evil when they received their allotment. Here's why…

First, the dominant paradigm of the Old Testament is the single nation of Israel as set apart by Yahweh to be a light to the darkened world of the Gentile nations, considered as a whole to be against God (Isa 49:6; Psa 2:1-2). All the nations worshipped gods that were not Yahweh. And even by the time of the New Testament, the Jews considered the word Gentile to be synonymous with sinner (Matt 5:47; 10:5; 18:17; Act 4:25-26). Paul writes in Galatians 2:15, "We ourselves are Jews by birth and not Gentile sinners." So the biblical understanding of "the nations" in Genesis 11, Deuteronomy 32 and Psalm 82 are Gentile nations who are idolaters. They do not worship Yahweh.

Second, let us not forget that all the nations created at Babel consisted of people in rebellion against Yahweh at the very start. The confusion of tongues and division of mankind was a judgment for sinful man who had sought deity with their pagan temples to the gods. So the context of Deuteronomy 32:8-10 is division as judgment, not as neutral separation.

Third, earlier in Deuteronomy, Moses clarifies God's command not to worship the heavenly host, defined interchangeably as both gods and as astronomical bodies (sun, moon and stars). *But he states that he allotted those gods to all the other peoples.*

> Deuteronomy 4:19–20
> And beware lest you raise your eyes to heaven, and when you see the sun and the moon and the stars, all the host of heaven, you be drawn away and bow down to them and serve them, things that Yahweh your God has allotted to all the peoples under the whole heaven. But Yahweh has taken you and brought you out of the iron furnace, out of Egypt, to be a people of his own inheritance.

This allotment of the gods/host of heaven to the peoples is reminiscent of the description of God "giving up" pagans to their idolatrous worship of creation in Romans 1.

> Romans 1:21–28
> For although they knew God, they did not honor him as God or give thanks to him, but they became futile in their thinking, and their foolish hearts were darkened. Claiming to be wise, they became fools, and exchanged the glory of the immortal God for images resembling mortal man and birds and animals and creeping things. Therefore **God gave them up** in the lusts of their hearts to impurity, to the dishonoring of their bodies among themselves...For this reason **God gave them up** to dishonorable passions... And since they did not see fit to acknowledge God, **God gave them up** to a debased mind to do what ought not to be done.

The contrast of God setting apart Israel "to be a people for his own inheritance" in Deuteronomy 4:20 after the allotment of the heavenly host in verse 19 is a reiteration of the allotment contrast in Deuteronomy 32. These verses refer to the same allotted inheritance.

In Deuteronomy 4 it's clear that Yahweh did not give the nations to be ruled by righteous heavenly host who then fell through accepting undeserved worship. Rather, Yahweh gave the host of heaven to all the peoples to worship as their gods *because they were already idolaters*. He was "giving them up" to their idolatry and giving the false gods their own people to rule over.

On first glance the phrase "to all the peoples under the whole heaven," would appear to mean that God allotted the heavenly host to everyone, including Israelites. But the context contradicts that inclusion when Moses says, "But Yahweh has taken you (Israel) to be a people of his own inheritance." "All the peoples under the whole heaven" is contrasted with

Israel, not included with her.

Another passage in Deuteronomy reinforces this notion of sinful nations allotted to fallen gods. In Deuteronomy 29:26 Moses tells the Israelites that when they entered the land of Canaan, they "went and served other gods and worshiped them, gods whom they had not known and whom he had not allotted to them." This passage affirms that God allotted these fallen gods of the heavenly host to the Gentile nations of Canaan.

So, why does Psalm 82 read as if these Sons of God were righteous beings to start? Well, I don't think it does. Look closer at the passage:

> Psalm 82:1–4
> God has taken his place in the divine council;
> in the midst of the gods he holds judgment:
> "How long will you judge unjustly
> and show partiality to the wicked? *Selah*
> Give justice to the weak and the fatherless;
> maintain the right of the afflicted and the destitute.
> Rescue the weak and the needy;
> deliver them from the hand of the wicked."

Verse one depicts Yahweh convening his council to judge the gods. Then he tells them, "How long will you judge unjustly and show partiality to the wicked?" So these gods *are already ruling unjustly* when God convenes the council. Then Yahweh commands those unjust gods to "give justice," "maintain rights," and "rescue the weak." So, the question is, why would God command wicked gods to rule justly?

I think it is the same principle involved with the giving of the Mosaic Law to humans. God did not give the Law to a righteous people, hoping they would keep it and then they failed to achieve that righteous obedience. Rather, God gave the law to an *already sinful* people to show them their sin and justify their condemnation (Rom 5:12-14). In the same way, God "gives up" fallen humanity to their fallen gods who rule over them in their fallen state. And then Yahweh justifies their judgment by commanding them to do justice—which they fail to live up to. Criminals are told to keep the law just as much as non-criminals are.

Though I am not dogmatic about the Sons of God being already fallen when they were allotted the nations, I would argue that if they were originally righteous, they must have fallen very quickly, maybe within a few years of Babel. Evidence of the earliest post-Flood civilization of which we know, ancient Sumer, already contains a developed sophisticated religion of idolatrous polytheism.

The earliest post-Flood cultures to which the Bible refers are all idolatrous and polytheistic to the core when we meet them: the Canaanites, the Egyptians, and the Amorites, from which God called Abraham (Gen 12). *We simply have no historical or biblical evidence of a period of righteous spiritual rulers or righteous worship of Yahweh after Babel*. If there was, it didn't last long enough to merit historical significance or inclusion in the Scriptures.

It makes more sense that Babel proved mankind's incorrigible depravity. Even after the Flood, they would not worship Yahweh. So Yahweh gave them over to the false gods they already worshipped. Since morality is inherently part of the creation and is not relative or subjective, even fallen angels who are awarded territory are still accountable for their behavior. The Sons of God could not claim they were just following orders or performing God's will at their spiritual Nuremburg Trial to come (Rom 9:19-23).

The Sons of God Are Also Called Watchers

One last aspect of the divine council is necessary to understand the big picture in Scripture: the Sons of God who have been allotted the Gentile nations are also called "Watchers," for the very simple reason that they were given the responsibility of watching over the nations to which they were allotted.

In Daniel 10:4-7 the prophet receives a vision at the Tigris River that includes a "man" described in terms reserved in Scripture for divine beings (see Ezekiel 1). Some scholars even argue he could be a pre-incarnate Jesus Christ.

That divine holy one then describes a scenario of heavenly "princes" at war.

> Daniel 10:13; 20-21
> "The <u>prince of the kingdom of Persia</u> withstood me twenty-one days, but Michael, one of the <u>chief princes</u>, came to help me, for I was left there with the kings of Persia…"
> Then he said, "Do you know why I have come to you? But now I will return to fight against the <u>prince of Persia</u>; and when I go out, behold, the <u>prince of Greece</u> will come. But I will tell you what is inscribed in the book of truth: there is none who contends by my side against these except <u>Michael, your prince</u>.

In this passage, we see that the notion of national principalities and powers ruling over earthly kingdoms continued even past the exile into Daniel's period. The previous prophecies of Daniel 2 and 7-8 had predicted Persia and Greece to be at war, as one kingdom was replaced by the other. But these princes in Daniel 10 are not the earthly rulers, but rather their heavenly counterparts. There is a spiritual prince of Persia, a spiritual prince of Greece, and Michael the archangel is considered the spiritual prince of Israel.

The biblical picture is that the heavenly and earthly rulers were tied together in unity, so that when there was a war on earth, there was a corresponding war in heaven. So much so, that the fates of both heaven and earth were linked. Here are a couple examples from Scripture that reinforce this theme:

In the time of the Judges when Israel fought the pagan kings of Canaan, the battle with Sisera at the river of Megiddo was described within the same paragraph from the perspectives of both heaven and earth.

> Judges 5:19–20
> "The kings came, they fought; then fought the kings of Canaan, at Taanach, by the waters of Megiddo; they got no spoils of silver. From heaven the stars fought, from their courses they fought against Sisera."

Identical language is used to link the fighting of the kings on earth with the fighting of heavenly stars. Again, remember, the heavenly host were often considered interchangeable with the heavenly rulers over the earth. When the kings on earth were at war, so were their allotted gods at war.

Another strong example of this equivalence between heavenly and earthly rulers is found in their predicted judgment in Isaiah, who describes a synchronized judgment of earthly kings and their heavenly rulers:

> Isaiah 24:21–23
> On that day the LORD will punish
> the host of heaven, in heaven,
> and the kings of the earth, on the earth.

Jeremiah also affirms the connection between earthly authorities and their heavenly principalities, when he prophesies Yahweh's judgment upon Egypt and her gods, including the high god, Amon, who was the patron deity of Thebes.

> Jeremiah 46:25
> Yahweh of hosts, the God of Israel, said: "Behold, I am bringing punishment upon Amon of Thebes, and Pharaoh and Egypt and her gods and her kings.

When Yahweh punishes heavenly rulers, he also punishes earthly rulers along with them, and vice versa.

But where do I get the idea that these heavenly rulers are called Watchers? Well, jumping back to Daniel 4, he has another vision where he tells us Watchers are holy ones that come down from heaven.

> Daniel 4:13, 17
> "I saw in the visions of my head as I lay in bed, and behold, a watcher, a holy one, came down from heaven…
> The sentence is by the decree of the watchers, the decision by the word of the holy ones, to the end that the living may know that the Most High rules the kingdom of men and gives it to whom he will and sets over it the lowliest of men.'

The Watchers are called "holy ones" (Deut 33:2-3; Jude 14), which we saw in Chapter 1 is another name for the heavenly host (1King 22:19) of the divine council (Psa 82:1), who are also called the Sons of God (Job 5:1; 15:15). We also see another reference to God allotting earthly territories to whomever he wills. So all these terms refer to the same divine beings. Though we do not see the term Watchers used specifically in Daniel 10, we see those ruling principalities of the nations that are also synonymous with the ruling gods/Sons of God/heavenly host of Psalm 82 and Deuteronomy 32.

The Watchers are the fallen Sons of God given the allotment of the nations, both land and people, as their inheritance.

Host of Heaven

One aspect of the Watchers in the Bible and other ancient Near Eastern sacred literature is their identification with the stars and planets in the heavens. The original context of heavenly host in the Bible is one of war. The Hebrew term for "host" (*saba*) was used as a reference to warriors. The term "Lord of Hosts" was then a designation of Yahweh as warrior king.

> Isaiah 13:4–5
> The sound of a tumult is on the mountains
> as of <u>a great multitude!</u>
> The sound of an uproar of kingdoms,
> of nations gathering together!
> The <u>LORD of hosts</u> is mustering
> a <u>host for battle</u>.
> They come from a distant land,
> from the end of the heavens,
> the LORD and <u>the weapons of his indignation</u>,
> to destroy the whole land.

In this passage, Isaiah likens the earthly armies of Babylon as Yahweh's own weapons used upon another nation. God is using Babylon providentially as his own host of warriors.

But there is a heavenly host of warriors as well. In Joshua 5, we are introduced to the leader of that heavenly host. Joshua was preparing to besiege Jericho, when an armed man appeared before him. But this warrior was more than a man. He proclaimed, "I am the commander of the host of the LORD" (5:14). And then, that commander, who was most likely the Angel of Yahweh (Jesus), said the exact same words that Yahweh proclaimed to Moses from the burning bush, "Take off your sandals from your feet, for the place where you are standing is holy" (5:15). Yahweh is a warrior king of a heavenly host of armies.

In 2 Kings 6, the prophet Elisha and his young assistant see the army of Syria surrounding Samaria. The servant worries that they are outnumbered. But Elisha tells him that there are more who are with Israel than with Syria.

He then asks Yahweh to show the young man the spiritual realm. "So the Lord opened the eyes of the young man, and he saw, and behold, the mountain was full of horses and chariots of fire all around Elisha" (6:17).

Seeing this military context of the "host" sheds light on Yahweh's reference to the Israelites leaving Egypt as a host. "And on that very day the LORD brought the people of Israel out of the land of Egypt by their hosts" (Exodus 12:51). In the story of the Exodus up until the Yam Suph crossing, Yahweh describes his people as the "host of Israel" in contrast with "Pharaoh and all his host of Egypt" (Exodus 14:17, 19-20). Anyone familiar with the story knows that the Israelites were not an army and they didn't fight against Pharaoh. They were the entire population of the Hebrews and other slaves, men, women and children. So why describe them in military terms as a "host"? Why would Yahweh use a military term for his civilian population? Because the entire Exodus is being framed by Yahweh as a war of gods and men. Israel vs. Egypt, Yahweh vs. Pharaoh and Yahweh vs. the gods of Egypt (see my book *The Spiritual World of Moses and Egypt* for further information) The glory of it all is that in this mighty spiritual war, the Israelites did not fight at all because Yahweh fought for them! As the Song of Moses declares,

> Exodus 15:2–11
> Yahweh is my strength and my song,
> and he has become my salvation…
> Yahweh is a man of war;
> Yahweh is his name.
> "Pharaoh's chariots and his host he cast into the sea,
> and his chosen officers were sunk in the Red Sea.
> The floods covered them;
> they went down into the depths like a stone.
> Your right hand, O Yahweh, glorious in power,
> your right hand, O Yahweh, shatters the enemy...
>
> "Who is like you, O Yahweh, among the gods?
>
> Who is like you, majestic in holiness,
> awesome in glorious deeds, doing wonders?

But war is not the only responsibility of Yahweh's heavenly host. They are also the millions who surround Yahweh's throne in heaven to glorify him and partake of his divine council as mentioned earlier in 1 Kings 22 and Job 1 and 2. Yahweh's heavenly host surround him, worship him (Nehemiah 9:6), but also counsel with him and then perform Yahweh's commands of tasks.

The question arises, how many are there of these heavenly host? Throughout the Bible, symbolic phrases are used to describe the numbers as innumerable, or uncountable. "Ten thousands" (plural) of these holy ones are depicted at Sinai (Deuteronomy 33:2). The New Testament author Jude quotes from 1 Enoch that says that the Lord will come with "ten thousands (plural) of his holy ones" (Jude 14-15). That phrase "ten thousands" is also translated as "ten million" (1 Enoch 1:9). Yahweh's heavenly chariots at Sinai were "twice ten thousand, thousands upon thousands" (Psalm 68:17). In Daniel's vision of heavenly host before Yahweh's throne, he sees "a thousand thousands served him, and ten thousand times ten thousand (one hundred million) stood before him" (Daniel 7:10). Jeremiah comes right out and says, "The host of heaven cannot be numbered" (Jeremiah 33:22).

Shining Ones and Stars

One more thing about this heavenly host. They are sometimes described as "shining." For example, in Daniel's vision on the Tigris River, he sees an unnamed heavenly warrior speaking of the various territorial principalities over the nations called "princes" or guardians of those lands (10:12-13, 20-21). The heavenly being is described as a man whose "body was like beryl [a gleaming gem], his face like the appearance of lightning, his eyes like flaming torches, his arms and legs like the gleam of burnished bronze" (10:6).

Heavenly creatures are often described in these shining terms in Scripture. Ezekiel's vision of the Cherubim also describe them as "gleaming beryl," glowing "burnished bronze," "gleaming metal," with "bright fire," "flashes of lightning and fire" around them (Ezekiel 1:4-16). Yahweh on his throne is described as the form of a man whose upper half was like "gleaming metal, like the fire enclosed all around," and "there was brightness all around him" (1:26-28).

At Mount Sinai, Yahweh and his host are both described in these terms of shining:

> Deuteronomy 33:2
> He said, "The LORD came from Sinai and dawned from Seir upon us; <u>he shone forth</u> from Mount Paran; <u>he came from the ten thousands of holy ones, with flaming fire</u> at his right hand.

In the New Testament, the angels who announced the resurrection of Jesus had "the appearance like lightning," and clothing "white as snow" (Matthew 28:3), described by Luke as "dazzling in apparel" (Luke 24:4). That was no designer clothes with bling, that was a shining brightness expressive of the heavenly realm.

In fact, even Moses began to shine with an unbearable brightness the more he was in Yahweh's presence in the tabernacle (Exodus 34:29-35).

Isaiah 14 gives a prophecy to the king of Babylon that many believe also refers to the satan. Yahweh taunts the human king who considered himself to be divine with intent to ascend above the very throne of God, "How you are fallen from heaven, O Day Star, son of Dawn!" (14:12). The first part of that name, "Day Star," is *helel* in Hebrew, which lexicons define as meaning "Shining One."[8] We will talk more about this passage in a second, but the context of it is clearly one of spiritual or heavenly connection. In his arrogant pride, the king of Babylon claims to be divine, like the shining beings of the heavenly host.

This "shining" was a well-known rendering of spiritual beings through all the ancient world. A fragment of the Dead Sea Scrolls speaks of "those who make knowledge shine among the divinities [gods] of light." [9] The Canaanite religious texts from Ugarit in Syria describe the same kind of divine council of gods around their supreme god, El. They are called, "the Shining Ones of the council."[10] As far away as ancient China, we find references to a supreme creator, Shang Di, also surrounded by lesser deities or spirits called, *shen*, which means, "bright ones."[11]

And in the popular Egyptian Book of the Dead, the deified dead scribe, now called Osiris Ani, speaks of the gods also as "Shining Ones" who "live in the rays of light," as emanations of the sun god Ra.[12]

> I may lift up the earth; that the shining ones may open their arms unto me; that the company of the gods may speak with the words of the shining ones unto Osiris Ani; that the hearts of the gods may direct [him]; and that they may make him powerful in heaven among the gods who have taken unto themselves visible forms.[13]

So, why all this brightness and shining of the gods? Is it just a manifestation of spiritual glory or is there more to it than that?

A closer look reveals that the shining of heavenly host reflects a strong literary and theological identification of the gods with stars. Some passages appear to address the "host of heaven" as the stars in the sky; and other passages appear to address the "host of heaven" as the spiritual beings around God's throne. This is because the stars and gods were thought of as interchangeable in their identities. Stars were equated with gods and gods were equated with stars. This explains the development of astrology as the stars determining our destiny: because the ancient mind thought of the stars as gods

---

8 "Shining one" Francis Brown, Samuel Rolles Driver, and Charles Augustus Briggs, *Enhanced Brown-Driver-Briggs Hebrew and English Lexicon* (Oxford: Clarendon Press, 1977), 237.

9 4Q403 1.2.35 - Florentino García Martínez and Eibert J. C. Tigchelaar, *"The Dead Sea Scrolls Study Edition (translations)"* (Leiden; New York: Brill, 1997–1998), 823.

10 E. Theodore Mullen, Jr., *The Divine Council in Canaanite and Early Hebrew Literature* (Chico, CA: Scholars Press, 1980), 240.

11 John Ross, *The Original Religion of China*, (New York, NY: Eaton and Mains, 1909), 172.

12 Book of the Dead LXXVIII (78). E. Wallis Budge, *The Egyptian Book of the Dead: The Papyrus of Ani* (1895), 333.

13 Book of the Dead CXXIV (174:10-12). Budge, *The Egyptian Book of the Dead,* 331. Pharaoh Pepi was also deified and described as standing "among the gods, among the shining ones." Budge, *The Egyptian Book of the Dead,* 57-58

and the gods controlled their lives. So then, the stars controlled their lives because they were manifestations of the gods.

When Moses warned the Israelites of worshipping the Canaanite deities, he likened the sun, moon and stars to "all the host of heaven."

> Deuteronomy 4:19-20
> And beware lest you raise your eyes to heaven, and when you see the sun and the moon and the stars, all the host of heaven, you be drawn away and bow down to them and serve them, things that the LORD your God has allotted to all the peoples under the whole heaven. But the LORD has taken you and brought you out of the iron furnace, out of Egypt, to be a people of his own inheritance, as you are this day.

On the surface, this looks like he is saying that the pagans worship the sun, moon and stars as deities. That is true. But not true enough. Notice the language that Yahweh has "allotted" those host to the peoples under heaven, while keeping Israel as his own "inheritance." This phrase and terminology is repeated with the same juxtaposition of Israel and the peoples later in Deuteronomy 32.

> Deuteronomy 32:8–9
> When the Most High gave to the nations their inheritance,
> when he divided mankind,
> he fixed the borders of the peoples
> according to the number of the sons of God.
> But the LORD's portion is his people,
> Jacob his allotted heritage.

In both Deuteronomy 4 and 32, we see the same repeated pattern of God allotting the peoples (nations) to the Sons of God—who are the host of heaven—as an inheritance, but keeping Israel (Jacob) as his own allotted inheritance. Earlier, we found that the Sons of God were in fact the divine beings around Yahweh's throne (who had rebelled). So we see that the Sons of God are equated with the host of heaven as both gods and as astronomical bodies. It is a case of both/and, not either/or. The Sons of God are the heavenly host, which is both a personal divine being from God's throne, and represented in the sun, moon and stars that were worshipped by pagans.

The Jews also equated the heavenly host as both stars and gods, but they refused to worship them. And remember, the phrase, "gods" in Hebrew was *elohim*, which was synonymous with the Sons of God in Yahweh's divine council (Psalm 82:1 with Job 1:6). Thus, Job ties the two together when he describes the Sons of God as "morning stars" singing together at God's creation of the universe.

Job 38:7
when the morning stars sang together and all the sons of God shouted for joy.

This verse uses a very common technique called "parallelism" that is ubiquitous in the Old Testament. Parallelism uses a doublet of phrases to convey the same thing in two different ways. "Morning stars singing" is another way of saying "sons of God shouting for joy." They are not two different things, but the same thing repeated with different words. The conjunctive "and" in Hebrew means "even" in this context. So, the text is not saying morningstars *and* all the sons of God, as if they are two different items, but rather, "morningstars, *even* all the sons of God."

Daniel also uses this parallel doublet in a passage identifying spiritual principalities with stars. Notice the conjunctive *and* again as meaning *even.*

Dan. 8:10-11
"It grew great, even to the host of heaven. And some of the host **and** some of the stars it threw down to the ground and trampled on them. It became great, even as great as the Prince of the host [Michael]"

The spiritual "princes" over the nations in this passage are also called "host of heaven" and "stars."

This poetic technique now makes more sense of Psalm 148:

Psalm 148:2–3
Praise him, all his angels;
praise him, all his hosts!
Praise him, sun and moon,
praise him, all you shining stars!

This Psalm also uses parallel doublets as well. Its call to praise is not a listing of separate things created by God: angels, hosts, sun and moon, shining stars; it is a parallel synonym of angels, who are his hosts, which are also his shining stars!

Now, remember that prophecy of Isaiah to the king of Babylon we brought up earlier in this chapter? That "Day Star, Son of the Dawn" in Hebrew is *Helel ben Shachar* which literally means "shining one, son of the dawn," and is actually a well known ancient reference to the planet Venus, known to the ancients as the "bright morning star."[14] The shining of astronomical bodies was the same shining of the divine Sons of God/gods/Watchers.

---

14 Michael S. Heiser, *The Unseen Realm: Recovering the Supernatural Worldview of the Bible*, First Edition (Bellingham, WA: Lexham Press, 2015), 85

As I explained in more detail in my previous book, When Giants Were Upon the Earth, this Isaiah passage is not really about "Satan's fall from heaven," but rather a mockery of the king of Babylon's fall from earthly power by placing him into a retelling of a Canaanite myth of the god Athtar's own failed ambitions. The king thought he would be like a god, but he will end up dead and in Sheol like every rebel.

> Isaiah 14:3, 12–15
> You will take up this taunt against the king of Babylon:
> "How you are fallen from heaven,
> O Day Star, son of Dawn!
> How you are cut down to the ground,
> you who laid the nations low!
> You said in your heart,
> 'I will ascend to heaven;
> above the stars of God
> I will set my throne on high;
> I will sit on the mount of assembly
> in the far reaches of the north;
> I will ascend above the heights of the clouds;
> I will make myself like the Most High.'
> But you are brought down to Sheol,
> to the far reaches of the pit

Scholar Michael S. Heiser definitively explains the linguistic and narrative referent of Helel ben Shahar (Day Star, son of the Dawn) as being the Ugaritic god Athtar from the epic Baal Cycle of myths at Ugarit. Heiser reveals that Athtar was equated with the planet Venus. Athtar sought to raise himself above "the stars of El," (gods as stars, again) a reference to the divine council or heavenly host that surrounded the high god of the Canaanite pantheon. He tried to do so by seeking to sit on the throne of Baal, referred to as "the Most High," upon the "mount of assembly" in the north called Saphon—just like in the prophecy of Isaiah. But Athtar was not powerful enough for the position of power and was cast to earth/Sheol.[15]

In the New Testament, Jude writes about another fall of divine beings in the days of the Flood, "angels who did not keep their own domain, but abandoned their proper abode" and fell to earth. God then imprisoned them "in eternal chains under gloomy darkness until the judgment of the great day" (Jude 6). Jude calls these imprisoned fallen angels "wandering stars" (v. 13), in line with Enoch's "prison house for the stars and the powers of heaven… they are the ones which have transgressed the commandments of God"

---

[15] Michael Heiser, "The Mythological Provenance of Isaiah 14:12-15: A Reconsideration of the Ugaritic Material" Liberty University https://digitalcommons.liberty.edu/lts_fac_pubs/280/

(1Enoch 18:14-15).[16]

This astralization of deities now brings some clarification to the poetic imagery used in many biblical prophesies of a collapsing universe. Falling stars, darkening suns, blood red moons and skies rolling up like a scroll are not scientific descriptions of the physical universe crumbling, they are a common mythopoeic image of heavenly rulers (Watchers) falling from power along with their earthly kingly counterparts. We saw previously in this chapter that the ancient Hebrew mind conceived of the earthly authorities as linked with their heavenly principalities. So then, Yahweh's judgment upon earthly powers and their heavenly counterparts is described as the astronomical heavens crashing down in defeat.

Here is a list of some passages that use astronomical catastrophe as symbol of spiritual and earthly powers at war:

- Judges 5:19-20 – kings of Canaan fighting on earth are described as "stars fighting from heaven."
- Isaiah 13:1-17 – the fall of Babylon to the Medes in 539 B.C. described as stars of heaven and the constellations not flashing forth their light, the sun darkened and the moon not shedding light.
- Haggai 2:6 – the promise of a New Covenant described as "shaking the heavens and earth." (See with this, Hebrews 12:26-28)
- Amos 8:9 – the fall of Samaria in 722 B.C. described as the sun going down at noon and the earth dark in broad daylight.
- Isaiah 30:25-26 – Israel's defeat of Sennacherib in 701 B.C. described as the moon being as a bright as the sun and the sun seven times brighter.
- Psalm 18:6-15 – David's deliverance from Saul described as earth reeling, mountains quaking heavens coming down with thick darkness, and the foundations of the earth laid bare.
- Joel 2:30–31 – Wonders in the heavens, the sun turning to darkness and the moon turning to blood are all described by the apostle Peter as being fulfilled in the first century in the fall of Israel and Jerusalem to the power of Rome (Acts 2:16, 20-21).

Centuries after Moses, in the 6th century B.C., Yahweh would destroy Egypt "by the hand of Nebuchadnezzar king of Babylon" (Ezekiel 30:10-11). Pagan Babylon would be a weapon of judgment in Yahweh's hand. Yahweh describes the judgment poetically, "I will dry up the Nile…I will bring desolation upon the land" (Ezekiel 30:12). Drying up the Nile was an obvious figurative image of "drying up" Egypt's wealth, since the river was the essence of her wealth (v. 10) The Nile never literally dried up. Then he gives this revealing description of astronomical catastrophe:

---

[16] James H. Charlesworth, The Old Testament Pseudepigrapha, vol. 1 (New York; London: Yale University Press, 1983), 23.

> Ezekiel 32:7–8
> When I blot you out, I will cover the heavens and make their stars dark; I will cover the sun with a cloud, and the moon shall not give its light. All the bright lights of heaven will I make dark over you, and put darkness on your land, declares the Lord GOD.

This destruction occurred around 580 B.C. But we have no records of these astronomical events occurring along with the historical ones. While these descriptions are certainly possible as physical phenomena, they are not necessarily so, because as I've noted elsewhere, the entire Exodus story is framed as a war of Yahweh on Pharaoh and the gods of Egypt. So whether this is literal or not, the meaning is certainly that Yahweh would "put the lights out" of both earthly Egypt and her heavenly principalities that ruled over her.

But there are many other examples of this astronomical language that is clearly not literal astronomical phenomena, but metaphorical reference to the fall of powers. Many of them refer to the same Babylonian campaign of conquest in the same time period.

When Babylon invaded Judah in 587 B.C., it also took out Edom. And the prophet Isaiah predicted that fall of kingdoms as "All the host of heaven shall rot away, and the skies roll up like a scroll. All their host shall fall, as leaves fall from the vine, like leaves falling from the fig tree." (Isaiah 34:4).

Edom fell in the 6th century B.C., but these astronomical events never occurred, because of course, if the sky rolled up like that and all the stars fell, we wouldn't be here. There would be no universe left. That could not possibly be literal. It was the description, not of physical phenomena, but spiritual events of earthly and heavenly powers being overthrown.

And when that same Babylon destroyed Israel and led her into captivity in that same time period, the same prophet Isaiah predicted it in vivid poetic language as the "earth will be completely laid waste and despoiled" (Isaiah 24:3), the earth is "split and broken asunder" (24:19), something that could not and did not happen physically or scientifically, but was symbolic. And then Isaiah says that in this event of judgment, God will simultaneously punish the earthly rulers together with their heavenly counterparts, the "host of heaven," or the Watchers, principalities of power over the peoples.

> Isaiah 24:21–23
> On that day the LORD will punish <u>the host of heaven, in heaven, and the kings of the earth, on the earth</u>. They will be gathered together as <u>prisoners in a pit</u>; they will be shut up in a prison, and after many days they will be punished. Then <u>the moon will be confounded and the sun ashamed</u>.

The "confounding" of the moon and "shaming" of the sun is a poetic way of saying the principalities and powers will be humbled by their defeat. One cannot confound the physical moon or shame the physical sun.

One last example gives this notion of astronomical catastrophe a clear metaphorical reference to the spiritual realm. When Babylon ended up destroying Jerusalem and the temple in its 6th century campaign of conquest, Jeremiah the prophet described it as if the entire world was being returned to a pre-creation state of chaos. The very spiritual cosmos of the covenant as incarnate in the temple was being undone. Jeremiah uses the creation language of Genesis 1 but retells it as if creation is being undone. Chaos is overtaking the order established by God.

> Jeremiah 4:23–28
> I looked on the earth, and behold, it was <u>without form and void;</u>
> and to the <u>heavens, and they had no light</u>.
> I looked on the <u>mountains</u>, and behold, they were <u>quaking</u>,
> and all the <u>hills moved to and fro</u>.
> I looked, and behold, there <u>was no man</u>,
> and all the <u>birds of the air had fled</u>.
> I looked, and behold, the fruitful <u>land was a desert</u>,
> and all its cities were laid in ruins
> before the LORD, before his fierce anger.
> For thus says the LORD, "The <u>whole land shall be a desolation; yet</u>
> <u>I will not make a full end</u>.
> "For this the <u>earth shall mourn</u>,
> and the <u>heavens above be dark</u>."

The language should tip off the reader that this is a symbolic literary connection to Genesis 1. He says the earth "was without form and void," the exact same Hebrew words of Genesis 1:1 that described the chaos before God started creating. This obviously is not literal but symbolic, because the earth was not physically returned to that chaos state in 586 B.C. It is a statement of spiritual chaos, not literal physical destruction of the earth.

Then Jeremiah describes a kind of emptying of the things of heaven and earth created in the six days. No more birds in the air undoes the creation on the fifth day. No more vegetation on the earth is an undoing of the third day of creation. The elimination of all humans ("no man") is the elimination of the sixth day of creation. Obviously all the humans on earth were not killed in 586 B.C. The heavens going dark is a description of the spiritual realm being emptied of the power and influence they were created with on the fourth day. The heavens going dark is an undoing of the first act of creation and a return to the primeval darkness. Astronomical catastrophe was a metaphor to describe the fall or judgment of both earthly powers and their spiritual principalities, the heavenly host.

For more in depth study of the language of cosmic collapse in biblical prophecy, see my book <u>End Times Bible Prophecy: It's Not What They Told</u>

You (affiliate link).

But what of the judgment of these rebellious Watchers in Psalm 82? What is it and when does it occur?

Chapter 3: The Judgment of the Watchers

In chapters 1 and 2, I examined Psalm 82 to discover that it talks about God having a heavenly host of divine beings around his throne that counsel with him and carry out his judgments or decisions. They are called "holy ones" (Deut 33:2-3; Jude 14), "heavenly host" (1King 22:19) "the divine council" (Psa 82:1), and "Sons of God" (Job 5:1; 15:15).

Then I showed how God had separated the seventy Gentile nations at Babel, placing them under the authority of fallen Sons of God, now also called Watchers (Dan 4:13, 17), who were supposed to rule with justice, but instead ruled unjustly and in darkness. This resulted in their punishment.

But what kind of punishment is it and when does it occur?

Like Men You Shall Die

I believe the Watcher's punishment is loss of both their immortality and their inheritance of nations at Babel. And I will argue that this was accomplished in the first-century complex of events of Messiah's death, resurrection, ascension and arrival of God's kingdom. Let's take another look at Psalm 82 to get a good reminder of the narrative.

> Psalm 82:6–8
> I said, "You are gods,
> sons of the Most High, all of you;
> nevertheless, like men you shall die,
> and fall like any prince."
> Arise, O God, judge the earth;
> for you shall inherit all the nations!

The first aspect of God's judgment upon the gods of the nations is in verses 6 and 7. Apparently, their punishment is the loss of immortality, resulting in death like mortal humans. Though they were gods with divine immortality, they will now die like men.

The question is, what is this death? Is it literal or metaphorical? If it is literal, then the text indicates that the immortal Watchers would lose their immortality and die just like earthly princes. It seems to be a humiliation of the heavenly princes who would otherwise survive their earthly princes' demise. But in this case, the gods are being stripped of their immortality and, thus, their divinity. Death does not become divine beings. So death would be a most serious punishment for such a creature.

Isaiah confirms this loss of immortality when he describes the day of Watchers' judgment:

> Isaiah 24:21–22
> On that day the LORD will punish the host of heaven, in heaven, and the kings of the earth, on the earth. They will be gathered together as prisoners in a pit; they will be shut up in a prison, and after many days they will be punished.

Notice how the fate of the Watchers is tied to the fate of their allotted nations. The divine host of heaven will die together with their earthly kings or princes. And death is described here in the common Old Testament image of "the pit" of Sheol or Hades, the underworld of the dead (Isa 38:18; Ezek 31:16; Pss 30:3; 88:3–4; Prov 1:12), followed by some kind of punishment.

The New Testament confirms this death of the Watchers that it calls the "rulers of this age" who are "doomed to pass away."

> 1 Corinthians 2:6
> Yet among the mature we do impart wisdom, although it is not a wisdom of this age or of the rulers of this age, who are doomed to pass away.

I will explain in Chapter 4 that these rulers are not merely earthly rulers, but the spiritual rulers over those earthly ones; and then in Chapter 5 that their passing away will be at the end of the age. But for now, I just wanted to address the "doom of passing away" as being a reference to the death or loss of immortality in Psalm 82. The Greek root word translated as "doomed to pass away" in this 1 Corinthians verse (*katargeo*) is the same root as that used later by Paul of the destruction of every ruler and authority and even of death itself at the end.

> 1 Corinthians 15:24–26
> Then comes the end, when [Jesus] delivers the kingdom to God the Father after destroying (*katargeo*) every rule and every authority and power. For he must reign until he has put all his enemies under his feet. The last enemy to be destroyed (*katargeo*) is death.

Katargeo is defined in lexicons as meaning "to destroy or render powerless."[17] So the fate of the ruling Watchers will be the same fate as that of death itself, namely destruction and powerlessness. But of what does this destruction, this death, this doom and punishment consist? Is it mere loss of authority, or do they actually die like human princes? Do they simply cease to

---

[17] Horst Robert Balz and Gerhard Schneider, *Exegetical Dictionary of the New Testament* (Grand Rapids, Mich.: Eerdmans, 1990–), 267.

exist? It is at this point that the lack of detail in the biblical text tempts us to consider texts that are outside the canon—though considered worthy by the canon—to answer the question.

The biblical source material of 1 Enoch suggests some detail that may shed light on the ancient Judeo-Christian understanding of the fate of the Watchers. As I have argued in a booklet on the book of 1 Enoch, the New Testament has drawn much from this pseudepigraphal text regarding the Watchers of the ancient world.

Jude paraphrases the storyline of 1 Enoch and then quotes verse 1:9 to describe God's coming judgment:

> Jude 14–15
> It was also about these that Enoch, the seventh from Adam, prophesied, saying, "Behold, the Lord comes with ten thousands of his holy ones, to execute judgment on all and to convict all the ungodly of all their deeds of ungodliness that they have committed in such an ungodly way, and of all the harsh things that ungodly sinners have spoken against him." [This is quoted from 1 Enoch 1:9]

Jude 6-7 and 1 Peter 3:18 draw from 1 Enoch to describe the sin of the Watchers before the Flood and their punishment of being chained in Tartarus "until the judgment of the great day."[18] One need not require acceptance of 1 Enoch as Scriptural canon to affirm its story of the Watchers as having some truth. After all, the New Testament authors do. How much of 1 Enoch is true is certainly up for debate, but it is a biblically legitimate resource for seeking some answers.

For a detailed argument of Evangelical Christian respect for the book of 1 Enoch, see my booklet on 1 Enoch.

The Judgment of Fire

1 Enoch 10 describes the fate of the pre-Flood heavenly Watchers who defied God by fornicating with earthly women. They are first bound beneath the rocks of the earth to await their judgment. And what is that judgment? Death. Just like the punishment explained for the post-Babel Watchers in Psalm 82:7. Then that "death judgment" is further unpacked as involving burning destruction. Here is the actual text:

---

[18] Lest anyone misunderstand Jude's reference to the location of the binding of the angels, Peter locates it right in Sheol, as Enoch did. He writes that God "did not spare the angels when they sinned, but cast them into hell and committed them to chains of gloomy darkness" (v. 4). The word for "hell" in this passage is tartaroo, not gehenna, the traditional designation for the English translation of hell. Tartaroo is a Greek word that refers to Tartarus, the deepest location in Sheol, where it was said in Greek lore that the gigantic Titans were chained. Enoch however says this is where the fallen angels, the Watchers, were chained (1 En. 63:10-64:1).

> 1 Enoch 10:11-15
> And to Michael God said, "Make known to Semyaza and the others who are with him, who fornicated with the women, that they will die together with them in all their defilement. And when they and all their children have battled with each other, and when they have seen the destruction of their beloved ones, bind them for seventy generations underneath the rocks of the ground until the day of their judgment and of their consummation, until the eternal judgment is concluded. In those days they will lead them into the bottom of the fire—and in torment—in the prison (where) they will be locked up forever. And at the time when they will burn and die, those who collaborated with them will be bound together with them from henceforth unto the end of (all) generations. And destroy all the souls of pleasure and the children of the Watchers, for they have done injustice to man.[19]

These pre-Flood Watchers who fornicated with human women are not the same persons as the post-Babel Watchers who were allotted the nations, but their judgment of "death" is the same: the loss of their immortality through death. It is likely that the death in Psalm 82 involves the same fire as in 1 Enoch 10. And that fire is later described as the "furnace of fire."

> 1 Enoch 54:6
> Then Michael, Raphael, Gabriel, and Phanuel themselves shall seize [the sinful Watchers] on that great day of judgment and cast them into the furnace (of fire) that is burning that day, so that the Lord of the Spirits may take vengeance on them.[20]

Whether the "furnace of fire" is literal or not, it certainly pictures God's final judgment of destruction for those beings. This imagery of a fiery furnace of judgment is also used by Jesus in his parables when he describes the judgment of all sinners and law-breakers at the end of the age.

> Matthew 13:41–42
> The Son of Man will send his angels, and they will gather out of his kingdom all causes of sin and all law-breakers, and throw

---

[19] James H. Charlesworth, *The Old Testament Pseudepigrapha*, vol. 1 (New York; London: Yale University Press, 1983), 18.

[20] James H. Charlesworth, *The Old Testament Pseudepigrapha*, vol. 1 (New York; London: Yale University Press, 1983), 38.

> them into the fiery furnace. In that place there will be weeping and gnashing of teeth. (see also Matt 13:49-50)

Though the Matthean parable seems to be referring to human sinners, it is not too much of a stretch to conclude that law-breaking angels who cause sin will be included in that fiery judgment, especially since 1 Enoch describes a furnace of fire for the Watchers as well.

The book of Revelation describes a "lake of fire" where the beast, the false prophet, the devil, Death and Hades, and indeed, all unbelieving sinners will have their end (Rev 20:10, 15; 21:8). Is this lake of fire the same furnace of fire that Enoch and Jesus taught about? The similarities and connections are too strong to deny. They are both used to describe the punishment of sinful humans and Watchers in fire. And they both occur at the same time, the "end of the age," the "day of judgment."

Is it too speculative to posit that rebellious post-Babel Watchers over the nations would die the same death that involves the same judgment in the same lake (or furnace) of fire as rebellious pre-Flood Watchers and other spiritual and human sinners? Perhaps, but it seems far more speculative to suggest otherwise.

> Revelation 20:15; 21:8
> And if anyone's name was not found written in the book of life, he was thrown into the lake of fire...But as for the cowardly, the faithless, the detestable, as for murderers, the sexually immoral, sorcerers, idolaters, and all liars, their portion will be in the lake that burns with fire and sulfur, which is the second death."

Remember, Jesus himself said that the eternal fire (another synonym for Lake of Fire) was actually made "for the devil and his angels" (Matt 25:41). So eternal fire once again appears to be the final judgment for fallen angels or Watchers.

Stoicheia: The Elemental Spirits

I believe there is another possible hint at the fiery destruction of the Watchers in 2 Peter 3. The relevant passage reads,

> 2 Peter 3:10-12
> But the day of the Lord will come like a thief, and then the heavens will pass away with a roar, and the heavenly bodies will be burned up and dissolved... waiting for and hastening the coming of the day of God, because of which the heavens will be set on fire and dissolved, and the heavenly bodies will melt as they burn!

In this passage that refers to the judgment of the last days (2 Pet 3:3), I want to focus on the word "heavenly bodies." In Greek, that word is *stoicheia*. Though some believe *stoicheia* is a reference to astronomical bodies like the sun, moon and stars, others believe it is better translated as "elements," such as the periodic table of the material universe. But these are both physical interpretations that reflect our modern scientific materialist bias.

There is another scholarly interpretation that argues for a spiritual interpretation of *stoicheia* in this passage. It is only used five other times in the New Testament. In three of those places, the context seems to refer to the "elementary principles" of the old covenant (Gal 4:3, 9; Heb 5:12). These have nothing to do with the physical periodic table of elements or astronomical bodies.

> Hebrews 5:12
> For though by this time you ought to be teachers, you need someone to teach you again the basic <u>principles</u> [*stoicheia*] of the oracles of God…

In the two other places *stoicheia* occurs (Col 2:8, 20), it is used in reference to the elementary principles of pagan worldviews.

> Colossians 2:8
> See to it that no one takes you captive by philosophy and empty deceit, according to human tradition, according to the <u>elemental spirits</u> [*stoicheia*] of the world, and not according to Christ.

But it is here that there is some ambiguity. Some translations render *stoicheia* here as "elemental spirits," because there is reason to believe the term is a spiritual one that refers to the bondage of the nations to the spiritual powers.[21] This would be consistent with the Deuteronomy 32 worldview of the Gentile nations under the Watchers' authority.

If this interpretation of *stoichea* is applied to 2 Peter 3:10-12, then what we see is a picture perfectly consistent with Psalm 82, 1 Enoch, Matthew and

---

[21] "We may consider the suggestion that stoicheia tou kosmou was Paul's particular way of referring to "local presiding deities" or "national 'gods' " who rule over territories and races. N. T. Wright has argued for this meaning in Colossians, understanding Paul to be engaged in a polemic against Judaism rather than some sort of Jewish-Hellenistic syncretism, and he sees the same meaning operative in Galatians (see Wright, 101–2, 115–16). Following and developing this line of interpretation we could understand ta stoicheia tou kosmou as a broad, inclusive term that embraced the whole host of spiritual beings known individually as principalities, powers, dominions and rulers, the equivalent to the angels or gods of the nations (see Principalities and Powers). In Galatians 4:8 Paul speaks of the Galatians as formerly enslaved to "those beings which by nature are no gods." This analysis of the Galatian Gentiles' former situation resonates with the Jewish notion that the gods of the nations are not really what they appear to be; they are but spiritual powers appointed as national guardians by Yahweh, ultimately subservient to him alone, but falsely regarded as "gods" by the nations."

Gerald F. Hawthorne, Ralph P. Martin, and Daniel G. Reid, eds., *Dictionary of Paul and His Letters* (Downers Grove, IL: InterVarsity Press, 1993), 232.

Revelation as described above. At the Day of the Lord, God will judge and burn up with fire those spiritual powers, the Watchers, who ruled unjustly over the nations along with their human equivalents.

But one question remains: When does this judgment of the Watchers' death take place? When are they thrown into the lake of fire? 1 Enoch says after seventy generations from the Flood. The New Testament says at the end of the age. But when is that? Is it in our future? Or did it already happen? The answer might shock you.

Chapter 4:
The Inheritance of the Nations

In previous chapters, I unpacked Psalm 82 to show that it talks about God having a heavenly host of divine beings around his throne. Some of these beings, called Watchers, were given the Gentile nations as an allotted inheritance in contrast with Israel as God's inheritance. But those heavenly host ruled their nations unjustly. This resulted in their punishment of death like humans, and most likely destruction in the lake of fire.

It is now the question of *when* this judgment of the Watchers occurs that I want to address. Many would assume it occurs at the end of the world in our future. But I think the text of Psalm 82 implies that it has already happened in our past.

Here is the relevant text of the Psalm to look at again:

> Psalm 82:5–8
> They have neither knowledge nor understanding,
> they walk about in darkness;
> all the foundations of the earth are shaken.
> I said, "You are gods,
> sons of the Most High, all of you;
> nevertheless, like men you shall die,
> and fall like any prince."
> Arise, O God, judge the earth;
> for you shall inherit all the nations!

The Foundations of the Earth are Shaken

There are three reasons in the Psalm that make me conclude that the capital punishment of the fallen Watchers occurred in the first century AD in conjunction with the coming of Messiah. 1) Verse 5 refers to "the foundations of the earth" being shaken. This is a reference to the consummation of the new covenant that came in Christ to overturn the Deuteronomic inheritance. 2) Verse 8 sets the context of the judgment at the resurrection of Messiah, which resulted in 3) Messiah's subsequent inheritance of the nations in the first century.

Let me explain each one.

First, the phrase "all the foundations of the earth are shaken" (v. 5) ties the context of the Watchers' judgment to the arrival of the new covenant. The concept of the shaking of heavens and earth is a common notion in the Old and New Testaments. It is used figuratively to describe the spiritual reality of an earthly event.

In Haggai 2:21-22, the prophet is told to tell the governor of Judah that God is going to "shake the heavens and the earth, and to overthrow the throne of kingdoms. I am about to destroy the strength of the kingdoms of the nations." This prophecy explains the shaking of heavens and earth as a symbolic reference to the destruction of the strength of kingdoms.

Shaking heavens and earth is commonly used as a metaphor for God overthrowing kingdoms or establishing a new authority (Isa 40:3-5; Hab 3:6-7, 9-10; Micah 1:3-7; Jer 4:23-30; Nahum 1:4-6; Psa 18:6-15; Judges 5:4-5).

The New Testament uses the imagery of shaking the heavens and earth as an expression of the spiritual impact of covenants. John the Baptizer's proclamation was described as a leveling of mountains and upheaval of valleys.

> Luke 3:3–6
> [John the Baptizer] went into all the region around the Jordan, proclaiming a baptism of repentance for the forgiveness of sins. As it is written in the book of the words of Isaiah the prophet, "The voice of one crying in the wilderness: 'Prepare the way of the Lord, make his paths straight. Every valley shall be filled, and every mountain and hill shall be made low, and the crooked shall become straight, and the rough places shall become level ways, and all flesh shall see the salvation of God.'"

This cosmic geological eruption occurred in the first century with the coming of Messiah. John the Baptizer was not pronouncing the second coming of Christ, he was pronouncing the first coming of Christ. So the terminology of the earth shaking was a spiritual reference to the impact of the New Covenant arrival. God becoming flesh in the savior Jesus is described as "all flesh seeing the salvation of God." That's obviously hyperbole. It was not literally physical as many Christians often mistakenly interpret prophecy. Why? Because it was a metaphor for the historic change of covenants and earthly powers.

In Hebrews 12, the creation of the old Mosaic covenant is described figuratively as God "shaking the earth," with the institution of his world-changing covenant. The new covenant in Christ is then referred to as a final shaking of the heavens and earth. The institution of the new covenant kingdom of God will never be shaken, that is, never be changed.

> Hebrews 12:26–28
> At that time [of the old covenant] his voice shook the earth, but now he has promised, "Yet once more I will shake not only the earth but also the heavens." This phrase, "Yet once more," indicates the removal of things that are shaken—that is, things that have been made—in order that the things that

cannot be shaken may remain. Therefore let us be grateful
for receiving a kingdom that cannot be shaken.

The arrival of the Mosaic old covenant was described in terms of God shaking the earth (v. 26). This is not a reference to physical earthquakes, but to the spiritual impact of covenant-making. We know this because the new covenant kingdom in Christ is described in like manner as a spiritual shaking of the heavens and earth of the old covenant, to replace it with a superior, permanent new covenant.

So the reference in Psalm 82:5 of God shaking the foundations of the earth is a symbolic reference to the arrival of the new covenant kingdom which is linked to the judgment of the Watchers. When the old covenant is abolished and replaced with the new covenant, God will take back the allotment of authority to the Watchers and judge them.

This connection between Psalm 82 and Hebrews 12 is made all the stronger when one realizes that Hebrews 12 is quoting Haggai 2 that prophesies the new covenant kingdom.

> Haggai 2:6–7
> For thus says the LORD of hosts: Yet once more, in a little while, I will shake the heavens and the earth and the sea and the dry land. And I will shake all nations, so that the treasures of all nations shall come in, and I will fill this house with glory, says the LORD of hosts.

Notice that the last part of that cosmic spiritual shaking of heavens and earth includes the drawing of the nations, the Gentiles, into God's house. The new covenant would involve the messianic inclusion of the Gentiles into the very house of God. That means that the allotted inheritance of the Gentiles to the Sons of God would be taken back by Messiah with the arrival of a new covenant, a new inheritance.

Remember, allotment and inheritance has to do with land and ownership in the old covenant. That leads us to the next element of our context, the inheritance of the nations.

The Inheritance of the Nations

The last verse of Psalm 82 places the event of the judgment of the Watchers at the time of the inheritance of the nations.

> Psalm 82:8
> Arise, O God, judge the earth;
> for you shall inherit all the nations!

Before we proceed, it must be noted that the English words that we read as *Gentiles* and *nations* are the same Greek and Hebrew word in the Bible (*ethnos* and *goyim*). "Gentiles" and "nations" are synonyms.

Scripturally, a Gentile was nothing more than a member of one of the seventy nations of Genesis 10 that were allotted to the Watchers in Deuteronomy 32. Sometimes, I will use the words together as "Gentile nations" only to remind the reader of that contextual reality.

This concept of inheriting the nations is messianic. The prophets predicted that when Messiah came, he would not only unite the houses of Judah and Israel, but he would bring the Gentile nations, previously cut off from his covenant, into his new covenant kingdom (Zech 2:6-11; Hos 1:10-11, 2:23; fulfilled in Rom 9:24-29).

At this point, it would be helpful to remember the Deuteronomy 32 worldview with which we started this narrative. God allotted the Gentile nations as an inheritance of the rebellious angelic Sons of God (Deut 32:8-9).

But now in Psalm 2, we read that God will inherit the nations. Or more specifically, Messiah will inherit the nations. God will take away the land deed of the Gentile nations from the Sons of God and give it to Messiah. How do we know this? Because the Psalm says so.

> Psalm 2:6–8
> "As for me, I have set my King on Zion, my holy hill." I will tell of the decree: The LORD said to me, "You are my Son; today I have begotten you. Ask of me, and <u>I will make the nations your heritage, and the ends of the earth your possession</u>.

Now, some would read this and argue that Jesus becoming king and his inheritance of the nations may not occur at the same time period in history. It is possible that he is enthroned as king now, but doesn't inherit the nations until later in our future. Others think Jesus is not yet enthroned as king. And both would be wrong.

In Acts 13:32-33, the apostle Paul quotes this same Psalm and connects it to the resurrection of Jesus.

> Acts 13:32–33
> "And we bring you the good news that what God promised to the fathers, this he has fulfilled to us their children by raising Jesus, as also it is written in the second Psalm, "'You are my Son, today I have begotten you.'"

Paul defines the context for Psalm 2 and Messiah's enthronement and inheritance of the nations *at the time of his resurrection.*

Do you see the powerful imagery here? The resurrection was a kind of birth from the dead that granted the inheritance of the nations to Jesus like the birthright of a firstborn son. To confirm this interpretation, Paul even uses the symbolic phrase "firstborn from the dead" of Jesus in reference to his resurrection in Colossians 1:18. Firstborn was a legal term of inheritance. When Jesus resurrected from the dead, he received the firstborn inheritance.

In Acts 2:30-35, Peter explains that "God had sworn with an oath to him that he would set one of his descendants on his throne, he foresaw and spoke about the resurrection of the Christ... being therefore exalted at the right hand of God."

So Christ was enthroned as universal king on heavenly Mount Zion at his resurrection and ascension (Heb 12:22-24). And that throne is over all authority, in heaven and on earth (Eph 1:20-22), including the Watchers and the nations.

At Babel, God gave over the rebellious Gentiles to the false gods they worshipped. He placed them under the authority of the fallen Sons of God. These spiritual princes ruled over their earthly kings and rulers and their fates were intertwined. But the gods of the nations had the title deed to the lands of the nations, and with it, their people.

It is my contention that when Messiah died, resurrected and ascended, he conquered those Watchers and took back the deeds to the nations, which allowed the Gospel of the kingdom to go out into all the world and draw people from every tribe and nation into the new covenant kingdom of God.

To see this narrative, we need to turn to the New Testament affirmation of the Deuteronomy 32 worldview.

New Testament Principalities and Powers

The idea of heavenly principalities over the earthly powers first instituted at Babel and continued on through Daniel is not lost on the New Testament writers.

Paul in particular alludes frequently to the heavenly/earthly connection of principalities and powers.

> Colossians 1:16
> For by him all things were created, in heaven and on earth,
> visible and invisible, whether thrones or dominions or rulers
> or authorities...

When Paul tried to encourage the Ephesian Christians suffering persecution from their local authorities, he did so by reminding them that those earthly powers were not the ultimate enemy; the heavenly powers behind them were. Those powers were led by the "prince of the power of the air" Satan (Eph 2:2).

> Ephesians 6:12
> For we do not wrestle against flesh and blood, but against
> the rulers, against the authorities, against the cosmic powers
> over this present darkness, against the spiritual forces of evil
> in the heavenly places.

But how would these powers be defeated? The secret was rooted in the

Gospel that Paul called the "mystery" that God kept from those powers (1 Cor 2:7-8). And guess what that mystery is? The Gospel adoption of Gentile nations into the new covenant kingdom of God through Christ.

> Ephesians 3:6
> This mystery is that the Gentiles are fellow heirs, members of the same body, and partakers of the promise in Christ Jesus through the gospel.

Remember how those Gentile nations were originally the allotted inheritance of the rebellious Sons of God? Remember how Messiah was promised to one day inherit the nations from those powers? Well, the unity of Gentiles with Jews in the Body of Christ, the Church, is the fulfillment of that messianic inheritance of the nations.

> Ephesians 3:10
> so that through the church the manifold wisdom of God might now be made known to the rulers and authorities in the heavenly places.

Exactly when did Jesus take back the territorial rights of the nations from the heavenly powers? *At his death, resurrection and ascension into heaven.*

Remember when Jesus told his disciples, after he had risen that "all authority in heaven and on earth has been given to me" (Matt 28:18)? He had *all* authority, not *some* authority. If Watchers still had authority over the nations, then Jesus would not have all authority, and he could not be the Messiah.

Paul links Christ's attainment of all authority to his resurrection and ascension to the right hand of God.

> Ephesians 1:20–22
> that he worked in Christ when he raised him from the dead and seated him at his right hand in the heavenly places, far above all rule and authority and power and dominion, and above every name that is named, not only in this age but also in the one to come. And he put all things under his feet.

So Christ's attainment of authority over all those heavenly powers occurred through his resurrection and ascension. His enthronement constitutes the legal authority taken away from the heavenly powers. The Watchers no longer own their allotted lands of inheritance.

Peter reiterates this submission of all heavenly powers with emphatic clarity.

> 1 Peter 3:22
> [Jesus] has gone into heaven and is at the right hand of God, with angels, authorities, and powers having been subjected to him.

There it is again, Jesus seated at the right hand of God as the ultimate conquest over all heavenly beings. So, all spiritual powers, including the Watchers, were subjected to Christ through his ascension. They simply do not have territorial authority anymore. They simply do not watch over the nations. Jesus Christ watches over the nations. He owns them.

In Chapter 3, I used 1 Corinthians 2:6 as a New Testament expression of the Watchers as heavenly authorities who were "doomed to pass away," or "die like men" (Psalm 82:7).

> 1 Corinthians 2:6–8
> Yet among the mature we do impart wisdom, although it is not a wisdom of this age or of the rulers of this age, who are doomed to pass away. But we impart a secret and hidden wisdom of God, which God decreed before the ages for our glory. None of the rulers of this age understood this, for if they had, they would not have crucified the Lord of glory.

Some might interpret this passage as a reference only to the earthly rulers who crucified Jesus (Acts 4:27-28; 2:23). But it should be clear by now, that Paul's use of the "rulers, authorities and powers" terminology is more in line with the Old Covenant notion of spiritual powers behind the earthly powers. Yes, earthly rulers crucified Jesus, but in truth, they were tools of the spiritual rulers just like the human rulers of Persia and Greece were the tools of the spiritual "princes" of Persia and Greece in Daniel's day (Dan 10:12-13, 20-21). And those spiritual rulers of "this age" were doomed to pass away with the age to come, the age of Messiah. More on that in the next Chapter 5.

Triumphal Procession

But there is more. Paul also reveals the ascension of Christ as involving a violent overthrow of the Watchers. He quotes Isaiah to show that after Christ ascended, he then descended to earth to give spiritual gifts to the Church through the Holy Spirit.

> Ephesians 4:7–10
> But grace was given to each one of us according to the measure of Christ's gift. Therefore it says, "When he ascended on high he led a host of captives, and he gave gifts to men." (In saying, "He ascended," what does it mean but that he had also descended into the lower regions, the earth?)

Notice that Christ's ascension is described as "leading a host of captives." Some Christians assume these are human captives freed from Hades through Christ's sacrifice. But that is not what the phrase means. It is actually a reference to the common ancient Roman triumphal procession, which involved military victors parading their conquered foes, dead or alive, through the streets of a city. It was rubbing the noses of the vanquished in their defeat and declaring the victor's new authority over those conquered foes.

Scholar Mary Beard describes the ancient Roman Triumph:

> To be awarded a triumph was the most outstanding honor a Roman general could hope for. He would be drawn in a chariot—accompanied by the booty he had won, the prisoners he had taken captive, and his no doubt rowdy and raucous troops in their battle gear—through the streets of the city to the Temple of Jupiter on the Capitoline hill, where he would offer a sacrifice to the god. The ceremony became a by-word for extravagant display…
> As the triumphal parade was reaching its last lap, passing through the Forum and about to ascend the Capitoline hill, the prisoners—or at least the most prominent, famous, or dastardly among them—were hauled off for execution and worse, probably in the nearby prison. [22]

Through analogy, Paul is saying that when Christ ascended to his throne at the right hand of God, he led the conquered and captive gods of the nations through spiritual streets as a victorious general and king, and executed them.

This interpretation is reinforced in Colossians where Paul writes that through the cross Jesus "disarmed the rulers and authorities and put them to open shame, by triumphing over them in him" (Col 2:15).

Beard describes the story from ancient Jewish historian Josephus of the triumph of Vespasian and Titus over Simon bar Gioras that occurred after the Roman destruction of Jerusalem in A.D. 70, the very time period in which Paul wrote his references to Christ's triumph over the powers.

> "Once they had reached the Temple of Jupiter Capitolinus, they stopped. For it was ancestral custom to wait at that point for the announcement of the death of the enemy commander. This was Simon, son of Gioras. He had been led in the procession amongst the prisoners of war; then, a noose round his neck, scourged by his guards, he had been taken to that place next to the Forum where Roman law prescribes that condemned criminals be executed. After the announcement came that he had met his end and the

[22] Mary Beard, *The Roman Triumph* (Mass: Harvard, 2007), 1, 128.

> universal cheering that followed it, Vespasian and Titus began the sacrifice."[23]

Beard points out that though there were certainly historical cases of imprisonment in place of execution for the Roman Triumph, its mythology or imagery included execution. This becomes relevant for understanding the proper context of when the Watchers will be judged to "die like men" (Psalm 82:8). The imagery of Triumph in Paul's writing suggests their deaths are tied in with the conclusion of the procession, not in some prophetic future.

Christ's apparent defeat at the cross led to the surprise victory of the resurrection and ascension to universal authority. Captivating, disarming, shaming and triumphing are all violent military words of subjugation that paint a clear picture of disinherited Watchers who no longer have the power and authority they were once allotted in primeval days. And that defeat includes the imprisonment and execution of the vanquished in the triumphal procession.

That triumphal procession to death is hinted at when Paul uses the same imagery of the Apostles as being led in an earthly Triumph to their deaths.

> 1 Corinthians 4:8-9 (NIV)
> You have begun to reign—and that without us! How I wish that you really had begun to reign so that we also might reign with you! For it seems to me that God has put us apostles on display <u>at the end of the procession, like those condemned to die in the arena</u>. We have been <u>made a spectacle</u> to the whole universe, to angels as well as to human beings.

In this passage, Paul is not referring to the spiritual authorities, but he is using the Triumph imagery again. And notice the reign of new kings follows upon the vanquishing of other authorities, in this case, the apostles! Notice that the assumption is the triumphal procession ends *with the execution of the vanquished in the arena*. "Spectacle" in Greek is the word from which we derive our English word, "theater." To the ancient mind the theater of the procession and arena was symbolic and expressive of the defeat and execution of enemy powers. And the Kingdom of God that Paul was preaching was relevant to both heaven and earth, the heavenly authorities of "angels" as well as the earthly "human beings."

Later, Paul extends the metaphor of Triumph to an ongoing display of the suffering of Christians as a means of converting others.

---

[23] Beard, *The Roman Triumph*, 129.

> 2 Corinthians 2:14
> But thanks be to God, who in Christ always leads us in triumphal procession, and through us spreads the fragrance of the knowledge of him everywhere.

Just as the apparent earthly "defeat" of Jesus at the cross would turn around and achieve the real spiritual victory over the powers, so too would the suffering of Christians, and their subjugation to Christ, become an ironic influence on spreading the truth of the Gospel.

There can be no doubt that the principalities and powers, those Sons of God who were allotted the nations at Babel, were finally conquered at the cross and led captive at the ascension of Christ to his enthronement over all powers and authorities in both heaven and earth. But the imagery of Roman Triumph that Paul uses also includes the execution of the "powers and principalities."

Under His Feet

There is another military image that the Scriptures use to describe complete victory over and subjugation of one's enemies, and that is the notion of "placing them under the feet."

A victorious general placing his foot on the necks of the vanquished ruler was a common symbolic activity in the ancient world. Joshua did it to the kings of Canaan when he conquered the Promised Land:

> Joshua 10:24–26
> Joshua summoned all the men of Israel and said to the chiefs of the men of war who had gone with him, "Come near; put your feet on the necks of these kings." Then they came near and put their feet on their necks. And Joshua said to them, "Do not be afraid or dismayed; be strong and courageous. For thus the LORD will do to all your enemies against whom you fight." And afterward Joshua struck them and put them to death.

Notice also that the execution of the vanquished was the consummation of that symbolic activity of putting the defeated beneath the victor's feet. This is not a mere symbol of power and authority, it is an incarnation of violent subjugation, followed immediately by execution.

Yet, this is exactly the image used of Christ's victory over the principalities and powers, the Watchers and their minions. As already noted, Ephesians 1:22 says that when Christ was enthroned in heaven, he "put all things under his feet." As a matter of fact, this phrase is part of the most-quoted Old Testament verse in the New Testament, Psalm 110.

Psalm 110:1
The LORD says to my Lord: "Sit at my right hand, until I put
your enemies under your feet."
(See also Psa 47:2-3; Isa 18:37-38)

Jesus and the apostles affirm that this prophecy of putting enemies under the feet was spoken to the Son of David as part and parcel of his enthronement in heaven, accomplished at his death, resurrection and ascension to the right hand of God (Matt. 22:44; Mark 12:36; Luke 20:42, 43; Acts 2:34, 35).

Now, if you're an informed Bible reader, you will probably be thinking of another connected messianic image that is woven into the tapestry of Scripture. I'm referring to Messiah crushing the head of Satan, the serpent.

In Genesis 3, God curses the serpent because of his deception of Adam and Eve in the Garden. He gives what theologians call the "protoevangelion," the first messianic promise of the Gospel.

Genesis 3:15 (NIV)
And I will put enmity between you [the serpent] and the
woman, and between your offspring and hers; he will crush
your head, and you will strike his heel."

Is this defeat of Satan in our future or in our past or something else? Later, I will argue that it occurred in our past in the first century (Rom 16:20). For now, just notice that the complex of events of Christ dying, resurrecting and ascending to his throne is described as a violent military style subjugation and stripping of authority from spiritual powers, including the Watchers, a placing of them under his feet, followed by their execution, and crushing the head of the serpent also under his feet.

Psalm 82 confirms that connection of the resurrection to the time of Messiah's inheritance of the nations.

Arise, O God

Psalm 82:8
Arise, O God, judge the earth;
for you shall inherit all the nations!

"Arise, O God…" is on the surface, a call to action for God to stand from his seated throne of judgment and actively perform his judgments (Psa 44:26-27; 74:22; 76:9-10).

But I think it goes deeper. I believe that Psalm 82 is referring to the complex of events surrounding Messiah's death, resurrection and ascension.

You see, the word for "arise" (*anasta*) in the Greek Old Testament is a word used of resurrection in the New Testament (Mark 5:41; Acts 9:40; Eph 5:14). I think Psalm 82 is making a veiled reference to the resurrection of Messiah as the foundation of the inheritance of the nations.

But I am not making this symbolic connection from my own poetic imagination; I got it from the apostle Paul. In Romans 15, he writes about Jesus and his resurrection being the catalyst that brings in the Gentiles, as foretold in Isaiah.

> Romans 15:12
> Isaiah says, "The root of Jesse will come, even he who arises to rule the Gentiles; in him will the Gentiles hope."

But when you go back and look at the passage in Isaiah that Paul quotes, we see a slightly different interpretation of the "arising."

> Isaiah 11:10–12
> In that day the root of Jesse, who shall stand as a signal for the peoples—of him shall the [Gentiles] nations inquire, …
> He will raise a signal for the nations…

Paul quotes the Greek Old Testament here that interpretively changes the raising of a battle standard into the raising of a person. Paul claims that person is Jesus who arose (*anasta*). And it's that same Greek word, *anasta,* that is used in the Greek version of Psalm 82:8 ("Arise, O God").

As New Testament scholars like N.T. Wright point out, the fulfillment of Christ "arising" to rule the nations (Gentiles) is an obvious contextual pointer to Christ's resurrection. So the claim of seeing the resurrection in the statement, "Arise O God, judge the earth. For you shall inherit all the nations (Gentiles)," is not only consistent with apostolic interpretation, it fits the parameters of the new covenant kingdom of Messiah that brings judgment and salvation for all.

The resurrection of Christ permeates Psalm 82. It is the very context that results in and includes Messiah's enthronement as well as his inheritance of the nations.

Some Christians believe that there are still Watchers with territorial control over nations today. That there is still a heavenly "prince of Russia" or "prince of Persia," etc. They justify this by appealing to the fact that many countries are still majority pagan, atheist or Muslim and therefore in bondage to the elemental spirits about which Paul wrote.

But if this is true, it would be equivalent to saying that Jesus did not triumph over the powers at his resurrection (Col 2:15); that he did not lead them captive to imprisonment (Eph 4:8); that Jesus is not enthroned at the right hand of God above all principalities and powers (Eph 1:21); that the Watchers are not under his feet (Eph 1:22); and executed at the conclusion of the triumphal procession (1 Cor 4:8-9); that Messiah did not inherit the nations (Psa 2:6-8); that the Gentiles cannot come into the kingdom because they are still in bondage to those spiritual powers (Rom 15:12); because all these things are tied together as occurring in and through the death, resurrection and ascension of Christ.

The very reason why people from all tribes and peoples and languages are becoming Christians through the Gospel is because Jesus the Messiah has freed them, because Messiah has disinherited the Watchers and has inherited the nations.

Simply stated, the Messiah could not draw people from any of the nations if there were still Watchers with any authority over them. The Watchers were disinherited, judged and died as Psalm 82 predicted; they were disarmed, shamed and triumphed over (Col 2:15), their necks placed under the feet of the conquering Messiah and they were executed. The spiritual authorities were not released to return back to their nations.

But after establishing this narrative of Christus Victor, Christ's victory over the powers, there remains one big glaring issue: If the powers were defeated at the cross, if they were led captive at Christ's ascension, then why did the New Testament describe Christians as still in a wrestling match with them? (Eph 6:12). Does this mean that this struggle with those Watchers over the nations remain for us today? I'll take a look at that next.

Chapter 5:
The End of the Age

I analyzed Psalm 82 to uncover the narrative of Christ's victory over the powers. In it, we saw a reiteration of the Deuteronomy 32 worldview that depicted fallen Sons of God from Yahweh's heavenly host being allotted the Gentile nations as an inheritance, while Yahweh kept Israel for his own inheritance.

These Watchers over the nations were unjust in their governance, so Yahweh declared he would judge them with death through the resurrection of Messiah, which would take back the allotment from the Watchers and give it to Messiah to inherit the nations.

But if Jesus triumphed over the spiritual powers at the cross and then led them captive in a military style triumphal procession, ending in execution, then how is it that the New Testament speaks of an ongoing struggle with those heavenly principalities and powers for the Christian? Are these territorial powers still an issue for us today?

My short answer is that the principalities and powers are not an issue for us today, but they were in Paul's day because when he wrote his New Testament letters, the new covenant had been legally inaugurated at the cross, resurrection and ascension, but was not historically consummated until the destruction of the earthly incarnation of the old covenant, the holy temple in Jerusalem in AD 70. That event was the historical completion of the spiritual truth begun a generation earlier.

Paul was writing in a transition period between covenants. The new had been spiritually inaugurated but not historically consummated until the old had been done away with in the physical world. The old covenant was fading out but had not yet vanished with the destruction of the historical temple (Heb 8:13; 9:8-9).

Thus, the spiritual powers had lost their legal right to the Gentile nations at the complex of events that climaxed with the ascension of Jesus Christ. But their actual judgment of death in the fires of Gehenna took place when the consummation of the inheritance of the nations occurred at the end of the old covenant age.

Many Christians assume that the end of the age or the "last days" is the end of the world. Thus when Jesus speaks of casting sinners into the furnace of fire at the end of the age, they assume this has not yet happened. After all, does not Isaiah place the inheritance of the Gentiles in a future "last days"?

Isaiah 2:2
It shall come to pass in the last days that the mountain of the house of the LORD shall be established as the highest of the mountains, and shall be lifted up above the hills; and all the nations shall flow to it…

But I will show that the judgment of the Watchers in Psalm 82 occurred with the inheritance of the Gentiles which actually began in the book of Acts and was completed by AD 70 in the destruction of the temple.

The "last days" occurred in the first century and they were the last days of the old covenant, not the last days of history or the earth. Those last days of the old covenant began with the arrival of Messiah and lasted through the forty years after the cross until the old covenant incarnation, the holy temple, was destroyed in AD 70. So in effect, the forty years from AD 33 or so until AD 70 was a period of transition between covenants, where the new covenant had been inaugurated in the heavenly realm, but not yet consummated in the earthly realm until the earthly incarnation of the old covenant was destroyed. So, in effect, it was an overlap of covenants for forty years.

That's kind of hard for our brains to understand because we want a clean cut break between covenants. But the problem is that God is not a God of mere abstraction and philosophy. He is a God of history. And history is messy. So let me try to help clean up some of the apparent mess.

Acts and the Inheritance of the Gentile Nations

In Acts 2, we read about the first explosion of the Gospel with the first baptism of the Holy Spirit. It was the thing that Jesus had told them to wait for, which would launch them into all the world with the Good News (Acts 1:4).

Pentecost would be the historical inauguration of the heavenly new covenant achieved by the death, resurrection and ascension of Christ. It would be the pouring out of God's Spirit upon his people (Isa 32:12-19; 44:5; Ezek 36:25-28; 37:14).

The disciples asked Jesus if this was the time of the restoration of Israel (1:6). Jesus told them that the regathering or restoration of Israel would begin when the Holy Spirit came upon them soon.

And what was the restoration? The pouring out of God's Spirit and the regathering of Jews from all over the known earth in a metaphorical resurrection (Ezek 37). That's pretty strongly restorative. So when the disciples were baptized with the Spirit at Pentecost and began to speak in foreign tongues, that was the fulfillment of God's pouring out of his Spirit (Acts 2:16-17).

But it was also the beginning of the regathering of Jews because "there were dwelling in Jerusalem Jews, devout men from every nation under heaven" (Acts 2:5). The list of nations that is described (Acts 2:9-11) just happens to be a representative sampling of the seventy nations of Genesis 10, *the very nations that were allotted as an inheritance to the Watchers*.

But those seventy nations were also "all the nations" to which the Jews were scattered (Amos 9:9). And the scattering of the tribes of Israel was described as being swallowed up by the nations (Hosea 8:8). In other words, the tribes of Israel had become so intermingled with the Gentile nations that for Diaspora Jews to return to Jerusalem and follow Messiah constituted the nations being drawn into the new covenant kingdom of God. According to the apostle Luke, Pentecost of AD 30 was not only the ingathering of the tribes of Israel, it was the beginning of the inheritance of the Gentile nations.

Pentecost, AD 30, was the beginning of regathering the scattered Jews AND the reclamation of the divided nations. Pentecost was the undoing of both Exile and Babel.

Scholar Michael Heiser explains this connection of Pentecost to Babel and Exile:

> There are two key terms in [Acts 2] that connect it back to Babel in an unmistakable way. The flaming tongues are described as "divided" (Greek: *diamerizo*), and the crowd, composed of Jews from all the nations, is said to have been "confused" (Greek: *suncheo*).
>
> The second term, *suncheo* (v. 6), is the same word used in the Septuagint version of the Babel story in Genesis 11:7: "Come, let us go down and **confuse** [Septuagint: *suncheo*] their language there." The multiplicity of nations represented at Pentecost is another link to Babel. Each nation had a national language. More importantly, all those nations referred to in Acts 2:9–11 had been disinherited by Yahweh when they were divided.
> The other word of importance (*diamerizo*; v. 3) is also used in the Septuagint, but not in Genesis 11. It is found exactly where one would expect it if one were thinking in cosmic-geographical terms—Deuteronomy 32:8 (Septuagint: "When the Most High ***divided*** [*diamerizo*] the nations, when he scattered humankind, he fixed the boundaries of the nations"). This is a strong indication that Luke is drawing on the Septuagint, and specifically the Tower of Babel story in Genesis 11 and Deuteronomy 32:8–9, to describe the events on Pentecost.[24]

The inheritance of the nations involved the gathering of Gentiles together

---

[24] Michael S. Heiser, *The Unseen Realm: Recovering the Supernatural Worldview of the Bible*, First Edition (Bellingham, WA: Lexham Press, 2015), 298.

with the Jews that occurred all throughout the book of Acts. Notice these passages that say that the evangelism of Acts is the very fulfillment of the promise to gather the Gentiles with the Jews as his people:

> Acts 15:13–19
> After they finished speaking, James replied, "Brothers, listen to me. Simeon has related how God first visited the Gentiles, to take from them a people for his name. And with this the words of the prophets agree, just as it is written.

> Acts 26:23
> [Paul:] "that the Christ must suffer and that, by being the first to rise from the dead, he would proclaim light both to our people and to the Gentiles."

The "ingathering" of Gentiles with Jews was based upon unity of belief in Jesus as Messiah. Isaiah had prophesied that when Messiah first came (the branch of Jesse), *in that very day*, the Lord would "recover the remnant that remains of his people" from all the nations. "In that day," the root of Jesse would be "raised [resurrected] as a signal for the nations," and would "assemble the banished of Israel and gather the dispersed of Judah from the four corners of the earth" (Isa 11:1-2, 10-12). *In that day* of Messiah's arrival and resurrection (his raising as a signal), he would draw both the remnant of Israel as well as Gentile believers.

Paul likened that raising of the signal to Christ's resurrection and confirmed this Isaianic promise as already being fulfilled *during his ministry*:

> Romans 15:8–9, 12
> For I tell you that Christ became a servant to the circumcised to show God's truthfulness, in order to confirm the promises given to the patriarchs, and in order that the Gentiles might glorify God for his mercy…And again Isaiah says, "The root of Jesse will come, even he who arises to rule the Gentiles; in him will the Gentiles hope.

What were the promises given to the patriarchs that Paul says were confirmed ("verified") in Christ's resurrection? All of them, including the regathering (Acts 3:24; 32; 15:13-15; 24:24; 26:6). In fact, most of the prophecies about the regathering of Israel almost always add the inclusion of Gentiles as a simultaneous event.

Some Christians argue that God is currently bringing in the Gentiles, but he has yet to regather Israel. But Paul writes explicitly that the Isaianic prophecy about the gathering of the remnant *along with* the Gentiles was already being fulfilled *in his own day*, not in some distant future.

The Last Days of the Old Covenant

Back to Pentecost. In Acts 2, Peter then preaches a sermon about how this baptism of the Spirit meant that they were in the last days as Joel described, a time when the "Day of the Lord" was coming for Israel.

That Day of the Lord was the destruction of Jerusalem and the temple in AD 70. This has to be the case because Peter clearly states that the "last days" and "Day of the Lord" of Joel were being fulfilled in AD 30, not in a distant future (Acts 2:16). See my book *End Times Bible Prophecy* for the details on this.

> Acts 2:15–17
> For these people are not drunk, as you suppose, since it is only the third hour of the day. But this is what was uttered through the prophet Joel: " 'And in the last days it shall be, God declares, that I will pour out my Spirit on all flesh…

There could be no more explicit claim of Joel's "last days" being fulfilled in their day than Peter saying, "This is what was uttered through the prophet Joel." *This is* what was uttered. Not "this is yet to come," or "this *is like* what was uttered." ***This is*** what was uttered—or prophesied.

Pentecost was the beginning of the promise of God's outpoured Spirit, and it meant they were in the last days *in the first century*.

So the last days are not the last days of earth or of history. They must be the last days of something else.

The rest of Joel that Peter also quotes predicts the Day of the Lord. Christians tend to assume that the Day of the Lord is a reference to a universal end-of-time judgment. But in the Bible, it is not. In the Bible, "Day of the Lord" is used to describe a variety of local judgments by God on nations, peoples or cities (Zeph 1:7-15; Isa 13:6-19). So in their ancient Jewish mindset, every time a city, people or nation was judged by God, it was called "the Day of the Lord" for that local historical entity. Modern Christians tend to impose their own cultural bias, removed by thousands of years and thousands of miles, upon the text to make "Day of the Lord" mean the end of history judgment of all people that have ever existed. That's just not how the ancient mind thought.

The Day of the Lord to which Peter refers in Acts 2 is not a worldwide universal judgment but rather the localized national and city judgment of God. And what city or people were going to be judged in the coming Day of the Lord? Jesus said it would be Israel and her city and temple in Jerusalem (Matt 23:37-24:2; 21:37-45; 22:1-9; Luke 19:41-44).

Jesus described the Day of the Lord for Israel in his generation. He called it the "days of vengeance," with "wrath upon his people." That Day of the Lord was Yahweh using the Romans to destroy the holy city and temple in AD 70 because that generation of Jews as a whole did not accept the "time of the visitation" of Messiah (Luke 19:43-44). That was not a prophecy about some distant future, it was a prophecy that was fulfilled within a generation, within forty years—just like Jesus predicted (Matt 23:36; 24:34).

> Luke 21:20–24
> "But when you see Jerusalem surrounded by armies, then know that its desolation has come near. Then let those who are in Judea flee to the mountains, and let those who are inside the city depart, and let not those who are out in the country enter it, for these are days of vengeance, to fulfill all that is written. Alas for women who are pregnant and for those who are nursing infants in those days! For there will be great distress upon the earth and wrath against this people. They will fall by the edge of the sword and be led captive among all nations, and Jerusalem will be trampled underfoot by the Gentiles, until the times of the Gentiles are fulfilled.

Messiah would arrive in the last days of the old covenant to bring the new covenant, making the first obsolete. It was the age of Messiah that brought an end to the previous ages. And the historical event that marked the end of that old covenant age was the destruction of the old covenant temple and judgment of those who refused to let it go (I detail this historical fulfillment fully in narrative form in my novel series Chronicles of the Apocalypse).

The apostles said explicitly that they were in the last days, *in their own day*—also referred to as the "end of the ages":

> Hebrews 1:1–2
> Long ago, at many times and in many ways, God spoke to our fathers by the prophets, but in these last days he has spoken to us by his Son, whom he appointed the heir of all things.

> Hebrews 9:26
> for then [Jesus] would have had to suffer repeatedly since the foundation of the world. But as it is, he has appeared once for all at the end of the ages to put away sin by the sacrifice of himself.

> 1 Corinthians 10:11
> Now these things happened to them [in the old testament] as an example, but they were written down for our instruction, on whom the end of the ages has come.

The New Testament repeatedly states that those who lived in the first century were in the last days, or the end of the age(s). The Hebrews 9:26 verse says that Jesus' sacrifice on the cross marked the purpose of that age. His death and resurrection would herald the arrival of the Messianic age to come to which Jews everywhere looked forward. The last days or end of the age, were the last days of the old covenant because the Messiah brought in the new covenant age.

The common Jewish understanding was that there were basically two ages, the present age and the age to come, the age of Messiah. They were living in the "present age" that would be replaced by the messianic age to come (see 1 Tim 6:17; Titus 2:12; Heb 9:8-9; Eph 1:21; 1 Cor 2:6-8; Matt 12:32).

The old covenant age was the "present age" that would vanish when its symbol, the earthly Jerusalem temple, was destroyed. The writer of Hebrews knew this because Jesus said it would happen (Matt 24:1-2), and the author was writing before the temple was destroyed. So he likened the old covenant and its earthly temple to a temporary tabernacle that was about to vanish away.

> Hebrews 8:13
> In speaking of a new covenant, he makes the first one obsolete. And what is becoming obsolete and growing old is ready to vanish away.

He was writing during the transition period between covenants. The old covenant was becoming obsolete and was ready to vanish away, which means it had not yet done so. The new covenant had been inaugurated spiritually with the cross (Luke 22:20) but not yet consummated temporally in the destruction of the old covenant and its temple.

> Hebrews 9:8–9
> By this the Holy Spirit indicates that the way into the [heavenly] holy places is not yet opened as long as the first [earthly] tabernacle is still standing (which is symbolic for the present age).

Here, the writer of Hebrews explains that the earthly temple is symbolic of that present old covenant age that they were still in at the time of the writing of Hebrews, because that temple had not yet been destroyed. It was "still standing." When it was destroyed, it would mark the end of the present age and the full arrival of the Messianic age to come, the reign of Messiah on his heavenly throne.

Therefore, the last days could not have been the last days of the whole earth but rather the last days of the old covenant, the end of the old covenant age.[25]

And those last days/end of the age would include the destruction of the spiritual powers over the nations that were a part of that old covenant Deuteronomy 32 worldview. The passage I have referenced in previous

---

[25] See "Chapter 9: End of the Age/Last Days," Brian Godawa, _End Times Bible Prophecy: It's Not What They Told You_ (Embedded Pictures, 2017), 70-80.

chapters about the Watchers being "doomed to pass away" was also predicted by Paul to occur at the end of the age. They were in fact, the "rulers of this age" that was about to end with the temple destruction.

> 1 Corinthians 2:6
> …the rulers of this age, who are doomed to pass away.

As I explained earlier, 2 Peter 3 describes those last days as the Day of the Lord, when the *stoicheia* (the elemental spirits over the nations) would be burned up in judgment along with unbelieving sinners (Rev 20:15; 21:8).

The judgment of the Watchers that Jude said would occur at "the judgment of the great day" (Jude 6) occurred in AD 70 with the destruction of the old covenant and all its earthly and spiritual elements. *Space does not permit an explanation of how 2 Peter and Revelation were fulfilled in the first century (see my book End Times Bible Prophecy).*

Now the last days of Isaiah 2 makes more sense. Messiah arrived in the last days of the old covenant to usher in the mountain of the kingdom of God (Dan 2:44-45), accepting the Gentiles that were previously under the authority of the Watchers.

> Isaiah 2:2
> It shall come to pass in the last days [of the old covenant]
> that the mountain of the house of the LORD shall be
> established as the highest of the mountains, and shall be
> lifted up above the hills; and all the nations shall flow to it…

That messianic mountain was also predicted by Daniel to begin in the time of the Roman Empire with the coming of Messiah as a heavenly cornerstone of a kingdom that would overcome all kingdoms and grow to be a mountain that filled the earth (Dan 2:35, 44-45). Jesus was that stone who came in the time of ancient Rome (Acts 4:11), his kingdom was established in the first century (Matt 12:28), and it is currently growing to fill the earth (Matt 13:31-33), just as Daniel prophesied.

All About the Narrative

So here is the summary narrative of what I have sought to exegete from Psalm 82 in conjunction with the rest of Scripture:

- The Watchers had been allotted the Gentile nations in their ancient rebellion and God kept Israel as his own allotment.
- But in the last days of the old covenant, Messiah came to take back that inheritance.
- His death, resurrection and ascension to the right hand of God was his enthronement that empowered him to overthrow the Watchers and take back their territorial rights over the Gentile nations.
- He then regathered his remnant of Jews from all the nations through the

gospel proclamation of his new covenant kingdom.

- But this spiritual inauguration of the kingdom was not historically consummated until the old covenant temple was destroyed.
- That new covenant now includes the Gentiles, no longer in bondage to the powers, who now flow into the heavenly Mount Zion, the New Jerusalem, the Body of Christ.
- There are no longer territorial Watchers who have power over the nations because Christ vanquished them through the cross, resurrection and ascension.
- At that time, he took back their inheritance and judged them by stripping them of immortality and most likely casting them into the lake of fire.
- He did this in the first century when the old covenant that included the Gentile allotment was completely abolished at the destruction of the old covenant temple in AD 70.

But we are still not done with this examination of Psalm 82. There is one other ramification to address in light of this narrative: If those spiritual principalities and powers were defeated and maybe even destroyed in the past, then how are we to understand the demonic evil that seems to plague our modern world?

That will be explored in the next chapter.

Chapter 6:
The Watchers Did Not Make You Do it

Having supported the supernatural interpretation of the gods of Psalm 82, I now want to address one of the tendencies that I see occurring within the community of those persuaded by the divine council worldview. They are often so focused on the heavenly principalities and powers that they can fall into a misunderstanding of human responsibility for evil in this world.

Since the Sons of God are understood within this view as being supernatural beings, then the interpretation of Genesis 6:1-4 places some of the cause of the great Flood upon the actions of those angelic divinities.

In that controversial passage, rebellious supernatural Sons of God come to earth and mate with human women in a violation of the heavenly/earthly divide (Jude 6-7). Their progeny were the cursed Nephilim, to whom the Bible links the cursed giants of Canaan (Num 13:32-33) (I can't take the space here to prove that interpretation. See my book *When Giants Were Upon the Earth* for the biblical evidence).

But the context of that Genesis 6 passage is that the physical corruption by the heavenly beings was part of the reason for the judgment of the flood.

> Genesis 6:11–13
> Now the land was corrupt in God's sight, and the land was filled with violence. And God saw the land, and behold, it was corrupt, for all flesh had corrupted their way on the land. And God said to Noah, "I have determined to make an end of all flesh, for the land is filled with violence through them. Behold, I will destroy them with the land.

Though the Bible gives no details beyond the violence and "corruption" of flesh, some Bible researchers draw from 1 Enoch to fill in the gaps of knowledge left out in Genesis. I've already explained that though 1 Enoch is not Scripture, it is certainly a source used by Scripture, so it carries some weight when it comes to understanding biblical context.

In 1 Enoch, we read an extended exposition of Genesis 6. It tells us that the Sons of God, also called the Watchers, were guilty of teaching mankind the arts of wickedness, from adultery and war, to sorcery, astrology and other forbidden dark arts.

> 1 Enoch 7:1-8:4
> And [the Watchers] took wives unto themselves, and everyone (respectively) chose one woman for himself, and they began to go unto them. And they taught them magical medicine, incantations, the cutting of roots...And Azaz᾽el taught the people (the art of) making swords and knives, and shields, and breastplates; …and alchemy. And there were many wicked ones and they committed adultery and erred, and all their conduct became corrupt… And (the people) cried and their voice reached unto heaven.[1]

1 Enoch paints a picture of humanity maliciously influenced by Watchers before the Flood. That means that the Watchers had some responsibility for the corruption that filled the land with violence (Gen 6:11). Under the Deuteronomy 32 worldview, the Old Testament extends that evil influence after Babel and all the way up to the arrival of Messiah.

But if what I am saying is true, that the Watchers are not only disinherited from the nations, but have been judged and possibly even destroyed in the first century AD, then that would mean that they are no longer active in this world.

Supernatural Evil or Human Evil?

One of the most common questions I get from those who are following my argument is that if what I say is true, then how do I explain the great evil that this world still experiences, from world wars to genocides? Certainly, that is demonic, is it not? And how do I explain all the apparent demonic activity that still seems to captivate our world? Even if we dismiss the charlatan exorcists and psychological explanations of many alleged supernatural cases, there still seems to be real apparent demonic activity in our world. How can that be if there are no demonic gods over the nations? And besides, didn't Paul write about the very real struggle going on with "principalities and powers" after the resurrection and ascension of Christ? (Eph 6;12). Isn't Satan spoken of as still being the Prince of the power of the air (Eph 2:2), the "god of this world" (2 Cor 4:4)?

My first charge is that despite the real evil that the Watchers did in the cosmos, they are still not the cause of evil inside human hearts. We are. A Watcher didn't make Cain commit the first homicide that typified our murderous human nature.

The Watchers may have been part of the reason for the Flood, they may have *influenced* humanity, but they were not *the cause* of human evil. That was found in humanity's own depravity.

---

[1] James H. Charlesworth, *The Old Testament Pseudepigrapha, vol. 1* (New York; London: Yale University Press, 1983), 16.

> Genesis 6:5–6
> The LORD saw that the wickedness of man was great in the land, and that every intention of the thoughts of his heart was only evil continually. And the LORD regretted that he had made man on the land, and it grieved him to his heart.

The text indicates that the wickedness and evil of humanity resided in their own hearts, not outside of them in other beings. We are not puppets of someone else's evil.

But there is something else to notice in Genesis 6. Though the behavior of the Sons of God is implicated, it is not explicitly stated as the reason for the flood. The text goes out of its way to focus emphatically on the "wickedness and evil heart of man" as God's main motive for the flood, without any reference to the Sons of God/Watchers. God makes "an end of all flesh, for the land is filled with violence through them" (Gen 6:11). The focus in Genesis is on the evil caused by humans (flesh) not Watchers.

Even in the most wicked period of history, God does not shift the blame of monstrous world evil onto external demonic spiritual forces. The heavenly and earthly are linked in both behavior and fates, but God blames the evil inside the human heart on humanity.

The wicked heart of man is a common refrain throughout the Old Testament, highlighting an internal origin of human evil, not an external one.

> Genesis 8:21
> The intention of man's heart is evil from his youth...

> Jeremiah 17:9
> The heart is deceitful above all things, and desperately sick;
> who can understand it?
> (see also Job 14:4; 15:14; Ps. 51:5; Jer 13:23)

The New Testament picks up this notion of internal sin nature and reaffirms it even after the kingdom of God has come in the new covenant.

> James 1:13–15
> Let no one say when he is tempted, "I am being tempted by God," for God cannot be tempted with evil, and he himself tempts no one. But each person is tempted <u>when he is lured and enticed by his own desire</u>. <u>Then desire when it has conceived gives birth to sin, and sin when it is fully grown brings forth death.</u>

External forces can tempt us, but in the chain of causation, we are the originating source of our evil. Human nature does not need Watchers to explain the heinous "demonic" evil of world wars, genocide and other atrocities that saturate our newspapers and history books. We can accomplish all of that on our own.

Adolf Hitler, Josef Stalin, Mao, Dahmer, Bundy, Gacy, the 9/11 terrorists and their successors; none of them needed to be demon-possessed to do what they did. As Jesus said, "For out of [man's] heart come evil thoughts, murder, adultery, sexual immorality, theft, false witness, slander."

Paul wrote a long list of human depravity that comes from the human "lust of our own hearts" and "debased minds." No demons or Watchers required.

> Romans 1:29–32
> [Sinful humanity is] filled with all manner of unrighteousness, evil, covetousness, malice. They are full of envy, murder, strife, deceit, maliciousness. They are gossips, slanderers, haters of God, insolent, haughty, boastful, inventors of evil, disobedient to parents, foolish, faithless, heartless, ruthless. Though they know God's righteous decree that those who practice such things deserve to die, they not only do them but give approval to those who practice them.

Again, this is an internal wickedness so thorough that no external supernatural entity is needed to explain it. It comes from within the heart of unredeemed humanity. And Paul was no stranger to demonic reality. He knew demons when he saw them (Acts 16:16-18; 19:12; Eph 6:12). But he didn't explain the worst of human wickedness by appealing to them in Romans 1.

If one thinks that the disinheriting of the Watchers' authority over nations means that there is no explanation for the evil in humanity, then perhaps one has forgotten that human evil is not located in heavenly beings but in humans themselves.

What the Devil is Going On Here?

This doesn't mean there are no demons or evil spirits anymore. Watchers are not demons; they are a separate category of beings from demons. Demons are evil spirits in search of a human host (Luke 11:24-25). But Watchers are not merely spirits, they are angelic divine rulers with heavenly flesh (Jude 7-8) that can fornicate with humans (Gen 6:1-4) and eat food (Gen 18:8). Watchers are *not* pure spirit like demons.

Watchers are more like generals in a spiritual war, and demons are like the troops. Assassinating the generals doesn't necessarily destroy the troops.

Just because the Watchers have been conquered or destroyed does not mean that there are no more evil spirits. I am not aware of any biblical description of evil spirits being destroyed from the earth, so I am agnostic on the issue. But I know that if there are demons, they are not Watchers or "rulers, authorities and cosmic powers in the heavenly places" that Paul wrote about in his day (Eph 6:12). Those were the Watchers of the nations.

Jesus said that the eternal fire was made for the devil and his angels (Matt

25:41), and since "angels" in Greek means messengers, it most likely includes demons. But Jesus' parables about Gehenna seem to only mention humans being thrown there at the end of the age (AD 70). I am not aware of any passage that directly says when the demons will end up there, so we would have to speculate as to when. They may still be around today. But that would make them more like terrorist cells without any central command.

It seems reasonable that the demons would be thrown into the Lake of Fire along with Satan at the end of the Millennium. But it is not explicitly written so (Rev 20:10).

Don't Forget

But what about Paul's reference to spiritual powers in his epistles such as Ephesians 6? Isn't the satan still the god of this world like the New Testament says? As we already discussed, those letters were written in the "last days" of the old covenant (Heb 1:1-2), before the temple had been destroyed and before the new covenant kingdom had been historically consummated. So the Watchers had been legally disinherited, paraded in Triumph, but not yet judged or executed. That would come with the final earthly destruction of the old covenant.

Remember, the temple was the incarnation of the old covenant. Its earthly presence marked the presence of that covenant still on earth. And the old covenant included the territorial spiritual powers as part of its paradigm (Deut 32:8-10). So if the old covenant was still in effect on earth until that temple destruction in AD 70 (Heb 9:8-9), then the Watchers were still at war with Yahweh and his Messiah during the transition period between covenants (Heb 8:13).

But when Jesus abolished the old covenant by destroying the earthly temple, he received the new covenant kingdom and the Watchers lost their power and were judged with the fire of execution They were burned up as *stoicheia*.

And that brings us to the next issue.

The Already and the Not Yet

Another attempt at addressing the apparent presence of supernatural evil in our modern world in the face of Christ's defeat and disinheritance of the Watchers is the suggestion that Christ's victory and triumphal procession was a legal or spiritual reality that is now being worked out historically.

What that means is that there can still be evil supernatural entities who have power over sinful humanity, but have limited power in relation to the Gospel. So, they may not have authority, but they still have power. Much like a criminal has no legal authority, but may have power in doing evil. This is commonly coined "the already and the not yet" explanation.

I actually believe there is some truth to this theological concept. But I don't think it provides a satisfactory answer to the question of the Watchers. Let me explain.

Here is the basic argument: Jesus Christ has indeed triumphed over the spiritual powers and has been enthroned as king over all the nations. Everything is under his feet, but this is only a legal or theological truth that is still working its way out in history.

Therefore, even though Christ has been victorious, the spiritual powers still rule over the nations, but Christ is exercising his superior rule over their rule by saving Gentiles from the nations. He is reigning *now* from heaven, but this is a spiritual sovereignty that is *not yet* historically incarnate on earth. It will be so in our future. It is gradually replacing the "already" with the "not yet"–step by step.

One Scripture that seems to teach this "already and not yet" is Hebrews 2.

> Hebrews 2:7–8
> You made [Jesus] for a little while lower than the angels; you have crowned him with glory and honor, <u>putting everything in subjection under his feet</u>." Now in putting everything in subjection to him, he left nothing outside his control. <u>At present, we do not yet see everything in subjection to him</u>.

The writer of Hebrews affirms the prophetic fulfillment of the messianic enthronement Psalm 110 (everything under his feet), but explicitly qualifies that as a heavenly truth that is in process historically ("at present, we do not yet see everything in subjection to him"). It is spiritually true but historically coming true. The already (heavenly) and the not yet (earthly).

Here is another passage that expounds on this historical "process" of subjugation:

> 1 Corinthians 15:24–27
> Then comes the end, when [Jesus] delivers the kingdom to God the Father after destroying every rule and every authority and power. <u>For he must reign until he has put all his enemies under his feet</u>. The last enemy to be destroyed is death. <u>For "God has put all things in subjection under his feet</u>."

I cannot exegete the entire complex chapter of 1 Corinthians 15, so I will just explain that I understand this to be referring to the end of history, when Christ returns. The idea here is that Christ is reigning right now from his heavenly throne at the right hand of God with all things legally or covenantally under his feet (Eph 1:20-22).

Jesus then makes true on earth what is already true in heaven (Matt 18:19), step by step, subject by subject. He has already conquered the spiritual authorities and executed them, but now, he is conquering the humans that used to be under their authority through Gospel conversion. This is much like an earthly king who reigns over a nation whether the people like it or not. As he employs his power, he gets his subjects to obey him, until they are all willing in their loyalty to the king.

But remember, the kingdom of God is not of this world (John 18:36); it is a spiritual kingdom (Luke 17:21). Its "conquering" is a spiritual conquering through conversion, not earthly compulsion. As people receive the Holy Spirit and are brought into God's kingdom, they become his subjects "under his feet" historically.

Jesus enacts his reign by working out in history what is already true in the heavenlies. As more people convert and are placed under his feet, the kingdom of God grows to be a mountain that fills the whole earth (Dan 2:35). It begins as a small speck of leaven, but soon expands to leaven the whole lump of dough (Luke 13:20). It starts as the smallest seed but grows to be the largest tree in the garden (Luke 13:19). So, while the kingdom is spiritual in its operations, it is earthly in its ramifications.

So, doesn't this support the notion that the Watchers may still have power without authority?

No. And here's why…

As we have already seen, the actual New Testament texts use the Roman Triumph as the picture of what occurred through the ascension of Christ and his judgment of AD 70. That picture was one of execution of the prisoners not release of them back into the nations. The forty-year transition period with old and new covenants overlapping explains how the principalities and powers were still around at that time. Because even though the new covenant had been inaugurated in the heavenly realm, the earthly old covenant temple still stood, so the old covenant still had some earthly effect. But with the destruction of the temple, so came the final destruction of the old covenant along with the Watchers. Their authority *and* power was rooted in the old covenant.

1 Corinthians 15:24-27 describes the *historical process* of Jesus "destroying every rule and authority and power." But it is a process that involves not merely the already and the not yet, but also the "before now." In other words, it involves the past, the present and the future.

The historical order is this:

1) Jesus disinherited the spiritual powers at his ascension and placed all authorities under his feet in the heavenly realm. The earthly fulfillment of that heavenly accomplishment is the destruction of the old covenant and temple in AD 70. That heavenly "already" eventually overcame and replaced the earthly "not yet" with the historical judgment of AD 70, and that heavenly "already" will continue to do so until God's will is fully done on earth as it is in heaven (Matt 6:10).

2) Jesus is now in the historical process of placing all humans under his feet on earth through spiritual conversion. On earth as it is in heaven.

3) Jesus will destroy the last enemy, death, at the end of history.

Past, present, future.

So, yes, there is an "already and not yet" aspect of heavenly truth and earthly impact, but the "not yet" does not include the Watchers because, as we have already seen in previous chapters, the spiritual powers were already conquered *in the heavenly realm*, where they resided. The heavenly realm is the "already." The earthly realm of history was the "not yet" that was fulfilled in the temple destruction. Final execution of the spiritual powers is part of the past accomplishment of Jesus' Days of Vengeance (Luke 21:20-22) in AD 70. The Watchers were triumphantly dragged through the streets, shamed, and disinherited from their allotments (Col 2:15). Then they were judged by being cast into the Lake of Fire in AD 70 with the destruction of the old covenant. As Psalm 82:7 says, they lost their immortality and died like any other prince. They're gone.

The rule of the Watchers is part of the old covenant that Messiah did away with. The heavenly realm is accomplished; it is the remaining "not yet" aspects of the earthly realm that continue to occur historically.

The Watchers were already conquered and destroyed. Their corresponding earthly powers are currently being conquered. Death will ultimately be conquered.

Amen.

•••••

To see how the rule of the fallen Watchers over the Gentile nations may have played out in history, read my novel series, *Chronicles of the Nephilim* and *Chronicles of the Watchers*.

To see what the Watcher's final destruction might have looked like, read my series *Chronicles of the Apocalypse*.

For more theological explanation of the last days and eschatology see my book *End Times Bible Prophecy.*

If you liked this book, then please help me out by writing an honest review of it on Amazon here. It's usually pretty easy. That is one of the best ways to say thank you to me as an author. It really does help my exposure and status as an author. Thanks! — *Brian Godawa*

•••••

Chapter 6: The Watchers Did Not Make You Do It

The Spiritual World of Moses and Egypt

Biblical Background to the Novel

Moses: Against the Gods of Egypt

By Brian Godawa

The Spiritual World of Moses and Egypt: Biblical Background to the Novel Moses: Against the Gods of Egypt
1st Edition

Warrior Poet Publishing
www.warriorpoetpublishing.com

ISBN: 978-1-942858-83-6 (paperback)
ISBN: 978-1-942858-84-3 (ebook)

Scripture quotations taken from *The Holy Bible: English Standard Version*. Wheaton: Standard Bible Society, 2001.

Acknowledgments
Thanks to Robert Cruickshank Jr. for his feedback and research connections of common interest. And to my editor, Jeanette Windle.

Get the novel *Moses* that is based on the biblical research of this book you are reading.

The Gods of Egypt Will Not Let the Hebrews Go Without a Fight.

An epic Bible novel about Yahweh and Moses in supernatural conflict with Pharaoh and the gods of Egypt. Respected Christian author Brian Godawa reveals the unseen realm like never before in this biblically faithful spiritual warfare novel.

https://godawa.com/get-moses/
(*affiliate link*)

Chapter 1
The Story

Scripture and History

Writing a novel about the life of Moses was daunting. First off, I was under the shadow of the 1956 Cecile B. DeMille movie *The Ten Commandments* with Charlton Heston as Moses and Yul Brenner as Pharaoh Ramesses. Though we now know some of the film's inaccuracies, it remains a dominant influence on people's understanding of the Exodus story, both consciously and unconsciously.

The problem is that DeMille did the best he could do with the information available to him at the time. He was also bound by constraints of a medium that was primarily visual, which led to creative choices not always in line with the research in order to make the story work as a movie. I do not condemn those choices since I too was bound by the constraints of storytelling in a reading medium, though this medium offered more latitude to integrate historical research.

There aren't many extrabiblical and archeological facts about the Exodus story that are certain. There is also significant lack of certainty in the interpretation of quite a few of those facts. But I found the information fascinating and worthy of this study regardless of whether one reads the novel or not.

Scripture vs. History

As an orthodox Christian, I believe in Sola Scriptura, that is, "Scripture alone is the primary and absolute source for all doctrine and practice (faith and morals)."[1] But notice this quote says "source of all doctrine and practice," not "source of all facts whatsoever." It is self-evident that the Bible does not tell

---

[1] Norman L. Geisler and Ralph E. MacKenzie, "What is Sola Scriptura?" CRI Online. https://www.equip.org/article/what-is-sola-scriptura/

everything that ever happened in the history of Judaism or Christianity, let alone the world. It leaves a lot of details out, especially in the life of Moses.

In the book of Exodus, we are only told of a few incidents in Moses's life before the Exodus: his birth, his murder of an Egyptian, his flight to Midian, and his introduction to the Midianites. That's all we know *of his first eighty years of life*.

The burning bush episode is when all the action starts that leads to the amazing story of the Exodus and the last forty years of Moses's life. But Moses had been a prince of Egypt for forty years prior. He may have been in line to become Pharaoh! That is significant. It shaped who Moses had become.

According to the Bible, it is not necessary for God's purposes of doctrine and practice related to the Exodus to know those details that were left out. That doesn't mean those facts are without value. And it certainly doesn't mean we can't learn something from other sources of history. But we must be careful and thoughtful about our usage.

Readers of all my Chronicles series know that I draw from many historical sources from the ancient world in order to "fill in" gaps in the story between what the Bible tells us and what is left out. I use them, not as inerrant scripture, but as helpful bridges toward understanding the biblical narrative through the ancient eyes of its original writers and readers. I also do so to give context and meaning to ancient godless narratives through the lens of a biblical worldview. Throughout the course of all my series, I have drawn from pagan stories like The Epic of Gilgamesh and The Baal Cycle as well as ancient Jewish apocrypha like the book of Jubilees and pseudepigrapha like the book of 1 Enoch. I have added to that well of knowledge from ancient Jewish historians like Josephus and pagan historians like Tacitus and Suetonius.

Unfortunately, there were not many extrabiblical historical sources available for the story of Moses. But I explain in the pages to follow some of those sources used for the novel. The ancient Jewish historians Josephus and Artapanus wrote of an interesting episode from Moses's life, not available in the Bible but incorporated into my novel, about his conquering of the Kushite kingdom while he was a prince and general of Egypt. A legendary text also exists about the two Egyptian magicians, Jannes and Jambres, who faced off with Moses in Pharaoh's court. Keep reading and you'll learn about those fascinating details.

Because I write theological novels that use fantastical imagery to speculate about the unseen spiritual realm, I incorporate some of that theology in a creative way. For example, the sea dragon of chaos, Leviathan, a reappearing monster in all my series, shows up at the Red Sea crossing in the Moses novel. I draw this obvious spiritual symbol from Scripture itself in

Psalm 74, where Yahweh's deliverance at the Red Sea was described in terms of him "crushing the heads of Leviathan," and Israelites feasting on its flesh in the desert as a way of describing the establishment of God's covenant order through Moses. I have explained Leviathan and his spiritual meaning in the Bible in much detail in my book When Giants Were Upon the Earth[2] (affiliate link), but I have some new material in this book. My goal is to do in my novel what Scripture does, interweaving spiritual symbol and meaning with historical fact into the same narrative.

The Problem of Ancient Names

I want to start with a note about my naming conventions in this novel as well as the others in the series. My goal is to create a balance between familiarity and novelty. Doing research sometimes reveals that commonly accepted names for historical characters and places are wrong or imprecise or victims of translation. Using more accurate names can be a way of bringing a fresh feel to a well-known story. However, too much change can make that well-known story become unfamiliar to the reader and cause confusion.

One of the problems is that ancient names, especially Egyptian names, are notoriously fluid. And when one translates them to English, variations abound. For example, many names of Egyptian gods are known to us through English translations of Greek versions of the original Egyptian. Here is a table of some samples:

Egyptian Name	Greek Translation
Ra	Helios
Set	Seth
Aset	Isis
Heru Sa Aset	Horus
Usir	Osiris

2 Brian Godawa, *When Giants Were Upon the Earth: The Watchers, the Nephilim, and the Biblical Cosmic War of the Seed*, (Los Angeles, CA: Embedded Pictures Publishing, 2014), pp 79-88.

Over time, names change and are combined with other names of gods. But that is not consistent nor are such changes time-stamped. Different ancient cities used numerous versions of names for various deities as well.

I decided to use mostly the Greek versions of these names because many people still know so little about the religion of ancient Egypt. So using Egyptian names would make it too unfamiliar. But sometimes I do use the Egyptian version if I like it better. For instance, I use the Greek Isis and Horus instead of the Egyptian Aset and Heru Sa Aset, but I use the Egyptian Set and Ra instead of the Greek Seth and Helios. Some versions fit the collective memory better than others. Some fit the narrative better.

The gods' identities evolved over time as well. Ra was a sun god as was Atum. They were eventually combined to be Ra-Atum. But Ra was also merged with Amun, the supreme head of the pantheon in the New Kingdom, to be Amun-Ra or Amon-Re. It can all get quite contradictory and confusing, so as a storyteller I had to simplify and commit to specific incarnations or spellings to fit the purposes of both history and narrative.

The same can be true of a person's name, place names, and cities as well. One example is the Egyptian adoptive mother of Moses. The Bible does not give her name. The ancient Jewish historian Artapanus calls her Merris. David Rohl suggests that Merris was most likely the Greek equivalent of the Egyptian Mereryt or Merestekhi (which are themselves English translations of the real Egyptian spelling and pronunciation). The Jewish historian Josephus calls her Thermuthis, the Greek version of Egyptian Tawaret. With so many options, sometimes the choice is simply subjective or preferential. And this fluidity of names is true for much Greek and Hebrew as well as Egyptian. In the chapters to follow, I explain some of my creative choices of names based on historical research.

When was the Date of the Exodus?

One of the biggest questions that determines a lot of details in the story of Moses is when the Exodus actually occurred in history. This question is often rooted in debating the historicity of the biblical text. Unfortunately, this issue has become a scholarly quagmire of debate for centuries with no certain conclusion in sight. I cannot reproduce the arguments for all the options as anything more than the basics here, so I refer the reader to Egyptologist David Rohl's works, the scholarly source from which I've drawn the most. His latest book Exodus: Myth or History?[3] (affiliate link) provides an in-depth explanation of this most fascinating area of research related to the stories of Joseph, Moses, the Exodus and the Conquest. I've also drawn from filmmaker Tim Mahoney's excellent documentary series, "Patterns of Evidence."[4]

Of all the possible dates suggested for the Exodus, there are two dominant ones that I will address here. The first is the traditional early date of approximately 1447 B.C. The second is the more liberal late date of approximately 1250 B.C.

Up until the mid-twentieth century, the traditional date for the Exodus was computed from the biblical text in conjunction with attested dates of other ancient events or literature. The key scripture is:

> 1 Kings 6:1
> In the four hundred and eightieth year after the people of Israel came out of the land of Egypt, in the fourth year of Solomon's reign over Israel, in the month of Ziv, which is the second month, he began to build the house of the LORD.

The scriptural claim here is that the Exodus occurred 480 years before Solomon began to build the temple in Jerusalem. But when did Solomon build the temple? If we can find a fixed historical date for his reign, we can work backward with the numbers to arrive at the biblical date for the Exodus.

In 1943, noted scholar Edwin Thiele provided a chronology to establish some fairly certain dates of biblical events that remains the most respected scholarship on the topic. He had used astronomical science combined with ancient Assyriological documentation in synchronization with the biblical books of Kings and Chronicles to establish the dates of the reigns of the kings of Judah and Israel. One of those fairly certain dates was the reign of Solomon beginning approximately 967 B.C. Subtracting 480 years from that date brings us back to 1447 B.C. for the Exodus.[5]

---

[3] David Rohl, *Exodus: Myth or History?* (MN: Thinking Man Media, 2015). Rohl's other books provide some overlapping information, but also additional material related to the issues. See his A Test of Time: The Bible - From Myth to History (U.K. Century, Ltd.), 1995 for more details on Egyptian chronology and Moses as well as Solomon, David and other biblical historical events within the New Chronology timeline.

[4] In fact, my own view is more in line with Mahoney's than with Rohl's. Mahoney is a mature Christian believer. Rohl is an agnostic, so Rohl sometimes claims biblical error where Mahoney seeks a biblical solution. Mahoney's excellent series does a fantastic job of simplifying the scholarship and issues about Moses for the layman. At the time of this writing, the two videos available on Amazon rental or purchase are *Patterns of Evidence: The Exodus*, and *Patterns of Evidence: The Moses Controversy*. The next two parts on the Red Sea Miracle are a must-see, but only available on the website for Patterns of Evidence. I recommend everything at that site store. https://patternsofevidence.com

[5] David Rohl, *Exodus: Myth or History?* (MN: Thinking Man Media, 2015), p 42-43.

A second biblical passage supports this date as well. Judges 11:26 says that the reign of Judge Jephthah was 300 years after the conquest of Canaan by the Israelites. Thiele's chronology establishes Jephthah's reign as 1100 B.C., which places the conquest in 1400 B.C., approximately 40 years after the Exodus (1447 B.C.), just like the Bible says (Exodus 16:35).

But there is a problem. The view of a 1250 B.C. Exodus also originated in a "literal" interpretation of the Bible, in particular one text that seemed to argue for the pharaoh of Exodus as being Ramesses the Great, whose reign (1279—1213 B.C.) was a couple hundred years later than the 1447 B.C. date. That verse talked about the Israelites in bondage to Egypt afflicted with heavy burdens by their taskmasters.

> Exodus 1:11
> They built for Pharaoh store cities, Pithom and Raamses.

Rohl explains that the city Raamses (Pi Ramesse in Egyptian) was named after its founder Ramesses the Great, producing a synchronism that lies at the heart of the modern misdating of the Exodus and Conquest.[6]

Ramesses had one of the longest reigns of Egyptian monarchs and engaged in many building projects from his residence in Goshen, which on the surface seems to line up with the biblical story. There's only one problem. It creates a contradiction in the biblical text with those passages previously sighted. Ramesses reigned in the 13th century B.C., but 1 Kings and Judges indicate a Hebrew Exodus over 200 years earlier in the 15th century B.C. Is the Bible contradicting itself with different timelines?

I do not believe the Bible contradicts itself, so there must be a way of understanding this term that is not apparent in a simplistic "literal" reading of the texts. What the Bible writers intended is not always apparent on the surface of the text. We must plumb the depths.

Well, there is a way that makes sense of all these passages, and we don't have to make something up or cover up the problem with a word salad. The Bible itself gives us the key. The original name of the city during the time of Moses was not Raamses. It was changed by a later writer/editor of the text to update that city name to its latest version for later readers. Rohl proves that the original name of the city was Avaris (*Hawara* in Egyptian), and it was later changed to Pi Ramesses (Raamses in Hebrew) during the reign of Ramesses the Great.[7]

---

[6] Rohl, *Exodus,* 17.

[7] Rohl, *Exodus,* 119-129.

This technique was not deceptive. In fact, it was done elsewhere in the Bible because the readers of a later time would not be familiar with the older name of the location no longer being used. So the newest city name was a placeholder for that original city location.

Let the Bible illustrate this again as seen in the story of Joseph.

> Genesis 47:11, 27
> So Joseph settled his father and his brothers in Egypt and gave them property in the best part of the land, the region of Rameses, as Pharaoh directed…
> Now the Israelites settled in Egypt in the region of Goshen.

In this passage, we see a reference to the Hebrews settling in the "region of Rameses," which is also called "the region of Goshen." So this is talking about the same exact location where the Hebrews are still dwelling in the days of Moses (Exodus 8:22).

But there's one big problem. Joseph arrived in Egypt in "the region of Rameses" around 1658 B.C. *That's 400 years before Ramesses the Great became king of Egypt*. So the Bible is naming a region for King Ramesses long before Ramesses existed. Is this an error? By no means. Rohl explains this common technique that occurs in other places in the Bible as well.

> So when the Genesis 47:11 passage states that Joseph settled his father Jacob "in the land of Ramesses" centuries before the city of Pi Ramesse was built by the 19th Dynasty pharaohs, this statement is clearly recognized by scholars as an anachronism. A later biblical redactor has amended or added the text to locate that part of the Egyptian delta in which Jacob settled in terms of the geography or toponymy of his own day. He did so because the people living in his time would have known the location of Ramesses but probably not its older name of Goshen. So the redactor helps out his readers by editing the text to give the "modern" toponym of Jacob's Egyptian home.[8]

So we see clearly that the Bible writers or editors will speak of older locations using newer names of those locations for newer readers, called "anachronisms."

Another biblical text that seems to synchronize the Exodus with Ramesses is 2 Chronicles 12:9, which says that the king of Egypt, named

---

[8] Rohl, *Exodus*, 20-21.

Shishak, plundered the Jerusalem temple during the reign of Judah's king Rehoboam in 925 B.C. Biblical scholars have linked this name Shishak to the Egyptian king Shoshenk I of the 22nd Dynasty. This has become one of the few "absolute dates" that modern scholars have accepted for synchronization between Israel and Egyptian timelines. Working back through the king lists of Egypt then confirms Ramesses as the Pharaoh of the Exodus.

I hate to be redundant, but there are some big problems with this scheme that David Rohl examines which prove disastrous for the late date view. While similarity of names between languages may often occur, it is not always the case. It is a logical fallacy to link names merely because they sound similar. As it happens, there is another Pharaoh with a name similar to Shisak, and it isn't Shoshenk. There must be other facts to prove identity.

Rohl deconstructs the arguments for this alleged pillar of certainty to show that it does not hold up under scrutiny. The entire edifice of the Ramesses-as-Exodus-Pharaoh theory falls beneath a tidal wave of problems. He uncovers bad translations, mistaken interpretations, and historical incongruities between the reigns and campaigns of Shishak in the Bible and Shoshenk in Egypt. He ends up revealing that the biblical Shishak is actually Ramesses II, who had an Egyptian nickname of Shysha (Shisha in English), which is the etymological connection being sought for—and with a Canaanite campaign to match the biblical facts.[9]

Rohl explains that the Ramesses-as-Exodus-pharaoh view must engage in a "conjuring trick" to harmonize the date of 1250 B.C. with the 1 Kings and Judges passages that otherwise clearly place the Exodus 200 years earlier around 1447 B.C. They take the 480 years of 1 Kings 6:1, and make it a rounded off number symbolic of the numbers 40 times 12. 40 represents a generation and 12 is the number of generations between Moses and Solomon. They go on to propose that a generation in those days was really more like 23 years. So if you multiply 23 by 12, you get 276 years. Go back 276 years from 967 B.C. (the date of the fourth year of Solomon), and we arrive at 1243 B.C., the date of Ramesses the Great.[10]

That's a rather desperate and unconvincing conjuring trick indeed!

---

[9] Such nicknames are common in the Bible: "Pharaoh Amenemhat I was known as 'Ameny', the Bible refers to Tiglath-pileser III as 'Pul' [2 Kings 15:19] and Shalmaneser V as 'Shalman' [Hoshea 10: 14]." Rohl, *Exodus*, 61.

For the full detailed argument about Shishak by Rohl, see Rohl, *Exodus*, 49-69. Also see the seminal paper by J.J. Bimson, "Shoshenk and Shishak - A Case of Mistaken Identity?" (ISIS Journal, Volume 06, 1993), pp 19-32. http://www.newchronology.org/cgi-bin/somsid.cgi?type=pdf&page=06a019&code=h1dxvgjh&session=884142A&record=77&subpage=0

[10] Rohl, *Exodus*, 43-44.

There are more evidences and issues that Rohl works through to discredit the later date of 1250 B.C. and prove his argument that the Exodus occurred in the traditional early date of 1447 B.C. But one of the most powerful of the arguments is archaeology.

Twentieth century archaeological excavations have almost universally discredited the thirteenth-century date for the Exodus and Conquest of Canaan. Liberal scholars appeal to it to prove that the biblical events never happened. The fall of Jericho occurred centuries before the late date Ramesses scenario. It wasn't even inhabited when Joshua was supposed to have overthrown it in the scheme of the late date. And most of the thirty cities that Joshua conquered were also not inhabited in the thirteenth century either. Canaanite cities did not have fortifications in the days after Ramesses as the Bible says they did. The biblical conquest narrative simply contradicts archaeological facts if one places the Exodus in 1250 B.C.

But Rohl's work and the documentary Patterns of Evidence: The Exodus (affiliate link) show that a shifting of the Exodus date back to 1447 B.C. synchronizes all the archaeological and historical evidence with the biblical narrative of Exodus and Conquest.[11] It's a powerful argument for the historical reliability of Scripture.

So I went with the date of 1447 B.C. for the Exodus. Which leads to the next question.

Who were the Pharaohs of Moses's life?

With apologies to Yul Brenner's memorable performance in the movie *The Ten Commandments, the pharaoh of the Exodus was most likely not Ramesses the Great.* Then who was? The answer can lead us into another quagmire of unending questions and complicated answers without much certainty, so I will try to summarize this as well to explain my choices for the novel. After all, I have to have a specific Pharaoh in my story or I don't have a specific story to tell. I have followed David Rohl's work in this area as well.

If the Exodus occurred in 1447 B.C., different researchers have suggested various options in accordance with conventional Egyptian chronology as to who was pharaoh at that time: Amenemhet III, Amenhotep II, Thutmose III, Neferhotep I, and others. Why so many options? That's because there is a problem with conventional Egyptian chronology.

---

[11] Rohl, *Exodus,* 263-327. See also the book by Timothy Mahoney, *Patterns of Evidence: The Exodus* (Thinking Man Media, 2015).

Egyptian chronology is notoriously unreliable and a mess. Starting around 3000 B.C., for 2800 years of Egyptian history there are over 30 dynasties of almost 400 different pharaohs. Scholars have tried to compile a list of the pharaohs with dates based upon king lists found on papyrus and engraved on monuments. The problem is that many of these lists are damaged, incomplete, contradict each other, and do not always differentiate overlapping reigns.[12] The differences of interpretation create disparities between some chronologies of hundreds of years.

David Rohl is part of a scholarly movement called The New Chronology that has successfully brought legitimate doubt upon conventional Egyptian dating and proposed a different chronology to solve the problems of the consensus view. This scenario shifts the royal dynasties by as much as three hundred years. And well, yes, you guessed it, that has created another quagmire. But Rohl's books provide a scholarly defense of the New Chronology as it relates to the Bible. And when it comes to the pharaohs in Moses's life, he provides some rather interesting offerings.

The Bible never gives the names of the pharaohs in question. So we are left with synchronizing other historical evidence to try to deduce their identities. One of those helpful pieces of evidence comes to us from an ancient Jewish historian of Persian descent named Artapanus. He was commissioned to write a history of the Jews for the Ptolemaic pharaohs in the second century B.C. He used the Great Library of Alexandria in Egypt for his sources. That famous library surely had ancient documents that went back to the time of Moses. Sadly, Artapanus's writings did not survive the Great Alexandrian Fire, nor did his sources. But we do have excerpts of his work quoted or paraphrased in two church fathers, Clement and Eusebius of Alexandria.

Artapanus claims that Moses's great-grandfather was named Palmanothes and the royal princess who adopted him was named Merris.

> …likewise of the king of Egypt, his son Palmanothes succeeded to the sovereignty…He begat a daughter Merris, whom he betrothed to a certain Khenephres [Chenephres], king of the regions above Memphis (for there were at that time many kings in Egypt); and she being barren took a supposititious child from one of the Jews, and called him

12 One of the most helpful lists that is used as a foundation for the conventional Egyptian chronology is titled *Aegyptiaca*, by Greek historian Manetho written around 270 B.C.

For an in-depth scholarly approach to the New Chronology see the archive of the Institute for the Study of Interdisciplinary Science (with the unfortunate acronym of ISIS) http://www.newchronology.org/cgi-bin/open.cgi?page=index2

> Moüsos (Moses): but by the Greeks he was called, when grown to manhood, Musaeus.[13]

Rohl points out that the Greek translations of the Egyptian names here are so distorted we cannot be sure which Egyptian pharaoh the name Palmanothes refers to. But Merris's husband's name Khenephres reveals a more probable Egyptian connection.

The Greek *Khenephres* is re-vocalized in Egyptian as *Kha-nefer-re*. Khaneferre was the coronation name of Sobekhotep IV, the 29th ruler of the 13th Dynasty and the only king in the whole of pharaonic civilization named Khaneferre.[14] That was one of the dynasties which also fit Artapanus's claim of Egypt being a divided kingdom at the time with different pharaohs in Upper and Lower Egypt. Kheneferre Sobekhotep IV brought unity back to Egypt. He was probably the pharaoh who sought to kill Moses when Moses went into exile in Midian. Unfortunately, we have very little information on this pharaoh.

But Artapanus tells an extra-biblical story of Moses becoming a prince of Egypt under Kheneferre and commanding the Egyptian army. We will look at this story later, but here is what Artapanus tells us next.

> But when Khenephres [Kheneferre Sobekhotep IV] perceived the excellence of Moses he envied him, and sought to slay him on some plausible pretext.[15]

So according to Artapanus, Sobekhotep IV was the pharaoh who tried to kill Moses when he fled to Midian.

Rohl draws from a well-known king list called the Royal Canon of Turin to reveal that there are approximately 42 years between the death of Sobekhotep IV and the accession of a ruler named Dudimose to the throne. Since we know Moses had returned to Egypt after 40 years in Midian, then the pharaoh who ruled Egypt when Moses returned was most likely this Dudimose.[16]

Roman historian Tacitus calls the Pharaoh of the Exodus, Bocchoris, another incoherent Greek bastardization of the original name.[17] Ancient

---

[13] Eusebius of Caesarea, Evangelicae Praeparationis Libri XV, ed. E. H. Gifford (Oxford: Oxford University Press, 1903), 462.

[14] Rohl, *Exodus*, 131-133. David Rohl, *A Test of Time*, 283.

[15] Eusebius of Caesarea, Evangelicae Praeparationis Libri XV, ed. E. H. Gifford (Oxford: Oxford University Press, 1903), 463.

[16] David M. Rohl, *A Test of Time: Volume One – The Bible from Myth to History*, (Random House, London, 1995) 280-284.

[17] Tacitus, *Histories* 5.3-4.

Jewish historian Josephus quotes Greek historian Manetho about Egypt being "smote" by God under a Pharaoh he names Tutimaos (Dudimose).[18] We will take a closer look at that passage below.

Unfortunately, we have even less historical information on this pharaoh of the Exodus. But an Egyptian artifact called a *stela*, a stone with engravings on it, has been discovered that depicts Dudimose's son Khonsuemwaset as a charioteer and leader of the army of Edfu.[19] Thus, I chose to depict him as the leader of Pharaoh's chariots who goes after Moses in the Red Sea crossing.[20] Since it was most common for pharaohs to lead their armies at the head, it is most likely that Dudimose drowned in the Red Sea.[21] Psalm 136:15 states that Yahweh "overthrew Pharaoh and his host in the Red Sea," which strongly implies that Pharaoh was drowned with his army.

Ramesses of the late date view of Exodus did not drown in the sea and he did not die until many years after the alleged Exodus of that view. We have his mummy in the Egyptian museum in Cairo. There is no historical indication that his rule suffered the massive loss of his chariot forces or his army and therefore his power.

So let it be written. So let it be done.

Why is the City of Ramesses Renamed Avaris?

In my novel *Moses,* I portray the Jews enslaved to Egypt as living in the city of Avaris in the land of Goshen on the vast delta. As mentioned earlier, the Bible says that Joseph originally moved his family to "the region of Rameses" or "the region of Goshen" (Genesis 47:11, 27). But we saw that Rameses was a later name applied anachronistically for later readers. I also argued that the name given for the city the Jews built in Moses's day was another anachronistic reference to the same readers about the same area and city. Well, if Rameses wasn't the name of their city, then what was it?

Since the 1960s, archaeologists have been excavating a mound in the Egyptian delta called Tel ed-Daba. It is a city called Hawara in Egyptian, or Avaris in English. The site has revealed several layers of populations important to our story.

---

18 Flavius Josephus, *Against Apion* 1.14.

19 This little artifact also discredits the "Rameses as Exodus Pharaoh" argument that says there were no chariot corps of significance before Rameses the Great. There were chariots led by the king's son long before in the days of Dudimose.

20 Rohl, *A Test of Time,* 185-186.

21 Ramesses was buried and we have his mummy, another argument against him being the Pharaoh of the Exodus.

By way of introduction, Hebrews were Semites. The Egyptians called Semites "Asiatics." But there is no evidence of a large population of Semites in this area of Goshen during the time of the early 13th century B.C., the very time period of Ramesses that the late date view claims the Hebrews were sojourning in Egypt. This would be the New Kingdom of Egypt or the Late Bronze Age. This is crucial for the historical reliability of the Bible because many scholars now argue that there is no evidence of the Exodus story as told in the Bible. And if one supports the consensus view of a 1250 B.C. Exodus, then these facts become fatal to the view.

If however, one looks to lower layers of excavation that represent hundreds of years earlier in the Middle Bronze Age, or what is called the Second Intermediate Period of Egyptian history, one finds that the population in Goshen was almost entirely Semitic. This would be the time period before the Exodus of 1447 B.C. The time period where Joseph's people settled and became fruitful upon the land.

Then came Moses.

Rohl describes two amazing discoveries at Avaris that match the biblical narrative of Moses and support the city of Avaris as his birthplace amongst the Hebrews. The first is an archaeological allusion to the enslavement of the Hebrews after they had thrived under Joseph. Then an allusion to Pharaoh's command to kill the Hebrew male infants. I will quote Rohl extensively here because God is in the details.

> According to the archaeological evidence at Tell ed-Daba, conditions [after Joseph's day] began to deteriorate with skeletal remains in the graves showing signs of malnutrition. Anthropological studies show that adults were dying in their early thirties. Strangely, there were far more burials of infants and young children (50%) than normal (25%) for this sort of ancient civic society. Moreover, there were more females than males in the adult grave population. For every three females there were only two males. Where had the adult males gone? The Bible provides the answer. The opening chapter in the Book of Exodus tells us that the Egyptians first enslaved the Israelites, then culled the male infants because the slave population was getting too large and Pharaoh perceived this as a threat. Obviously, in archaeological terms, this would mean an increase in infant

> burials and a skew in the adult population in favor of females.[22]

So the archaeology of Avaris in the area of Goshen, shows Semites living and dying in great numbers that match the biblical story. It's almost as if that's evidence that confirms Scripture (that's sarcasm).

Rohl describes another excavated layer at Avaris that seems to reflect the devastation of the tenth plague.

> At the end of stratum G/1 at Tell ed-Daba, which is roughly dated to the middle of the 13th Dynasty, Bietak and his archaeological team began to uncover a gruesome scene. All over the city of Avaris they found shallow burial pits into which the victims of some terrible disaster had been hurriedly cast. These were no careful interments of the deceased. The bodies were not arranged in the proper burial fashion but rather thrown into the mass graves, one on top of the other. There were no grave goods placed with the corpses as was usually the custom. Bietak is convinced that we have here direct evidence of plague or some other sudden catastrophe at Avaris.
>
> What is more, analysis of the site archaeology suggests that a large part of the remaining population of the town abandoned their homes and departed from Avaris en masse. The site was then reoccupied after an interval of unknown duration by Asiatics who were not 'Egyptianised' like the previous population of stratum G.[23]

The archaeologist Bietak mentioned here is not a believer, so he does not acknowledge the connection with the Bible. But Rohl explains that this fits perfectly the biblical narrative of the tenth plague killing a large amount of people, followed by the Hebrews (Semites) evacuating Egypt, which was then easily invaded by other Semites the Egyptians called the Hyksos (Canaanites/Amorites). The Hyksos took over the area of Goshen and were not Egyptianized as the Hebrews had been—just as the excavated layers reveal.

One other relevant historical fragment is a statement by that ancient historian Manetho, who writes about the time of Pharaoh Dudimose (spelled *Tutimaos* in Greek). The Jewish historian Josephus quotes him:

---

22 Rohl, *Exodus*, 127

23 Rohl, *A Test of Time*, 279.

> Tutimaos [Dudimose]. In his reign, for what cause I know not, God smote us [the Egyptians]. And, unexpectedly, from the regions of the east, invaders of obscure race marched in confidence of victory against our land…
>
> [and whose new pharaoh resided at] a city called Avaris.[24]

Rohl explains that this "smiting" by God corresponds quite well to the plagues against Egypt. It was at this time that foreign invaders (the Hyksos) marched into Egypt virtually unopposed to set up a hundred years of dynastic reign. The most reasonable historical setting for something like that to happen to one of the most powerful nations on earth would be if the male population numbers were decreased—you know, like maybe in a plague on the firstborn. And if Pharaoh and his army were not available to defend against the invaders—you know, like maybe because they were all drowned in the sea.

Any other possibility defies reason.

The Number of Hebrews in the Exodus

One element of *Moses: Against the Gods* that may cause some concern with believers in the Bible is my census of about 6,000 warriors and 70,000 Hebrews in the Exodus. For those acquainted with the English translations, it seems that the Bible says there were 603,550 warriors and by implication, about 2,000,000 to 3,000,000 total men, women, and children in the Exodus (Num. 1:46).

This is not my attempt to deny or change holy writ. The fact of the matter is that the consensus of both liberal and conservative scholarship is that the English translation of 600,000 warriors cannot possibly be literally accurate for both artifactual and biblical reasons.[25]

David Fouts's dissertation on the large numbers in the Bible examines archaeological excavations, ancient urban density calculations, relevant ancient manuscripts, population demographics, and statistics to conclude that, even by the time of the Iron Age (shortly after the Exodus), the entire population of Palestine, was less than 1,000,000.[26]

---

[24] Flavius Josephus, *Against Apion* 1.14. as quoted in Rohl, *A Test of Time,* 280-281.

[25] David Mark Fouts, *The Use of Large Numbers in the Old Testament: With Particular Emphasis on the use of 'elep."* (Dissertation, Dallas Theological Seminary, 1992),

[26] Fouts, *The Use of Large Numbers,* 53-67. See also John H Walton, *Zondervan Illustrated Bible Backgrounds Commentary* (Old Testament): Genesis, Exodus, Leviticus, Numbers, Deuteronomy, vol. 1 (Grand Rapids, MI: Zondervan, 2009), 344.

Contrast this fact with the biblical statement of Canaanite inhabitants and one sees that the literal numbers in the Hebrew census are not what they seem.

> Deuteronomy 7:1, 7
> "When the LORD your God brings you into the land that you are entering to take possession of it, and clears away many nations before you…seven nations more numerous and mightier than you…for you were the fewest of all peoples.

If there were seven nations more numerous than little old Israel at a suggested 3 million, that would make the total population of Canaan to be well over 21 million people, which does not comport well with the archaeological fact of only 1 million inhabitants.[27] 21 million Canaanites is simply absurd. And appealing to "miracles" to fill in the gaps of absurdity will not do. God miraculously parted a sea, but he didn't deceptively take all evidence of 20 million inhabitants out of the archaeological, scientific, and historical record.[28]

Numbers 3 lists the numbers of first-born males of Israel (v. 43) and compares it to the number of males in the tribe of Levi (v. 39). If the total population of Israel was 3 million, the average family would have 100 sons each![29] Another absurdity that cannot be dismissed with glib appeals to miracles. These numbers are clearly hyperbolic. Something other than a shallow surface reading is necessary to discern their meaning.

The census numbers under King David are not only different between 2 Samuel 24 and 1 Chronicles 21, but like the Numbers census, they are entirely too large to fit the facts of the region and time period. There are many more biblical examples that Fouts examines, but he concludes from the evidence that this tiny little nation that is supposed to be smaller than all the others seems to use the largest numbers in its records. "The historical literature of the Old Testament employs more numbers in excess of 100,000 than does all the major published historical literature of the ancient Near East. The Old

---

27 The modern population of Israel and Palestine is about 13,000,000.

28 Pharaoh's fear, "Behold, the people of Israel are too many and too mighty for us" (Exodus 1:9) is an obvious exaggeration of hyperbole used to justify violence against them. Classic victim delusion. 600,000 warriors would outnumber the men of Pharaoh's army according to Herodotus, Colin,J. Humphreys, "How Many People Were in the Exodus from Egypt?" *Science & Christian Belief*, Vol 12, No. 1, 18.

29 "Num. iii 43 states that the number of firstborn males a month or more old was 22,273. However, if the number of males over twenty years old was 603,550, this implies a total number of males a month or more old of about one million, hence a ratio of all males to firstborn males of about 50 to 1. The average mother must then have had about 100 children (50 sons and 50 daughters)." Humphreys, "How Many People Were in the Exodus?", 18.

Testament also contains the largest numbers extant in the historical literatures of the ancient Near East."[30]

As a believer in the Bible, I am not suggesting that Scripture is somehow a faulty or lying witness. But rather that there is something very different about the ancient Hebrew tabulation of population numbers that differs from our modern desire for raw mathematical precision. And this is not to say either that all such hyperbolic numbers would therefore be reducible to symbolism alone. As it turns out, the most troubling of the large numbers are usually related to military context or cultic ritual.

This hints at a possible answer. Fouts looks at certain genres of writing in the ancient Near Eastern world to see if there is a pattern we can learn from. He uncovers the fact that ancient Sumerian, Mesopotamian, and Assyrian royal inscriptions and annals of military and civilian calculation of population and property all engaged in hyperbolic numbering. Their purpose was to glorify the reigning monarch, whether in peace or war. It is no heresy or leap of logic to conclude that Hebrew scribes would write in a similar genre as those around them when they wanted to glorify their God and their king in comparison.

And we'll see later in chapter 3 that the Exodus story is told using military language as a battle between Yahweh and Pharaoh with his gods of Egypt. So the military context fits the narrative.

As an added revelation, Fouts reveals that many of the hyperbolic numbers of Sumer and Assyria are divisible by 6 or 60 because their arithmetic was based on a sexagesimal system. In contrast, the Hebrews, following their Egyptian captors, used the decimal system, which may explain their own hyperbolic numbers in terms of tens or hundreds or even thousands.

I quote Fouts's conclusion at length here for its clarity and impact.

> The intentional, purposeful embellishment of the numbers (hyperbole) [in the Bible] is for the purpose of glorifying King Yahweh, King David, or King Solomon (and a few lesser kings of the divided monarchy). By analogy with the practices of other ancient Near Eastern cultures who also embellished numbers, the large numbers of the Old Testament may be safely reduced to 1/10 in the case of Pentateuchal numbers, and possibly to as little as 1/100 or even 1/1000 in such passages as 1 Kings 20:30, as an approximation of what the actual totals may have been. It is

---

[30] Fouts, *The Use of Large Numbers*, 2.

> furthermore thought that understanding the large numbers as hyperbole is the only tenable solution to the problems encountered by their occurrences which satisfies both the demands of Scripture and the artifactual data currently available.[31]

Though Fouts offers a strong biblical argument for symbolism in the hyperbole of large biblical numbers, there is another theory championed by J.W. Wenham and more recently by Colin J. Humphreys that interprets the number problem linguistically. In this view, it is revealed that the Hebrew word for the number 1,000 is *'lep*, but it can also mean units of military troops or tribes.[32] Colin Humphrey explains, "In many languages the same word can have different meanings with the meaning being determined by the context. Thus in English the word crab can mean sea crustacean, zodiacal constellation, nebula, wild apple, or a specialized rowing term.[33] So in this case, the original ancient intent has been misinterpreted at a later time and references to "troops" of men has been translated as "thousands" of men.

In this view, therefore, the numbers of military worthy men described in Numbers 1 should be read quite differently than our modern English translations. 45,650 men of the tribe of Gad (1:24) should be 45 troops of 650 men in total. The 74,600 of the tribe of Judah (1:26) should be translated as 74 troops of 600 men in total, and so on.

Humphreys then uses rigorous mathematical calculations to show that his theory applies consistently in this and other passages. He concludes that the number of fighting men in the Numbers census was not 603,550 men (Numbers 1:46), but rather 598 troops of 5,550 men in total.[34] The

---

[31] This is from Fouts' summary article of his dissertation: David M. Fouts, "A Defense Of The Hyperbolic Interpretation Of Large Numbers In The Old Testament," *JETS* 40/3 (September 1997), 378.

[32] Hebrew numbers were not numerical like ours, they used letters to represent numbers, so meaning can be misunderstood.

Of "elep: "There are, however, several specialized usages. One is in the basic sense of the largest basic division of leadership in political oversight or military leadership (Ex 18:21; Num 1:16; 31:4; Deut 1:15; I Chr 13:1; 27:1; Amos 5:3)." Jack B. Scott, "109 אֶלֶף," ed. R. Laird Harris, Gleason L. Archer Jr., and Bruce K. Waltke, Theological Wordbook of the Old Testament (Chicago: Moody Press, 1999), 48.

[33] Humphreys, "How Many People Were in the Exodus", 20.

[34] Humphreys, "How Many People Were in the Exodus", 24. Why is this not interpreted consistently as 603 troops of 550 men for the total? Because the word "elep is unfortunately being used in two different ways, as both "thousand" and "troops," in the same passage. Humphreys explains, "we suggest the total in the original text was of the form 598 'lp (troops) and 5 'lp (thousands) and 550 men, and the original readers understood that there were 598 troops containing 5550 men. At a later date, when the original meaning was lost, a scribe conflated the numbers and ran together the two 'lp figures (598 + 5), to yield 603 thousand, not realising that two different 'lp meanings were intended." Page 28. Though some Christians and Jews do not like to admit inconvenient facts, there are many textual problems with the Old Testament manuscripts that we have, and this suggestion is not out of line with the kind of things that have occurred in translations of other biblical texts.

corresponding total population of men, women and children in the Exodus then works out to approximately 20,000. Wenham gave more leeway on interpretation to conclude 70,000 Israelites.[35]

I have included on the ChroniclesoftheWatchers.com website the articles quoted here for the reader under the "Scholarly Research" page.

Red Sea, Reed Sea, or Something Else?

I have previously referred to the Red Sea in passages above. But that is a misnomer. I now want to explain why the sea I named in the novel as Yam Suph (based on the Hebrew Bible), the sea that God parted for Israel's crossing, is not accurately translated as Red Sea. Shocking, I know. But biblical, you'll see.

For these next few sections, I have drawn heavily from material written by Glen Fritz, PhD. in environmental geography. He has surveyed the real-world geography as it relates to the Exodus and combined it with solid exegesis of Scripture to come up with viable arguments for the identity of Yam Suph, the Exodus route, and the location of Mount Sinai—all at odds with the traditional views.[36]

Let's take a look first at the "Red Sea." The actual biblical name for the famous body of water in the Hebrew text is *Yam Suph*. By now, many people know about the more controversial claim that Yam Suph did not mean "Red Sea" but "Reed Sea," one of the smaller lakes to the north of the Red Sea. We'll deal with that problem in a moment. There's a bigger issue to start with.

The biggest problem is that the words *Yam Suph* simply do not mean "Red Sea." As Bible scholar Bernard Batto explains, "Yam indeed means sea; that much is clear and agreed. But the word for red is *adam*, not sûp. Literally, Red Sea should be Yam Adam, not Yam Sûp."[37] The reason why this has totally escaped the attention of so many of us is because tradition has blinded us to the ancient understanding.

But wait, did not the ancients understand Yam Suph to mean Red Sea? Some did. But Glen Fritz lays out the evidence to show that there is an older

---

[35] J.W. Wenham, "Large Numbers in the Old Testament," *Tyndale Bulletin* 18 (1967) 19-53. See also

[36] His two volumes contain impressive scholarly research. Glen A. Fritz, *The Lost Sea of the Exodus : A Modern Geographical Analysis* 2nd Edition (FL: GeoTech, 2007, 2017) and Glen A. Fritz, *The Exodus Mysteries: of Midian, Sinai & Jabal al-Lawz* (FL: GeoTech, 2019). Best to purchase them from his website: https://ancientexodus.com

[37] Bernard Batto, "Red Sea or Reed Sea?" *Biblical Archaeology Review* 10:4, July/August 1984. https://www.baslibrary.org/biblical-archaeology-review/10/4/3&

tradition that Moses and the Hebrews did not read it that way. It all begins with the Septuagint (also referred to as LXX).

The Septuagint is the oldest Greek translation of the Bible from the original Hebrew.[38] It was completed around 250 B.C. by Jewish scholars in Alexandria, Egypt. That makes their understanding of the original Hebrew to be pretty ancient. The problem is, it's not ancient enough. The Greek words used to translate *Yam Suph* are *Eruthra Thalassa*. *Yam* does mean "sea" as does the Greek *thalassa*. But *suph* does not mean "red" as *eruthra* does.

Fritz explains:

> [T]his Septuagint rendering was not a translation. It was a geographical interpretation reflecting the scholars' knowledge of the two great seas near Egypt, the Mediterranean on the north and the Red Sea on the south. Based on contemporary writings such as Herodotus, they would have understood this sea as a long shaft of water passing along Arabia and ending near Egypt. The Red Sea termination near Egypt is now known as the Gulf of Suez [in modern times].[39]

Fritz drops the bomb when he adds, "the Greek Red Sea concept did not include the Gulf of Aqaba as we know it because the Greeks were ignorant of its geography." The Gulf of Aqaba, a modern name, is shown on the map below (Figure 1) as a second prong of the Red Sea that created the Sinai Peninsula. The Gulf of Suez on the left, the Gulf of Aqaba on the right.

Ancient Greek maps of this region do not tend to have the Gulf of Aqaba on them. They didn't even know of the existence of the Gulf of Aqaba, so they didn't include it in their maps. The only sea the translators of the LXX knew of in that region was the Red Sea prong now called the Gulf of Suez.[40] You can see how lack of knowledge can create a tradition of assumptions that may not be true.

---

38 It is important to note that the Hebrew text we have of the Bible is not necessarily more accurate to the original than the LXX. That's because the Hebrew text we have is from the middle ages of the ninth century A.D. by Masoretic scribes (that's 1000 years later than the LXX). That later date means that the Masoretic Hebrew is not always in line with the more ancient Hebrew understandings in the LXX. The problem is that both Greek and Hebrew versions are sometimes right, sometimes wrong, but we can't always know which is which. It is also relevant to note that both Jesus and the apostles quoted from the LXX, so they accepted it as a legitimate translation, imperfect as it has sometimes been found to be. God's Word is not bound by the imprecision of translation.

39 Glen A. Fritz, *The Lost Sea of the Exodus : A Modern Geographical Analysis* 2nd Edition (FL: GeoTech, 2007, 2017), xxiii.

40 Fritz provides many reproductions of ancient maps illustrating this fact throughout the book *The Lost Sea of the Exodus.*

This ignorance of the Gulf of Aqaba is exposed in three passages of the Bible where Yam Suph is not translated as Red Sea (Judges 11:16; I Kings 9:26; Jeremiah 49:21). In those passages, Yam Suph is used in Hebrew of the sea at the edge of Edom. Edom was known by the ancient Greek translators to be southeast of Canaan, a long way away from Egypt and the "Red Sea" as they understood it. When the translators read "Yam Suph," they knew it could not be the Red Sea as they understood it, so they translated it differently. But if you look up those passages you find that it is the same Yam Suph of the Exodus crossing as well as of the land of Edom. Yam Suph is described as bordering Edom, but Edom is not in the modern-day Sinai Peninsula. It is beside the Gulf of Aqaba.

Fritz concludes that most scholars through much of history simply did not know of the existence of the Gulf of Aqaba to even consider it as a candidate for Yam Suph. They only knew of the one sea, the Gulf of Suez, as the Red Sea, so it was logical that they would translate Yam Suph geographically as the Red Sea, despite knowing that Yam Suph *did not linguistically mean* Red Sea.

But Fritz argues that this Gulf of Aqaba was exactly the Yam Suph of the Bible. So on my map below, I named the Gulf of Aqaba on the right as the Yam Suph of the Bible. Fritz found evidence that later Egyptians called both gulfs Yuma Sekot (*sekot* meaning circle).[41] I found the earliest Egyptian reference to the Red Sea as Mew Kedew (MW KḎW) around 1164 B.C.[42] So I named the Gulf of Suez as Mew Kedew.

This places Yam Suph far, far away from what is traditionally understood as the Red Sea crossing. We will discuss the biblical issues related to this in a moment. For now, take special note that the Bible itself points to the Gulf of Aqaba as Yam Suph rather explicitly in a way that discredits the Red Sea theory. Of course in the modern world, we understand both these gulfs to be part of the Red Sea, but we name them as different "gulfs" of that same sea. The ancients would give different names as well, but they did not call them "gulfs," they called them "seas."

Let's take a closer Scriptural look.

Yahweh himself defines the boundaries of the Promised Land to Moses this way:

---

[41] Fritz, *Lost Sea*, 41.

[42] Maurice Copisarow, "The Ancient Egyptian, Greek and Hebrew Concept of the Red Sea," *Vetus Testamentum, Vol. 12, Fasc. 1* (Jan., 1962), 4. ANE expert Michael S. Heiser gave me the English translation, Mew Kedew. Personal correspondence email August 2, 2021.

> Exodus 23:31
> And I will set your border from the Red Sea [Yam Suph] to the Sea of the Philistines, and from the wilderness to the Euphrates, for I will give the inhabitants of the land into your hand.

The boundaries of the Promised Land as delineated in the biblical text cannot possibly include what is today called the Sinai Peninsula (not its ancient name) if Red Sea means the Gulf of Suez. No Bible scholar worth his degree would ever suggest such extended boundaries. The territory of the Promised Land goes from the Euphrates in the north to the Mediterranean Sea in the west to the Gulf of Aqaba in the south, not to the Gulf of Suez (Red Sea) in the far south west. The Gulf of Aqaba must be the biblical Yam Suph, or the Bible would be saying that the Promised Land includes the entire Sinai Peninsula.

What Does Yam Suph Mean?

The Reed Sea theory. The belief that Yam Suph means Sea of Reeds or Reed Sea or Sea of Rushes has origins as far back as the Middle Ages, based on writings of classical authors. Some influential scholars like Martin Luther thought the Red Sea should be called the Reed Sea because they thought *suph* meant reeds. But this could not possibly be true because the Red Sea is salt water and reeds do not grow in salt water.[43]

The theory spread in the 19th century when many different scholarly options were offered for Yam Suph that were part of a line of inland lakes north of the Red Sea called the Bitter Lakes. These were lakes connected geographically to the larger body of water south of them, thus being able to be considered part of the Red Sea and thus warrant a generic reference to "Red Sea." But these lakes were fresh water, so reeds might actually grow there.

The reader need not fear such theories as "liberal" attempts to discredit the Bible by making Yam Suph a mere small lake that was dried up by natural means, followed by a tidal wave of natural causes. The Bible does often use poetic language, and we must be ready to understand it in their ancient context rather than in our own modern context. As I will describe later, the Bible certainly does use mythological and poetic symbolic language in some passages about the Exodus. So we must not assume that everything written is hyperliteral.

---

[43] Bernard Batto, "Red Sea or Reed Sea?" *Biblical Archaeology Review* online 10:4, July/August 1984. https://www.baslibrary.org/biblical-archaeology-review/10/4/3& Bi

But even if it was true that Yam Suph was a small lake, the Exodus crossing would still be miraculous in its timing and in the fact that God would have drowned the entire Egyptian army in a small lake. That's arguably a dramatic supernatural display of God's power. So I make the argument that the reader should not react from conservative bias any more than liberal bias but rather seek to understand and accept the meaning of the text whatever it may say—not *what our bias wants it to say*.

But back to the meaning of *suph*. Claims are made that the Hebrew word *suph* is derived from the Egyptian word *twf* (pronounced "thoof"), which means papyrus or reeds. But Bible scholar Bernard Batto dismisses the connection with much effect when he writes of *twf*, "The phrase appears a number of times in Egyptian texts. It refers, however, to a papyrus marsh area or district, not to a lake or body of water."[44]

Then why is the word *suph* translated as reeds, weeds, or rushes in the Bible? Actually, there are only four places where that botanical rendering is the case (Exodus 2:3-5; Isaiah 19:6; Jonah 2:5). Fritz analyzes each one of those four cases to show that they are better translated not as reeds or papyrus, but as something else.

A lexical analysis of the word family of *suph* yields the fact that its root meaning is *end* or *ending.*[45] *In all four scriptural cases above, the odd botanical rendering is not the most accurate to the Hebrew, but rather that it should in each case be rendered as something like "a place where the water ends*."

In Exodus 2:3-5, Moses's sister made a basket of papyrus or reeds and placed Moses's basket not "among *the reeds* by the river bank," but "by *the edge* of the river bank."[46]

Isaiah 9:6, Fritz writes, "contains the phrase: '…the branches of Egypt's Nile will diminish and dry up, reeds and rushes [*suph*] will rot away.' In this

---

44 Batto explains, "In some texts *p´-t_wf* is used to designate a district or area not only where papyrus grows but also where animals are pastured and agricultural enterprises undertaken.In hieroglyphic writing an unpronounced sign, called a determinative, is often included in the spelling to indicate the class of noun the word falls into. Thus the determinative for god is added to the phonetic signs for gods, so we know which names refer to gods. *P´-t_wf* is always written with the determinative for plant. Occasionally it is written with the determinative for town, but never is it written with the determinative for lake or water."

Bernard Batto, "Red Sea or Reed Sea?" https://www.baslibrary.org/biblical-archaeology-review/10/4/3&

45 Fritz, *Lost Sea*, 164-165.

46 "A noun *sûp̱* allegedly also existed, originally with the meaning "end, boundary," as a designation for the banks of the Nile, in whose region the Israelites lived during their sojourn in Egypt." H. Lamberty-Zielinski and M. Ottosson, "סוּף," ed. G. Johannes Botterweck, Helmer Ringgren, and Heinz-Josef Fabry, trans. Douglas W. Stott, *Theological Dictionary of the Old Testament* (Grand Rapids, MI; Cambridge, U.K.: William B. Eerdmans Publishing Company, 1999), 191.

case, 'banks' work, giving an alternative reading: '...the branches of Egypt's Nile will diminish and dry up, the reeds and the banks [*suph*] shall wither.' A river's bank is its ending!"[47]

In Jonah 2:5, Jonah describes his sinking into the depths of the sea and how the "weeds (*suph*) were wrapped around my head." But there is a problem here. Suph cannot mean "reeds" in this text because there are no reeds in the salt water of the sea. So the translators arbitrarily changed the translation of the word *suph* from reeds to weeds to maintain their bias rather than follow the root meaning of "ending." The Septuagint is more accurate in translating this same phrase as "Water was poured around me to the soul: the lowest deep (*suph*) compassed me, my head went down."[48] Suph here means the sea floor as the *end of the water*. He reaches the bottom of the sea, its ending, its *suph*.[49]

Yam Suph should not be translated as Red Sea. Fritz concludes:

> Based on Hebrew grammar, the suph word family meaning, and the geographical context of Yam Suph, its likely translations are "sea of ending" or "sea of boundary."[50]

Batto agrees, saying that Yam Suph "was regarded by the ancients as the sea at the end of the world."[51] In my novel, I used Yam Suph as the name of the sea of crossing. But I also call it "Sea of Ending" and even suggest a possible common folk translation as "Sea at the End of the World" because for the Hebrew everything else beyond it was the end of their world, both while they were living in Egypt and later in Canaan.

Where Was the Sea Crossing?

Determining the location of Yam Suph is not enough. One must also find a place for crossing that is geographically possible if the waters were held back for the Israelites to pass through as well as for Egyptian chariots to roll through. Fritz has an entire section describing the geography of the prime location for the crossing at the Gulf of Aqaba. It is a large beachhead (with the modern name of Nuweiba) about halfway down the gulf that is accessed by a long cavernous wadi (a deep gully carved by water). The key comparison with

---

47 Fritz, *Lost Sea*, 167.

48 Lancelot Charles Lee Brenton, *The Septuagint Version of the Old Testament: English Translation* (London: Samuel Bagster and Sons, 1870), Jon 2:4–7.

49 Fritz, *Lost Sea*, 169.

50 Fritz, *Lost Sea*, 102.

51 Bernard Batto, "Red Sea or Reed Sea?" https://www.baslibrary.org/biblical-archaeology-review/10/4/3&

other possible crossing locations is that it alone offers a passable "land bridge" for people to cross if water is held back.

The Gulf of Suez is a shallow sea with an average depth of 155 feet, but its declines are too steep for people, much less chariots, to cover if the waters were held back. The Gulf of Aqaba on the other hand is exceedingly deep with depths as much as 1500 feet. But there is a geological anomaly of a submarine sill only nine hundred feet deep with gentle slopes that would be traversable by people and chariots. And that is located exactly at the single large beachhead of Nuweiba. If the waters were pulled back, it would create a land bridge approximately 9.7 miles long and several miles wide, that would enable the large number of Israelites to cross it in time.[52]

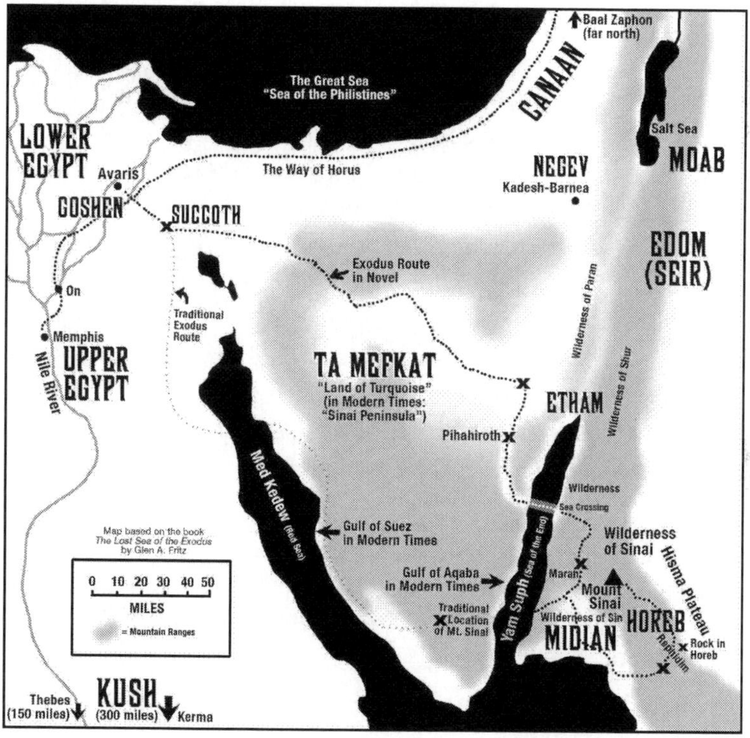

Figure A

Walls of Water

When anyone pictures what the parting of the sea would look like in their mind's eye, just about everyone sees the images from the 1956 epic *The Ten*

---

[52] Fritz, *Lost Sea*, 195-197.

Commandments. Huge walls of water forming a canyon-like pathway for the Israelites to walk through. But is this accurate or just more Hollywood hyperbole?

The terrible blasphemous movie of recent years, *Exodus: Gods and Kings*, takes a different approach. It depicts the strong east wind of Exodus 14:21 but attempts to give a more naturalistic interpretation by using an offshore earthquake to create a tsunami. The water pulls back from the shoreline, and the Israelites cross the exposed lakebed. Then when the Egyptians are crossing, a huge wall of water comes rushing in to drown them. This is relatively accurate to how a major tsunami might work.

As I've already written, I am not against naturalistic descriptions of miraculous events per se, so I thought it was still a pretty awesome depiction with much more realistic special effects than the old classic.

But is it possible?

As a believer who trusts the veracity of the biblical text, I can't say that it is. First, Yam Suph is not described as a lake with a slender lakebed as depicted in the recent movie. It is a deep and mighty sea with roaring waves (Exodus 15:8, 10; 14:27).[53]

Secondly, Fritz provides geological evidence that the path for crossing the sea was as much as a few miles wide, due to the land bridge beneath the surface.[54] But also, such a wide path would provide enough distance for the Egyptian army to be willing to cross. That would make those walls of water quite far in the distance from the crossing. It wouldn't seem an immediate threat to them in their pursuit of Israel. It would seem *almost natural.* This is exactly what Jewish historian Josephus suggests:

> …but the Egyptians were not aware that they went into a road made for the Hebrews, and not for others; that this road was made for the deliverance of those in danger, but not for those that were earnest to make use of it for the others' destruction.[55]

This means that the movie versions of a few hundred feet wide pathway are not as feasible.

---

53 See also Isaiah 43:16: 51:10, 14; Jeremiah 31:35.

54 Fritz, *Lost Sea*, 195-198.

55 Josephus, *Antiquities of the Jews* 2.16.3 (342-344) Flavius Josephus and William Whiston, *The Works of Josephus: Complete and Unabridged* (Peabody: Hendrickson, 1987), 76.

But this doesn't mean the waters were simply drawn back to look as if there was a crossing between two seas. The text explicitly claims that the waters were "heaped up" on the right and on the left.

> Exodus 15:8
> At the blast of your nostrils the waters piled up; the floods stood up in a heap; the deeps congealed in the heart of the sea.
>
> Psalm 78:13
> He divided the sea and let them pass through it, and made the waters stand like a heap.
>
> Exodus 14:21–22
> Then Moses stretched out his hand over the sea, and the LORD drove the sea back by a strong east wind all night and made the sea dry land, and the waters were divided. And the people of Israel went into the midst of the sea on dry ground, the waters being a wall to them on their right hand and on their left.

What are we to make of waters "piling up," "standing like a heap," "being a wall of water" on the right and left, with the "deeps congealed in the heart of the sea"? William Propp suggests "congealing" is a key word having to do with freezing of water.

> The poet has been developing a progressively paradoxical and miraculous image: the waters are first piled up (*neʿermû*), not unusual in a storm, but then they actually stand upright (*niṣṣəbû*)! How? Because some of the waters, the "Deeps," have congealed, presumably into ice (cf. Philo's *krystallōthentos* 'crystallized/frozen' [*Moses* 2.253]). To heighten the miracle, the ice does not float to the surface (cf. Sir 43:20), but remains vertical "in Sea's heart" until melted by Yahweh's second blast (v 10, cf. v 7).[56]
> I shall suggest that Yahweh *freezes* the Sea. If so, the reference to Yahweh's *burning* anger in v 7 becomes more appropriate. Yahweh's first blast turns the Deeps to ice. His second (v 10) melts the gelid waters.[57]

---

[56] William H. C. Propp, *Exodus 1–18: A New Translation with Introduction and Commentary*, vol. 2, Anchor Yale Bible (New Haven; London: Yale University Press, 2008), 523.

[57] Propp, *Exodus*, 520.

Regarding the waters "standing up in a heap," Noel Osborn suggests the meaning of "heap" is not certain, so a variety of translations result: "wall" (TAN, NIV), "bank" (REB), "dyke" (NJB), "mound" (NAB), "stack" (Durham), and "hill" (Childs)."[58] This was the ambiguity from which I imagined my depiction of the parting of Yam Suph in the *Moses* novel.

What Was the Mysterious Exodus Route?

The map above (Figure 1) was used in my novel of Moses. It shows the Exodus route my narrative follows and compares it to one of the traditional Exodus routes to illustrate some of the differences. Of course, once Yam Suph is established in an entirely different location than the traditional one, the route to that Yam Suph will also be quite different.

Unfortunately, there are many different suggestions for the Exodus route because no one knows for sure. The problem is that Moses references only five major landmarks before they reach Yam Suph, and none of the landmarks are known with certainty today.

Here is the Scripture.

> Numbers 33:5–7
> So the people of Israel set out from Rameses [Avaris] and camped at Succoth. And they set out from Succoth and camped at Etham, which is on the edge of the wilderness. And they set out from Etham and turned back to Pi-hahiroth, which is east of Baal-zephon, and they camped before Migdol.

The five landmarks before they reached Yam Suph are Succoth, Etham, Pi-hahiroth, Baal Zaphon and Migdol. Fritz examines each in detail and compares them with the real geography of the area that matches elements in the biblical text.

On the map, I show the Exodus route I used in the novel. It traverses the upper peninsula to the Gulf of Aqaba, where the sea-crossing leads them into Midian. This view will be quite new to those committed to some version of the traditional view. On the map, I also show a rough approximation of the traditional view that shows it crossing the Red Sea and going somewhere in the southern Sinai Peninsula for Mount Sinai.

---

[58] Noel D. Osborn and Howard A. Hatton, *A Handbook on Exodus*, UBS Handbook Series (New York: United Bible Societies, 1999), 362.

Keep in mind that the name *Sinai Peninsula* was not the ancient name for that location in Egypt. *Sinai Peninsula* only came into use in the 19th century A.D. because religious believers had thought Mount Sinai had been located there based on arguments only begun in the 4th century. We will look at Mount Sinai near Midian vs. Mount Sinai in the Sinai Peninsula later. But Fritz's book The Lost Sea of Exodus was very helpful in laying out all the details of this journey in a way that addresses the reality of the geography, something other views often fail to take into account.

One of the first objections that is raised to this "upper route," as I will call it, is that the distance of Yam Suph from Egypt in this view places Mount Sinai much farther away than the traditional view, which I will call the "lower route." This upper route places Mount Sinai at a minimum of three or more weeks distance from their starting point in Avaris, Egypt. But the lower route view argues that Mount Sinai was only three days away. After all, doesn't the Bible say so?

> Exodus 3:18
> You and the elders of Israel shall go to the king of Egypt and say to him, "The LORD, the God of the Hebrews, has met with us; and now, please let us go a three days' journey into the wilderness, that we may sacrifice to the LORD our God." (see also Exodus 5:1 and 8:27)

There are several problems with this interpretation that Mount Sinai is supposed to be three days from Avaris. First, the text does not say God wants to take them to Sinai in either of the two requests. *It never mentions Mount Sinai.* It simply shows that God was testing Pharaoh, drawing him out by asking for a mere three day's reprieve from their bondage in order to sacrifice in the desert—away from the Egyptian idols (Exodus 8:25-26). That's not Sinai.

The fact is, at this moment in history, the Hebrews could have sacrificed anywhere in the desert, since no location for sacrifice had been established by God yet. Three days are close enough to ask for a temporary leave of absence, while drawing out Pharaoh's hard heart, but a 60-day request (if Sinai was the intent) would be on the surface ludicrous.[59] No ruler would be expected to allow their slaves to go so far away. Pharaoh wouldn't be hardening his heart but simply using good common sense.

---

[59] Exodus 19:1-2 says the Israelites arrived at Mount Sinai "in the third month" of their exodus from Egypt. Even if you consider them wandering around a bit before arriving at the mountain, that is nothing like being three days' distance.

If we go back to the five encampments, some say that these are far too few of encampments for the 200 mile upper route to the Gulf of Aqaba as Yam Suph. But the itinerary listed is not intended to be an exhaustive description of every place they stopped, merely the key places. And the text is known for large abbreviations of time in between events. Moses's first 40 years of life was summarized in a few verses (Exodus 2:1-10). His middle 40 years only referenced a couple events (Exodus 2:11-4:17). The Israelite's 30-day journey in Midian was abbreviated to a mere three encampments (Exodus 19:1). Abbreviation of the Exodus itinerary would be considered stylistically normal.

But there is something more interesting about the five itinerary stops of the Exodus: Succoth, Etham, Pi-hahiroth, Baal Zaphon and Migdol. While most scholars assume these are names of cities, Fritz makes strong arguments that they are more geographical landmarks that Moses referred to in a mostly vacant wilderness.

First, if there were tens of thousands of Hebrews (let alone 1.5 to 3 million as the traditional view supposes), there is no way they could stay in cities. They would suffocate those populations. The Hebrews would have to stay in large open areas.

Secondly, Fritz explains the meanings of the words as being more general references to geographical areas. Succoth is a plural Hebrew word that means temporary booths. It is an experience that they will ultimately celebrate with the Feast of Booths later. "Succoth likely referred to a general region in the Wadi Tumilat [one day's journey from Avaris] that would be associated with predictable water resources."[60] Etham was not a city but a large wilderness area that extended to the far side of Yam Suph into Edom.[61]

Pi-hahiroth, Baal Zaphon and Migdol were far more meaningful than cities.

> Numbers 33:7 (LEB)
> Then they set out from Etham and [turned back] to Pi-Hahiroth, which faces Baal Zephon, and they camped before Migdol. (see also Exodus 14:2, 9, RSV)

Migdol is a Hebrew word that means "tower," describing the towering mountain range that Moses saw to the south as they crossed the upper route wilderness.[62] Pi-hahiroth means something like "mouth of the caves," which

---

60 Glen A. Fritz, *The Exodus Mysteries: of Midian, Sinai & Jabal al-Lawz* (FL: GeoTech, 2019), 217.

61 Fritz, *The Exodus Mysteries,* 219.

62 Fritz, *The Exodus Mysteries,* 237.

happens to be an apt description of the cavernous Wadi Watir that travels along the Gulf of Aqaba to the beach of the proposed Exodus crossing. With the sun low on the horizon, this sole pathway to the beach looks like a tunnel.[63]

That wadi opening faces due north where Baal Zaphon is. Baal Zaphon is not some local Egyptian city but a Semitic term that refers to the cosmic mountain of Baal in northern Syria, familiar to the Hebrews and therefore a generic reference to the north.[64]

There is much more to these biblical references, but I give these here as an example of what my descriptions of the Exodus journey in the novel are based upon.

Where was Mount Sinai?

If the Yam Suph crossing is not at the Gulf of Suez of the Red Sea, but farther east at the Gulf of Aqaba, then the location of Mount Sinai is somewhere near the land of Midian in Arabia, a vastly different location than the traditional views of somewhere on the Sinai Peninsula.

The holy mountain of God has as many theories as there are theories of Exodus routes and Yam Suph crossings. And just as many uncertainties that keep scholars to this day from settling on any one mountain as the certain choice. But I discovered some very fascinating geographical and biblical facts from Glen Fritz's book, *The Exodus Mysteries: of Midian, Sinai & Jabal al-Lawz*.

First, it is mostly agreed that the land of ancient Midian to which Moses traveled before and after the Exodus is located in the northwest region of modern Saudi Arabia or ancient Arabia Felix (Arabia for short). On the map of Figure 1 above, it can be seen on the southeast corner of the Gulf of Aqaba (Yam Suph) with a mountain range surrounding its territory.

In Galatians, the apostle Paul makes an allegorical connection between Hagar and Mount Sinai that contains a simple geographical reference to the holy mountain's location.

> Galatians 4:25
> Now Hagar is Mount Sinai in Arabia…

---

[63] Fritz, *The Exodus Mysteries*, 244-248.

[64] Fritz, *The Exodus Mysteries*, 237-242.

In the ancient world, the Sinai Peninsula was not called the Sinai Peninsula. The Egyptians called it *Ta Mefkat*, or "Land of Turquoise."[65] And it was not part of Arabia. Arabia consisted of land around Israel/Canaan all the way down to the Gulf of Aqaba. But it did not include what we now call the Sinai Peninsula, so Mount Sinai could not be located there.

Glen Fritz tracks the travel route the Israelites must have trod based on biblical descriptions of their journey compared with the geography of the surrounding region of Midian. He concludes the location of Mount Sinai must fulfill several biblical criteria of evidence.

> **Condition 1**: The route to the mountain must be accessible by a multitude.
> **Condition 2**: The mountain must have terrain suitable to host the multitude and its herds for 11 months.
> **Condition 3**: Mount Sinai was the tallest peak in the region according to Josephus (1960, Ant. II.xii.1; III.v.1) and Philo (Moses II.xiv.70).
> **Condition 4**: Relative to Midian, Mount Sinai was located at the rear of a wilderness.
> **Condition 5**: Mount Sinai was in a highland setting.[66]

Fritz then goes through the evidence to conclude that the mountain meeting those requirements is Jabal al-Maqla in the Jebal al-Lawz mountain range north of the Midian location. On the map of Figure 1 above, that mountain range sits at the "rear of the wilderness" on the Hisma Plateau, a highland setting indeed.[67] Jabal al-Maqla is the tallest peak in that region and is certainly accessible by a multitude—all in ways more fitting for Mount Sinai than other candidates.

For those unfamiliar with the actual geography of the area, this means little. But Fritz's research of that mountain and its surrounding geography was paramount for me capturing the world that Moses and Yahweh's people were traveling through. The topography, sights, sounds, and smells, flora and fauna all contribute to a sensory imagination that brings the biblical story of the Exodus alive for the reader.

---

65 Fatma Keshk, "Forgotten archaeological gems: The ancient turquoise mines of South Sinai" *Egypt Independent* Online https://www.egyptindependent.com/forgotten-archaeological-gems-ancient-turquoise-mines-south-sinai/

66 Fritz, *The Exodus Mysteries,* 88.

67 As Fritz explains, "The Bible does not mention the Hisma, but it does cite a region called Horeb, which hosted the Mountain of God, the wilderness of Sinai, and Rephidim. Based on Horeb's etymology, it was presumably an arid region. Horeb's association with the rear of the mountain wilderness, and with aridity, raises the likelihood that Horeb was an ancient analog of the Hisma." Fritz, *The Exodus Mysteries,* 176. These are all depicted on the map of Figure 1 above.

Some will argue that this places Mount Sinai in Midian, and according to the Bible Mount Sinai could not be in Midian. Exodus 18:27 and Numbers 10:30 clearly describe Jethro and Hobab departing from Mount Sinai "to their own land" in Midian. But as Fritz explains, "The Bible does not state whether Mount Sinai was inside or outside of the land of Midian. It does place it within "the wilderness of Sinai" (Exo. 19:1-2), the "wilderness" that Moses and Jethro traveled to from Midian to reach the Mountain of God (Exo. 3:1; 18:1-5). Moses's excursion with Jethro's flock also suggests that some degree of travel was required between the mountain of God and Midian."[68]

A careful look on the map in Figure 1 shows that the mountain range is close to Midian, but it is not in Midian. In fact, it is in Horeb.

Many Bible readers have interpreted the name Horeb to be a synonym for Mount Sinai. Others argue for Sinai and Horeb as two different mountain peaks near each other. The word for Horeb appears 17 times in the Old Testament. Most of those uses can be understood as describing a region rather than a mountain. But a few appear to use the name Horeb interchangeably with Mount Sinai. The first case is exemplary.

> Exodus 3:1 (KJV 1900)
> Now Moses kept the flock of Jethro his father in law, the priest of Midian: and he led the flock to the backside of the desert, and came to the mountain of God, *even* to Horeb.

In those questionable cases, the underlying Hebrew reveals something different than the English translations. Fritz explains this problem with Exodus 3:1. The translation traditions mistake "mountain of God" as being identical with "Horeb," which actually obscures the geographical reality of Horeb.

> In explanation, "even to Horeb" is not a literal translation, with the italicized *even* signaling that it was not derived from the underlying Hebrew. Furthermore, the translators overlooked an important point of Hebrew grammar. In the underlying Hebrew, khorev (spelled hrb) is written hrbh (pronounced horevah), giving the explicit meaning of Horeb-ward or toward Horeb. Hence, hrbh is an adverb...
> In summary, the meaning of Horeb describes the conditions of a dry or desolate place. In the region surrounding Midian, the previously described Hisma plateau would match these

---

[68] Fritz, *The Exodus Mysteries,* 119.

> conditions. If so, Horeb described the arid region lying beyond the mountain wilderness east of Midian.[69]

After examining all the biblical and geographical evidence, Fritz concludes:

> 1. Horeb and Sinai were not equivalent terms for the same mountain.
> 2. Horeb and Sinai were not the names of separate mountains.
> 3. Horeb was not a mountain.
> 4. Horeb was a region in which Mount Sinai was located.[70]

Of course there is so much more to explore with these issues, which is why I recommend the books by Fritz for an exciting journey of imagination in the Exodus through Yam Suph and all the way to Mount Sinai in the region of Horeb.[71]

---

[69] Fritz, *The Exodus Mysteries,* 130-131.

[70] Fritz, *The Exodus Mysteries,* 131.

[71] Glen A. Fritz, *The Lost Sea of the Exodus : A Modern Geographical Analysis* 2nd Edition (FL: GeoTech, 2007, 2017) and Glen A. Fritz, *The Exodus Mysteries: of Midian, Sinai & Jabal al-Lawz* (FL: GeoTech, 2019). Best to purchase them from his website: https://ancientexodus.com

Chapter 2
The Characters

Moses

His Egyptian Name

Attempting to write a novel about one of the most known and beloved heroes of the Bible was daunting. The specter of cliché and redundancy hovers over the writer like a dark cloud. As a storyteller, I sought to be unique and bring a fresh approach to the narrative, but as an intellectual dedicated to the integrity of the text, I wanted to make it theologically consistent with the Bible. My mourning of this apparently difficult dichotomy turned to dancing when research uncovered information previously unknown or unused in other versions. I have already described some of those transforming discoveries above related to the events and characters of the Exodus. Some of those discoveries related directly to the man himself.

If we return to the dating of the Exodus at about 1447 B.C., and combine that with David Rohl's New Chronology restructuring of the Egyptian dynasties, we find some fascinating possibilities for the novel retelling of this classic story.

I explained that according to Rohl's New Chronology, the pharaoh of the Exodus was most likely Djedneferre Dudimose, last of the 13th Dynasty, not the assumed Ramesses II of the 19th Dynasty around 1250 B.C. Rohl also concludes that Neferhotep I (13th Dynasty) is the pharaoh of Lower Nile when Moses was born (not Seti as in the movie). His daughter, the princess, then marries the son of the pharaoh of the Upper Nile, Sobekhotep IV. This becomes an important identifier for Moses's name.[1]

In the story of Moses's birth, his mother places her three-month-old son in a basket on the Nile. Moses's sister watches from a distance as Pharaoh's daughter discovers the basket. Miriam comes out of hiding and tells the Egyptian that she knows a woman who can be a nursemaid for the babe, which happens to secretly be Moses's own mother. Unwise to the deception,

---

[1] David Rohl, *Exodus: Myth or History?* (MN: Thinking Man Media, 2015), 137.

Pharaoh's daughter agrees to the arrangement for a little while until she officially adopts Moses as her own.

> Exodus 2:10
> When the child grew older, she brought him to Pharaoh's daughter, and he became her son. She named him Moses, "Because," she said, "I drew him out of the water."

While it appears that the Hebrew word for Moses means "drew him out of the water," this is not quite what is going on. Moses in Hebrew does not mean "one who is drawn out" [of water], it means "one who draws out." As famed Jewish Bible commentator Umberto Cassuto explains,

> The explanation does not fit the name accurately, because the form of the word is active not passive…The author of the verse undoubtedly had a fine feeling for the Hebrew language, and he knew quite well the difference between *mōše* ['one who draws out'] and *māšūy* ['one who is drawn out']. It is also difficult to suppose that Scripture attributed to the Egyptian princess a knowledge of Hebrew and the choice of a Hebrew name. The naming is to be explained in a different way. First, it is stated that 'he became her son; and she called his name *Mōše'*, that is, *son* in Egyptian (an Egyptian word that was actually pronounced thus—*Mōse*—at that period and in that locality).[2]

Egyptologist John Currid agrees, noting that "Mose" was a common Egyptian word meaning "son of." "Many Egyptian names employ it in conjunction with other words: Thutmosis (son of Thut) and Ahmosis (son of Ah), for example." In the name Moses, however, the genitive has no object. He is simply 'the son of'."[3]

One could interpret the royal daughter's reasoning behind the naming, as reflecting a symbolic birth reference. Natural birth was often referred to as "born of water," since the infant follows the release of the water from the

---

[2] U. Cassuto, *A Commentary on the Book of Exodus,* trans. Israel Abrahams (Jerusalem: Magnes Press, 1997), 20–21. Walter Brueggemann concludes, "What may be a royal Egyptian name is transposed by the proposed etymology into Israelite praise for deliverance." Walter Brueggemann, "The Book of Exodus," in *New Interpreter's Bible,* ed. Leander E. Keck, vol. 1 (Nashville: Abingdon Press, 1994–2004), 700.

[3] John D. Currid, *A Study Commentary on Exodus: Exodus 1–18*, vol. 1, EP Study Commentary (Darlington, England; Carlisle, PA: Evangelical Press, 2000), 64.

In Egyptian, "Mose" could also be a reference to the sonship itself. Thus Dudimose's name could have meant "He (whose) birth has been granted." From personal Facebook correspondence with scholar David Rohl.

Another source translates Dudimose's name as Dedumose, which means "A god has fashioned/given him." See http://everything.explained.today/Dedumose_II/

womb. In this way, she could be meaning that she calls him "son" (Mose) because he was *symbolically* born of the water of the Nile, the holy source of life in Egypt from which she drew him.

In other words, Mose(s) is technically an incomplete nomenclature. It could be what is called a hypocoristicon, a shortened version of a longer name, much like a nickname. So if Mose's adoptive father was Sobekhotep IV, then what might his full Egyptian name be? David Rohl suggests a couple reasonable options for an original full name: "Sobekmose ('born of the crocodile god Sobek') or Hapimose ('born of the Nile flood')."[4]

But he offers one more powerful piece of archaeological evidence related to Moses's step-father that made me decide to use the first option.

> Interestingly, on the Wadi Hammamat stela [a monument in Egypt's eastern desert], the first of Sobekhotep IV's four sons is called Sobekhotep Mio (Egyptian Miw), and it is tantalizing to consider that this might be an actual mention of the boy Moses, here being referred to by his pet name or hypocoristicon 'Mio' [Mio being a derivative of Mose][5]

Professor Kim Ryholt in his major work on the period concludes that this Sobekhotep Mio must be the eldest son and designated successor of the Pharaoh.[6] Just imagine that Moses might have been in line to be Pharaoh of Egypt. The novel *Moses: Against the Gods of Egypt* imagines just that.

A Doubting Moses and Anger Issues

Charlton Heston's performance in *The Ten Commandments* burned a picture into the cultural imagination of what Moses may have been like that is hard to surpass. His rugged masculine looks, deep commanding voice, and charismatic presence is unparalleled in movie history (equaled only by Yul Brenner's Ramesses). There's just one problem with that articulate persona of faithfulness. It's not biblical. At least not entirely.

When Yahweh calls Moses to go back to Egypt, confront Pharaoh, and bring his people out of Egypt, Moses balks. "Who am I that I should go to Pharaoh and bring the children of Israel out of Egypt?" (Exodus 3:11).

As the exchange continues, we learn that this is not a mere rhetorical question. It's doubt. Moses reveals a hesitancy due to a lack of confidence both in God and in his own skills and ability to pull off his duty.

---

[4] David Rohl, *Exodus: Myth or History?* (MN: Thinking Man Media, 2015), 137.

[5] Rohl, *Exodus,* 137.

[6] Rohl, *Exodus,* 138.

When Yahweh affirms that he is the one delivering, Moses asks the now-famous question: "If I come to the people of Israel and say to them, 'The God of your fathers has sent me to you,' and they ask me, 'What is his name?' what shall I say to them?" (Exodus 3:13).

This is not a mere clarification of a lack of knowledge. It is more skeptical doubt. In the ancient world, names and especially the names of gods embodied the identities of the nameholder. Moses is questioning the very reputation and power of this deity now before him. We know this because when Yahweh gives him his name, I AM, and expands on the majestic signs and wonders of judgment he will perform, Moses is still not buying it. And he doesn't think his people will either. "They will not believe me or listen to my voice, for they will say, 'Yahweh did not appear to you'" (4:1).

Yes, he is skeptical, but I think beneath his doubt is an underlying lack of confidence. When Yahweh "proves" his miraculous ability to Moses by performing a simple miracle on the spot, Moses still does not believe him. Moses finally reveals what has been bothering him. "Oh, my Lord, I am not eloquent, either in the past or since you have spoken to your servant, but I am heavy of mouth and of tongue…Oh, my Lord, please send someone else" (4:10, 13). God gets angry with Moses's stubborn hesitation. He accommodates Moses's fears by telling him to bring his brother Aaron with him to be his mouthpiece. Then he promises miraculous provision: "I will be with your mouth and with his mouth" (4:15).

Later after Moses confronts Pharaoh, Dudimose responds by blaspheming Yahweh and increasing his oppression of the Israelites. Moses is discouraged. Fair enough. But look closely at his words and see that lack of confidence, increasing doubt, desire to avoid the battle, and complaining attitude.

> Exodus 5:22–23
> Then Moses turned to the LORD and said, "O Lord, why have you done evil to this people? Why did you ever send me? For since I came to Pharaoh to speak in your name, he has done evil to this people, and you have not delivered your people at all."

This pessimistic attitude of doubt and complaining remains with Moses to the end of his life. Even after seeing many of Yahweh's signs and wonders, the plagues, the sea crossing, speaking to Yahweh face to face, Moses still has trust issues. Like doubting Thomas, Moses tells Yahweh, "See, you say to me, 'Bring up this people,' but you have not let me know whom you will send with me. Yet you have said, 'I know you by name, and you have also found favor in my sight.' Now therefore, if I have found favor in your sight, please show me now your ways, that I may know you in order to find favor in your sight" (Exodus 33:12). What a man of contradictions. He struggles with confidence and doubt, yet has the boldness to argue with the living God!

That boldness translated into a bad temper as well. When Moses came down from Mount Sinai with the two tablets of God's testimony, he discovered the golden calf idolatry. "And as soon as [Moses] came near the camp and saw the calf and the dancing, Moses's anger burned hot, and he threw the tablets out of his hands and broke them at the foot of the mountain" (Exodus 32:19).

One could argue that this was righteous anger. After all, Yahweh would justifiably destroy thousands of those idolaters with a plague. But I do not think this is righteous anger in Moses because he doesn't just pour out his anger upon the evil people but on the holy tablets of God.

This anger is more explicitly chastised by God later when God tells Moses to speak to a rock at Meribah in order to miraculously provide water from that rock for the people to drink. In a fit of anger, Moses does not speak to the rock but strikes it twice with his staff. Yahweh then responds:

> Numbers 20:12
> And the LORD said to Moses and Aaron, "Because you did not believe in me, to uphold me as holy in the eyes of the people of Israel [by hitting the rock in anger, instead of speaking to it], therefore you shall not bring this assembly into the land that I have given them."

That outburst of anger caused Moses to forfeit his own entry into the Promised Land. His anger issues haunted him his entire life and finally caught up with him.

Heavy of Mouth and of Tongue

Now let's go back to one of Moses's first recorded statements of his lack of confidence to address another frailty of his human condition.

> Exodus 4:10
> And Moses said to Yahweh, "Please, Lord, I am <u>not a man of words</u>, neither recently nor in the past nor since your speaking to your servant, because <u>I am heavy of mouth and of tongue</u>."

Exodus 6:12
But Moses said to the LORD, "Behold, the people of Israel have not listened to me. How then shall Pharaoh listen to me, for I am of uncircumcised lips?"

Moses's lack of confidence in his eloquence of speaking is more than being a strong, silent type or a man of few words. Moses had a speech impediment. For decades, scholars have explored the meaning of these enigmatic Hebrew words for "heavy of mouth and of tongue" and "uncircumcised lips" and have debated the options of Moses's problem. Jeffry Tigay's seminal article on the issue explains the two possible categories. "(1) a speech impediment, often said to be caused by a structural defect or injury of the mouth, and (2) a linguistic problem."[7]

Tigay considers the common argument that Moses's "heaviness of mouth" was simply a figurative expression of linguistic problems. Maybe Moses had been away from Egypt for so long that he had lost his skill of the Egyptian language. Or that he didn't know Hebrew well enough. Or maybe he was just "a man of few words" (Exodus 4:10) with minimal skills of persuasion and oratory.

This is surely a possible prospect for interpreting Moses's complaint. After all, he does say, "I am not a man of words." Some translations read, "ineloquent," both apparent cases of mere linguistic problems. But the idea that Moses would lose his indigenous language skills is not believable. Egyptian was a native language to him. He didn't learn it later in life. He was raised to think and speak Egyptian (along with Hebrew, no doubt).

But the important context is that Moses does not stop with the mere claim. He tells God *why*—the reason he is a man of few words. "I am heavy of mouth and of tongue…I am of uncircumcised lips." These are not merely figurative ways of saying "I am not persuasive" or "I am not very good with words." These are terms that indicate a *physical medical defect that results in stuttering*.

In the Bible, *kabed* is the Hebrew word for "heavy," and the concept of "heaviness" or "uncircumcision" of an organ refers to the malfunction of that organ, at least when it comes to the ears, heart, and eyes.

Isaiah 6:10
Make…their ears heavy [*kabed*], and blind their eyes; lest they see with their eyes, and hear with their ears...

---

[7] Jeffry H. Tigay, "Heavy of Mouth" and "Heavy of Tongue": On Moses's Speech Difficulty, *Bulletin of the American Schools of Oriental Research*, No. 231 (Oct., 1978), 60.

Jeremiah 6:10
Behold, their ears are uncircumcised, they cannot listen…

Genesis 48:10 (YLT)
And the eyes of Israel have been heavy [*kabed*] from age, he is unable to see…

Exodus 7:14
Pharaoh's heart is hardened [*kabed*]: he refuses to let the people go.

In the Bible, when eyes, heart, or ears are said to be "heavy," it is because they are not functioning physically as they ought to, even in a figurative or metaphorical context.

When it comes to the tongue, several prophetic passages that describe foreign languages as "stammering" or "stuttering," use the same Hebrew word for "heavy of tongue" as an interchangeable synonym with "stuttering."

Ezekiel 3:5–6 (YLT)
For, not unto a people deep of lip and heavy of tongue *art* thou sent—unto the house of Israel; not unto many peoples, deep of lip and heavy of tongue, whose words thou dost not understand.

Isaiah 33:19
You will see no more the insolent people, the people of an obscure speech that you cannot comprehend, stammering in a tongue that you cannot understand.

Bible scholar Edward Young explains, "These appear to be mere unintelligible mutterings, so that those who hear will hear gibberish. The following phrase, however, shows that the reference here is to another language. Hence God will speak to the nation in a language that it does not know. They had regarded His speaking through the prophet as so much nonsense; as a matter of fact, He would now speak to them in such a way that they would not understand, but would only hear sounds which would seem to them as vain babblings."[8]

To insiders of any language, foreign languages sound like babbling or stuttering. As Bible commentator Hans Wildeberger explains: "It is a

---

[8] Edward Young, *The Book of Isaiah, Chapters 19–39*, vol. 2 (Grand Rapids, MI: Wm. B. Eerdmans Publishing Co., 1969), 277.

commonly held impression that foreign nations stammer; one might compare for example Greek (*barbaros*) and Sanskrit *barbara* = "stammering, speaking in a way that cannot be understood."[9] "Barbar" is onomatopoeia, a word that sounds like the thing it is describing. Foreign languages sounded like stuttering: bar bar bar.

Stuttering is used by Isaiah to mock drunken revelers who reject God's word. Those apostates first mock Isaiah's call to God's Law as "Order on order, order on order, line on line, line on line" (Isaiah 28:10). In the underlying Hebrew of this phrase, there is a wordplay that sounds like stuttering. It reads, "*ṣaw lāṣāw ṣaw lāṣāw*!"

So Isaiah responds by mocking back:

> Isaiah 28:11–13 (NASB95)
> Indeed, [Yahweh] will speak to this people <u>through stammering lips and a foreign tongue</u>…So the word of the LORD to them will be, "Order on order, order on order, Line on line, line on line…

Stammering lips meant stuttering. Brevard Childs explains: "To a people who refused to hear the divine offer of salvation (v. 12; cf. 30:15), the word of God will be turned into gibberish for them, and from the lips of alien conquerors they will hear the same incomprehensible nonsense: *ṣaw lāṣāw ṣaw lāṣāw*!"[10]

A popular apocryphal Jewish legend says that Moses burned his tongue on a coal as an infant, which remained as his speech impediment for life.[11] Though I don't follow that particular legend, I do have Moses as struggling with a stuttering problem that Yahweh himself miraculously suspends to give forth his Word.

Interestingly, these two passages (Exodus 4:10; 6:12) are the only places that refer to Moses's stuttering. Was it just to make the point that God can overcome our physical defects or personal frailties to show his power? In my research, I found another possible reason why the author draws attention to it.

We will explore the nature of Egyptian magic below. But one of the elements of magic is the *spoken word* of the magicians. As expert Ritner explains: "Productive and destructive, the force of magic animates and permeates the cosmos, resident in the word, in the bodies of gods and men,

---

[9] Hans Wildberger, *A Continental Commentary: Isaiah 28-39* (Minneapolis, MN: Fortress Press, 2002), 24.

[10] Brevard S. Childs, *Isaiah: A Commentary*, ed. William P. Brown, Carol A. Newsom, and Brent A. Strawn, 1st ed., The Old Testament Library (Louisville, KY: Westminster John Knox Press, 2001), 207.

[11] Tigay, "Heavy of Mouth," 57.

and in the plants and stones of earth."[12] The spoken word harnesses that magic to the bidding of the magician or god.

In Egytpian mythology it was the spoken words of Ptah that created the heavens and earth as well as the other gods, something also reflected in Moses's account of creation by Yahweh in Genesis 1.[13] Words, spoken or written, in spells and enchantments could harness that magic to do the god's or magician's bidding with well-known phrases such as "spells/magic of your utterances" or "spells/magic on your mouth."[14] Ritner extrapolates:

> Thus Thoth, the god of writing, is regularly qualified as "excellent of magic" in his capacity as "Lord of hieroglyphs". Similarly, Heka [god who is magic] may be directly identified with the spoken word. Spells are specifically labeled as "god's words", and in the "Apophis Book," the reciter warns the demon: "Retire, turn back at this magic which has come forth from my mouth for Pharaoh!" Depictions of the god Heka are also instructive…he is described at Dendera as "excellent of words."[15]

Egyptologist Wallis Budge describes this power of words residing in the utterances of magicians, who were called, "lector-priests."

> By pronouncing certain words or names of power in the proper manner and in the proper tone of voice [the priest/magician] could heal the sick, and cast out the evil spirits which caused pain and suffering in those who were diseased, and restore the dead to life, and bestow upon the dead man the power to transform the corruptible into an incorruptible body…and in obedience to his commands, inanimate figures and pictures became living beings and things which hastened to perform his behests. The powers of nature acknowledged his might, and wind and rain, storm

---

12 Robert Kriech Ritner, *The Mechanics of Ancient Egyptian Magical Practice* (Chicago, IL: The Oriental Institute of Chicago, 1993), 23.

13 I do not here suggest Genesis 1 is about God using magic to create. But the notion of "speaking forth" a reality is certainly common notion that the text shares with magical understanding. It is a similar notion with different definitions.

14 Ritner, *Mechanics*, 42-43. Though Ritner argues that it is not words alone that are the power, but rather words in combination with ritual and material that are the power of magic.

15 Ritner, *Mechanics*, 35.

> and tempest, river and sea, and disease and death worked evil and ruin upon his foes.[16]

The claims of the power of words used by magician-priests are all things which Yahweh would ultimately perform in the story of Moses's confrontation with Pharaoh and his magicians. It was to be miracle vs. magic. Moses was raised in the court of Pharaoh and knew the magicians and their power. Regardless of how real or unreal the modern reader may think of that power, Moses thought he didn't have what it took to face them. His stuttering would be impotent words compared to their eloquent and powerful words of magic. But Yahweh's response, "I will be with your mouth" (Exodus 4:12), confirms that what Moses was about to say and do was not magic, but rather the words and power of God himself. A power that would eat the magician snakes for lunch.

What Did Moses Know and When Did He Know It?

A significant plot point in the novel is a scene where Moses discovers his true identity as a Hebrew. I place this in the storyline near his battle with Kush, when he is around 40 years old. In truth, the Kush campaign may have happened many years earlier, as would his self-discovery. But for the purposes of the story, I compressed that timeline to create a quicker story progression toward Moses's exile.

The Bible says that when Moses killed the Egyptian at age 40, he already knew he himself was a Hebrew.

> Exodus 2:11–12
> One day, when Moses had grown up, he went out to his people and looked on their burdens, and he saw an Egyptian beating <u>a Hebrew, one of his people</u>. He looked this way and that, and seeing no one, he struck down the Egyptian and hid him in the sand.

So the murder of the Egyptian was based on Moses being defensive of his own people, even though he was still an Egyptian royal. But here's the thing. The story before this one was the nativity of Moses. Then it jumps from his birth all the way to when he was 40 years old. So we don't really know

---

[16] E.A. Wallis Budge, *Egyptian Magic*, (London: Kegan, Paul, Trench and Trübner & Co., 1901), xi-xii.

when he learned of his Hebrew identity. It could be anytime between his adoption and 40 years of age.[17]

Some argue that he was taught his Hebrew identity when he was a small child. They cite Exodus 2, where the infant Moses is discovered by Pharaoh's daughter. But then Moses's sister Miriam tricks the Egyptian and says that she knows of a Hebrew wet nurse the princess could use, since the maiden would not have the capacity nor interest for nursing the babe. But Miriam does not tell her that wet nurse is Moses's actual mother. Nice plot twist.

> Exodus 2:9–10
> And Pharaoh's daughter said to her, "Take this child away and nurse him for me, and I will give you your wages." So the woman took the child and nursed him. When the child grew older, she brought him to Pharaoh's daughter, and he became her son. She named him Moses.

The phrase "when the child grew older" is sometimes interpreted as meaning Moses could be as much as 10 years or so old when he is brought back to Pharaoh's daughter and is adopted. Some Jewish hagiographic traditions try to maintain this long separation to avoid tainting Moses's background with paganism. In that scenario, certainly Moses has been deeply and thoroughly educated in his Hebrew origins and living in two worlds for much of his life.[18]

But I think this makes too much of the text for several reasons. First, "take this child away" and "brought to her" are not terms of remoteness and distance (as from the palace), but rather generic terms of immediate presence. Moses wasn't taken away from the palace altogether. He was taken away from the princess's immediate presence to nurse *within the palace*.

Secondly, it wouldn't make sense to take the infant completely away from the palace back to the Hebrew community. That would have immediately jeopardized Moses's life since the genocide of Hebrew males was still going on. That would have been a foolish act of endangerment not consistent with the characters or the story.

---

[17] There are several places where Moses's age is given helping us to place his chronology. In Acts 7:23 Stephen says Moses was 40 years old when he struck the Egyptian. Acts 7:30 says that the burning bush occurred after Moses was 40 years in Midian, making him 80 years old at that time. Exodus 7:3 says he was 80 when he and Aaron first confronted Pharaoh. Numbers 32:13 says that Israel wandered for 40 years in the wilderness and Deuteronomy 34:7 says Moses was 120 years old when he died. This is why most scholarship divides his story into increments for both narrative and theological purposes: 0-40 in Egypt with the Hebrew sojourn; 40-80 in exile in Midian; and 80-120 in the Exodus and wilderness.

[18] See Philo, *Life of Moses* 1.23-26 and Louis Ginsberg, *The Legends of the Jews* 2.4.65-66.

Thirdly, Pharaoh's daughter was moved by the plight of a precious little innocent baby. Her heart was touched. She "drew him out of the water," a very personal term connecting the two of them. It would not make sense for her to then let him leave her entirely and then adopt him as a juvenile. There would be no personal connection to justify that interest. He would have been forgotten if his adoptive mother did not keep him in the palace all those years.

Fourthly, bringing an older child into the palace and then all of a sudden adopting him would not be tolerated by Pharaoh. Keeping him there from the time of his newborn status (3 months old—Exodus 2:2) would make him endeared and connected to the royal family from the start.

The context makes more sense to mean that the baby Moses remained in the palace, but the wet nurse was paid to come and care for him like any servant would for a royal princess—in the palace. But of course breastfeeding and basic care would be done "away" from the princess, as is the usual case for royalty. "When the child grew older" most likely refers to a year to three years later, when the wet nursing would no longer be necessary and a newly adopted name could still take hold.

None of this disallows the possibility of Moses learning his true identity as a young man. But what is possible is not always what is probable. The fact is that for Moses to have become a prince in the Egyptian court means that his adoption had been accepted with significance. In Acts 17:22, Stephen says that Moses was "instructed in all the wisdom of the Egyptians." That means he would have been thoroughly educated in Egyptian culture, religion, and philosophy, otherwise he would not have risen as high as he did. And he would not have been allowed such status and authority had he not participated fully in that idolatrous system.

We have a hint that Moses became a prince of Egypt by the statement of the offended Hebrew who complained, "Who made you a prince and judge over us?" (Exodus 2:14) in response to Moses breaking up a Hebrew fight. The context is clear that Moses is considered Egyptian by the Hebrew. The Hebrews have their own cultural judges, but they had no princes. The Hebrew was saying, "You are a prince of Egypt, but you're no prince of Israel."

As we discovered earlier, there are some ancient traditions that indicate Moses did indeed become a prince of Egypt, even a general of the Egyptian army, and possibly in line to be Pharaoh. So it is most likely that he was considered to be in the royal lineage as a prince and therefore a thoroughly paganized Egyptian. He may have learned his Hebrew identity sometime later in his life. But he surely kept it at a distance from himself until he was 40, or he would not have been able to participate in the Egyptian system.

A further evidence of Moses's lack of Hebrew knowledge is that when he meets Yahweh in the burning bush at age 80, he doesn't know his name.

> Exodus 3:13–15
> Then Moses said to God, "If I come to the people of Israel and say to them, 'The God of your fathers has sent me to you,' and they ask me, 'What is his name?' what shall I say to them?"

God tells Moses his name is both Yahweh and I Am Who I Am. This is very significant. Moses did not know the name of Israel's God until he was 80 years old. In context, knowing God's name means knowing his identity. Which means that Moses knew about his people the Hebrews, but they never told him about their God. How is that possible, unless they also did not know the name? The burning bush was not the first revelation of Yahweh's name to the Hebrews. Yahweh was in fact known by name to Moses's forefathers Abraham, Isaac, Jacob and others, hundreds of years earlier (Genesis 14:22; 15:8; 26:22).[19] Could it be that the Israelites had lost the knowledge of Yahweh over the hundreds of years of slavery under Egypt? In that case, both Moses and the Israelites were so Egyptianized that they may have all been worshipping Egyptian deities together.

A Pagan Spin on Moses

One of the satisfying things about research is the discovery of understanding an opposing viewpoint. Sometimes a lot can be learned about an opponent by seeing how they misunderstand what you know to be true. One of my favorite passages that illustrates the ignorance of pagan thought is from the "erudite" Roman historian Tacitus (1st century A.D.) describing what he has heard about Moses and the Exodus. He mentions a disfiguring disease (echoes of the plagues) that breaks out in Egypt on account of the accursed Jews, no less! Those Jews were kicked out to the desert, and Moses took over.

---

[19] Then what of Exodus 6:3 where Yahweh says of these forefathers, "by my name Yahweh I did not make myself known to them"? Bruce Wells explains that it could be because the context of what Yahweh is indicating is the knowledge of his identity as tied in with the covenant promise of the land. "For Abraham, Isaac, and Jacob not to have "known" God by the name Yahweh may have meant that the biblical narrative never portrays them as experiencing the fulfillment of the Yahweh-promise. The later Israelites possess the land of Canaan in ways their forefathers would probably never have imagined and thus come to "know" Yahweh in the sense of experiencing the realization of the promise." John H Walton, *Zondervan Illustrated Bible Backgrounds Commentary (Old Testament): Genesis, Exodus, Leviticus, Numbers, Deuteronomy,* vol. 1 (Grand Rapids, MI: Zondervan, 2009), 184.

See how distortions and misinterpretations are defined by the pagan's own bias, derived from his religious views, and worsened by hearsay, rumors, and gossip:

> Tacitus, *Histories* 5.3-4
> Most writers, however, agree in stating that once a disease, which horribly disfigured the body, broke out over Egypt; that king Bocchoris, seeking a remedy, consulted the oracle of Hammon, and was bidden to cleanse his realm, and to convey into some foreign land this race detested by the gods. The people, who had been collected after diligent search, finding themselves left in a desert, sat for the most part in a stupor of grief, till one of the exiles, Moyses [Moses] by name, warned them not to look for any relief from God or man, forsaken as they were of both, but to trust to themselves, taking for their heaven-sent leader that man who should first help them to be quit of their present misery. They agreed, and in utter ignorance began to advance at random. Nothing, however, distressed them so much as the scarcity of water, and they had sunk ready to perish in all directions over the plain, when a herd of wild asses was seen to retire from their pasture to a rock shaded by trees. Moyses [Moses] followed them, and, guided by the appearance of a grassy spot, discovered an abundant spring of water. This furnished relief. After a continuous journey for six days, on the seventh they possessed themselves of a country, from which they expelled the inhabitants, and in which they founded a city and a temple.
>
> Moyses [Moses], wishing to secure for the future his authority over the nation, gave them a novel form of worship, opposed to all that is practiced by other men. Things sacred with us, with them have no sanctity, while they allow what with us is forbidden. In their holy place they have consecrated an image of the animal by whose guidance they found deliverance from their long and thirsty wanderings. They slay the ram, seemingly in derision of Hammon, and they sacrifice the ox, because the Egyptians worship it as Apis.[20]

---

[20] Tacitus, *The Annals and The Histories*, ed. Mortimer J. Adler, Second Edition, vol. 14, *Great Books of the Western World* (Chicago; Auckland; Geneva; London; Madrid; Manila; Paris; Rome; Seoul; Sydney; Tokyo; Toronto: Robert P. Gwinn; Encyclopædia Britannica, Inc., 1990), 295.

Remember, Tacitus is a respected ancient historian! We trust much of what he says about historic events, and yet here he gets Moses and the Jews so terribly wrong, it just shows everything written, even by so-called reliable historians, must be read with a skeptical eye.

Tacitus contradicts himself in the same passage. After describing the Jewish temple as having an image of an ass or donkey as their deliverer in the desert, he later writes that Jews do not allow images to stand in their cities or temple.[21] Consistency is never a virtue in pagan attacks on the biblical God and his people. But scholar Assman explains the possible origin of this ignorance:

> The strange and particularly absurd motif of the god of the Jews being represented in the statue of an ass finds its explanation in Plutarch, who tells the story in a completely mythologized form. The god Seth, the murderer of Osiris, is driven out of Egypt and spends seven days fleeing into Palestine. There he fathers two sons, whom he calls Hierosolyma and Juda [Jerusalem and Judah]. Seth is usually associated with the donkey in Egyptian mythology. In Greco-Egyptian texts, the god *lao*—the Greek rendering of the Hebrew Tetragrammaton—is equated with Seth and the ass because the name—obviously onomatopoietic—sounded like the Egyptian word for ass.[22]

Of course we are all capable of misinterpreting others through our own biases, but the above is an example of how pagans have done so in a way relevant to our topic of Moses and Egypt. It serves as a warning for how we must remain cautiously skeptical of ancient historians and authors just as much as we should do so of historians and scholars today. Sometimes, it's all we've got to go with, but we must remember even historians draw from legends, apocryphal stories, rumors and gossip. Yes, words can be powerful magic, to deceive and blind with lies as much as to enlighten and reveal truth.

---

[21] "The Egyptians worship many animals and images of monstrous form; the Jews have purely mental conceptions of Deity, as one in essence. They call those profane who make representations of God in human shape out of perishable materials. They believe that Being to be supreme and eternal, neither capable of representation, nor of decay. They therefore do not allow any images to stand in their cities, much less in their temples." Tacitus, *Histories* 5.5.

[22] Jan Assman, *Moses the Egyptian: The Memory of Egypt in Western Monotheism* (Cambridge, MA: Harvard University Press, 1997), 37.

Zipporah and the Cushite Wife of Moses

One little verse in the Moses narrative has created a universe of speculation to this very day (okay, it's not the only one. I see a pattern here too). All the way near the end of their wandering, Israel is in Kadesh and about to send the spies into Canaan. Led and taught by Moses as Yahweh's mouthpiece, they have experienced all the miracles of deliverance and provision in the desert. Yet Aaron and Miriam let their egos flare up, and they challenge Moses's identity as sole authority over Israel. They think they should be able to speak for God too. But look at the reason why they challenge him.

> Numbers 12:1–2
> Miriam and Aaron spoke against Moses because of the Cushite woman whom he had married, for he had married a Cushite woman. And they said, "Has Yahweh indeed spoken only through Moses? Has he not spoken through us also?"

Scholarship has established with as much certainty as is possible that Cush (also spelled as Kush) was a kingdom south of Egypt in the area we now call Ethiopia, Africa. And Cushites were black-skinned people just as Ethiopians are today.

Moses had married a black woman from Kush/Cush. While it is tempting with our modern bias to reduce this to a case of "racist" anger in Miriam and Aaron, the ancient context doesn't warrant it. While the complaint is certainly an accusation of Moses doing something wrong by marrying the woman, the color of skin was an irrelevant issue to the Hebrews. Nationality however, was not.

Yahweh had demanded a separation of Israel from the nations (Deuteronomy 32:8-10), but Israel included aliens and sojourners who had converted to Torah, including peoples of all colors and nations (Exodus 12:48). In fact, the Exodus deliverance included people from those nations, called "a mixed multitude" (Exodus 12:38).

Miriam and Aaron weren't reacting to intermarriage with a person of another color. They were reacting to intermarriage with a person *of another nation (Gentile).* But this was not simplistic xenophobia like the modern political notion of "nationalism" is misused as.

Though God's command was not as exhaustive as it appears to be,[23] the principle of avoiding intermarriage with other nations was based upon

---

[23] The only strict command by God was to deny intermarriage with the seven condemned (*herem*) nations of Canaan. The fact is that the history of Israel includes many exceptions, including Ruth the Moabitess and Rahab the

religion, not race or politics. This principle is "You shall not enter into marriage with them, neither shall they with you, for surely they will turn away your heart after their gods." (1 Kings 11:1-2). Foreign nations were evil because they worshipped false gods, not because of race, politics or other modern notions.

But here's a complication. Exodus 12:21 says that Moses married a Midianite woman named Zipporah, a woman *from another nation.* The questions start to build up like congealed waters of Yam Suph. Why does this Kushite wife not show up anywhere else in Moses's story? Was she a deceased wife before Zipporah? Or was she a second wife after Zipporah's unmentioned death? Did Moses have two wives? Or was Zipporah herself the Kushite wife?

To tell my Moses story, I had to enter another quagmire and answer those questions. And the first angle to address was Zipporah's identity.

The text lays out clearly that Zipporah was a Midianite. As we have already discovered, Midian was way over in Arabia, and Kush was way over beneath Egypt, both separated by a wide peninsula of several hundred miles and two mighty seas. They are completely different peoples with different histories, and the Midianites were most likely not black-skinned.

Or were they? Some argue that Zipporah could have been "Kushite in ancestry and Midianite in culture."[24] Ancient historians, such as Strabo, had noted that Ethiopians lived on both shores of the Red Sea. But this assumes the Sinai Peninsula as the location of Midian, which has been discredited earlier. They're still too far away. Of course, it does not discount the idea that Midians as a nomadic people might have strayed into the "Land of Turquoise" and even intermixed to some degree with Kushites. Maybe one of Jethro's wives was a Kushite, and Zipporah was her daughter. That might make her Kushite in ancestry, Midianite by marriage and culture.

There is another intriguing possibility I discovered while reading the ancient Jewish historians Josephus and Artapanus. Both of these men write about a story of Moses that is not in the Bible but appears to be based on other ancient historical sources (with some differences). They tell of Moses as a general of Pharaoh's army fighting the Kushites/Ethiopians to gain back territory taken by their southern opponents. As it turns out, this fits the historical reality of that time period during Sobekhotep IV's reign as Pharaoh.

Canaanite harlot, both in the lineage of Jesus the Messiah! But the principle can be seen in general throughout the Old Testament. Solomon's wives as quoted in 1 Kings 11:1-2 were not all from the seven herem nations alone, yet they are condemned for the same principle of "turning away the heart after their gods."

[24] Ron M. Serino, "A Sign in the Dark: Moses's Cushite Wife and Boundary Setting in the Book of Numbers," *Biblical Interpretation* 24 (2016), 157.

Josephus adds an element of interest that fits the biblical reference to a Kushite wife. It says that Kush had conquered Egyptian cities up the Nile as far as Memphis. Moses was commissioned to regain Egyptian territory. He did so, pushing the invaders back to the Kushite city of Saba/Kerma, where he set up a difficult siege. The daughter of the king, a Kushite princess named Tharbis, saw Moses and fell in love with him. She offered surrender of the city in exchange for their marriage, a common ancient form of peace negotiation between warring kingdoms. Here's the text of Josephus as he tells it:

> Josephus, *Antiquities of the Jews* 2.10.2 (251-253)
> However, while Moses was uneasy at the army's lying idle (for the enemies durst not come to a battle), this accident happened:—Tharbis was the daughter of the king of the Ethiopians [Kushites]: she happened to see Moses as he led the army near the walls, and fought with great courage; and admiring the subtility of his undertakings, and believing him to be the author of the Egyptians' success, when they had before despaired of recovering their liberty…she fell deeply in love with him; and upon the prevalency of that passion, sent to him the most faithful of all her servants to discourse with him about their marriage. He thereupon accepted the offer, on condition she would procure the delivering up of the city; and gave her the assurance of an oath to take her to his wife; and that when he had once taken possession of the city, he would not break his oath to her. No sooner was the agreement made, but it took effect immediately; and when Moses had cut off the Ethiopians, he gave thanks to God, and consummated his marriage, and led the Egyptians back to their own land.[25]

Egyptologist David Rohl suggests an Egyptian version of the Greek name Tharbis as Tjarbit, so I used that name in my novel.[26]

There is archaeological evidence supporting this story in the form of a life-sized monument to Sobekhotep IV in one of the Kushite cities near Kerma, deep in the heart of ancient Kush. Such kingly statues indicate victory

---

[25] Flavius Josephus and William Whiston, *The Works of Josephus: Complete and Unabridged* (Peabody: Hendrickson, 1987), 70.

[26] David Rohl, *From Eden to Exile: The Five-Thousand-Year History of the People of the Bible* (London: Random House, 2002), 186.

and authority over the region. Sobekhotep was the Pharaoh for whom Moses fought.[27]

But there are some problems with the marriage of Moses to this Kushite princess Tharbis. He supposedly marries her before he leaves Egypt, sometime before he is forty years old. But when he embarks on his journey to Midian, he is described as being alone in the biblical text (Exodus 2:11-22). There is never any mention of this woman—as if she doesn't exist. While it is true that the story does not always reveal every detail of reality, this is a detail that would be significant if left out.

If Moses did not bring Tharbis with him, then he would have left her in Egypt. But that would be a cruel thing for Moses to do that is not consistent with his character. In that ancient culture, the wife and family of a man condemned to death by Pharaoh would surely have been punished with Pharaoh's wrath. Moses would never leave his beloved to such fate.

If he did leave her, he would have been doubly cruel because he had no intentions of returning, another inconsistency with his integrity. If he had left her and she was *not* harmed by Pharaoh, then Moses would have returned to her after 40 years, causing quite a bit of traumatic pain and problems with his other wife. Yet again, her existence isn't even hinted at in a scenario like this.

So one other possibility is that Tharbis could have died before Moses left. This would maintain Moses's moral character without violating the text. But this is not mere speculation. It is also rooted in another non-canonical story of Moses from Artapanus.

Remember that Egyptian campaign against Kush? Artapanus has some elements missing from Josephus: It describes Moses's exalting victory over Kush, which then breeds envy in Pharaoh Sobekhotep's heart. He fears Moses's glory will surpass his own, so he hatches a plot to assassinate the general—his own adopted son—on a false pretext. He orders an assassin Chanethothes to do the dirty deed:

> Eusebius of Caesarea., *Preparation for the Gospel* 9.27
> But when the Egyptians were alienated from [Pharaoh Kheneferre Sobekhotep IV], he bound his friends by an oath not to report to Moses the plot which was being contrived against him, and he appointed the men who were to kill [Moses].

[27] David Rohl, *A Test of Time: The Bible From Myth to History* (U.K. Century, Ltd., 1995), 263.

> When however no one would obey him, Chenephres [Pharaoh Sobekhotep] reproached Chanethothes, who promised to make the attempt when he found an opportunity. And Merris [Moses's adopted Egyptian mother] having died about this time, [Pharaoh Sobekhotep] professed to give the body to Moses and Chanethothes to carry it over into regions beyond Egypt and bury it, supposing that Moses would be slain by Chanethothes.
> But while they were on the way, one of those who were cognizant of the plot reported it to Moses; and he being on his guard buried Merris himself.
> Then Aaron the brother of Moses, having learned about the plot, advised his brother to flee into Arabia [Midian]; from Memphis.
> But when Chanethothes was informed of the flight of Moses, he lay in ambush intending to kill him; and when he saw him coming, he drew his sword against him, but Moses was too quick for him, and seized his hand, and drew his sword and slew Chanethothes.[28]

At the advice of Egyptologist David Rohl, I changed the spelling of Chanethothes to the more Egyptian spelling of Khanethothes for the novel.[29]

The astute reader will notice a problem with this story as it relates to the biblical narrative. It seems to indicate that this attempt to kill Moses instigates his fleeing to Midian rather than Moses's murder of the Egyptian taskmaster.

In order to maintain the essence of this story, I altered it a bit to integrate it into the biblical story, so that it would all fit and provide a stronger confirmation of the biblical story. But I won't spoil it for you. You'll have to read the novel to find out.

---

28 Eusebius of Caesarea, *Evangelicae Praeparationis Libri XV*, ed. E. H. Gifford (Oxford: Oxford University Press, 1903), 464.

29 Facebook Direct Message from David Rohl 4/19/20.

SIDEBAR
Moses's Kushite Campaign and Flying Snakes

As an aside, there is one more element of this story by Josephus that I used in the novel. He describes Moses's campaign in the area of Kush where there are flying snakes that impeded the advance of his army.

So Moses devised a strategy to overcome this natural enemy.

> Josephus, *Antiquities of the Jews* 2.10.2 (245-248)
> Moses invented a wonderful stratagem to preserve the army safe, and without hurt; for he made baskets like unto arks, of sedge, and filled them with ibes [ibises: meat-eating birds], and carried them along with them; which animal is the greatest enemy to serpents imaginable, for they fly from them when they come near them; and as they fly they are caught and devoured by them, as if it were done by the harts…As soon, therefore as Moses was come to the land which was the breeder of these serpents, he let loose the ibes, and by their means repelled the serpentine kind, and used them for his assistants before the army came upon that ground. When he had therefore proceeded thus on his journey, he came upon the Ethiopians [Kushites] before they had expected him; and joining battle with them he beat them.*

The Ibis bird (ibes) mentioned here was known to be a killer of snakes. But it was also considered a sacred bird in Egypt connected to Thoth, the god of scribes and knowledge.** Josephus may have been trying to draw a symbolic connection between Moses and Thoth.***

This story of flying snakes may not be as legendary as it may seem, since Numbers 21:6-9 talks about these creatures being sent by Yahweh to punish the Israelites for their complaining and unbelief.

> Numbers 21:6
> Then the LORD sent <u>fiery serpents</u> [*seraphim nachash*] among the people, and they bit the people, so that many people of Israel died.

The Hebrew word in this text, *seraphim*, is the one used of the winged serpentine celestial beings that guard Yahweh's throne in heaven.

> Isaiah 6:2–7

> Above him stood the seraphim. Each had six wings: with two he covered his face, and with two he covered his feet, and with two he flew.

This is not to say that Yahweh is sending those heavenly beings as his justice, but rather that these earthly snakes with a "fiery" bite probably had some kind of rudimentary ability to fly.

Other Scriptures talk about these flying serpents as well. Isaiah 14:29 and 30:6 refer to the same "flying fiery serpent" (*seraph*) in the wilderness "that originated in mythically conceived winged serpent deities."[30]

the Isaiah 30 passage describes these flying fiery serpents as the beasts of the Negeb, the same location for the fiery serpents of Numbers 21.

Jacob Milgrom argues that the bronze or copper snake that Moses put on the pole was a winged serpent. He concludes this from the link of the Hebrew *seraph* to the Egyptian *uraeus* serpent.

> Egypt is the home for images of winged serpents. For example, the arms on the throne of Tutankhamen consist of two wings of a four-winged snake (uraeus), which rise vertically from the back of the seat. Indeed, the erect cobra, or uraeus, standing on its coil is the symbol of royalty for the pharaoh and the gods throughout Egyptian history. Winged uraei dating from the Canaanite period have been found, proving that the image of the winged serpent was well known in ancient Israel.[31]

Scholar Karen Randolph Joines adds more to the Egyptian origin of this motif by explaining that the usage of serpent images to defend against snakes was also an exclusively Egyptian notion without evidence in Canaan or Mesopotamia.[32]

But the Bible and Egyptian culture are not the only places where we learn of flying serpents in the desert. Hans Wildberger points out Assyrian king Esarhaddon's description of flying serpents in his tenth campaign to Egypt in the seventh century B.C.

> "A distance of 4 double-hours I marched over a territory…there were two-headed serpents whose attack spelled death—but I trampled upon them and marched on. A distance of 4 double-hours in a journey of 2 days there were green [animals] [Tr.: Borger: "serpents"] whose wings were

> batting."[33]

The Greek historian Herodotus wrote of "sacred" winged serpents and their connection to Egypt in his *Histories*:

> There is a place in Arabia not far from the town of Buto where I went to learn about the winged serpents. When I arrived there, I saw innumerable bones and backbones of serpents...This place…adjoins the plain of Egypt. Winged serpents are said to fly from Arabia at the beginning of spring, making for Egypt...The serpents are like water-snakes. Their wings are not feathered but very like the wings of a bat. I have now said enough concerning creatures that are sacred.[34]

The notion of flying serpents as mythical versus real creatures appearing in the Bible is certainly debated among scholars, but this debate gives certain warrant to the imaginative usage of winged flying serpents appearing in *Moses: Against the Gods of Egypt.*[35]

* Flavius Josephus and William Whiston, *The Works of Josephus: Complete and Unabridged* (Peabody: Hendrickson, 1987), 69.

** George Hart, *The Routledge Dictionary of Egyptian Gods and Goddesses* (New York, NY: Routledge, 1986, 2005), 156.

*** Donna Runnalls, "Moses's Ethiopian Campaign," *Journal for the Study of Judaism*, Vol. XIV, no. 2., pp 151-152.

---

30 Brown, Francis, Samuel Rolles Driver, and Charles Augustus Briggs. *Enhanced Brown-Driver-Briggs Hebrew and English Lexicon.* electronic ed. Oak Harbor, WA: Logos Research Systems, 2000.

31 Jacob Milgrom, *Numbers*, The JPS Torah Commentary (Philadelphia: Jewish Publication Society, 1990), 459.

32 Karen Randolph Joines, "The Bronze Serpent in the Israelite Cult," *Journal of Biblical Literature*, Vol. 87, No. 3 (Sep., 1968), 251.

33 Hans Wildberger, *A Continental Commentary: Isaiah 28-39* (Minneapolis, MN: Fortress Press, 2002), 136. Quoting from James Bennett Pritchard, ed., *The Ancient Near East an Anthology of Texts and Pictures*, 3rd ed. with Supplement (Princeton: Princeton University Press, 1969), 292.

34 *Herodotus, Herodotus, With an English Translation* by A. D. Godley, ed. A. D. Godley (Medford, MA: Harvard University Press, 1920) Histories 2:75.1-76.3. Thanks to my editor, Don Enevoldsen, for this reference.

35 Scholars who acknowledge the evidence for mythical flying serpents, but argue against it: Wilhelm Gesenius and Samuel Prideaux Tregelles, *Gesenius' Hebrew and Chaldee Lexicon to the Old Testament Scriptures* (Bellingham, WA: Logos Bible Software, 2003), 796; R. Laird Harris, "2292 שָׂרָף," ed. R. Laird Harris, Gleason L. Archer Jr., and Bruce K. Waltke, *Theological Wordbook of the Old Testament* (Chicago: Moody Press, 1999), 884.

Jannes and Jambres

Magic was a form of power in ancient Egypt. Magicians were called "lector-priests" in Egyptian because they considered it part of their religious worldview. Magic was not mere tricks or sleight of hand to them. It was real, and magicians carried weight in Pharaoh's court.

In Exodus 7, Moses confronts Pharaoh with his miracles and Pharaoh calls his magicians to replicate what he thought was magic. They sought to do the same with each of the plagues—water turned to blood, the frogs—until they were unable to counter the miracles with their "secret arts." Then they warned Pharaoh that these were "the finger of God" (Exodus 8:19).

The Old Testament never names the magicians anywhere. *But the New Testament does*. When Paul wrote to Timothy about evil men opposing the gospel, he likened them to the magicians of Pharaoh's court.

> 2 Timothy 3:8–9
> Just as Jannes and Jambres opposed Moses, so these men also oppose the truth, men corrupted in mind and disqualified regarding the faith. But they will not get very far, for their folly will be plain to all, as was that of those two men.

The obvious question is where Paul obtained the names of the magicians if they weren't in the Old Testament. As I have written elsewhere, the Bible often draws from other non-canonical sources for much of its historical and even theological material.[36] In this particular case, there are some traditions in pseudepigraphal and apocryphal texts that reference the names of Jannes and Jambres. All the extant manuscripts we have are post-biblical but may point back to a more ancient origin.

The earliest occurrence of them comes from the Damascus Document of the Dead Sea Scrolls, which is dated about 100 B.C. Apparently referring to the Exodus, it states:

> …in ancient times, Moses and Aaron arose by the hand of the Prince of Lights and Satan [Belial] in his cunning raised

[36] Some sources used by biblical writers are *The Book of the Wars of Yahweh* (Num. 21:14), *The Book of Jasher* (Josh. 10:12-13; 2Sam. 1:19-27), *The Acts of Solomon* (1Kings 11:41), *Acts of Gad the Seer* (1Chron. 29:29), *Acts of Nathan the Prophet* (2Chron 9:29), *Prophesy of Ahijah the Shilonite* (2Chron. 9:29), *Visions of Iddo the Seer* (2Chron. 9:29), *Acts of Jehu Son of Hanani* (2Chron. 20:34), *Acts of the Seers* (2Chron. 33:19) and others. See Brian Godawa, *When Giants Were Upon the Earth: The Watchers, the Nephilim, and the Biblical Cosmic War of the Seed*, (Los Angeles, CA: Embedded Pictures Publishing, 2014), pp 117-128.

> up Jannes [Joḥana] and his brother when Israel was first delivered.[37]

There are scattered references to Jannes and Jambres in post-Christian rabbinic literature such as the Targums and Talmud and even a reference to them as adepts of magic with Moses by the 1st century A.D. pagan writer Pliny the Elder.[38]

One tradition of Jannes and Jambres is recorded in the Jewish Talmudic commentaries *Targum Pseudo-Jonathan* from some time around the 8th century A.D.[39] In this storyline, the two brother magicians are with Pharaoh in the days of Moses's birth. In fact, they are the ones who warn the king from a dream that there was to be a child born "by whose hand will be destruction to all the land of Egypt." This revelation leads to Pharaoh's slaughter of the Hebrew male infants.[40] Jannes and Jambres turn out to be the sons of Balaam, the Moabite sorcerer who tried to curse Israel. According to this story, they went with Balaam when his donkey saved him from the Angel of Yahweh's wrath.[41]

According to the *Anchor Bible Dictionary*, other tales of Jannes and Jambres find their way into the Jewish Common Era texts. They include the brothers at the confrontation of Pharaoh with Moses. "Outdone by Moses, they came to him to become proselytes and, against God's explicit directive, were accepted. Thus a "mixed multitude" (Exodus 12:38) with Jannes and Jambres at the head accompanied Israel out of Egypt. It was they who were the real culprits in Israel's idolatrous debacle at Sinai and consequently were killed by the Levites (*Yal. Reu.*; cf. *Midr. Tanh.*). Alternatively in Jewish tradition, Jannes and Jambres, flying above the Red Sea on self-made wings, were

---

37 A. Pietersma and R. T. Lutz, *"Jannes and Jambres: A New Translation and Introduction,"* in *The Old Testament Pseudepigrapha and the New Testament: Expansions of the "Old Testament" and Legends, Wisdom, and Philosophical Literature, Prayers, Psalms and Odes, Fragments of Lost Judeo-Hellenistic Works*, vol. 2 (New Haven; London: Yale University Press, 1985), 427.

38 "There is another sect, also, of adepts in the magic art, who derive their origin from Moses, Jannes, and Lotapea [Jambres?]," Pliny the Elder, The Natural History 30.2.11, ed. John Bostock (Medford, MA: Taylor and Francis, Red Lion Court, Fleet Street, 1855), 5425.

39 The following summary is taken from "Etheridges' Translation of the Palestinian Targum of the Book of Shemoth of the Exodus," on the online site, NTCS, The Newsletter for Targumic and Cognate Studies. http://targum.info/targumic-texts/pentateuchal-targumim/

40 *Targum Pseudo-Jonathan* on Exodus Section I http://targum.info/pj/pjex1-6.htm

"According to rabbinical tradition they were the two chiefs of the magicians at the court of Pharaoh who foretold the birth of Moses, "the destroyer of the land of Egypt," thereby causing the cruel edicts of Pharaoh (Soṭah 11a; Sanh. 106a)." From https://www.jewishencyclopedia.com/articles/8513-jannes-and-jambres

41 *Targum Pseudo-Jonathan* on Numbers, Section XL http://targum.info/pj/pjnum22-25.htm

destroyed by an angel dispatched by God (*Yal. Sim.*; cf. *Yal. Reu.; ChronJ* 54)." [42]

Ancient Christian writers also have their legends of Jannes and Jambres, some of which include: "Pharaoh's daughter reputedly entrusted Moses to Jannes and Jambres for instruction in wisdom (e.g., Bar Hebraeus). They were regarded as gods by the Egyptians (*Acts Pil.*), and Satan counted them his brothers *(Ques. Bart.)*. Moreover, Abezethibou, the demon from the Red Sea, claimed to have come to their aid *(T. Sol.)*; it was they who were responsible for leading Pharaoh astray until the king and his host met their death in the sea *(Mart. Pet. Paul; Pal. hist.)*. Moses, in the course of their altercations with him, afflicted their adherents with sores and sent the mother of one of them to their death (Philostorgius)."[43]

The Jewish Encyclopedia claims that according to rabbinical tradition, Jannes and Jambres, "were the two chiefs of the magicians at the court of Pharaoh who foretold the birth of Moses, "the destroyer of the land of Egypt," thereby causing the cruel edicts of Pharaoh (Soṭah 11a; Sanh. 106a)."[44] This legend plays into the storyline of the *Moses* novel.

All these are late legends pointing back to earlier sources for the names of the magicians. But there is one pseudepigraphal book by their names discovered in fragments from as early as the 3rd century A.D. With possible connections back to Artapanus (100 B.C.), *Jannes and Jambres* is most likely a Jewish pre-Christian text that tells a story of the magician brothers and intersects with the story of Moses. It is very fragmentary and therefore difficult to understand at some points, but Charlesworth's *The Old Testament Pseudepigrapha and the New Testament* provides the composition as coherently as possible.[45] Evidently, the 3rd century church father Origen believed this was the book from which Paul got the names of Jannes and Jambres he mentions to Timothy.[46]

It tells the story of Pharaoh summoning his wise men and magicians to observe some kind of plant whose branches seemed to sprout in a mere seven

---

[42] Albert Pietersma, "Jannes and Jambres (Persons)," ed. David Noel Freedman, *The Anchor Yale Bible Dictionary* (New York: Doubleday, 1992), 639.

[43] Albert Pietersma, "Jannes and Jambres (Persons)," ed. David Noel Freedman, *The Anchor Yale Bible Dictionary* (New York: Doubleday, 1992), 639.

[44] From https://www.jewishencyclopedia.com/articles/8513-jannes-and-jambres

[45] A. Pietersma and R. T. Lutz, "Jannes and Jambres: A New Translation and Introduction," in The Old Testament Pseudepigrapha and the New Testament: Expansions of the "Old Testament" and Legends, Wisdom, and Philosophical Literature, Prayers, Psalms and Odes, Fragments of Lost Judeo-Hellenistic Works, vol. 2 (New Haven; London: Yale University Press, 1985), 427-442.

[46] Pietersma and Lutz, "Jannes and Jambres", 430.

days. Jannes is ordered to sit beneath an apple tree. An earthquake and thunder occurs, breaking off some of the branches, so Jannes runs to his library for his magical books and tools.

Then two heavenly messengers in white visit him and tell him that "the Lord of the earth and the Overseer of the universe" have told them to come and take Jannes away to Hades. But for some unknown reason, they grant him a respite from his fate for 14 days.

Jannes's mother falls ill, and Jannes takes his brother Jambres to Memphis to give him a book of magic, admonishing him to keep it secret. He also warns Jambres not to "go forth" with Pharaoh when he marches out against the Hebrews.

In the next scene, Jannes is at a wedding for seven days. While there, emissaries come from the palace, telling him to "oppose Moses the Hebrew and his brother Aaron, who are performing signs and wonders to the amazement of all." He is struck with a fatal ulcer on the spot and retires, from where he sends a message of apparent regret to Pharaoh that he opposed Moses. He calls it "the finger of God" that he is unable to counter.

Jambres and possibly his mother visit Jannes, but a falling star seems to foretell his death. Jannes dies, and Jambres gives some kind of moving lament about how death changes our bodies to lifelessness. Soon after, the mother of the two brothers dies, and Jambres buries her next to her son.

Jambres then uses his magical books near the apple tree from the beginning of the story in order to perform necromancy and call up his brother's "shade" from Hades. Jannes exclaims that he is suffering justly in "the netherworld where there is burning and the pit of perdition" for having opposed Moses and Aaron. He exhorts his brother Jambres to do good because in death his abode is a 3 by 6 foot grave and in Hades there is suffering and "no forgiveness" for their idolatry. How Jambres responds and what happens to him, we do not know from the missing fragments. But it seems to convey the common imagery of Hades that Second Temple Literature was developing.

Much of the text is missing, leaving big questions and a somewhat unclear storyline. So, while I couldn't follow this text as a "Bible" for the Jannes and Jambres characters in my novel, I used it more as a non-canonical source of ideas upon which to imagine.

Amalekite Giants

In my previous book, When Giants Were Upon the Earth, I explore at great length, the existence of giants in the Bible and their purpose in the theological narrative of Scripture. By way of brief summary, that narrative originated in

Genesis 6:1-4 that describes fallen divine beings called "Sons of God" violating the heavenly/earthly divide and cohabiting with human women. Their progeny were these giants called "Nephilim," who were destroyed with sinful humanity by the Great Flood.[47]

But when Israel gets to the Promised Land of Canaan after the Exodus, it turns out that it is crawling with giants who are linked back to those original Nephilim of Noah's primeval days. And they are now called "sons of Anak."

> Numbers 13:32–33
> "The land [of Canaan], through which we have gone to spy it out, is a land that devours its inhabitants, and all the people that we saw in it are of great height. And there we saw the Nephilim (the sons of Anak, who come from the Nephilim), and we seemed to ourselves like grasshoppers, and so we seemed to them."

These sons of Anak, also called "Anakim," were considered the corrupted "Seed of the Serpent" that Yahweh commanded Joshua to wipe out from the holy land.

> Deuteronomy 9:1–2
> "Hear, O Israel: you are to cross over the Jordan today, to go in to dispossess nations greater and mightier than you, cities great and fortified up to heaven, a people great and tall, the sons of the Anakim, whom you know, and of whom you have heard it said, 'Who can stand before the sons of Anak?'

But there were other names for the giants in different regions and in different clans. They had names such as Emim, Rephaim and Zamzummim.

> Deuteronomy 2:10–11, 20-21
> The Emim formerly lived there, a people great and many, and tall as the Anakim. Like the Anakim they are also counted as Rephaim, but the Moabites call them Emim. (It is also counted as a land of Rephaim. Rephaim formerly lived there—but the Ammonites call them Zamzummim—a people great and many, and tall as the Anakim.

There are several other clans that are not explicitly said to be giants, but are implied as such by their inclusion in groupings of giants. One of those

---

[47] For the detailed biblical exegesis of these Nephilim and their meaning, see Brian Godawa, *When Giants Were Upon the Earth: The Watchers, the Nephilim, and the Biblical Cosmic War of the Seed*, (Los Angeles, CA: Embedded Pictures Publishing, 2014), pp 37-78.

clans was the Amalekites. Amalekite history goes all the way back to Genesis 14 and the Giant Wars in the days of Abraham. In that passage, Chedorlaomer leads his alliance of four Mesopotamian kings to wipe out specific giant clans in Canaan. The list of giant clans they take out are the Rephaim, Zuzim and Emim that we have already seen are called giants in Deuteronomy 2.[48] But they also list three other clans that Scripture implies contain giants: Horites (Deuteronomy 2:10-12) Amorites (Amos 2:9-10) *and Amalekites.*

> Genesis 14:5–6
> In the fourteenth year Chedorlaomer and the kings who were with him came and defeated the Rephaim in Ashteroth-karnaim, the Zuzim in Ham, the Emim in Shaveh-kiriathaim, and the Horites in their hill country of Seir...Then they turned back and came to (Kadesh) and defeated all the country of the Amalekites, and also the Amorites.

In the Zohar, a 13th century Jewish mystical text, there is a clear reference to the Amalekites as giants among the Nephilim, Anakim, and Rephaim.[49] The Arabs also have legends about Ad, the son of Amalek, being a giant.[50] This is not to say that *all* the Amalekites were giants, but only that they most likely had giants among their numbers.

Here's where all this comes into play with the story of *Moses: Against the Gods of Egypt.* After the Israelites cross Yam Suph and begin their journey to Mount Sinai, they encounter the nomadic Amalekites as a prelude to what they would face in the Promised Land 40 years later. Exodus 17 tells the story of how Joshua went to war with the Amalekites and if Moses raised his "staff of God" Joshua would prevail in the battle, but if Moses lowered his staff the Amalekites would prevail. Moses gets Aaron and Hur to help him keep his tired arms raised so Joshua would ultimately win and repel the Amalekites.

Yahweh then proclaims to Moses,

---

48 Zuzim is a shortened version of Zamzummim.

49 Special thanks to Doug Van Dorn for this bit of research. *Beresheet A,* 20.224, "There are five races of mixed multitude. These are the Nefilim (fallen), the Giborim (mighty), the Anakim (giants), the Refaim (shades) and the Amalekim." Van Dorn, Douglas (2013-01-21). *Giants: Sons of the Gods* (Kindle Locations 2629-2631). Waters of Creation. Kindle Edition. It is important to note however that the Zohar is of questionable origin, so it represents a much later tradition than is preferable for our ancient research.

50 "A tradition told in the famous Al-Khitat, a history of Egyptian lore compiled by al-Maqrizi (1364-1442 AD), recounts the teaching of one master Ibrahim bin Wasif Shah (d. 1203 AD) who said that King Adim (Ad) was, 'A violent and proud prince, tall in stature.'" Van Dorn, *Giants* (Kindle Locations 2605-2608).

> Exodus 17:14–16
> "Write this as a memorial in a book and recite it in the ears of Joshua, that I will utterly blot out the memory of Amalek from under heaven." …Yahweh will have war with Amalek from generation to generation."

The Amalekites would become one of the recurring enemies of Yahweh once Israel was settled in the Promised Land. But here's where the roaming Amalekites that Moses met in the wilderness may have included some other allies that show up in the novels *Joshua Valiant* and *Caleb Vigilant.* Egyptologist David Rohl explains that in the 1950s, a scarab bearing the name of Maaibre Sheshi was excavated from a tomb in Jericho. Scarabs were beetle-shaped seals that had reference to Egyptian rulers, and it turns out that Sheshi may have been one of the Hyksos warriors who invaded Egypt right after Moses led the exodus of Israelites out of that land. This scarab ties Sheshi both to Egypt and to the land of Joshua's conquest.[51]

As a side note, under conventional Egyptian chronology combined with the late date of the Exodus under Ramesses, the Hyksos invasion of Egypt allegedly came *before* Moses. But under David Rohl's New Chronology and early date for Exodus, the Hyksos invasion fits perfectly right *after* the Exodus. Those foreign attackers took over Egypt without a fight because Pharaoh and his army had been killed in the waters of Yam Suph.

Rohl concludes that these Amalekites that faced Israel at Rephidim were probably the "Hyksos" who afterward invaded Egypt. The word Hyksos is actually Egyptian for "shepherd kings," nomadic foreigners. The Amalekites were the Semites who took over the abandoned Hebrew city of Avaris and even brought Ba'al worship with them that eventually evolved into worship of the Egyptian god Set.[52]

Rohl explains that "Prior to the Israelite invasion of Canaan, [Sheshi's] influence had stretched far and wide. Scarabs bearing Maibre Sheshi's name have been found all over southern Palestine and were even recovered from the very last burials of the Middle Bronze Age cemetery at Jericho. These crucial finds suggest that Jericho fell to Joshua just a few years after Sheshi and the Amalekites had conquered Egypt."[53]

---

[51] David Rohl, *Exodus: Myth or History?* (MN: Thinking Man Media, 2015), 299-301. See also David Rohl, *From Eden to Exile: The Five-Thousand-Year History of the People of the Bible* (London: Random House, 2002), 248-252.

[52] Rohl, *From Eden to Exile,* 251.

[53] Rohl, *From Eden to Exile,* 251.

But here's another fascinating connection: *Rohl argues that Sheshi is the Anakim chieftain named Sheshai in the Bible.* Sheshai was one of three powerful "descendants of Anak" who ruled from the city of Hebron in Canaan.

> Numbers 13:22
> [The Israelites] went up into the Negeb and came to Hebron. Ahiman, Sheshai, and Talmai, <u>the descendants of Anak</u>, were there.

Remember, "descendants of Anak" or "sons of Anak" was a reference to the Anakim, the giants of the land of Canaan that Joshua sought to wipe out with his wars of conquest (Joshua 11:21-22). For those familiar with my series, Chronicles of the Nephilim, these three giant Anakim: Ahiman, Sheshai and Talmai, come to play a major role in the novels *Joshua Valiant* and *Caleb Vigilant*. That's because they were giant villains who played a major role in the biblical story of Joshua's conquest. It took Caleb's mighty valor to finally defeat them.

> Joshua 15:13–14
> [Joshua] gave to Caleb the son of Jephunneh a portion among the people of Judah, Hebron…And Caleb drove out from there the <u>three sons of Anak, Sheshai and Ahiman and Talmai, the descendants of Anak</u>. (see also Judges 1:10)

By the 13th century B.C., the Egyptians had become familiar with these Anakim giants of Canaan, describing them as Bedouin nomads who were "four or five cubits (7 to 9 feet) from their nose to their foot and [they] have fierce faces."[54] But evidently, the Egyptians had their own giants as well because one of the "descendants of the giants" who sought to kill King David centuries later was described in the Bible as being an Egyptian, 8 feet 6 inches tall (1 Chronicles 11:23).

Joshua's battle with these Amalekite giants was a foretaste of what they would be facing with the conquest of Canaan in the wars of Yahweh (Deuteronomy 9:1-3; 1:28; 2:10, 20-21; Joshua 11:21-22).

---

[54] Edward Frank Wente and Edmund S. Meltzer, vol. 1, *Letters from Ancient Egypt*, Writings from the Ancient World, 108 (Atlanta, GA: Scholars Press, 1990).

Chapter 3
The Spiritual World of Egypt

The Watchers

I explained in the Note to the Reader at the beginning of *Moses* that I employ the Deuteronomy 32 worldview, or divine council motif, as a fantasy element to tell the supernatural side of the story of Yahweh's war on the gods of Egypt. The basic premise is that there is a spiritual world of principalities and powers whose stories are linked to earthly rulers.

Deuteronomy 32 tells the story of Israel and how she had come to be God's chosen nation. Moses begins by glorifying God and then telling the Israelites to "remember the days of old."

> Deuteronomy 32:8–9:
> When the Most High gave to the nations their inheritance,
>   when he divided mankind,
> he fixed the borders of the peoples
>   according to the number of the sons of God.
> But the Lord's portion is his people,
>   Jacob his allotted heritage.

The context of this passage is the Tower of Babel incident in Genesis 11 when mankind was divided. Rebellious humanity sought divinity in unified rebellion, so God separated them by confusing their tongues, which divided them into the seventy nations (of Gentiles) described in Genesis 10 and their ownership of those bordered lands as the "inheritance" of those peoples.

But inheritance works in heaven as it is on earth. The people of Jacob (Israel) would become Yahweh's allotted inheritance while the other seventy Gentile nations were the allotted inheritance of the *Sons of God*.

So who were these Sons of God who ruled over the Gentile nations (Psalm 82:1-8)? Some believe they were human rulers. Others argue for their identities as supernatural principalities and powers. I am in the second camp. In my Psalm 82 book, I prove why they can't be humans and must be heavenly creatures.

The phrase "Sons of God" is a technical theological term that means divine beings from God's heavenly throne court (Job 1:6; 38:7), and they are referred to with many different titles. They are sometimes called "heavenly host" (Isaiah 24:21-22[1]), sometimes called "holy ones" (Deuteronomy 33:2-3[2]), sometimes called "the divine council" (Psalm 82:1[3]), sometimes called "Watchers" (Daniel 4:13, 17, 23), and sometimes called "gods" or *elohim* in the Hebrew (Deuteronomy 32: 17, 43; Psalm 82:1; 58:1-2). Yes, you read that last one correctly. God's Word calls these beings *gods*.

But fear not. That isn't polytheism. The word "god" in this sense is a synonym for "heavenly being" or "divine being" whose realm is that of the spiritual. It doesn't mean uncreated beings who are all-powerful and all-knowing. Yahweh alone is that God. Yahweh is the God of gods or "Elohim of elohim" (Deuteronomy 10:17; Psalm 136:2). He created the other *elohim* ("gods"). These "gods" are created finite angelic beings who are most precisely referred to as Sons of God.

The narrative is this. Before the Flood, some of these heavenly Sons of God rebelled against Yahweh and left their divine dwelling to come to earth (Jude 6), where they violated Yahweh's holy separation and mated with human women (Genesis 6:1-4). This was not a racial segregation but a spiritual one. Their corrupt hybrid seed were called "nephilim" (giants), and their effect on humanity included such corruption and violence on the earth that Yahweh sent the Flood to wipe everyone out, starting over again with Noah and his family.

Unfortunately, after the Flood humanity once again united in evil while building the Tower of Babel, a symbol of idolatrous worship of false gods. So Yahweh confused their tongues and divided them into the seventy nations. Since mankind wouldn't stop worshipping false gods, the living God gave them over to their lusts (Romans 1:24, 26, 28) and placed them under the authority of the fallen Sons of God whom they worshipped. Fallen spiritual rulers for fallen humanity (Psalm 82:1-7). It's as if God said to humanity, "Okay, if you refuse to stop worshipping false gods, then I will give you over to them and see how you like them ruling over you."

Deuteronomy 32 hints at a spiritual reality behind the false gods of the nations, calling them "demons" (Deuteronomy 32:17; also Psalm 106:37-38). The Apostle Paul later ascribes demonic reality to false gods as well (1

---

[1] See also Deut 4:19 with Deut 32:8-9; 1 King 22:19-23.

[2] See also Psalm 89:5-7; Heb 2:2.

[3] See also Psalm 89:5-7.

Corinthians 10:20; 8:4-6). The New Testament continues this ancient notion that spiritual principalities and powers lay behind earthly powers (Ephesians 6:12; 3:10). The two were inextricably linked in historic events. As Jesus indicated, whatever happened in heaven also happened on earth (Matthew 6:10). Earthly kingdoms in conflict are intimately connected to heavenly powers in conflict.[4]

When earthly rulers battle on earth, the Bible describes the host of heaven battling with them in spiritual unity. In Daniel 10, hostilities between Greece and Persia are accompanied by the battle of heavenly Watchers over those nations (described as spiritual "princes").

> Daniel 10:13, 20-21
> The prince of the kingdom of Persia withstood me twenty-one days, but Michael, one of the chief princes, came to help me, for I was left there with the kings of Persia.…Then he said, "Do you know why I have come to you? But now I will return to fight against the prince of Persia; and when I go out, behold, the prince of Greece will come. But I will tell you what is inscribed in the book of truth: there is none who contends by my side against these except Michael, your prince."

When Sisera fought with Israel, the earthly kings and heavenly authorities (stars or host of heaven) are described interchangeably in unity.[5]

> Judges 5:19–20:
> "The kings came, they fought; then fought the kings of Canaan…From heaven the stars fought, from their courses they fought against Sisera.

When Yahweh punishes earthly rulers, he punishes them along with the heavenly rulers ("host of heaven") above and behind them.

> Isaiah 24:21–22:
> On that day the LORD will punish the host of heaven, in heaven, and the kings of the earth, on the earth. They will be

[4] Daniel10:12-13, 20-21; 2Kings 6:17; Judges 5:19-20.

[5] See also 2 Kings 6:15-17 where Elisha's servant has his spiritual eyes opened to see the myriad of heavenly warriors surrounding Israel preparing to battle Syria.

> gathered together as prisoners in a pit; they will be shut up in a prison, and after many days they will be punished.[6]

Jeremiah also affirms the connection between earthly authorities and their heavenly principalities when he prophesies Yahweh's judgment upon Egypt and her gods, including the high god Amon, who was the patron deity of Thebes.

> Jeremiah 46:25
> Yahweh of hosts, the God of Israel, said: "Behold, I am bringing punishment upon Amon of Thebes, and Pharaoh and Egypt and her gods and her kings.

Yahweh is not using punishment upon the gods as mere generic rhetoric. He is specifically naming a deity that he will be punishing as the spiritual prince of that territory. When Yahweh punishes heavenly rulers, he also punishes earthly rulers along with them and vice versa.

This notion of territorial archons or spiritual rulers is biblical and carries over into intertestamental literature such as the Book of Enoch and others.[7] It is one of the foundational storylines behind my three book series *Chronicles of the Watchers*, *Chronicles of the Nephilim*, and *Chronicles of the Apocalypse*.

In the Bible, the term "Watchers" only appears in Daniel 4, where a Watcher, also called a "holy one," came down from heaven to proclaim to Daniel the "decree of the Watchers" that Nebuchadnezzar would go mad like a beast (Daniel 4:13-17, 23). Though the Watchers of Daniel 4 are not explicitly equated with the "princes" over the kingdoms of the nations in Daniel 10, they are considered by ancient Jews to be synonymous. The Watchers over the nations were the spiritual princes or principalities of those nations.

Two examples of how the ancient Jews interpreted Deuteronomy 32:8-9 illustrate this notion of territorial principalities watching over nations.

---

[6] Interestingly, this passage of Isaiah is not clear about what judgment in history it is referring to. But the language earlier in the text is similar to the Flood when it says, "For the windows of heaven are opened, and the foundations of the earth tremble. 19 The earth is utterly broken, the earth is split apart, the earth is violently shaken. 20 The earth staggers like a drunken man; it sways like a hut; its transgression lies heavy upon it, and it falls, and will not rise again." So this may be another passage that uses a Flood reference tied in with the Watchers and their punishment.

[7] 1 En. 89:59, 62-63; 67; Jubilees 15:31-32; Targum Jonathan Deut. 32, Sect. LIII; 3Enoch 48C:9, DSS War Scroll 1Q33 Col. xvii:7, Targum Jonathan, Genesis 11, Section II.

Jubilees 15:31-32:
(There are) many nations and many people, and they all belong to [Yahweh], but over all of them he caused spirits to rule so that they might lead them astray from following him. But over Israel he did not cause any angel or spirit to rule because he alone is their ruler and he will protect them.

Targum Jonathan, Deuteronomy 32, Section LIII:
When the Most High made allotment of the world unto the nations which proceeded from the sons of Noach [Noah], in the separation of the writings and languages of the children of men at the time of the division, He cast the lot among the seventy angels, the princes of the nations with whom is the revelation to oversee the city.[8]

It is the book of 1 Enoch that most commonly uses the term "Watchers" of these territorial princes or angels or spirits or holy ones. The Sons of God of Genesis 6 are called Watchers all throughout 1 Enoch.[9] And those Sons of God are described in the Old Testament as Yahweh's heavenly host that surround him in his divine council.

Job describes the Sons of God as divine beings who were a heavenly host present at the creation (Job 38:4-7) and who gathered around Yahweh, along with the satan, to council with him and perform his decrees (Job 1:6-7; 2:1-6). 1 Kings 22:19-23 depicts this same "host of heaven" as spirits surrounding Yahweh who do his bidding. Psalm 82 and 89 describes the assembly of heavenly host as his "divine council" of "gods," "holy ones," and "Sons of the Most High" (82:6). In other words, Sons of God.

All these terms are used synonymously for the divine beings of God's heavenly host, the Sons of God to whom Deuteronomy 32:8 declared were allotted the nations for an inheritance to watch over (territorial powers).

So the Bible says that there is demonic reality to false gods. But since those Sons of God who were territorial authorities over the nations were spiritually fallen Watchers, that makes them demonic or evil in essence. So what if they were the actual demonic beings behind the false gods of the

---

8 See also 1 Enoch 89:59; 90:25, 3Enoch 48C:9, DSS War Scroll 1Q33 Col. xvii:7, Targum Jonathan, Genesis 11, Section II; Philo, On the Posterity of Cain and His Exile 25.89; Concerning Noah's Work as a Planter 14.59; On the Migration of Abraham 36.202; 1 Clement 29; Origen, First Principles 1.5.1. Thanks to Don Enevoldsen for some of these passages. Walter Wink footnotes a plenitude of texts about the 70 angel "gods" over the 70 nations in the Targums in Walter Wink. *Naming the Powers: The Language of Power in the New Testament* (The Powers : Volume One) (Kindle Locations 2235-2242). Kindle Edition.

9 1 Enoch 10:9, 15; 12:2-6; 13:10; 14:1-3; 15:9; 16:1-2.

ancient world? What if the fallen Sons of God were masquerading as the gods of the nations in order to keep humanity enslaved in idolatry to their authority? That would affirm the biblical stories of earthly events occurring in synchronization with heavenly events.

That is the biblical premise of all three of my Chronicles series of novels, including *Chronicles of the Watchers*. The pagan gods like Isis, Horus, Set, Baal, Astarte, and others, are actually fallen Sons of God, Watchers of the nations, crafting false identities and narratives as gods of the nations that are connected with and reflected in the earthly events of human history and its rulers. For a detailed biblical defense of this interpretation, see my booklet *Psalm 82: The Divine Council of the Gods, the Judgment of the Watchers and the Inheritance of the Nations.* (affiliate link)

The Binding of Mastema

Through the entire *Chronicles* series, I have used a concept called "binding" of angels, demons, and Watchers. This binding is accomplished through imprisonment in the earth, the sea or the underworld.

The idea of binding spirits is a common one in ancient religion and magic. Michael Fishbane notes that in the ancient Near East, incantations and spells were used by sorcerers and enchanters to bind people and spirits in spiritual "traps, pits, snares, and nets," using venomous curses from their lips like serpents or arrows. In response to some of these verbal sorceries, the Psalmist himself calls upon Yahweh in similar utterances to reverse the spells upon his enemies that they would be trapped, ensnared and bound by their own magical devices as with God's arrows.[10]

> Psalm 64:7–8
> But God shoots his arrow at them; they are wounded suddenly. They are brought to ruin, with their own tongues turned against them.

David reverses an incantation ("mischief of their lips") against evildoers who curse him:

> Psalm 140:9–11
> As for the head of those who surround me, let the mischief of their lips overwhelm them! Let burning coals fall upon

---

[10] Michael A Fishbane, *Studies In Biblical Magic : Origins, Uses And Transformations Of Terminology And Literary Form* (Dissertation) Brandeis University, 1971. See also Edwin M. Yamauchi, "Magic In The Biblical World," The Institute For Biblical Research Lecture, 1981, *Tyndale Bulletin* 34 (1983).

> them! Let them be cast into fire, into miry pits, no more to rise! Let not the slanderer be established in the land; let evil hunt down the violent man speedily!

This is not merely a prayer request to God, but a reversal of their own words of curse.

Exorcists of the first century used incantations to cast out demons in Jesus' name (Acts 16:18), the same incantation attempted by demons *against* Jesus before being cast out (Mk 1:27).[11]

Ezekiel 13:18 refers to a specific form of hunting and binding spirits in a practice of women "who sew magic bands upon all wrists…in the hunt for souls!" These magic bands were supposed to protect the women and magically bind their enemies. In my novels, I reversed this pagan version of using magical bands by creating a heavenly version of the archangels with armbands of indestructible Cherubim hair for their hunting and binding of evil spirits. The hair is is used by the archangels as a rope to bind the Watchers' hands and feet: A fictional way to portray the theological meaning of binding.

The Egyptians also had detailed magical traditions of binding humans, spirits and gods. Tying ritual knots was believed to be a form of sympathetic magic that would bind all enemies natural or supernatural. As Egyptologist Geraldine Pinch explains,

> Rope was very important in ancient Egypt and was an essential part of many hunting techniques, all of which were used symbolically against supernatural enemies. Harmful spirits might be caught in a net, or with a lasso of rope, so a magician could use these objects to frighten off potential troublemakers. The Underworld Books are full of episodes in which the enemies of order and light are bound with ropes to restrain them. Human or semi-human figures called the 'Enemies of Ra' are shown with their arms tied behind their backs. Magical figurines representing enemies were treated in the same way.[12]

---

[11] Graham Twelftree, *Jesus the Exorcist: A Contribution to the Study of the Historical Jesus* (Eugene, OR: Wipf and Stock, 2010), 95, 139, 159-60.

[12] Geraldine Pinch, *Magic in Ancient Egypt* (London, England, British Museum Press, 1994) 84.

The Egyptian Book of the Dead describes various episodes of gods being bound as a part of a dead noble achieving his apotheosis into Osiris, "I have bound up the gods with divine tresses."[13]

The noble, then appropriates Osiris's powers through binding: "I bind together and I gather up your powers." "May it be granted that I bind his soul in the divine [solar] boat [of Ra]." "The gods were bound therewith." "Thine enemy is given to the fire, the evil one hath fallen; his arms are bound, and his legs hath Ra taken from him."[14]

As we have seen, Scripture itself subverts or turns this occult binding against pagan magicians through God's superior powers. But that binding is also appropriated against the elohim or gods in the Bible. Jesus, the Master himself, binds the "god of this world," Satan (2 Cor. 4:4) in order to take over the land as Messiah. Satan was declared to be the ruler of the known world of first century Rome (Jn. 12:31, 14:30-31, 16:11), in accordance with the territorial inheritance of the nations as described earlier in Deuteronomy 32:8-10. So when Jesus cast out demons, he explained the act as a spiritual colonization of the Promised Land, by casting out that world's god, Satan.

> John 12:31
> Now is the judgment of this world; now will the ruler of this world be cast out.
>
> Matthew 12:28–29
> But if it is by the Spirit of God that I cast out demons, then the kingdom of God has come upon you. Or how can someone enter a strong man's house and plunder his goods, unless he first binds the strong man [Satan]?

Biblical binding does not necessarily refer to a total inability of the spiritual being to do anything. Though Satan was bound by Jesus in his ministry, he was still able to prowl around like a roaring lion during the first century (1 Pet 5:8). That is because this binding is a metaphor for limitation of powers. The binding of Satan in Revelation 20:2-3 is described specifically as the inability to deceive the nations which allowed the Gospel to spread to those nations.

---

[13] From the Papyrus of Nu (British Museum No. 10,477, sheets 13 and 14), E.A. Wallis Budge, Ed., Epiphanius Wilson, A.M. *The Ancient Egyptian Book of the Dead* (New York, NY: Wellfleet Press, 2016) 133.

[14] E.A. Wallis Budge, *The Book of the Dead: The Papyrus of Ani in the British Museum* (scanned at www.sacred-texts.com, Oct-Dec 2000, 1895) 218, 224, 270, 247.

And this binding of Satan has a precursor in Jewish Second Temple literature. In the Dead Sea Scrolls of Qumran, Satan is called by the names of Belial and Mastema.[15]

In the pseudepigraphal book of Jubilees, Mastema is also equivocated with Satan (Jubilees 10:8-11) and described as being the spiritual "prince" who helped the Egyptian sorcerers in their magic against Moses. Mastema is then described as being bound during the Exodus and then released for the Yam Suph episode.

> Jubilees 48:15-18
> the [spiritual] prince Mastêmâ was bound and imprisoned behind the children of Israel that he might not accuse them. And on the nineteenth we let them loose that they might help the Egyptians and pursue the children of Israel.[16]

This is the basis in the novel *Moses* for the depiction of Mastema as taking on the identity of the god Ra, the ruler god of Egypt, as well as Ra being bound by angels until the Yam Suph deliverance.

Jubilees incorrectly depicts Mastema as the Destroying Angel of the Passover (Jubilees 49:2), which only proves that extra-biblical legends may be theologically helpful for narrative but are not inerrant Scripture.

Another well-respected pseudepigraphal book of the Second Temple period that described binding of ruling spirits was 1 Enoch. In this text, the fallen Sons of God from Genesis 6:1-3 are angelic beings called "Watchers" who reveal forbidden secrets to mankind, related to sorcery and war (1 Enoch 8). As in Genesis 6:11-12, their influence on mankind leads to genetic corruption of humanity and great violence (1 Enoch 7-8; 9:9).

So God binds them in the earth at the Flood to wait for their release unto judgment in the future.

> 1 Enoch 10:12-13
> Bind them for seventy generations underneath the rocks of the ground until the day of their judgment and of their consummation, until the eternal judgment is concluded. In

---

15 J. W. van Henten, "Mastemah," ed. Karel van der Toorn, Bob Becking, and Pieter W. van der Horst, *Dictionary of Deities and Demons in the Bible* (Leiden; Boston; Köln; Grand Rapids, MI; Cambridge: Brill; Eerdmans, 1999), 553-554.

16 Robert Henry Charles, ed., *Pseudepigrapha of the Old Testament*, vol. 2 (Oxford: Clarendon Press, 1913), 79.

> those days they will lead them into the bottom of the fire—
> and in torment.[17]

Though some might dismiss 1 Enoch as fanciful speculation without merit, the authors of the New Testament Scriptures did not. 1 Enoch was quoted and paraphrased in several New Testament books, including Jude and 2 Peter. Jude likens human apostate teachers of false doctrine to the apostate angels (Sons of God, Watchers) who taught the evil arts to mankind. Jude claims that those fallen angels were imprisoned in "eternal bonds" and Peter speaks of the same binding as occurring at the Flood (2 Peter 2:4-5):

> Jude 6 (NASB95)
> And angels who did not keep their own domain, but abandoned their proper abode, He has kept in eternal bonds under darkness for the judgment of the great day.

That reference to angels who did "not keep their own domain but abandoned their proper abode" is the same language as 1 Enoch 12:4 and 15:2-3: "The Watchers of heaven who have *abandoned the high heaven, the holy eternal place,* and have defiled themselves with women." Jude also likens depraved human apostates to "wandering stars, for whom the gloom of utter darkness has been reserved forever" (Jude 13). This same wandering star metaphor is used of the fallen Watchers in 1 Enoch who are "stars that change their courses" (1 Enoch 80:6) having been reserved for a "prison house" (1 Enoch 18:13-15) in the "deep, empty and dark abyss" (1 Enoch 88:1-3).

Jude then quotes 1 Enoch 1:9 verbatim when he says of these wandering stars,

> Jude 14–15
> 14 It was also about these that Enoch, the seventh from Adam, prophesied, saying, "Behold, the Lord comes with ten thousands of his holy ones, to execute judgment on all and to convict all the ungodly of all their deeds of ungodliness that they have committed in such an ungodly way, and of all the harsh things that ungodly sinners have spoken against him."

---

[17] James H. Charlesworth, The Old Testament Pseudepigrapha, vol. 1 (New York; London: Yale University Press, 1983), 18.

So, Jude and 2 Peter agree with 1 Enoch that fallen angelic Watchers were bound below the earth at the Flood, awaiting their coming judgment. Other Watchers, as described in Daniel, continue to be spiritual princes over earthly powers and nations until Messiah would come (Daniel 10:13, 20-21; 4:13, 17, 23).

Host of Heaven

One aspect of the Watchers in the Bible and other ancient Near Eastern sacred literature is their astronomical identification in the heavens. And the original context of "heavenly host" in the Bible is one of war. The Hebrew term for "host" (*saba*) was used as a reference to warriors. The term "Lord of Hosts" was therefore a designation of Yahweh as warrior king over an army.

> Isaiah 13:4–5
> The sound of a tumult is on the mountains
> as of a great multitude!
> The sound of an uproar of kingdoms,
> of nations gathering together!
> The LORD of hosts is mustering
> a host for battle.
> They come from a distant land,
> from the end of the heavens,
> the LORD and the weapons of his indignation,
> to destroy the whole land.

In this passage, Isaiah describes the earthly armies of Babylon subversively as Yahweh's own weapons used upon another nation. God is using Babylon providentially as his own host of warriors.

But there is a heavenly host of warriors as well. In Joshua 5, we are introduced to the leader of that heavenly host. Joshua was preparing to besiege Jericho when an armed man appeared before him. But this warrior was more than a man. He proclaimed, "I am the commander of the host of the LORD" (5:14). That commander, most likely the Angel of Yahweh (Jesus), then said the exact same words that Yahweh proclaimed to Moses from the burning bush: "Take off your sandals from your feet, for the place where you are standing is holy" (5:15). Yahweh is a warrior king of a heavenly host of armies.

In 2 Kings 6, the prophet Elisha and his young assistant see the army of Syria surrounding Samaria. The servant worries that they are outnumbered. But Elisha tells him that there are more who are with Israel than with Syria.

He then asks Yahweh to show the young man the spiritual realm. "So the Lord opened the eyes of the young man, and he saw, and behold, the mountain was full of horses and chariots of fire all around Elisha" (6:17).

Seeing this military context of the "host" sheds light on Yahweh's reference to the Israelites leaving Egypt as a host. "And on that very day the LORD brought the people of Israel out of the land of Egypt by their hosts" (Exodus 12:51). In the story of the Exodus up until the Yam Suph crossing, Yahweh describes his people as the "host of Israel" in contrast with "Pharaoh and all his host of Egypt" (Exodus 14:17, 19-20). Anyone familiar with the story knows that the Israelites were not an army and didn't fight against Pharaoh. They were the entire population of the Hebrews along with other slaves, men, women, and children. So why describe them in military terms as a "host"? Remember the census numbers of the Exodus we talked about earlier (Numbers 1). Those numbers were given as a military census in the ancient world. Why would Yahweh use a military term for his civilian population? Because the entire Exodus is being framed by Yahweh as a war of gods and men. Israel vs. Egypt, Yahweh vs. Pharaoh, and Yahweh vs. the gods of Egypt. The glory of it all is that the Israelites did not fight in this mighty spiritual war because Yahweh fought for them. As the Song of Moses declares:

> Exodus 15:2–11
> Yahweh is my strength and my song,
> and he has become my salvation…
> Yahweh is a man of war;
> Yahweh is his name.
> Pharaoh's chariots and his host he cast into the sea,
> and his chosen officers were sunk in Yam Suph.
> The floods covered them;
> they went down into the depths like a stone.
> Your right hand, O Yahweh, glorious in power,
> your right hand, O Yahweh, shatters the enemy...
> Who is like you, O Yahweh, among the gods?
> Who is like you, majestic in holiness,
> awesome in glorious deeds, doing wonders?

But war is not the only responsibility of Yahweh's heavenly host. They are also the millions who surround Yahweh's throne in heaven to glorify him and partake of his divine council as mentioned earlier. The prophet Micaiah describes the basic scenario from his vision:

> 1 Kings 22:19–22
> I saw the LORD sitting on his throne, and all the host of heaven standing beside him on his right hand and on his left; and the LORD said, "Who will entice Ahab, that he may go up and fall at Ramoth-gilead?" And one said one thing, and another said another. Then a spirit came forward and stood before the LORD, saying, "I will entice him." And the LORD said to him, "By what means?" And he said, "I will go out, and will be a lying spirit in the mouth of all his prophets." And [the LORD] said, "You are to entice him, and you shall succeed; go out and do so."

This scene matches up with the passages in Job 1 and 2 referenced earlier that showed this same gathering around God's throne of his heavenly host, also called "Sons of God." Yahweh's heavenly host surround him, worship him (Nehemiah 9:6), but also counsel with him and then perform Yahweh's commands of tasks.

The question arises just how many there are of these heavenly host. Throughout the Bible, symbolic phrases are used to describe the numbers as innumerable, or uncountable. "Ten thousands" (plural) of these holy ones are depicted at Sinai (Deuteronomy 33:2). The New Testament author Jude quotes from 1 Enoch that says that the Lord will come with "ten thousands (plural) of his holy ones" (Jude 14-15). That phrase "ten thousands" is also translated as "ten million" (1 Enoch 1:9). Yahweh's heavenly chariots at Sinai were "twice ten thousand, thousands upon thousands" (Psalm 68:17). In Daniel's vision of heavenly host before Yahweh's throne, he sees "a thousand thousands served him, and ten thousand times ten thousand (one hundred million) stood before him" (Daniel 7:10). Jeremiah comes right out and says, "The host of heaven cannot be numbered" (Jeremiah 33:22).

By any accounting, that's a lot of heavenly host.

Shining Ones

One more thing about this heavenly host of warriors. They are sometimes described as "shining." For example, in Daniel's vision on the Tigris River, he sees an unnamed heavenly warrior speaking of the various territorial principalities over the nations called "princes" or guardians of those lands (10:12-13, 20-21). The heavenly being is described as a man whose "body was like beryl [a gleaming gem], his face like the appearance of lightning, his eyes like flaming torches, his arms and legs like the gleam of burnished bronze" (10:6).

Heavenly creatures are often described in these shining terms in Scripture. Ezekiel's vision of the cherubim also describe them as "gleaming beryl," glowing "burnished bronze," "gleaming metal," with "bright fire," "flashes of lightning and fire" around them (Ezekiel 1:4-16). Yahweh on his throne is described as the form of a man whose upper half was like "gleaming metal, like the fire enclosed all around," and "there was brightness all around him" (1:26-28).

At Mount Sinai, Yahweh and his host are both described in these terms of shining:

> Deuteronomy 33:2
> He said, "The LORD came from Sinai and dawned from Seir upon us; he shone forth from Mount Paran; he came from the ten thousands of holy ones, with flaming fire at his right hand.

In the New Testament, the angels who announced the resurrection of Jesus had "the appearance like lightning" and clothing "white as snow" (Matthew 28:3), described by Luke as "dazzling in apparel" (Luke 24:4). That was no designer clothes with bling but a shining brightness expressive of the heavenly realm.

In fact, even Moses began to shine with an unbearable brightness the more he was in Yahweh's presence in the tabernacle (Exodus 34:29-35).

Isaiah 14 gives a prophecy to the king of Babylon that many believe also refers to the satan. Yahweh taunts the human king who considered himself to be divine with intent to ascend above the very throne of God, "How you are fallen from heaven, O Day Star, son of Dawn!" (14:12). The first part of that name, "Day Star," is *helel* in Hebrew, which lexicons define as meaning "Shining One."[18] We will talk more about this passage shortly, but the context of it is clearly one of spiritual or heavenly connection. In his arrogant pride, the king of Babylon claims to be divine, like the shining beings of the heavenly host.

This "shining" was a well-known rendering of spiritual beings through all the ancient world. A fragment of the Dead Sea Scrolls speaks of "those who make knowledge shine among the divinities [gods] of light." [19] The Canaanite religious texts from Ugarit in Syria describe the same kind of divine

---

[18] "Shining one" Francis Brown, Samuel Rolles Driver, and Charles Augustus Briggs, *Enhanced Brown-Driver-Briggs Hebrew and English Lexicon* (Oxford: Clarendon Press, 1977), 237.

[19] 4Q403 1.2.35 - Florentino García Martínez and Eibert J. C. Tigchelaar, *"The Dead Sea Scrolls Study Edition (translations)"* (Leiden; New York: Brill, 1997–1998), 823.

council of gods around their supreme god, El. They are called "the Shining Ones of the council."[20] As far away as ancient China, we find references to a supreme creator, Shang Di, also surrounded by lesser deities or spirits called *shen*, which means "bright ones."[21]

And in the popular Egyptian Book of the Dead, the deified dead scribe, now called Osiris Ani, speaks of the gods also as "Shining Ones" who "live in the rays of light" as emanations of the sun god Ra.[22]

> I may lift up the earth; that the shining ones may open their arms unto me; that the company of the gods may speak with the words of the shining ones unto Osiris Ani; that the hearts of the gods may direct [him]; and that they may make him powerful in heaven among the gods who have taken unto themselves visible forms.[23]

So, why all this brightness and shining of the gods? Is it just a manifestation of spiritual glory, or is there more to it than that?

A closer look reveals that the shining of the heavenly host reflects a strong literary and theological identification of the gods with stars. Some passages appear to address the "host of heaven" as the stars in the sky. Other passages appear to address the "host of heaven" as the spiritual beings around God's throne. This is because the stars and gods were thought of as interchangeable in their identities. Stars were equated with gods, and gods were equated with stars. This explains the development of astrology as the stars determining our destiny. The ancient mind thought of the stars as gods, and the gods controlled their lives. Since the stars were manifestations of the gods, the stars therefore controlled mankind's lives and destiny.

As mentioned earlier, when Moses warned the Israelites against worshipping the Canaanite deities, he likened the sun, moon, and stars to "all the host of heaven."

> Deuteronomy 4:19-20
> And beware lest you raise your eyes to heaven, and when you see the sun and the moon and the stars, all the host of heaven, you be drawn away and bow down to them and serve them, things that the LORD your God has allotted to all

---

20 E. Theodore Mullen, Jr., *The Divine Council in Canaanite and Early Hebrew Literature* (Chico, CA: Scholars Press, 1980), 240.

21 John Ross, *The Original Religion of China*, (New York, NY: Eaton and Mains, 1909), 172.

22 Book of the Dead LXXVIII (78). E.A. Wallis Budge, *The Egyptian Book of the Dead: The Papyrus of Ani*, 333.

23 Book of the Dead CXXIV (174:10-12). Budge, *The Egyptian Book of the Dead*, 331. Pharaoh Pepi was also deified and described as standing "among the gods, among the shining ones." Budge, *The Egyptian Book of the Dead*, 57-58.

> the peoples under the whole heaven. But the LORD has taken you and brought you out of the iron furnace, out of Egypt, to be a people of his own inheritance, as you are this day.

On the surface, this looks like he is saying that the pagans worship the sun, moon, and stars as deities. That is true. But not true enough. Notice the language stating that Yahweh "allotted" those host to the peoples under heaven while keeping Israel as his own "inheritance." This terminology of allotted inheritance is repeated with the same juxtaposition of Israel and the peoples later in Deuteronomy 32.

> Deuteronomy 32:8–9
> When the Most High gave to the nations their inheritance,
> when he divided mankind,
> he fixed the borders of the peoples
> according to the number of the sons of God.
> But the LORD's portion is his people,
> Jacob his allotted heritage.

In both Deuteronomy 4 and 32, we see the same repeated pattern of God allotting the peoples (nations) to the Sons of God—who are the host of heaven—as an inheritance, but keeping Israel (Jacob) as his own allotted inheritance. Earlier, we found that the Sons of God were in fact the divine beings around Yahweh's throne (who had rebelled). So we see that the Sons of God are equated with the host of heaven as both gods and as astronomical bodies. It is a case of both/and, not either/or. The Sons of God are the heavenly host, which is both a personal divine being from God's throne and represented in the sun, moon, and stars that were worshipped by pagans.

The Jews also equated the heavenly host as both stars and gods, but they refused to worship them. Remember that the phrase "gods" in Hebrew was *elohim*, which was synonymous with the Sons of God in Yahweh's divine council (Psalm 82:1 with Job 1:6). Thus, Job ties the two together when he describes the Sons of God as "morning stars" singing together at God's creation of the universe.

> Job 38:7
> [at creation,] when the morning stars sang together
> and all the sons of God shouted for joy.

This verse uses a very common technique called "parallelism" that is ubiquitous in the Old Testament. Parallelism uses a doublet of phrases to convey the same thing in two different ways. "Morning stars singing" is another way of saying "sons of God shouting for joy." They are not two different things but the same thing repeated with different words. The conjunctive "and" in Hebrew means "even" in this context. So the text is not saying morning stars *and* all the sons of God, as if they are two different items, but rather "morning stars, *even* all the sons of God."

Daniel also uses this parallel doublet in a passage identifying spiritual principalities with stars. Notice the conjunctive *and* again as meaning *even.*

> Dan. 8:10-11
> It grew great, even to the host of heaven. And some of the host **and** some of the stars it threw down to the ground and trampled on them. It became great, even as great as the Prince of the host [Michael]

The spiritual "princes" over the nations in this passage are also called "host of heaven" and "stars."

This poetic technique now makes more sense of Psalm 148:

> Psalm 148:2–3
> Praise him, all his angels;
> praise him, all his hosts!
> Praise him, sun and moon,
> praise him, all you shining stars!

This psalm uses parallel doublets as well. Its call to praise is not a listing of separate things created by God: angels, hosts, sun and moon, shining stars. It is a parallel synonym of angels, who are his hosts, which are also his shining stars.

Let's go back then to Isaiah's prophecy addressed to the king of Babylon we brought up earlier in this chapter. "Day Star, Son of the Dawn" in Hebrew is *Helel ben Shachar*. which literally means "shining one, son of the dawn." It is actually an ancient reference to the planet Venus, well-known to the ancients as the "bright morning star."[24] The shining of astronomical bodies was the same shining as of the divine Sons of God/gods/Watchers.

As I explained in more detail in my previous book, When Giants Were Upon the Earth, (affiliate link) this Isaiah passage is not really about "Satan's fall from heaven," but rather a mockery of the king of Babylon's fall from earthly power by placing him into a retelling of a Canaanite myth of Athtar's

---

[24] Michael S. Heiser, *The Unseen Realm: Recovering the Supernatural Worldview of the Bible*, First Edition (Bellingham, WA: Lexham Press, 2015), 85

own failed ambitions. The king thought he would be like a god, but he will end up dead and in Sheol like every rebel.

> Isaiah 14:3, 12–15
> You will take up this taunt against the king of Babylon:
> "How you are fallen from heaven,
> O Day Star, son of Dawn!
> How you are cut down to the ground,
> you who laid the nations low!
> You said in your heart,
> 'I will ascend to heaven;
> above the stars of God
> I will set my throne on high;
> I will sit on the mount of assembly
> in the far reaches of the north;
> I will ascend above the heights of the clouds;
> I will make myself like the Most High.'
> But you are brought down to Sheol,
> to the far reaches of the pit."

Scholar Michael S. Heiser definitively explains the linguistic and narrative referent of Helel ben Shahar (Day Star, son of the Dawn) as being the Ugaritic god Athtar from the epic Baal Cycle of myths at Ugarit. Heiser reveals that Athtar was equated with the planet Venus. Athtar sought to raise himself above "the stars of El," (gods as stars, again) a reference to the divine council or heavenly host that surrounded the high god of the Canaanite pantheon. He tried to do so by seeking to sit on the throne of Baal, referred to as "the Most High," upon the "mount of assembly" in the north called Saphon—just like in the prophecy of Isaiah. But Athtar was not powerful enough for the position of power and was cast to earth/Sheol.[25]

In the New Testament, Jude writes about another fall of divine beings in the days of the Flood, "angels who did not keep their own domain, but abandoned their proper abode" and fell to earth. God then imprisoned them "in eternal chains under gloomy darkness until the judgment of the great day" (Jude 6). Jude calls these imprisoned fallen angels "wandering stars" (v. 13), in line with Enoch's "prison house for the stars and the powers of

[25] Michael Heiser, "The Mythological Provenance of Isaiah 14:12-15: A Reconsideration of the Ugaritic Material" Liberty University https://digitalcommons.liberty.edu/lts_fac_pubs/280/

heaven…they are the ones which have transgressed the commandments of God" (1Enoch 18:14-15).[26]

This astralization of deities now brings some clarification to the poetic imagery used in many biblical prophesies of a collapsing universe. Falling stars, darkening suns, blood-red moons, and skies rolling up like a scroll are not scientific descriptions of the physical universe crumbling. They are a common mythopoeic image of heavenly rulers (Watchers) falling from power along with their earthly kingly counterparts. We saw previously in this chapter that the ancient Hebrew mind conceived of the earthly authorities as linked with their heavenly principalities. So Yahweh's judgment upon earthly powers and their heavenly counterparts is described as the astronomical heavens crashing down in defeat.

Here is a list of some passages that use astronomical catastrophe as symbol of spiritual and earthly powers at war.

- Judges 5:19-20—kings of Canaan fighting on earth are described as "stars fighting from heaven."
- Isaiah 13:1-17—the fall of Babylon to the Medes in 539 B.C. described as stars of heaven and the constellations not flashing forth their light, the sun darkened and the moon not shedding light.
- Haggai 2:6—the promise of a New Covenant described as "shaking the heavens and earth" (with Hebrews 12:26-28).
- Amos 8:9—the fall of Samaria in 722 B.C. described as the sun going down at noon and the earth dark in broad daylight.
- Isaiah 30:25-26—Israel's defeat of Sennacherib in 701 B.C. described as the moon being as bright as the sun and the sun seven times brighter.
- Psalm 18:6-15—David's earthly deliverance from Saul described as earth reeling, mountains quaking, heavens coming down with thick darkness, and the foundations of the earth laid bare.
- Joel 2:30–31—Wonders in the heavens, the sun turning to darkness, and the moon turning to blood are all described by the apostle Peter as being fulfilled in the first century in the fall of Israel and Jerusalem to the power of Rome (Acts 2:16, 20-21).

---

[26] James H. Charlesworth, The Old Testament Pseudepigrapha, vol. 1 (New York; London: Yale University Press, 1983), 23.

Centuries after Moses, in the 6th century B.C., Yahweh would destroy Egypt "by the hand of Nebuchadnezzar king of Babylon" (Ezekiel 30:10-11). Pagan Babylon would be a weapon of judgment in Yahweh's hand. Yahweh describes the judgment poetically: "I will dry up the Nile…I will bring desolation upon the land" (Ezekiel 30:12). Drying up the Nile was an obvious figurative image of "drying up" Egypt's wealth, since the river was the essence of her wealth (v. 10). The Nile never literally dried up. Then he gives this revealing description of astronomical catastrophe:

> Ezekiel 32:7–8
> When I blot you out, I will cover the heavens and make their stars dark; I will cover the sun with a cloud, and the moon shall not give its light. All the bright lights of heaven will I make dark over you, and put darkness on your land, declares the Lord GOD.

This destruction occurred around 580 B.C. But we have no records of these astronomical events occurring along with the historical ones. While these descriptions are certainly possible as physical phenomena, they are not necessarily so, because we will see later that the entire Exodus story is framed as a war of Yahweh on Pharaoh and the gods of Egypt. So whether this is literal or not, the meaning is certainly that Yahweh would "put the lights out" of both earthly Egypt and her heavenly principalities that ruled over her.

There are other examples of this astronomical language that are clearly not literal astronomical phenomena but metaphorical reference to the fall of powers and authority. Many of them refer to the same Babylonian campaign of conquest in the same time period.

When Babylon invaded Judah in 587 B.C., it also took out Edom. The prophet Isaiah predicted that fall of kingdoms as "All the host of heaven shall rot away, and the skies roll up like a scroll. All their host shall fall, as leaves fall from the vine, like leaves falling from the fig tree" (Isaiah 34:4).

Edom fell in the 6th century B.C., but these astronomical events never occurred because, of course, if the sky rolled up like that and all the stars fell, we wouldn't be here. There would be no universe left. That could not possibly be literal or physical. It was the description, not of physical phenomena, but of spiritual events that involved earthly and heavenly powers being overthrown.

When that same Babylon destroyed Israel and led her into captivity in that same time period, the same prophet Isaiah predicted it in vivid poetic language as the "earth will be completely laid waste and despoiled" (Isaiah 24:3), the earth is "split and broken asunder" (24:19), something that could not and did not happen physically or scientifically but was symbolic. Isaiah then says that in this event of judgment, God will simultaneously punish the earthly rulers together with their heavenly counterparts, the "host of heaven," or the Watchers, principalities of power over the peoples.

> Isaiah 24:21–23
> On that day the LORD will punish the host of heaven, in heaven, and the kings of the earth, on the earth. They will be gathered together as prisoners in a pit; they will be shut up in a prison, and after many days they will be punished. Then the moon will be confounded and the sun ashamed.

The "confounding" of the moon and "shaming" of the sun is a poetic way of saying the principalities and powers will be humbled by their defeat. One cannot confound the physical moon or shame the physical sun.

One last example gives this notion of astronomical catastrophe a clear metaphorical reference to the spiritual realm. When Babylon ended up destroying Jerusalem and the temple in its 6th century campaign of conquest, Jeremiah the prophet described it as if the entire world was being returned to a pre-creation state of chaos. The very spiritual cosmos of the covenant as incarnate in the temple was being undone. Jeremiah uses the creation language of Genesis 1 but retells it as if creation is being undone. Chaos is overtaking the order established by God.

> Jeremiah 4:23–28
> I looked on the earth, and behold, it was without form and void;
> and to the heavens, and they had no light.
> I looked on the mountains, and behold, they were quaking,
> and all the hills moved to and fro.
> I looked, and behold, there was no man,
> and all the birds of the air had fled.
> I looked, and behold, the fruitful land was a desert,
> and all its cities were laid in ruins
> before the LORD, before his fierce anger.
> For thus says the LORD, "The whole land shall be a desolation; yet
> I will not make a full end.
> "For this the earth shall mourn,
> and the heavens above be dark."

The language should tip off the reader that this is a symbolic literary connection to Genesis 1. He says the earth "was without form and void," the exact same Hebrew words of Genesis 1:1 that described the chaos before God started creating. This obviously is not literal but symbolic since the earth was not physically returned to that chaos state in 586 B.C. when the temple was destroyed. It is a statement of spiritual chaos behind the historical event, not literal physical destruction of the earth.

Jeremiah then describes a kind of emptying of the things of heaven and earth created in the six days of Genesis 1. No more birds in the air undoes the creation on the fifth day. No more vegetation on the earth is an undoing of the third day of creation. The elimination of all humans ("no man") is the elimination of the sixth day of creation. Obviously, all the humans on earth were not killed in 586 B.C. The heavens going dark is a description of the spiritual realm being emptied of the power and influence they were created with on the fourth day. The heavens going dark is an undoing of the first act of creation and a return to the primeval darkness.

In chapter 6, we will see that the Genesis 1 creation is a metaphor for covenantal meaning. So this undoing of creation, or "de-creation," is a concept of spiritual meaning, not scientific observation. Astronomical catastrophe was a literary metaphor used to describe the fall or judgment of both earthly powers and their spiritual principalities, the heavenly host.

In chapter 5 on the ten plagues, we will look more closely at this concept of "decreation" that is a common technique of biblical authors. It becomes a stylistic device to express spiritual chaos that results from earthly wars and destruction.

For more in depth study of the language of cosmic collapse in biblical prophecy, see my book End Times Bible Prophecy: It's Not What They Told You (affiliate link).

Egyptian Magic

Lector-Priests of Heka

It's important for our modern western minds to be careful not to impose our scientific post-Enlightenment worldview upon the ancient world when seeking to understand them in their context. The modern concept of "magic" (outside of actual occult niches) carries the connotation of tricks of illusion or sleight of hand. That is not the ancient Near Eastern understanding of magic and certainly not the Egyptian view. They also did not have our dichotomy of religious spiritual beliefs separated from natural laws and secular life. The ancient Egyptian mind had a more integrated worldview that the gods were very much a part of the operations of the world around them. There was no view of a "natural world" or "laws of nature" apart from spiritual or divine agency. As Egyptologist Robert Ritner explains, to the Egyptian "the activity which he designated 'magic' was felt to be not supernatural but quintessentially a part of nature, being coeval with the creation of the natural order and used daily by the gods to maintain—not violate—that order."[27]

When the Egyptians saw the sun moving across the sky, they understood its activity in terms of the daily crossing of Amon-Ra, the sun god, on his "barque," or sun boat, protected by Thoth from the serpent of chaos, Apophis, in the waters. They conceived of Shu, the air god, holding up Nun, the sky goddess, to keep her from being united with Geb, the god of earth. Their interpretation of the reality behind what they experienced with their physical senses was not mere mythological story, but their way of understanding reality as an integrated interplay between the unseen realm of the gods and the seen realm of creation.

So magic, described as *heka*, was a cosmic force that manipulated reality in this world and the next. But Heka was also a deity in his own right, so the magic practiced by the Egyptians was an appeal through the use of words, objects, and rituals to achieve their goals with Heka's help, much as we use technology to make "nature" do our bidding. To them it wasn't so much supernatural as it was the natural way the world worked.

The common conception of Heka was humanoid in form, but he was supposedly generated by Atum in the beginning of creation. "As detailed in the recitation 'To Become the God Heka' (Coffin Text Spell 261), Heka was believed to have been formed 'before duality had yet come into being' as the force that at once animated, compelled, and protected the gods and subsequent creation."[28]

This is not to say that all Egyptian magic was "real." There were certainly tricks that magicians foisted upon a gullible public. But in the biblical view, there is a spiritual realm and there are deceiving spirits, so there could certainly have also been demonic deception or occult reality behind some of the magic.

The Hebrew word for "magician" was itself an interpretation because the Egyptians did not call themselves magicians. Rather, they used the term "lector-priests." Their operations of magic were a normal part of their religion, thus they were spiritual leaders. "Chief lector-priests" were members of the priestly caste and considered teachers of wisdom. As such, they could operate as advisors to Pharaoh.[29] Because they were heavily reliant upon written

---

27 Robert Kriech Ritner, *The Mechanics of Ancient Egyptian Magical Practice* (Chicago, IL: University of Chicago, 1993, 2008), 8.

28 Donald Redford, Ed. in Chief, *The Oxford Encyclopedia of Ancient Egypt Volume 2* (Oxford, England: Oxford University Press, 2001), 322.

29 John D. Currid, *Ancient Egypt and the Old Testament* (Grand Rapids, MI: Baker Books, 1997), 94.

spells, enchantments, and other formulas, the lector-priests were often scribes as well. The scriptorium where their sacred books and inscriptions were stored was called "The House of Life," and it was usually attached to the local temple of the city.[30]

There is a famous text called the Westcar Papyrus that tells stories of magicians to Pharaoh Khufu of the Old Kingdom 4th Dynasty. One is about the lector-priest Djadja-em-ankh on a boat in a lake with King Snefru and his entourage. A maiden drops a pendant in the lake. In an act reminiscent of the parting of Yam Suph, the lector priest "said his say of magic."

> He placed one side of the lake's water upon the other; and he found the pendant lying on a shard. He brought it and gave it to its owner...Then he said his say of magic and returned the waters of the lake to their place. [31]

The second story is about a lector-priest named Djedi who "said his say of magic" to reconnect the decapitated heads of a goose and an ox to impress the king. When he is taken into the palace, he prophesies about the three children who will succeed the crown. So in Egyptian magic, the utterance of words in a proper tone by a qualified priest could be efficacious. Those same words could be written upon papyrus, stone, or amulets to transmit their effect for the owner. But as Ritner cautions, "Nonetheless, speech alone cannot be considered the totality of heka...The ritual as well as the spell is crucial for the success of magic."[32] Egyptian magic was not mere propositions but a tactile and actionable cult.

In the confrontations between Moses and Aaron and the Egyptian lector-priests, Scripture makes it clear that Moses does not use spells, incantations, or words of magic to call forth God's miraculous power. But scholar Scott Noegel itemizes Yahweh's signs and wonders as deliberately mirroring well-known Egyptian magical practices. He explains this as a polemical tactic whereby Yahweh subverts the entire system of Egyptian belief within its own context.[33]

Let's take a look at some of that polemical mirroring.

---

[30] A. H. Gardiner, "The House of Life," *The Journal of Egyptian Archaeology*, 24(1), (1938), 157–179.

[31] Miriam Lichtheim, *Ancient Egyptian Literature: Volume I: The Old and Middle Kingdoms* (Berkeley: University of California Press, 1973–), 216-222.

[32] Ritner, *The Mechanics of Ancient Egyptian Magic,* 38.

[33] Scott B. Noegel, "Moses and Magic: Notes on the Book of Exodus," *Journal of the Ancient Near Eastern Society* 24 (1996), 45-59.

Staff of Moses, Rod of God

The staff of Moses became a powerful symbol of the confrontation of Yahweh and Moses with Pharaoh and the magicians of Egypt. Moses's staff was a humble shepherd's crook from his time in Midian (Exodus 3:1). Yet Yahweh would use it to mock the power of Pharaoh, the magicians, and their gods in several different ways.

In Egypt, the gods were often depicted as carrying "holy staffs" that symbolized their power and authority over the people. As Abraham Yahuda explains, "There were various types of rods for magical purposes, tipped with the heads of various gods and named after them, thus a 'holy rod of Aaron', a 'rod of Khnum', a 'rod of Amon-Ra', a 'rod of Horus of Edfu', a 'rod of Hathor' and many others.[34] In Moses's story, his staff is sometimes called "the rod of God" or "the staff of Elohim" (Exodus 4:20; 17:9).

But Pharaoh had a staff as well. It was a symbol of his royal power and authority. John Currid points out the ancient Pyramid Texts describing the king receiving his staff at his coronation, representing the symbol of his royal power and authority over all of Egypt.

> Stand (as king) over it, over this land which has come forth from Atum…
> Be (king) over it; be high over it…
> He comes to thee, O Re [Ra]…
> Let him grasp the Heavens
> And receive the Horizon;
> Let him dominate the Nine Bows
> And equip (with offerings) the Ennead.
> Give the crook into his hand.
> So that the head of Lower and Upper Egypt shall be bowed.[35]

Currid explains that the magicians of Egypt also carried staffs in order to perform the acts of magic:

> It is recorded that when attacked by enemies, the magician-king Nectanebo II (c. 360–343 BC) turned wax figures of soldiers and ships into an animate force by means of a magical rod. Numerous scarabs attest to that practice by containing scenes of magicians holding rods in their hands

---

[34] Quoted in John D. Currid, *Against the Gods: The Polemical Theology of the Old Testament* (Wheaton, IL: Crossway, 2013), 113.

[35] Pyramid Texts 196–203. Quoted in Currid, *Against the Gods*, 114.

> that could instantly be turned into snakes. Wallis Budge claims that the practice of rod divination operated among the magicians of Egypt and refers to "from time immemorial…a wonderful rod of which they worked wonders."[36]

In the Westcar Papyrus, we also read about Webaoner, a lector-priest who turns a wax figure of a crocodile into a real creature.[37] So transformation of objects into living creatures was a well-known tradition in Egyptian magic.

With all three of these institutional figures of gods, pharaohs, and magicians employing staffs, it becomes quite deliberately ironic and subversive that Yahweh would use the very iconic emblem that symbolized Egyptian power and authority to first humiliate, then divest them of all power and authority. Aaron's staff was miraculously turned into a snake that swallowed the magicians' staffs-turned-to-snakes (Exodus 7:9-12). Significantly, the text doesn't say that Aaron's *snake* swallowed the magicians' *snakes*, but rather that his "*staff* swallowed up their *staffs*" (7:12), which draws attention to that deified power and authority being swallowed by God. Swallowing was a common Egyptian magical concept of absorbing an opponent's essence or vital force.[38]

In his book on Egyptian magic, Robert Ritner explains, "Consumption entails the absorption of an object and the acquisition of its benefits or traits. Alternatively, the act can serve a principally hostile function, whereby 'to devour' signifies 'to destroy'—though even here the concept of acquiring power may be retained."[39]

Noegel gives some examples from Egyptian texts of this magical swallowing:

> Pyramid Texts (ca. 2400 BCE): "(King) Unas is one who eats men and lives on the gods…Unas eats their ḥeka, swallows their spirits" (spell 273).
> Coffin Texts: "I have swallowed the seven uraei-serpents" (spell 612), and "I have eaten truth (lit. Maat), I have swallowed ḥeka" (spell 1017).[40]

---

36 Currid, *Against the Gods*, 117.

37 Currid, *Against the Gods*, 29.

38 Currid, *Against the Gods*, 118.

39 Ritner, *The Mechanics of Ancient Egyptian Magic*, 103.

40 Scott B. Noegel, "The Egyptian 'Magicians'" *The Torah.com* https://www.thetorah.com/article/the-egyptian-magicians

Moses also used that same staff raised or struck to turn the Nile to blood (7:20), draw forth the plagues of frogs (8:5), gnats (8:17), hail (9:23), locusts (10:13-14), and ultimately to split the sea for crossing (14:16). Though Yahweh did not need a magic item to accomplish his miracles, he clearly worked within the symbolic system of Egyptian magic to prove that he was God of gods, king of kings, and, one might add with tongue in cheek, "Magician of magicians."

I quote Currid again at length for his profound summary conclusion:

> What the rod confrontation portrays is…a heavenly combat—a war between the God of the Hebrews and the deities of Egypt. For the biblical writer, the whole episode of Israel in Egypt was a matter of theology. It was a question of who was the one true God, who was sovereign over the operation of the universe, and whose will was to come to pass in heaven and upon earth.[41]

An additional element of this polemic is found in the fact that the staffs were turned into serpents. Noegel points out that this could *not* be the classic "snake charming" technique because such procedures were achieved through touching the serpent's head, whereas Moses picked it up by its tail (Exodus 4:4). But the particular Hebrew word for serpent in the story (*nachash*) could be a reference to the uraeus of power represented on Pharaoh's crown as a cobra poised to strike. The uraeus was a symbol of the cobra goddess Wadjet, who protected the king with her magic. So the swallowing of the serpents represented Yahweh's removal of the king's divine protection.[42]

In another article, Noegel lists multiple Egyptian paintings on coffins, tombs, and temples depicting both magicians and various gods carrying serpent staffs as emblems of their magical power. The several different gods include Heka (magic) as well as Horus, Thoth, Nehy, and Sekhmet.[43]

The giant serpent of chaos, Apophis, was known to be the hostile enemy of Ra as the sun god sought to drive his solar boat across the heavens. Yahweh was suppressing the agent of chaos that Ra had to deal with each day. When Moses "cast down" his staff (Exodus 7:8-9), this was a common phrase of Egyptian magicians in acts of exorcism and spells.[44]

---

[41] Currid, *Against the Gods*, 118.

[42] Noegel, "Moses and Magic," 47.

[43] Noegel, "The Egyptian 'Magicians'" https://www.thetorah.com/article/the-egyptian-magicians

[44] Noegel, "Moses and Magic," 48.

Execration and the Song of the Sea

In addition to the confrontation of serpent staffs, another mirror of Egyptian magical rhetoric is found in Moses's Song of the Sea in Exodus 15. It reflects a common magical practice of execration texts well-known in Egyptology. The magician would transfer the power and identity of one's enemy onto clay images or pottery. They would write the enemy's deeds or traits upon the object, then bury it, burn it, or smash it to pieces.

All these elements are found in the language of Exodus 15. The description of the Egyptians' impious statements and actions are listed in standard Egyptian pattern;

> Exodus 15:9
> The enemy said, "I will pursue, I will overtake,
> I will divide the spoil, my desire shall have its fill of them.
> I will draw my sword; my hand shall destroy them."

Then Yahweh's right hand "shatters the foe," "smashes his opponents" (15:6-7), words more conducive to execration than merely drowning. In 15:12, that drowning is described unusually as "the earth swallowed them," rather than the waters—just like an execration burial. And 15:7 proclaims out of context from the water, "You send forth Your burning anger, and it consumes them as chaff." Noegel concludes, "Like execration victims, then, Pharaoh's army is smashed, crushed, burned, and buried."[45]

The ultimate goal of execration was terror, fear, and dread in the enemy's hearts. So the Song of the Sea concludes with such execration language:

> Exodus 15:14–16
> The peoples have heard; they <u>tremble</u>;
>   <u>pangs have seized</u> the inhabitants of Philistia.
> Now are the chiefs of Edom <u>dismayed</u>;
>   <u>trembling seizes</u> the leaders of Moab;
>   all the inhabitants of Canaan have <u>melted away</u>.
> Terror and dread fall upon them.

The Finger of God

When Yahweh refers to his own actions, he uses the phrase "hand of God" (Exodus 3:19-20; 6:1). But when the Egyptian magicians become overwhelmed and unable to replicate Yahweh's wonders, they cry out with an

---

[45] Noegel, "Moses and Magic," 57.

Egyptian idiom, "This is the finger of God!" (8:19), a phrase they would use of their own god's performative powers (Finger of Thoth, Finger of Seth).[46]

The Bronze Serpent

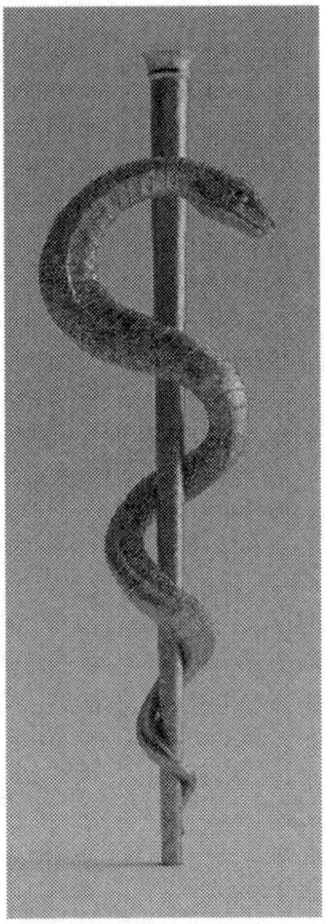

Numbers 21:4-9 is the story of the bronze serpent called Nehushtan (2 Kings 18:4). The Hebrews have crossed the sea and are now in the wilderness. Almost immediately, they begin complaining. "Why have you brought us up out of Egypt to die in the wilderness? For there is no food and no water, and we loathe this worthless food" (21:5). So Yahweh punishes them by sending "fiery" serpents into their midst, and many Israelites die. As explained earlier, "fiery serpents" was a way of describing the venomous bite of poisonous snakes. The irony is not lost on the reader that those fiery serpents represent the Pharaoh's power to which the Israelites want to return. Whoever said God is not sarcastic has not read the Old Testament very closely.

When the Israelites repent, Yahweh tells Moses, "Make a fiery serpent and set it on a pole, and everyone who is bitten, when he sees it, shall live" (21:8). He does so, and the Israelites are saved. A closer look reveals that this is yet another incident of Yahweh appropriating notions of Egyptian magic that the Israelites were used to and using them in a polemical way to make his point.

The bronze serpent operated as a standard or ensign. The use of standards was commonplace in Egypt as symbolic heralds of royalty, divinity and military. They might be carried in royal parades, in temples, or into war with troops. John Currid explains: "The principal purpose of the standards was to serve as a physical repository of the power of the gods. That is to say, these poles were empowered with the divine force. In reality, the gods were thought to be embodied in the standards."[47] To Egyptians, this did not merely mean symbolic representation but that standards were an actual carrier of the power of deity. For example, "a scene on the exterior north side and west end of Rameses III's funerary temple at Medinet Habu pictures the king going into battle on his chariot. Before him is a chariot bearing the standard of Amon. An

---

[46] Noegel, "The Egyptian 'Magicians'" https://www.thetorah.com/article/the-egyptian-magicians

[47] John D. Currid, *Ancient Egypt and the Old Testament* (Grand Rapids, MI: Baker Books, 1997), 151.

inscription over the standard reads: 'Utterance of Amon-Re, king of gods: 'Lo, I am before thee, my son, lord of the Two Lands.''"[48]

Frequently, the uraeus was engraved onto the standard as Pharaoh's glorious protector. They were used in battle, in coronation, and in other situations that would provoke either blessing or curse, depending on its use—a sure reflection of the operation of the bronze serpent Nehushtan.

Even more so, the bronze serpent was reminiscent of the Egyptian practice of fashioning images of threatening creatures like snakes, crocodiles, or scorpions as images of power to protect the user from the creatures or to be used as a magical protection *by* those creatures. Yahweh used a commonly understood form of Egyptian magic with a serpentine symbol of Pharaoh's power to show Yahweh's omnipotent power and authority.

The Egyptian Underworld

In the novel *Moses*, I tell the story of a lector priest having a dream vision of a journey to the underworld on the solar boat of Ra. The Egyptians called this underworld the Duat. The Bible calls it Sheol and Hades. Like Sheol, Duat was the place of the dead in an unseen realm called the underworld. But unlike Sheol, Duat was technically not below the surface of the earth. It was actually considered to be to the West, or more specifically accessed in the West, where the sun of Ra set. That access was through an opening in the great mountain range that surrounded Egypt as the center of the world and held up the sky. Duat was actually a valley that followed that circular disc of mountains with another chain of mountains on its other side. Like the Nile in Egypt, a river ran through the netherworld called the Wernes (or Urnes).[49] The Egyptians believed that the solar boat of Ra that carried the sun traveled through the Duat underworld during the twelve hours of the night to arrive back in the east for its morning rising.

For this journey in the novel, I drew from three of the most influential Egyptian texts of the afterlife, The Book of the Dead, The Amduat and the Book of Gates. While there are similarities between these books, they are not in agreement over what happens to the "Ba" soul of the dead or the solar boat of Ra on their passage through that netherworld region. In fact, they are not in agreement over much at all. Frankly, the Egyptian view of the afterlife

---

[48] Currid, *Ancient Egypt*, 152.

[49] E.A. Wallis Budge, *The Egyptian Heaven and Hell: The Contents of the Books of the Other World Described and Compared* (Lasalle, IL, Open Court Publishing, 1905), 88-90, 111.

presented in these documents is a confusing contradictory mess. So in the novel I simplified and picked elements from the texts that would tell the most entertaining narrative of the journey while communicating some of the significant themes of the mythology. I created order out of the chaos![50]

The Egyptian Book of the Dead, known to its original readers as the Book of Going Forth by Day is the most well-known to westerners. Its origin is ancient, sometime before Menes the first king of Egypt. It is essentially a book of close to two hundred spells for the dead to use on their tour through Duat, protecting and providing for various needs in the afterlife on their way to judgment or resurrection. Some spells guard against demons, or monsters like Apophis, the serpent of chaos. Some spells are intended to preserve and regenerate the physical corpse of the individual in order to return to it. And some spells help prepare the person to face the judgment hall of Osiris where their hearts will be weighed against the feather of Ma'at or justice.[51]

The Book of the Dead was originally applied exclusively to kings and then other rulers. It was painted on walls of tombs and on coffins so that the deceased royalty would have access to the spells in the Duat. As dynasties passed, such access was allowed to lesser mortals and those who could not afford tomb art would have a scroll of the book buried with their mummy.

The Amduat and Book of Gates both originate around the time of Moses, before the New Kingdom era. Both books tell a narrative of the expedition of the sun god Ra on his solar boat or barque through the twelve gates of Duat that each represent the twelve hours of the night. But whereas the Amduat focuses on the journey of Ra, the Book of Gates includes the deceased king (or later, any individual) in that quest. So the king or individual identifies with Ra in his death and resurrection from setting to rising, an ancient Egyptian version of the hero's journey.

Egyptian scholar Erik Hornung describes that heroic narrative this way:

> The book begins with the entry of the sun god, as a ram-headed ba ("soul"), into the interstitial realm of the first hour of the night, and it ends with his rebirth in the morning, after uniting with his corpse in the middle of his journey in the

---

[50] My sources were: Erik Hornung, *The Ancient Egyptian Books of the Afterlife* (Ithaca, NY, Cornell University, 1999); Garry J. Shaw. *The Egyptian Myths* (Kindle Edition). Thames and Hudson Ltd.; E.A. Wallis Budge, *The Egyptian Heaven and Hell: The Contents of the Books of the Other World Described and Compared* (Lasalle, IL, Open Court Publishing, 1905); Andreas Schweizer, trans. Erik Hornung, *The Sungod's Journey Through the Netherworld: Reading the Ancient Egyptian Amduat* (Ithaca, NY, Cornell University Press, 1994, 2010).

[51] Erik Hornung, *The Ancient Egyptian Books of the Afterlife* (Ithaca, NY, Cornell University, 1999) 17-12.

> sixth hour and overcoming the menacing serpent Apophis in the seventh hour.[52]

The midpoint of the night, the sixth hour (the sixth gate), marks the lowest depth of the underworld, from which the sun is united with Osiris and is reborn to begin his final half of his journey toward resurrection.

In the Amduat, it is in the seventh hour that the nemesis Apophis, that ancient sea serpent of chaos who had been held at bay until now, is fought and conquered by the gods on the barque (the tenth hour in the Book of Gates). They dismember him and render him powerless.[53]

This results in the Judgment of the Dead before the throne of Osiris. The blessed dead are on the steps of Osiris and the damned are consigned to the Place of Annihilation beneath his feet.[54] This is where we find a Lake of Fire for the punishment of the wicked, called the Second Death, an ancient precursor to the Lake of Fire and Second Death spoken of in the New Testament book of Revelation 20:10, 14-15. Egyptian scholar Andreas Schweizer explains the illustrations of the Amduat, one of the Egyptian afterlife texts on a tomb wall,

> The Lake of Fire is depicted in the lower register of the fifth hour of the Amduat. Beginning in the Middle Kingdom, with the Book of the Two Ways, the Lake of Fire was part of the topography of the netherworld. Its water annihilates the damned.[55]

The terms Lake of Fire and Second Death are found nowhere else in the Bible or other ancient Near Eastern literature, suggesting a strong link between the Egyptian and Hebrew concepts.

Hornung summarizes the psycho-spiritual connection to the inner human exploration that this divine quest through the underworld describes:

> The nightly journey of the sun is the focus of all the Books of the Netherworld, and consistent with this, it also furnishes

---

[52] Hornung, *The Ancient Egyptian Books,* 34.

[53] Hornung, *The Ancient Egyptian Books,* 38, 64.

[54] Hornung, *The Ancient Egyptian Books,* 62.

[55] Andreas Schweizer, trans. Erik Hornung, *The Sungod's Journey Through the Netherworld: Reading the Ancient Egyptian Amduat* (Ithaca, NY, Cornell University Press, 1994, 2010) 216.

"The phrase "to die the second death" (mt m whm) occurs frequently in the Coffin Texts and the Book of the Dead (Zandee, Death, 186–88; Faulkner, Coffin Texts 1:88 [spell 83]; 1:134 [spell 156]; 1:267 [spell 203]; 2:69 [spell 423]; 2:76 [spell 438]; 2:88 [spell 458]; 2:308 [spell 787]), referring to the total destruction of the ba, "soul," after bodily death. David E. Aune, *Revelation 17–22, vol. 52C, Word Biblical Commentary* (Dallas: Word, Incorporated, 1998), 1092.

the ordering and creative principle for the spaces in the hereafter. This nocturnal regeneration of the sun demonstrates, by way of example, what powers of renewal are at work on the far side of death. At the same time, the journey occurs in the spaces of the human soul, in which a renewal from the depths becomes possible. That it is an odyssey of the soul is emphasized by the Egyptians through the indication that the sun god descends into the depths as a *ba*-soul (and thus is ram-headed, since *ba* is also the word for ram); herein lie significant antecedents of modern psychotherapy.[56]

---

56 Hornung, *The Ancient Egyptian Books,* 27.

Chapter 4
The Gods of Egypt

The history of Egypt is a history of gods and kings. There were over 2,000 deities in the Egyptian pantheon. These evolved over the centuries and between provinces within Egypt such that there is no single canon of stories or interpretations. I quote Egyptologist Garry Shaw at length on their divine narrative world:

> The Egyptian gods are a vibrant and eclectic group; they squabble, fight, murder, form relationships and can die of old age (before being reborn, illustrative of the Egyptian love of cyclical time). They could also manifest in a variety of forms, in various locations simultaneously, whilst their true selves remained distant and invisible in the sky; though malleable in form, they were, nevertheless, neither omniscient nor omnipresent. Charged with specific divine responsibilities (Osiris for regeneration, Min for fertility, for example), they were restricted in their powers, and had to merge with each other to share each other's powers for a short time, if they needed to achieve a goal beyond their cosmic remit: thus, lacking the ability and power to re-energize himself, the ailing sun god merges with Osiris each night, using this god's regenerative force to enable him to be born again in a new dawn. Sometimes, when one god assumed the characteristics of another, (s)he transformed into that other deity; so, when Hathor, as Eye of Re [Ra], attacked mankind, her violent rage transformed her into the overtly bloodthirsty goddess Sekhmet.[1]

My sampling here will be based on connections to the biblical story of the Exodus. Additional gods appear in the novel *Moses: Against the Gods of Egypt*.

---

[1] Garry J. Shaw. *The Egyptian Myths* (Kindle Locations 146-154). Thames and Hudson Ltd.

Pharaoh

I have previously explained that I am following David Rohl's New Chronology for Egypt's history, which argues for a 1447 B.C. date of the Exodus and therefore, Khaneferre Sobekhotep IV as Moses's adopted father and Djedneferre Dudimose as the Pharaoh of the Exodus. But in this section on the gods of Egypt, I want to examine the office of Pharaoh as divine and how Yahweh interacted with it.

From earliest of days, the king/Pharaoh was considered to be the incarnation of the god Horus, the son of Ra on earth. As god-man, the king was the royal mediator between the gods and humans. But his divinity was expressed in different ways for different purposes. For instance, he was also considered begotten of the creator Amon-Ra through the queen mother. "As regards his divine potency, he was Horus, the son of [the goddess] Hathor. As the legitimate successor to the throne (a notion with cosmic implications), he was Horus the son of Osiris and Isis, the grandson of Geb, the earth."[2] His titles were often grand titles of divinity that might include such epithets as these:

> Horus (the god of Lower Egypt)
> Son of Ra (the sun god)
> The Two Ladies (a manifestation of Wadjet, cobra goddess of Lower Egypt, and Nekhbet, vulture goddess of Upper Egypt)
> The Two Lords (a manifestation of the gods Horus of Lower Egypt and Set of Upper Egypt)
> Divine of Forms
> Divine of Births[3]

As Frankfort points out, in many Egyptian texts Pharaoh is simply called "the god," "the great god," or "the good god."[4] As we will see below, one of the founding myths of Egypt was of Horus ascending the throne as "Lord of Heaven." So Pharaoh ascends to the throne of Egypt as Horus on earth.

But just as Horus's father Osiris died and was resurrected to become Lord of the Underworld, so when a Pharaoh died, he became Osiris and his successor became the new Horus. The Egyptians had complex ceremonies for

---

2 Henri Frankfort, *Kingship and the Gods: A Study of Ancient Near Eastern Religion as the Integration of Society & Nature* (Chicago, IL: University of Chicago Press, 1948, 1978), 299.

3 Frankfort, *Kingship and the Gods,* 46.

4 Frankfort, *Kingship and the Gods,* 36, 39.

that succession, of which Frankfort concludes: "Better than any other feature of Egyptian kingship, it shows that the monarchy was conceived as a reality in the world of the gods no less than in the world of men."[5]

As god, Pharaoh was responsible to maintain "ma'at," which "meant the 'right order'- the inherent structure of creation, of which justice is an integral part."[6] Ma'at was also personified as a goddess of that cosmic order. Egypt had a troubled history of conflict and hostility between its northern (Lower Egypt) and southern (Upper Egypt) halves. Menes, the first pharaoh to bring unity between the "Two Lands" of Upper and Lower Egypt, established an essential responsibility of the king as being a unifier that would last for three thousand years of dynastic kingship. As Frankfort explains,

> That form was the dual monarchy, the kingship of Upper and the kingship of Lower Egypt united in the single person of the ruler. This extraordinary conception expressed in political form the deeply rooted Egyptian tendency to understand the world in dualistic terms as a series of pairs of contrasts balanced in unchanging equilibrium. The universe as a whole was referred to as "heaven and earth." Within this concept "earth" was again conceived dualistically, as "north and south," the "portions of Horus and the portions of Seth," "the two lands," or "the two (Nile) banks."[7]

The Serpent

One of the signifying elements of Egyptian deity was the uraeus, the image of a cobra in striking position that was on the crown of Pharaoh. The serpent diadem symbolized all power, sovereignty, and magic residing in the king. It also represented the guardian goddesses of Upper and Lower Egypt, Wadjet and Nekhbet. The uraeus was a symbol of Pharaoh's venomous power to be both respected and feared in the hearts of all. From the Bible's perspective, of course, this serpentine divinity was an apt incarnation of the seed of the Serpent at war with the seed of Eve.

Because of the cobra's venomous bite, it was called "Fiery One" or "fiery snake," which gives context to the fiery snakes that attacked the Hebrews in the wilderness.[8] They were not snakes that were on fire. Rather, they were most likely cobras with bites that burned like fire. Perhaps their launched

---

[5] Frankfort, *Kingship and the Gods,* 33.

[6] Frankfort, *Kingship and the Gods,* 51.

[7] Frankfort, *Kingship and the Gods,* 19.

[8] John D. Currid, *Ancient Egypt and the Old Testament* (Grand Rapids, MI: Baker Books, 1997), 91–93.

attacks made it look as though they were flying. Though it is interesting to point out that ancient authors do claim that these snakes did actually fly in the air.[9]

But this serpentine symbol of the uraeus also gives more context to the meaning of Moses's staff-turned-to-snake that gobbled up the pharaonic staffs-turned-to-snakes. John Currid writes: "The Egyptians described Pharaoh as eternal, worthy of worship, and omniscient; he imbued Egypt with existence and power. They taught that he was *ka*, the life force and soul of Egypt. And the serpent-crested coronet symbolized his deification and majesty. When Moses had Aaron fling the rod-snake before Pharaoh, he was directly assaulting that token of pharaonic sovereignty—the scene was one of polemical taunting."[10] And I might add, one of many echoes in Scripture of "crushing the serpent's head."[11] The divine ophidian protectors of Egypt were about to be eaten, head first.

Egyptologist John Currid argues that this serpent confrontation "is also paradigmatic in that it defines for the reader the true issue at stake in the entire Exodus struggle. The hostilities were not primarily between Moses and Pharaoh, or between Moses and the Egyptian magicians, or for that matter between Israel and Egypt. What the serpent contest portrays is a heavenly combat—a war between the God of the Hebrews and the deities of Egypt."[12]

Strong Right Arm

Another way that Yahweh mocks Pharaoh's divine claims is in his usage of "strong right arm." The concept of a strong arm of Pharaoh begins in the Middle Kingdom around the 12th Dynasty and is often used in royal and military inscriptions. Dudimose, our Exodus pharaoh, was in the 13th Dynasty, so the phrase would have been common by then. Senusret I is described as "a mighty man who achieves with his strong arm a champion without equal." Hyksos kings Apophis and Thutmose IV are both described as "possessor of a strong arm." Thutmose II bore the Golden Horus name "Great of Power, Mighty of Arm." Thutmose III's military victories are

---

9 See SIDEBAR: "Moses's Kushite Campaign and Flying Snakes" in this book, Chapter 2.

10 Currid, *Ancient Egypt*, 93–94. Some have argued that the fiery flying serpents (*seraph nachash*) of Numbers 21:6, Isaiah 14:29 and 30:6 were these cobras because when they prepared to strike, their hoods stretched out and looked like wings.

11 James Hamilton, "The Skull Crushing Seed of the Woman: Inner-Biblical Interpretation of Genesis 3:15" *The Southern Baptist Journal of Theology* · *SBJT* 10/2 (Summer 2006) https://sbts-wordpress-uploads.s3.amazonaws.com/equip/uploads/2010/07/sbjt_102_sum06-hamilton.pdf

12 John D. Currid, *Ancient Egypt and the Old Testament* (Grand Rapids, MI: Baker Books, 1997), 86.

described as "…victory with my very own arm." Amenhotep III's Golden Horus name was "Great of Arm, Smiter of Asiatics." Amenhotep II was he "who smites foreign rulers of the far north, he is a god whose arm is great."[13]

Yahweh himself draws on this "strong arm/hand" imagery to describe Pharaoh in an almost affirming way:

> Exodus 6:1
> But the LORD said to Moses, "Now you shall see what I will do to Pharaoh; for with a strong hand he will send them out, and with a strong hand he will drive them out of his land."

We see that this description of Pharaoh's "strong hand" is only a set up for Yahweh to mock Pharaoh because God then uses that same language of "mighty hand" or "outstretched arm/hand" of power to describe Yahweh's own action against the king.[14]

> Exodus 6:6
> I am the LORD, and I will bring you out from under the burdens of the Egyptians, and I will deliver you from slavery to them, and I will redeem you with an outstretched arm and with great acts of judgment.

> Exodus 3:19–20
> But I know that the king of Egypt will not let you go unless compelled by a mighty hand. So I will stretch out my hand and strike Egypt with all the wonders that I will do in it; after that he will let you go.

Egyptologist James Hoffmeier concludes that this arm wrestling contest between Yahweh and Pharaoh was like a final match of ultimate power:

> What better way for the exodus traditions to describe God's victory over Pharaoh, and as a result his superiority, than to use Hebrew derivations or counterparts to Egyptian expressions that symbolized Egyptian royal power. The drama of the exodus narratives in describing the struggle between God and Pharaoh's arms is heightened when it is realized that the arm of the Egyptian king was thought to be

---

[13] James K. Hoffmeier, "The Arm of God Versus the Arm of Pharaohin the Exodus Narratives," *Biblica* Vol. 67, No. 3 (1986), pp. 378-387.

[14] Hoffmeier notes that the Hebrew words for "hand" and "arm" are yād and zerod', and "both mean hand or arm, but metaphorically mean power or strength." Hoffmeier, "The Arm of God," 379. These terms are used all over the text: Exod 3:19; 6:6; 13:3; 14:16; 32:11; Deut 9:29; 26:8; 3:14; 6:21; 9:26.

> infused with strength of the supreme god Amun, or the war gods Seth or Montu.[15]

God is essentially saying that Pharaoh is not God. Yahweh is God. In fact, Yahweh's strong arm drowns the "god" Pharaoh like all storm gods defeat the sea god of chaos.

> Exodus 15:4–6
> Pharaoh's chariots and his host [Yahweh] cast into the sea, and his chosen officers were sunk in Yam Suph. The floods covered them; they went down into the depths like a stone. Your right hand, O LORD, glorious in power, your right hand, O LORD, shatters the enemy.

Though the Bible does not say explicitly that Pharaoh was drowned with his army,[16] it was standard practice for him to lead his chariots into battle, and Exodus 14:28 affirms that "not one" of the host of Pharaoh's chariots and horsemen remained. Josephus implies that Pharaoh was killed in the waves: "And thus did all these men perish, so that there was not one man left to be a messenger of this calamity to the rest of the Egyptians."[17] "Not one man left," not even Pharaoh.

Thus Says a God

Another expression that Yahweh uses against the god-king of Egypt is, "Thus says..." Bible readers are familiar with this phrase from the mouths of prophets speaking for Yahweh. But those books were written long after the time of Moses. In fact, the very first time God uses the phrase "Thus says the Lord [Yahweh]," is in Exodus 4:22 in relation to Moses's confrontation with Pharaoh.

Why would that be?

Egyptians and their Hebrew captives were already familiar with the phrase "thus says" as an authoritative utterance of deity within their culture. For example, in the Egyptian Book of the Dead, a section called "The Primeval

---

[15] Hoffmeier, "The Arm of God," 387.

[16] One possible exception is Exodus 15:19 that seems to indicate a distinction between Pharaoh's horse (singular) and all the chariots and horsemen (plural) going into the sea. "For the horse of Pharao went in with the chariots and horsemen into the sea, and the Lord brought upon them the water of the sea" (Brenton LXX).

[17] Josephus, Antiquities of the Jews 2.16.3 (344) Flavius Josephus and William Whiston, *The Works of Josephus: Complete and Unabridged* (Peabody: Hendrickson, 1987), 76.

Establishment of Order," the creator god Atum uses the authoritative phrase "Thus spoke Atum" several times.[18]

In Exodus 5:1, Yahweh tells Moses to speak to Pharaoh: "Thus says Yahweh, the God of Israel, 'Let my people go.'" The Egyptian taskmasters use the same language in their rebellious response: "Thus says Pharaoh, 'I will not give you straw'" (5:10). The contest of gods begins in the language of divine verbal utterance. Yahweh would soon mock every element of that spiritual authority of both Pharaoh and the gods that would climax in the ten plagues.

Pharaoh as Dragon

In the sixth century B.C., the prophet Ezekiel spoke Yahweh's word of judgment upon Pharaoh Hophra. He likened the pharaoh to a "dragon" (*tannin* in Hebrew) lying in the Nile.[19] The Nile river was the boast of Egypt's greatness. There were many deities connected to it, one of them being Sobek the crocodile god. So Ezekiel most likely used that divine imagery of Pharaoh as Sobek lying proudly in the waters.

> Ezekiel 29:3–6
> Thus says the Lord GOD: "Behold, I am against you, Pharaoh king of Egypt, the great dragon that lies in the midst of his streams, that says, "My Nile is my own; I made it for myself." I will put hooks in your jaws…and I will draw you up out of the midst of your streams...And I will cast you out into the wilderness...To the beasts of the earth and to the birds of the heavens I give you as food. Then all the inhabitants of Egypt shall know that I am the LORD.

This will be explored in more detail in the chapter on Leviathan. But we see here that Yahweh likens the pharaoh to the reptilian god Sobek so that Yahweh's subjugation of him is that much more humiliating. Another possibility is that this *tannin* is a reference to Apophis, the serpent of chaos that waits in the waters to attack the sun god's solar boat. We will discuss Apophis in chapter 6. But the point here is that the reptilian "god" is nothing more than Yahweh's fishing catch. That river of glory and power is just a stream of dishonor.

---

[18] James Bennett Pritchard, ed., *The Ancient Near Eastern Texts Relating to the Old Testament , 3rd ed. with Supplement* (Princeton: Princeton University Press, 1969), 9.

[19] John Day, *God's Conflict with the Dragon and the Sea: Echoes of a Canaanite Myth in the Old Testament* (Cambridge University Press, 1985), 94-95.

But Ezekiel's prophecy goes one step further in that it likens the Egyptian "god" to Leviathan, well known to the Hebrews as a dragon (*tannin*) of chaos that is described as hooked by Yahweh (Job 41:1-2) and eaten in the wilderness of the Exodus (Psalm 74:13-14). Ezekiel is saying that this so-called god of Egyptian order is actually a creature of chaos that Yahweh will hook, reel in, and give as food to scavengers. The predator is actually the prey.

Hardening Pharaoh's Heart

One of the controversial phrases repeated throughout the Exodus story is that of God "hardening Pharaoh's heart."[20] The action has to do with Pharaoh not allowing the Hebrews to leave Egypt even for a mere three days journey into the desert to sacrifice to their God. It is depicted as Yahweh controlling Pharaoh's will in order to achieve God's purposes of displaying his power and glory.

> Exodus 4:21–23
> And the LORD said to Moses, "When you go back to Egypt, see that you do before Pharaoh all the miracles that I have put in your power. But <u>I will harden his heart, so that he will not let the people go</u>. Then you shall say to Pharaoh, 'Thus says the LORD, Israel is my firstborn son, and I say to you, "Let my son go that he may serve me." If you refuse to let him go, behold, I will kill your firstborn son.'"

For Christians who believe that God does not violate the free will of autonomous humans, this becomes a theological difficulty because it clearly negates the heart of their definition of free will. They believe that if God changes the heart of an individual, then they are no longer free. If God can have any control over a person's will, then God is in some way a puppet-master. They believe that the final causation of a human's will must be rooted in the human person themselves and not in God or that would make God unfair or unjust in some way.

In the ancient Near Eastern mind of Moses and his contemporaries, there was no such conceptual separation of human autonomy from divine control. Behind the actions, good or evil, of humans, Yahweh was the ultimate causal agent of it all.

---

[20] Exodus 4:21; 7:3; 9:12; 10:1, 20, 27; 14:4, 8.

> Exodus 5:22–23
> Then Moses turned to the LORD and said, "O Lord, why have you done evil to this people? Why did you ever send me? For since I came to Pharaoh to speak in your name, he has done evil to this people, and you have not delivered your people at all."

Notice the exact equivalency of language used, "done evil to this people." In context, the same acts of bondage and refusal had both the human agency of Pharaoh and the divine agency of Yahweh. Pharaoh was certainly considered responsible for his evil, but God was considered to be sovereignly determining Pharaoh's actions.[21]

I have written more extensively on the biblical theological issue of God's sovereignty,[22] so I will focus here on other ramifications related to the spiritual warfare theme.

Egyptologist John Currid sets the stage for the Egyptian understanding of the heart in this story:

> Ancient Egyptian sacred texts taught that the heart (*i'b*) was the essence of the person. The *i'b* was to be distinguished from the *ba* ("soul, spirit, body") and the *ka* ("a manifestation of the vital energy"), which were both complex and broad concepts. The *i'b* was the inner spiritual center of the self. It was arguably the most important part of the human in ancient Egyptian religion.[23]

The Egyptian Book of the Dead (called by Egyptians "The Book of Going Forth By Day") depicts the judgment hall of the underworld god Osiris "in which hearts are weighed" against the feather of justice. If it was too heavy, the sinner would be judged. It tells the journey of a scribe named Ani to the underworld where he must be judged for his deeds.[24] In different vignettes of illustrations, "the deceased is represented: (1) seated, and addressing his heart, which stands on a support; (2) standing, holding in his hands a heart, which he

---

[21] This is the same kind of "dual agency" behind individual human acts that is attested in Genesis 50:20 when Joseph says to his brothers who sold him into slavery, "As for you, you meant evil against me, but God meant it for good, to bring it about that many people should be kept alive, as they are today." Joseph considered the single act of being sold into slavery to have two separate agencies and intents, both human and divine. This is a ubiquitous view throughout the entire Old Testament.

[22] See my article, "Whatsoever Comes to Pass: A Personal Pilgrimage Towards God's Sovereignty" https://godawa.com/wp/wp-content/uploads/2019/04/Whatsoever-Comes-to-Pass.pdf

[23] John D. Currid, *Ancient Egypt and the Old Testament* (Grand Rapids, MI: Baker Books, 1997), 96.

[24] Though Ani was a scribe, and not a Pharaoh, Pharaohs were routinely embalmed with pages of the Book of Dead woven into their wrapping or sarcophagus. These were made individually for the deceased.

offers to three deities. Another vignette represents a priest tying a heart on to a statue of the deceased."[25]

In one passage Ani says to Osiris, "Ye who steal hearts, and who make the heart of a man to come into existence according to that which hath been done by him; may [my heart] be made strong by you."[26] In the Egyptian worldview, the heart of Pharaoh was in the hands of the gods.

In a seminal article on this hardening phenomena in Exodus, theologian G.K. Beale expanded on the Egyptian understanding of the heart as "the 'seat of destiny,' determining one's life…and it even came to be said 'that the heart of a man [is] his God himself.' The heart was also seen as a divine instrument through which a god directed a man and the organ by which man could receive and comprehend divine commandments."[27]

In the Memphite Theology, the world and all things in it were in the control of the heart and tongue of Thoth and Horus.

> It has evolved that heart [Thoth] and tongue [Horus] have control of all limbs, showing that he [Ptah] is preeminent in every body and in every mouth — of all the gods, all people, all animals, and all crawling things that live — planning and governing everything he wishes.[28]

So when Yahweh was "hardening Pharaoh's heart" and speaking with his tongue, "Thus says…" he was mirroring the language of the Egyptian worldview of the "heart and tongue" of divine control. As Beale concludes, "The hardening may be viewed as a polemic against the Egyptian idea of Pharaoh's deity and the belief that Pharaoh's heart was the all-controlling factor both in history and society."[29]

But it was also a not-so-veiled reference to the weighing of the heart against the feather of justice mentioned earlier. In Hebrew, two word families are used for "harden" throughout the story. One of them means to "grow strong," as in our understanding of harden. But the other means "to make heavy." Yes, God is pressing down on Pharaoh to make him do God's will. But Yahweh was also using the Egyptians' own concepts to communicate that

---

[25] E. Wallis Budge, *The Egyptian Book of the Dead: The Papyrus of Ani* (1895), 307.

[26] Budge, *The Egyptian Book of the Dead,* 312.

[27] G.K. Beale, "An Exegetical and Theological Consideration of the Hardening of Pharaoh's Heart in Exodus 4-14 and Romans 9," *Trinity Journal* 5 NS (1984) 133. Beale examined the Hebrew concept of the heart and found it quite similar in volitional, emotional, intellectual and spiritual aspects with the Egyptian understanding, Beale, "An Exegetical and Theological Consideration," 132.

[28] William W. Hallo and K. Lawson Younger, *The Context of Scripture* (Leiden; New York: Brill, 1997–), 22.

[29] Beale, "An Exegetical and Theological Consideration," 149.

he was making Pharaoh's heart heavy with injustice so that he would be judged against the feather of justice on those afterlife scales.

Ra the Sun God

Ra (or Re) was the creator sun god and "father of the gods," whose main cult was in the Egyptian city of Iunu or Onu (Heliopolis in Greek and On in the Bible—see Genesis 41:45). His rays permeated the heavens, the earth, and the underworld, and he was the quintessence of all sun deities. Other gods were combined with him to enhance their divinity (Ra-Atum and Amun-Ra).[30] His physical manifestation was a falcon or falcon-headed humanoid with the fiery sun disk over his head, encircled by a serpent. In the underworld of Duat, his form was the ram-headed male.

Pharaoh was considered the first-born son of Ra, whose earthly rule corresponded with Ra's heavenly rule over all. Pharaoh's supremacy was assured in his responsibility to maintain the ma'at, or underlying order established by Ra. According to the Egyptian creation myth, Ra emerged from the primeval waters on the primordial hill (hillock). The creation of Ra was the first sunrise that was repeated every day in the earthly sunrise. The Egyptian notion was that every day Ra sailed in his solar barque across the heavens aided by the gods Thoth, Set, and Ma'at with Horus as steersman. They fought to keep the sea serpent of chaos, Apophis, from attacking the boat. At sunset, Ra was swallowed by Apophis. He then journeyed through the underworld until he left the throat of Apophis and arrived for the sunrise again the next day.[31]

G.A. Rendsburg surveys various passages in the Pentateuch story of the Exodus where the Egyptian sun god Ra is attacked polemically by the author. As one of the high gods of Egypt deeply connected to the reign of Pharaoh, Yahweh was at war with Ra and with Pharaoh as Ra's "son."[32]

In the 8th plague of locusts, we read: "When it was morning, the east wind had brought the locusts...They covered the eye of the whole land, so that the land was darkened" (Exodus 10:13, 15). In the Egyptian worldview, the morning was the victorious rising of Ra to start his daily journey across the sky. The phrase "eye of the land" was used of the sun, which was also called

---

30 "Ra" in George Hart, *The Routledge Dictionary of Egyptian Gods and Goddesses* (New York, NY: Routledge, 1986, 2005), 133.

31 E.A. Wallis Budge, *The Gods of the Egyptians: Or Studies in Egyptian Mythology* (London, Methuen and Co., 1904), 323.

32 G. A. Rendsburg. "The Egyptian Sun-God Ra in the Pentateuch." Henoch 10 (1988): 3–15.

"the eye of Ra" that watched over all things with its light. Darkening the eye of the land was another way of saying Yahweh was giving Ra a black eye. Yahweh was already taunting the sun god, using the locust plague as a prelude or mere warm-up for the climactic attack.[33]

Yahweh then destroys Ra in the 9th plague, which is described as "a thick darkness in all the land of Egypt for three days…a darkness that could be felt" (Exodus 10:21-22). This was more than merely blotting out the sun with cloudy skies. This was an existential darkness that could actually be *felt*. It's as if Yahweh was returning their world to the primeval darkness before the creation of any light/Ra. In the next chapter, we will see that Yahweh is not merely warring against the gods of Egypt but is undoing the creation that the Egyptians believed was controlled by the gods, at the head of which was Ra.

The 10th plague, the death of the firstborn, not only occurs at midnight (Exodus 11:29), the time of Ra's absence and therefore impotence, but takes the life of Pharaoh's firstborn, who was to be the next ruler and therefore the next son of Ra.[34]

Another literary reference to Ra might be seen in the golden calf incident. When Moses comes down the mountain and asks Aaron in frustration what the people did to inspire Aaron to create the golden calf, Aaron answers him: "You know the people, that they are set on evil. For they said to me, 'Make us gods who shall go before us'" (Exodus 32:21-22).

Rendsburg looks closely at the Hebrew word for "evil" in context, *be-ra-ah*, to conclude that Aaron is using a wordplay that connects Ra with the evil. After all, the Israelites had just come from hundreds of years beneath the rule of the sun god, so it makes sense that they would be familiar and even comfortable with the common image of a bull or calf since such were images of the high god Ra. Though Rendsburg suggests the golden calf is of Ra, other scholars make stronger arguments that it is an image that represents Yahweh, not Ra. But the connection with Ra can still be seen in that bovine cults flourished in Egypt. Currid points out: "Apis was the most important of the Egyptian sacred bulls; Isis, queen of the gods, bore cow's horns on her head, and Hathor had a bovine head."[35] And Rendsburg's evidence cannot be denied that there are multiple examples "where Ra or Amon-Ra is described as a bull…Amon-Ra is called 'the young bull with sharp pointed horns.' The

33 A.S. Yahuda, "The Language of the Pentateuch in its Relation to Egyptian" (London: Oxford University, 1933) 62-3. Referenced in Rendsburg. "The Egyptian Sun-God."

34 Rendsburg. "The Egyptian Sun-God," 7.

35 John D. Currid, *A Study Commentary on Exodus: Exodus 19–40*, vol. 2, EP Study Commentary (Darlington, England; Carlisle, PA: Evangelical Press, 2001), 271.

famous Hymn to Amon-Ra refers to this deity as 'the bull residing in On'...Finally, the Pharaoh; considered the son of Ra as well as the human incarnation of Ra, is termed, 'the mighty bull', in Egyptian literature."[36]

In conclusion, rather than the golden calf being an image specifically of Ra, the ubiquitous context of bovine imagery in their recent Egyptian past, specifically connected to the high god Ra and his son Pharaoh, it would be a natural response for the Israelites to also cast a bull image for Yahweh, their new high god and deliverer, to replace their old one. They would be drawing from their most readily accessible pantheon of imagery.

Another confrontation between Yahweh and Ra can be found in the Yam Suph episode. When the Israelites found themselves facing the sea with the Egyptians at their backs, the angel of God in the form of a pillar of cloud went behind the Israelites to block access to them by the Egyptians (Exodus 14:19).

> Exodus 14:19–20
> And there was the cloud and the darkness. And it lit up the night without one coming near the other all night.

In this strange wording we see the pillar creating both "darkness" and "lighting up the night." John Currid explains: "A good and proper interpretation of this verse is that one side of the cloud brought light and the other side gave darkness. The Egyptians were clothed in darkness, and the Hebrews were bathed in light. Amon-Re and Pharaoh, the incarnation of the sun-god, could not bring light to their people."[37]

Ra was again humiliated and left in the dark by Yahweh.

I Am Who I Am

My final example of Yahweh's war on Egypt's god Ra is found in the name Yahweh gives himself when asked by Moses at the burning bush.

> Exodus 3:13–15
> Then Moses said to God, "If I come to the people of Israel and say to them, 'The God of your fathers has sent me to you,' and they ask me, 'What is his name?' what shall I say to them?" God said to Moses, "I AM WHO I AM." And he said, "Say this to the people of Israel: 'I AM has sent me to you.' " God also said to Moses, "Say this to the people of Israel: 'YAHWEH, the God of your fathers, the God of

[36] Rendsburg. "The Egyptian Sun-God," 7.

[37] John D. Currid, *Against the Gods: The Polemical Theology of the Old Testament* (Wheaton, IL: Crossway, 2013), 128.

> Abraham, the God of Isaac, and the God of Jacob, has sent me to you.' This is my name forever, and thus I am to be remembered throughout all generations."

First, it is important to note that Moses did not know the name of Yahweh. As we pointed out earlier, Moses was most likely a thoroughly Egyptianized idolater. But Currid explores this name phenomenon to uncover another polemic of Yahweh against the god Ra/Amon-Ra.

He reveals an ancient Egyptian text, the Book of the Heavenly Cow, that is inscribed on tomb walls dated to around 1300 B.C., with possible origins that go back to 2000 B.C. The opening of the book is called "The Destruction of Mankind." It tells the story of Ra discovering that mankind is plotting to rebel against him. But Ra declares instead, "I am who I am. I will not let them take action."[38] In the tomb of Seti I (1300 B.C.), the Pharaoh also takes on the name "I am who I am," because he is believed to be the incarnation of Ra.[39]

Currid points out that the root of the name Yahweh in Hebrew is the verb "to be" (*hyh*) which is the same as the Egyptian (*yw*), which means they are using the exact same language to say the exact same thing. In Exodus 3:14, Yahweh calls himself "I Am Who I Am," and in the "Destruction of Mankind," Ra declares himself to be "I Am Who I Am."[40]

Liberal scholars would try to claim that this means the Hebrews stole the name from the Egyptians and appropriated it for their own god. But as we have seen, the authors of the Bible were more sophisticated than modern scholars give them credit. The ancient writers would often subvert the opponent's cultural language in order to make a theological claim.

As Currid puts it, "the cannibalizing of symbols and names of foes was a means of consuming them and seizing their power. In other words, it was a way of ingesting another's power and character into oneself."[41] For example, in Canaanite myth Baal the storm god was referred to as "Rider on the Clouds."[42] So Isaiah wrote that "Yahweh rides a swift cloud" (Isaiah 19:1) as if to say, "Baal is not the storm god. Yahweh is the storm god."

Interestingly, in this case we may have the reverse scenario. The Hebrews may have brought the name Yahweh with them into Egypt through Abraham.

---

[38] William Kelley Simpson (Editor), *The Literature of Ancient Egypt: An Anthology of Stories, Instructions, Stelae, Autobiographies, and Poetry* 3rd Revised Edition (Yale University Press, 2003), 294.

[39] Currid, *Against the Gods*, 105

[40] Currid, *Against the Gods*, 101.

[41] Currid, *Against the Gods*, 107.

[42] N. Wyatt, Religious *Texts from Ugarit*, 2nd ed., Biblical Seminar, 53 (London; New York: Sheffield Academic Press, 2002), 296.

So it may actually be the Egyptians who sought to undermine the Hebrew god by using Yahweh's epithet as Ra's own.

> By doing so, the Egyptians were attempting to vanquish and mock the Hebrew God. Re [Ra] and Pharaoh would then also have ingested the character and traits of the God of the Hebrews. They alone would, therefore, be the sovereign, eternal, and all-powerful deities of the universe.[43]

But Ra and Pharaoh would eventually find themselves at war with Yahweh, a war they could not win. They would be the ones "swallowed" in the waters and ingested by Yahweh as the true sovereign eternal and all powerful creator of the heavens and earth.

There is one further element of this story that brings illuminating context and understanding to that war of gods and men. The Egyptians believed that Ra had a secret name that embodied his power. For human and god alike, knowing the deity's secret name would give one power over him. A Theban text from the 14th century B.C. called "The God and His Unknown Name of Power" tells the story of Isis tricking Ra into giving her his secret name to get power over him. She creates a snake from the spittle of Ra, which stings the old god, making him sick. He pleads with the gods to help him figure out the cause and try to heal him. Isis then promises that she can find the cure if he tells her his secret name. He eventually gives in and Isis achieves her goal of power. The story was used as a charm for scorpion or snake bites.

So the story of Moses asking for Yahweh's name may carry another polemic against Ra. Though Moses does not carry the same devious intent of Isis, he is nevertheless highly learned in the Egyptian worldview, which included this notion of the secret name of the high god. Moses and the Egyptians did not know the name of Yahweh. So they might be inclined to hope for discovering the secret of this new high god challenging Pharaoh and Ra's supremacy. Yahweh's response is a kind of reversal of the secret name of power. He commands Moses to speak clearly in his name to Pharaoh. There is no secret magical name and no power over Yahweh by any created being.

One might even find a veiled reference to this notion of a secret name of power when Moses questions Yahweh after telling the people his name.

> Exodus 5:22–23
> Then Moses turned to Yahweh and said, "O Lord, why have you done evil to this people? Why did you ever send me?

---

[43] Currid, *Against the Gods*, 109.

> For since I came to Pharaoh to speak in your name, he has done evil to this people, and you have not delivered your people at all."

It's almost as if Yahweh is baiting Pharaoh, making him think that, like Isis, Pharaoh can use Yahweh's name against him and foil his deliverance. All for Yahweh to make his point with a stronger emphasis when he lets the hammer drop to judge Pharaoh and the gods. The name of Yahweh is not his weakness but rather the authority of his will that no creature—man or god—can thwart.

Isis and Osiris

Pharaoh was considered the incarnation of the god Horus, son of Ra. In some ways this was unique among ancient Near Eastern nations, whose kings were considered to be sons of gods rather than actual gods of the pantheon. Scholar Garry Shaw explains the Egyptian understanding: "The king might have been the product of the union of a human mother and a god, but he did not enter the ranks of the divine until his coronation. During this grand ceremony, the royal ka—the spirit of kingship—entered the mortal man's body and transformed him into a pharaoh. Through the coronation rituals, the man was reborn, his physical body infused with divine power."[44]

Yahweh would use Moses to confront Pharaoh and the gods of Egypt. So the biblical text mocks and deconstructs Pharaoh's claims, using the Egyptians' own mythological understanding. To see this spiritual warfare, we must first become acquainted with the ancient Egyptian narrative of Horus.

The story of the birth of Horus and his rise to kingship over Egypt was the main myth that legitimized Pharaoh's divine kingship as Horus incarnate. There are several versions depending on when and where they were written. Shaw synthesizes them to tell the story.[45]

The god Osiris had not always been the mythological king of Egypt. But his co-reign with his sister-wife goddess Isis before the reign of the pharaohs was considered the origin of many of the social customs, institutions, and laws of the Black Land.[46]

---

[44] Garry J. Shaw. *The Egyptian Myths* (Kindle Locations 1337-1340). Thames and Hudson Ltd.

[45] Shaw. The Egyptian Myths (Kindle Locations 805-1270).

[46] The "Black Land" was a reference to the fertile Nile River valley in Lower Egypt and the civilization that went with it. Shaw, *The Egyptian Myths* (Kindle Locations 826-828).

Set, the brother of Osiris, was a violent god of chaos who sought to take the throne from his brother. Set is depicted as a male human body with an unknown animal head, probably a fusion of an aardvark with a jackal or canine of some kind. Set traps Osiris in a wooden box, which he seals and sends upriver into the Mediterranean Sea.

Osiris's queen, Isis, was a goddess of strong magic, depicted as an anthropomorphic woman with a crown of cow-horns and a sun disk. Seeking her husband's floating coffin, Isis finds it up north in the coastal city of Byblos. In it is the body of her dead husband (Egyptian gods could die). She returns with it to Egypt, but Set finds the corpse and cuts it up into 14 pieces (or 26, depending on the version), scattering them across Egypt. Isis hunts the pieces down and puts her beloved's body back together, lacking one lost piece, his phallus, which Isis replaces with one fashioned through magic.

Isis then uses her magic to resurrect Osiris for one night where she unites with him and gets impregnated. But his resurrection is not complete. Osiris is unable to return fully to the land of the living. Shaw explains:

> Osiris's resurrection was confined to the Duat [underworld], where he ruled over the blessed dead as king. He was confined to this place and could only communicate with those in the living world through messengers. As the force of regeneration in the world, Osiris united with the ailing sun god [Ra] in the middle of each night, filling him with enough energy to rise in the east each morning and continue his circuit. He also presided over the judgment of the dead, watching as the heart of the deceased was weighed against the feather of maat.[47]

This transformation of Osiris from overworld king to underworld king is expressed in his depiction in Egyptian art as having green skin and being wrapped in tight white mummy linen. The color green indicated not merely his death but his effect on fertility of the land.

Osiris's son Horus would eventually become king of Egypt, enfleshed in Pharaoh. So in real history, the coronation of a new pharaoh becoming the incarnation of Horus would be accompanied by an additional ceremony wherein the previous deceased pharaoh would then become Osiris, king of the blessed dead. The pharaonic succession of deity would continue.

But the story is not over.

---

[47] Shaw, *The Egyptian Myths* (Kindle Locations 1004-1008).

Horus and Set

With Osiris now dead, Set takes the throne of Egypt and reigns for anywhere from 29 to over a 100 years, depending on the version of the myth. During that time, Horus is born in a papyrus thicket. Isis uses her magic to stay hidden in the delta region, raising the child with the help of other goddesses as servants and nursemaids. Horus is depicted as a falcon or as a human male with a falcon head.

> Papyrus MMA 35.9.21
> O evil-doer [Set], your crime is directed against you. Our lord is in his house and shall not fear. The child is greater than you. He will live and his father will live.[48]

When Horus comes of age, he confronts his uncle Set to claim his rightful inheritance of the throne. Set refuses. They bring it before the divine council of the gods, called the Ennead, and Ra the "All-Lord." Some gods side with Horus (Thoth, Shu, Neith) and some side with Set. So a series of both legal and physical contests over 80 years between the two are recorded in the Egyptian manuscript "The Contentions of Horus and Set."[49]

During one of these contentious battles, Set takes either one or both of Horus's eyes, depending on the version. But Horus is healed by Isis, Thoth, or Hathor (again, depending on the version). This element becomes a mythic expression of the restoration of order after disorder in the kingdom.

Ultimately, Horus is declared the winner and crowned king. Set is exiled to the land of the Asiatics in some versions, only to return and become king later with the arrival of the Semitic Hyksos invaders.

This perpetual battle between Horus of the North and Set of the South represents the historic political division of Egypt into Upper and Lower kingdoms. Though pharaohs beginning with Menes united those two kingdoms, there were periods where they divided and had multiple kings concurrently ruling in the north and south. The time of Moses's birth during the reigns of Neferhotep I and Sobekhotep III was one of those times.

Biblical scholar Gary Rendsburg makes a persuasive argument in his article "Moses as Equal to Pharaoh" that the story of Moses vs. Pharaoh is

---

48 Shaw, *The Egyptian Myths* (Kindle Locations 1028-1030).

49 Miriam Lichtheim, *Ancient Egyptian Literature: Volume II: The New Kingdom* (Berkeley: University of California Press, 1973–), 214-223.

written as an analogy of the story of Horus contending with Set for divine kingship of the land.[50]

Before I summarize some of his biblical findings, I want to address a negative response that may arise in the thoughts of readers who believe that the Bible is God's Word. Some may think that the suggestion that Moses's story is told to liken him to Horus is the equivalent of liberal unbelievers who try to argue that the Bible just took other stories and rewrote them as their own without any historical reality. That this is somehow an attack on the inspiration of Scripture.

This may indeed be what liberals and critical scholars may say. But it is not what I am saying. Let me assure the reader that finding parallels with other mythical or historical persons does not mean mere plagiarism or even evolution of a story. This is simply another case of polemical writing. In other words, using that which is known to the original readers as a paradigm of change into another paradigm or worldview.

As a professional storyteller, I can tell you with confidence that all stories, even those claiming historical reliability, *are not* raw facts. Storytellers use a presupposed worldview that they have for interpreting what they think happened in history. Even if they seek to follow confirmable facts, they still organize their stories into pre-determined storytelling structures to express the meaning of the story as they see it. Story structure is the worldview that brings order to the chaos of so-called raw facts. It guides us about which facts to include in our stories, which to exclude, and how to make story connections between those facts that are not "self-evident." What is cause? What is effect? What is the meaning behind the outward actions of the agents? Writing history is itself a "fictionalizing" process of "finding the story" that gives it real meaning. This is why people of different belief systems like politics or religions can look at the same facts of an event and have two completely opposite interpretations of the real story.

This is not to say that truth is entirely subjective but only that we as humans are subjective. We seek to discover what is the objective truth, but we are nevertheless limited by our own finite subjective perspective. So even though there are an almost infinite number of interpretations of reality by religions and other worldviews, that does not mean they are all acceptable or that reality is unknowable (relativism). It only means that we should be cautious and humble about how we see the world and remain open to

---

[50] Gary A. Rendsburg, "Moses as Equal to Pharaoh," Gary Beckman, Theodore J. Lewis, Eds., *Text, Artifact, and Image: Revealing Ancient Israelite Religion* (Providence, RI: Brown Judaic Studies,), 201-219.

discovering our own biases as we seek to understand objective reality and the truth so that we can align our subjective interpretation with reality rather than seek to mold reality to our interpretation.

Earlier, we gave an example of this dilemma of reinterpretation in the view that Roman pagan historian Tacitus had of Moses's story. Because of his Greek worldview, Tacitus misinterpreted many aspects of Moses's story through his bias. That was his way of trying to make sense of what he had heard by trying to find the story in it. He accepted what he heard that fit with his preconceived view and rejected or "spun" what didn't fit.

This kind of storytelling is not inherently "wrong" or fallacious. We all do it in differing degrees. Someone who believes that George Washington was a hero much like the Roman warrior Cincinnatus will organize the facts of Washington's life to reflect similarity with those in the Roman warrior's life, then tell the story with that context or meaning.[51] This is not lying or even manipulative. It is simply a way of organizing the facts of a story and expressing its meaning through parallels and connections. This is such a frequent technique of storytelling, and indeed of biblical storytelling, that it is quite frankly non-controversial.

Now I want to explain why the story of Moses is told in this same way, likening Moses to Horus and Pharaoh to Set in order to denigrate and undermine Pharaoh's claim to divinity and the throne of Egypt while painting Moses as the one who truly deserves the honor, despite the fact that he will not take it.

Shaw begins his analysis with two scriptures that on the surface appear to be biblically unique.

> Exodus 4:16
> [Aaron] shall speak for you to the people, and he shall be your mouth, and <u>you shall be as God to him</u>.
>
> Exodus 7:1 (KJV 1900)
> And the LORD said unto Moses, See, I have <u>made thee a god to Pharaoh</u>: and Aaron thy brother shall be thy prophet.

Of course there are similes in Scripture of men representing God in legal disputes (Exodus 18:19) or being God's spokespersons (Hebrews 1:1). But this is different. Though many translations render the phrases in these passages

---

[51] This Washington/Cincinnatus comparison was common even in Washington's own day. https://www.mountvernon.org/library/digitalhistory/digital-encyclopedia/article/cincinnatus/

as "you shall be as God," and "made you like God," the Hebrew text hints at something stronger than mere simile.

In 4:16, the Hebrew behind "shall be" (*hyh*) is the same root as that in God's name earlier in the story (Exodus 3:15).[52] So God is not saying Moses shall be Yahweh. That would be heretical nonsense. Rather, he is using the divine "shall be" of Yahweh's name to indicate a literary transformation of Moses into the god that Pharaoh only claims to be in comparison.

Regarding 7:1, Umberto Cassuto explains:

> *I have made you a god to Pharaoh.* You will not only be a god vis-à-vis your brother Aaron (4:16)—that is, you will instruct him what to say, just as God instructs His prophets—but I have also made you a god before Pharaoh. Although Pharaoh is himself considered a deity, he is nevertheless accustomed to hear the prophets of Egypt address him in the name of their gods; now you will appear before him as one of the divinities.[53]

The standard understanding of Moses and Aaron is as prophet and priest of Yahweh. True enough. But in this text, Cassuto shows that Yahweh is establishing Moses as a pharaoh god-king and Aaron as "a spokesman mediating between [Moses] and the people, after the manner of the high Egyptian official who was designated 'the mouth of the king' and acted as an intermediary between the deity Pharaoh and the officials below him."[54]

So even though the biblical worldview maintains a strict ontological distinction between the Creator and humanity—his created representative image—in this case, God is drawing upon the Egyptian worldview *to use it against itself.* Rendsburg explains: "The summit conference between the two leaders of the two peoples demands that the two appear as equals. Accordingly, since Pharaoh was understood to be a god by his people, for the purposes of this story, Moses is elevated to divine status."[55]

And since Pharaoh claimed to be the god Horus, Yahweh is going to subvert the Egyptian myth and paint Moses in terms of Horus and Pharaoh in terms of Set, the god of chaos exiled from Egypt.

---

52 "A final and brief word may be said about the meaning and interpretation of Jehovah/Yahweh. It seems beyond doubt that the name contains the verb hāyâ 'to be.'" Victor P. Hamilton, "491 הָיָה," ed. R. Laird Harris, Gleason L. Archer Jr., and Bruce K. Waltke, *Theological Wordbook of the Old Testament* (Chicago: Moody Press, 1999), 214.

53 U. Cassuto, *A Commentary on the Book of Exodus,* trans. Israel Abrahams (Jerusalem: Magnes Press, 1997), 89.

54 Cassuto, *Exodus*, 51.

55 Rendsburg, "Moses as Equal to Pharaoh," 203.

The birth of Moses is now a well-known literary motif in history that is often referred to as "the exposed child" narrative. These stories all depict the hero as a vulnerable infant or child left to die in the elements, and under attack by his arch-nemesis whose throne or power the child will one day overthrow. Though many scholars believe that Moses's birth story is drawn from the birth story of Sargon of Akkad (from 900 years earlier), Rendsburg and others argue that the Egyptian context of Exodus is more genetically akin to the story of Horus than to an Akkadian one.

The parallels between the biblical story and the Egyptian one include:

- An emphasis on the mother protecting the infant.
- The mother hiding the child.
- The presence of the papyrus thicket of the Nile.
- Another woman appearing as a protectress of the newborn, the goddess Nephthys in Horus's story, and Miriam, Moses's sister, in his story.
- An emphasis on suckling the child.
- Like Set, Pharaoh seeking the child to murder him.

Most critically, Rendsburg points out that the Horus and Moses stories alone share a totally unique plot point. All other "exposed child" narratives have the parents "exposing" the child to nature to be rid of him. The Horus and Moses narratives alone have the mother protecting the child rather than giving him over to destructive forces.[56]

In Exodus 7, Moses confronts Pharaoh, and his staff turns into a serpent that consumes the serpent staffs of the magicians. We have already noted in the chapter on magic that the act of "swallowing" was considered to be emblematic of absorbing the opponent's essence and power into one's self in victory and control over the opponent. We also saw that serpent staffs were a common pictorial device in Egyptian hieroglyphs of the gods—such as Horus.[57]

In Exodus 4:4, Yahweh instructs Moses regarding his shepherd's staff that was turned into a serpent to grab it by its tail. The normal way of picking up a snake, let alone a deadly venomous one, is to grab it by its head. There is more going on here than Yahweh making Moses perform a dangerous ploy. Ancient Jewish readers steeped in Egyptian culture would remember the many

---

56 Rendsburg, "Moses as Equal to Pharaoh," 207.

57 Rendsburg, "Moses as Equal to Pharaoh," 209-211.

pictorial depictions on various stelae of Pharaoh as Horus holding a serpent staff *by the tail* as a herdsman of his people.[58]

B. Section of the Metternich Stela of Horus holding snake staffs by the tail. By E A Budge - The Gods of the Egyptians, t.2, Public Domain

Exodus 7:7 makes a point that Moses was 80 years old when he first spoke to Pharaoh after returning from exile. There is, of course, a chronological element to the story. The division of Moses's life is in increments of 40 years (a common biblical symbolic number). But the Egyptian-minded reader would hear of this 80 years in reference to the confrontation between Moses and Pharaoh, and they would be reminded of the famous Egyptian myth "The Contendings of Horus and Seth." In that story, Thoth writes a letter to Re-Atum about the ongoing contention between Horus and Set. He asks, "What shall we do about these two people, who for 80 years now have been before the tribunal, and no one knows how to judge between the two?"[59] Like Horus and Set, Moses and Pharaoh have been at odds for 80 years, and now it's time for the final climactic confrontation. Who is the true god-king?

---

58 Rendsburg, "Moses as Equal to Pharaoh," 213.

59 Miriam Lichtheim, *Ancient Egyptian Literature: Volume II: The New Kingdom* (Berkeley: University of California Press, 1973–), 215. Quoted in Rendsburg, "Moses as Equal to Pharaoh," 215.

The ten plagues then become that final conflict, wherein Yahweh uses Moses as his "god" on earth to humiliate and subjugate all the gods of Egypt, especially Pharaoh as Horus, first-born of Ra the sun god. In this story that God is retelling for his purposes, Pharaoh becomes Set who is then destroyed in the sea of the desert just like Set, who was exiled to the desert for his failure.

Rendsburg makes one final parallel between Horus and Moses in Exodus 34. Though questionable, it remains an interesting possibility. It concerns the statement of the skin of Moses's face "shining" after speaking with Yahweh on the mountain.

> Exodus 34:29–30
> As he came down from the mountain, Moses did not know that the skin of his face shone because he had been talking with God. Aaron and all the people of Israel saw Moses, and behold, the skin of his face shone, and they were afraid to come near him.

This passage remains contentious between scholars over the interpretation of the Hebrew word translated "shone." Older translations like the Latin Vulgate translated it as Moses having horns. Thus the depiction of Moses in older works of art like Michelangelo's Moses sporting two horns from his head. Most modern translators prefer the word that indicates radiance. Some have combined the interpretations to say that it speaks of Moses shining rays of light that look like horns.

Rendsburg then sides with the older translations of horns because he argues this was another reference to the deity of Pharaoh residing in Moses. He provides artwork of Pharaohs in the New Kingdom sporting ram-like horns usually on their cheeks or around their ears. Since horns were a ubiquitous symbol of deity throughout the Near East, as was shining, Rendsburg concludes that these were probably horns of deity claimed by Pharaoh but provided by Yahweh for Moses in the context of the Horus literary connection.[60]

---

[60] Rendsburg, "Moses as Equal to Pharaoh," 217.

Ancient Egyptian Gods

Amun

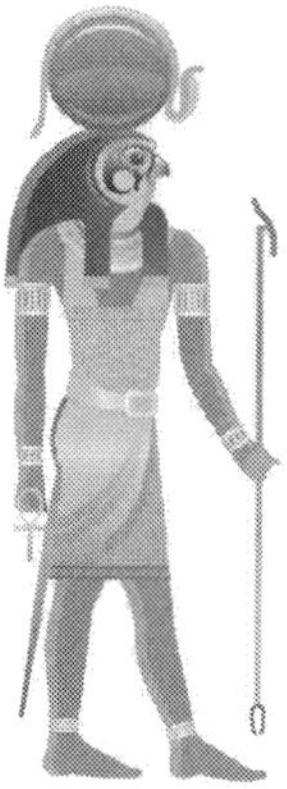

Ra

Pharaoh

Osiris

Isis

Horus

Set

Sobek

Maat

Ancient Egyptian Gods

Khnum

Ptah

Thoth

Sekhmet

Geb

Anubis

Hathor

Hapi

Bastet

Chapter 5
The Ten Plagues

The plagues of Egypt were the part of Moses's story that inspired the genesis of the novel *Moses: Against the Gods of Egypt*. Because the Chronicles series of novels seeks to retell biblical stories with the Watcher gods in them, this story appeared to have a strong element of this spiritual reality behind the idols of Egypt and God's war on them. Yahweh explicitly states,

> Exodus 12:12
> On all the gods of Egypt I will execute judgments: I am Yahweh.
>
> Numbers 33:4
> On their gods also Yahweh executed judgments.

A similar statement by Yahweh occurs later in the 6th century when Yahweh proclaims judgment upon Egypt's gods using Babylon as his weapon. We see the same language as in Moses's day.

> Jeremiah 46:25
> Yahweh of hosts, the God of Israel, said: "Behold, I am bringing punishment upon Amon of Thebes, and Pharaoh and Egypt and her gods and her kings."[1]

Amon was the patron god of Thebes. He was called "The Hidden One" and was combined with Ra around 1550 B.C., becoming Amon-Ra, the eventual new head of the Egyptian pantheon. The point here is that when Yahweh uses historical means as judgment upon cities and nations, especially of Egypt, he describes it as executing judgment upon those gods as well. The judgment is described as the destruction of their religious temples and carrying away of their gods' images (Jeremiah 43:12). But as we have seen throughout the Bible, this is more than a mere metaphor of religious warfare. Yahweh considered pagan gods to have real spiritual demonic reality behind them

---

[1] Thanks to Robert Cruickshank Jr. for this reference.

(Deuteronomy 32:17; Psalm 106:37-38). So Yahweh's spiritual war was on real demonic beings (*shedim*).

In the Exodus verses above that speak about this spiritual war, the context is the final plague on the firstborn of Egypt. But this is not a reference to a sole plague as being the only judgment on the gods of Egypt. Like the tenth plague, it is a climactic summary judgment of all the previous plagues as well.

Ziony Zevit's influential article "Three Ways to Look at the Ten Plagues" explains the three interpretations of this war of Yahweh.

1) The plagues are natural phenomena linked to Egypt's ecosystem.

2) They are Yahweh's war on the Egyptian pantheon of gods.

3) They are a literary "de-creation" or undoing of the cosmos.[2]

Let's look at each of these three options to see how we can understand the plagues in their spiritual context.

Plagues as Natural Phenomena

First, the naturalistic option argues that each of the plagues has a scientific explanation as effects within the biological and environmental ecosystem. The first six plagues are sequentially connected in cause and effect. Zevit summarizes this sequence in detail.

> The naturalistic account is connected initially with the violent rain storms that occur in the mountains of Ethiopia. The first plague, blood, is the red clay [and red algae] swept down into the Nile from the Ethiopian highlands. The mud [and algae] then choked the fish in the area inhabited by the Israelites. The fish clogged the swamps where the frogs lived; the fish, soon infected with anthrax, caused the frogs (the second plague) to leave the Nile for cool areas, taking refuge in people's houses. But, since the frogs were already infected with the disease, they died in their new habitats. As a consequence, lice, the third plague, and flies, the fourth plague, began to multiply, feeding off the dead frogs. This gave rise to a pestilence that attacked animals, the fifth plague, because the cattle were feeding on grass which by then had also become infected. In man, the symptom of the same disease was boils, the sixth plague.[3]

---

[2] Ziony Zevit, "Three Ways to Look at the Ten Plagues," *Bible Review* 6:3, June 1990 online: https://www.baslibrary.org/bible-review/6/3/13

[3] Zevit, "Three Ways."

He then explains that the last four plagues are more climactic or atmospheric. The sixth and seventh plagues, hail and locusts, are common enough occurrences in Egypt, and the ninth plague of darkness was probably caused by a Libyan dust storm. The tenth plague, while more difficult to naturalize, could be a reference to a high infant mortality rate at the time.

But there are too many scientific problems with this theory to legitimize it. Russell Grigg of Creation.com credits the origin of this theory to a scholar named Greta Hort in 1957. He then deconstructs it with scientific rigor into absurdity.[4]

He points out that the "red algae" Hort referred to was not red in flowing water but green. Not only that, no scientists have ever found those algae forms in the Nile because they are only found in cold climates! Algae could not have suffocated the fish because lack of oxygen only occurs after the algae blooms, and algae doesn't bloom in muddy water. Nile mud is brown, not red. Anthrax occurs in the soil, not in the water of the Nile. Fish could not get anthrax because it does not infect aquatic animals. Flies do not spread anthrax. All the flooding, humidity for hail, and massive mud saturation she predicts for her scenario discounts the possibility of a dust storm that requires extremely dry conditions. A plague that only kills the firstborn of Egyptians but not Hebrews has no possible naturalistic explanation in mortality rates.

The naturalistic causal interpretation is a tempting one for the modern reader with a materialistic anti-supernatural bias, but it fails on its own merits. Most of the plagues were indeed natural elements that existed in varying degrees at varying seasons in Egypt, such as frogs, flies, hail, and locusts. But again, the precise timing and scenarios coupled with sheer impossibilities like a blood Nile, "thick" darkness, and precision firstborn deaths make this option unreasonable.

---

[4] Russell Grigg, "The Ten Plagues of Egypt: Miracles of 'Mother Nature'?" Creation 27(1):34–38, December 2004 Creation.com online: https://creation.com/the-ten-plagues-of-egypt

SIDEBAR
The Plagues in Egyptian Records

Debates about the historicity of the Exodus story sometimes address the comparison of the Bible with known Egyptian manuscripts. The basic purpose is that if there is corroboration between different cultural texts, then the historicity of an event is more likely. One of the main criticisms of the Bible is that there are virtually no references to Moses or the Jews in relation to Egypt beyond the monumental inscription of the Merneptah Stela (9th century B.C.).

The problem is that ancient documents do not often translate with clarity between cultures. People, places, and things can often have completely different names and/or spellings between different languages, which requires studied interpretation to discover the referents (i.e.: Chenophres in Greek by Artapanus refers to Khaneferre Sobekhotep in Egyptian, and these names you are reading are English translations of the originals. And remember Daniel, Hananiah, Meshial, and Azariah who were Belteshazzar, Shadrach, Meshach, and Abednego to the Babylonians.).

Besides the archeological evidence of a massive population of Semites (Jews were Semites) in Avaris in the 15th-16th century B.C. (time of Joseph and Moses), we have already seen a possible Egyptian reference to Moses as Sobekhotep's son Mio. But there are others. David Rohl argues that there are many references to King Saul, David, and their kingdoms in the Egyptian El Amarna manuscripts from the 11th century B.C. that match up similar events with different names in the different languages.*

But there is another fascinating Egyptian document that appears to refer to the Ten Plagues. It is called "The Admonitions of an Egyptian Sage" by a scribe named Ipuwer, and the most recent assessment of its dating is during the Second Intermediate Period sometime after the 12th Dynasty, the very time period where we are suggesting the plagues occurred.

Egyptologist David Rohl walks through the highlights of the manuscript and shows its corroboration with the biblical narrative of the plagues. It is not a perfect one-to-one correlation. But it doesn't have to be. Every culture interprets similar events through different worldviews. Their resulting interpretations focus on different things. They include facts and exclude facts based on their purposes and interpret all facts through their worldview grid. But in this case we can see a rather close connection between key elements of the plagues.

Here is a sample of those connections as translated by Rohl:

Exodus 7:20-22: Nile River turning to blood.

Ipuwer: "The river is blood! As you drink of it you lose your humanity and thirst for water."

Exodus 9:31, 9:6, 10:15: Destruction of crops, death of livestock.

Ipuwer: "Gone is the grain of abundance. Food supplies are running short. The nobles hunger and suffer. Upper Egypt has become a wasteland. Grain is lacking on every side. The storehouse is bare. Women say, 'Oh that we had something to eat!'"

Exodus 10:7: Egypt is ruined.

Ipuwer: "What can we do about it? All is ruin!"

Exodus 10:22: Darkness covers the land.

Ipuwer: "Those who had shelter are now in the dark of the storm. The whole of the delta cannot be seen."

Exodus 14:17: The hardening of the Egyptian hearts and regret.

Ipuwer: "There is fire in their hearts! If only he (earlier Pharaoh Amenemhat) had perceived their nature in the first generation! Then he would have smitten the evil - stretched out his arm against it. He would have destroyed their seed and their heritage."

Exodus 12:29-30: Death of firstborn Egyptians.

Ipuwer: "Behold, plague sweeps the land; blood is everywhere with no shortage of the dead. Children are dashed against the walls. The funeral shroud calls out to you before you come near. Woe is me for the grief of this time. He who buries his brother in the ground is everywhere…Wailing is throughout the land mingled with lamentations."

Exodus 12:35-36: Jews plunder the Egyptian's wealth before leaving.

Ipuwer: "The slave takes what he finds. What belongs to the palace has been stripped. Gold, lapis lazuli, silver, and turquoise are strung on the necks of female slaves. See how the poor of the land have become rich whilst the man of property is a pauper."

* This is a controversial argument, but see David Rohl, *A Test of Time: The Bible -*

From Myth to History (U.K. Century, Ltd., 1995), 300-385 for a detailed exegesis.

** David Rohl, *Exodus: Myth or History?* (MN: Thinking Man Media, 2015), 150-153. For the full text of the Admonitions of Ipuwer, see William W. Hallo and K. Lawson Younger, *The Context of Scripture Vol. 1* (Leiden; New York: Brill, 1997–), 93–104.

Plagues as Yahweh's War on Egyptian Gods

The second option for contextualizing the plagues is the interpretation that they are judgments on the gods of the Egyptian pantheon. As shown above, Scripture explicitly points to this but without explanation (Exodus 12:12; Numbers 33:4).

On the surface, the plagues are certainly manifestations of natural phenomena run amuck. And the Egyptian gods are connected to those various elements of nature such as the Nile, frogs, and other creatures touched by the plagues. An obvious connection might be that Yahweh is cursing or abusing the god of the particular creature in each plague. Many have tried to lay out charts of the plagues and which gods were affected. Common suggestions involve the god of the Nile for the first plague, the frog god Hekhet for the second plague, Ra the high sun god cursed by the ninth plague of darkness. But all these charts break down on a few points.

First, the Egyptian pantheon had thousands of gods. Ten would be inconsequential to address such numbers with real impact.

Secondly, while there can be direct correspondence of some plagues with some gods, like Hapi as the spirit of the Nile, Hekhet as the frog god, Apis as the bull god (livestock), or Ra as the sun god (darkness), the rest of the plagues do not have a similar application to specific deities. There is no god of flies. Apis is only a bull, but the plague struck all livestock including sheep and other herd animals. There is no god of boils, hail, locusts, or firstborn. The gods suggested for those plagues are indirect, not direct representations of the creatures. So Kheprer the scarab beetle god gets connected to the flies or gnats. Nut the sky goddess gets connected to the hail, presumably because hail comes from the sky. The locusts are connected to Senehem, the god of protection against pests. Sekhmet the goddess of plagues or Seraphis the god of healing are mocked by the boils indirectly.

The problem with this endeavor of connecting plagues to individual gods is that it creates far too many varying interpretations. Yahweh could be accused of not being very clear about his judgments.

Thirdly, even if one accepted this direct connection to specific gods, most of them are minor or inconsequential in the pantheon. Sure, Ra the sun god addressed by the ninth plague is a major deity, and Pharaoh as the firstborn "Son of Ra" was as well. But the others, such as the frog goddess Hekhet, are minor deities. The creator gods, Amun, Ptah, and Thoth are nowhere directly attacked. The Ennead of Heliopolis are nine major deities of which Ra is only one. Most of the major deities get no honor of a plague devoted to them, yet they carried much of the mythology that drove Egypt's identity. Atum the head of the Ennead surely deserved to be cursed. Others included Isis and Osiris, whose love story defined the heart of Egypt, and Set the god of chaos necessary to the struggle of order within their cosmos. These are just a few of the major deities of consequence who have no plague dedicated to them. If Yahweh were directing plagues at specific deities, he sure didn't target the right ones.

A fourth problem comes from the fact that the pantheon evolved much over time and not all the deities shared the same time periods, let alone that of Moses's era, the 13th Dynasty of the Second Intermediate Period.

While these issues make it difficult to draw specific parallels with specific deities being judged, nevertheless Yahweh's words require some kind of judgment upon the gods. Rather than a one-to-one correspondence, I see the plagues as an attack *on the entire system*, the pantheon of gods as a whole. The Egyptian cosmic picture was a sacralization of nature. When Yahweh broke down their environment and infected living things, he was reducing the gods to impotence because nature to the ancient Egyptian was in essence an interacting pantheon of deities. It's not that there were specific deities of specific creatures or processes like a modern scientific itemized attribution. Rather, it was more like a narrative of multiple deities with many different manifestations and duties all interacting to create, stabilize, and maintain the cosmos of creation.[5] So Yahweh's plagues were breaking down that story, that system, and the elements and creatures tied to it. The plagues were not exhaustive of all of nature and biology, but they were certainly representative of the system that Yahweh was deconstructing, or rather de-creating.

For example, Ra was the sun god who would seem to be addressed by the plague of darkness. But he was not the only sun deity. Atum, Horus, Khepri, Horakhty, Tem, Sekhmet, and others were either sun gods or connected in

---

5 "So perhaps the best approach is not to work so hard at teasing the Egyptian deities apart, but, instead, to view them as a gigantic whole, responsible for the cosmos in all its various predictable and unpredictable events, and thus having myriad parts that reflect that regularity and that capriciousness." Donna Jo Napoli. *Treasury of Egyptian Mythology* (Kindle Locations 1685-1687). National Geographic Society.

some way to the sun's part in the cosmos. And in different times and places, gods like Ra were combined with other gods to represent new storylines of mythology. So Ra was combined with Atum the creator god to be Ra-Atum. Ra was combined with Amun to become Amun-Ra and with Khnum to be Khnum-Ra.

Also, most deities like Ra had various manifestations and duties that went far beyond a simplistic "the sun is Ra" symbolism. For instance, Ra was most commonly manifested as a human figure with a falcon's head. But he also had an underworld form as a ram-headed god.[6] So was Ra merely affected by the plague of darkness, or did he also represent birds of the sky affected by the plague of hail? As a ram god, could he not also be considered part of the livestock touched by the plague of pestilence?

The manifestations, emanations, and symbolism of the gods are endless and evolving. This is because in the Egyptian cosmos they are an integrated *collective system* of deities that work together in varying overlapping ways behind the cosmic order of the natural world around them. Instead of one centralized canon of sacred definitions and identities, there are multiple sources and traditions with varying views. This is why God's plagues address the ecosystem in a systemic way rather than an individualistic way. The pantheon was a collective, so Yahweh's judgments were representative of that collective. Yahweh controlled the natural order around them. Their gods did not.

Here is a chart of a sampling of the many gods I could find connected with each of the plagues from which I drew to depict in my *Moses* novel.[7]

---

6 See "Ra" in George Hart, *The Routledge Dictionary of Egyptian Gods and Goddesses* (New York, NY: Routledge, 1986, 2005), 133.

7 This chart was made with help from John J. Davis, *Moses and the Gods of Egypt* (BMH Books, 1971, 1986), 87-137; George Hart, *The Routledge Dictionary of Egyptian Gods and Goddesses* (New York, NY: Routledge, 1986, 2005); David Padfield, *Against All the Gods of Egypt* (2002), online: www.padfield.com

Plague	Egyptian deities and sacred creatures affected
1. Nile Exodus 7:14-25	**Hapi**—God of the Nile flood (manifest as crocodile). **Khnum**—Guardian of the Nile. **Satet**—Goddess consort of Khnum associated with Nile flood. **Anket**—Goddess of the cataracts of the Lower Nile. *Khnum, Satet, and Anket linked to annual Nile flood.* **Osiris**—Nile was his bloodstream. Underworld god drowned in Nile, resurrected to become a giver of rebirth. Symbol of Nile's death and life cycle. **Sobek**—Crocodile god of the Nile. **Nun**—God of the primeval waters, source of Nile and waters. **Nu**—God of the life of the Nile. **Taweret**—Hippopotamus goddess of the Nile. **Hatmehyt**—Fish goddess of the delta. **Neith**—War goddess protected the largest fish, the *lates.* **Sothis/Sopdet**—Goddess heralds the annual flood of Nile. **Tatenan**—God symbolizing emergence of fertile Nile soil. **Aten**—Provides invisible Nile in sky for Syria without Nile. **Geb**—Earth god whose body is decorated with Nile reeds. **Isis**—Goddess whose urine is "the Nile flood between my thighs". **Neper**—God of grain whose abundance depends upon Nile silt. **Ra**—Creator god instituted seasons around flood of Nile.
2. Frogs Exodus 8:1-15	**Heket**—Frog goddess of birth. **Hapi**—Nile god has a harem of frog goddesses. **Nun, Heh, Kek, Amun**—Four gods of the Ogdoad who have the heads of frogs.

3. Gnats Exodus 8:16-19	*Sometimes translated as "lice," "sand flies," or "fleas."* **Geb**—Earth god. Gnats were made from "dust of the earth." **Tatenan**—name means "exalted earth." Combined with Ptah to become creator god and primal mound of earth in creation. Also connected to Geb. **Khepri**—Creator sun-god in form of a scarab beetle. Dung beetle. Not a gnat or fly, but a fellow insect. **Sepa**—Centipede god. Insect family. **Ta-Bitjet**—Wife of Horus. Had power against poisonous bites.
4. Flies Exodus 8:20-32	*Moses does not use the word "flies," but the more generic word for "swarms of pests."*[8] *Some translate as biting "dog flies."*[9] **Khepri**—Creator sun-god in form of a scarab beetle. Represents Egypt as a whole. **Amon-Ra**—Creator, king of the gods. Had head of a beetle. **Sepa**—Centipede god. Technically not an insect. **Ta-Bitjet**—Wife of Horus. Had power against poisonous bites. **Osiris** — represented by the Jewel Beetle, a sacred insect that may have represented rebirth. **Neith**—Goddess of protection associated with the Click Beetle amd the honey bee. **Honey Bees**—Associated with sun god **Ra** and **Neith**, goddess of protection. **Flies**—Fly amulets protected against misfortune and disease.

[8] "Exactness is not possible, but the term from עָרַב, mingle with, be intermixed with, may indicate a swarm of mixed insects." Willem VanGemeren, ed., *New International Dictionary of Old Testament Theology & Exegesis* (Grand Rapids, MI: Zondervan Publishing House, 1997), 525.

[9] "The noun ʿārōḇ, "dog fly," is usually connected with this root." Heinz-Josef Fabry and H. Lamberty-Zielinski, "ערב," ed. G. Johannes Botterweck and Helmer Ringgren, trans. David E. Green, *Theological Dictionary of the Old Testament* (Grand Rapids, MI; Cambridge, U.K.: William B. Eerdmans Publishing Company, 2001), 331.

5. Livestock Exodus 9:1-7	*Exodus 9:3 says, " Livestock, horses, donkeys, camels, herds, and flocks."* **Apis**—a bull. Was the image of Ptah, Ra, and Isis. **Ptah**—Creator god, living image was Apis the bull. **Ra**—Sun god. The disk between the bull's horns. **Isis**—Mother of Horus. As a cow, she gave birth to Apis the sacred bull. **Hathor**—Cow-headed goddess. Mother of Pharaoh. **Khnum**—Guardian of Nile, had head of a ram. **Mnevis**—Sacred bull of the sun god of Heliopolis. **Sekhmet**—Goddess of pestilence. **Haurun**—A shepherd god. **Banebdjedet**—A ram god.
6. Boils Exodus 9:8-12	**Sekhmet** –Goddess of plagues and healing. **Amon-Ra**—Healer. **Serapis**—Egyptian/Greek hybrid god of healing. **Imhotep**—God of medicine and healing. **Thoth**—God of medical learning. **Isis**—Goddess of healing. She reassembled Osiris. **Astarte**—Goddess of healing. **Khonsu**—God of healing.

7. Hail Exodus 9:13-35	*Actually, "thunder, lightning, and hail" in storm. Sky and storm god terminology. Birds are affected.* **Set—**Lord of the sky and storm god. **Mut**—Goddess whose crown represented a vulture. **Nekhbet**—Vulture goddess of Upper Egypt. **Thoth**—God of scribes sometimes manifest as an Ibis bird. **Horus**—Hawk-headed sky god of Upper Egypt. **Nut**—The sky goddess and vault of heaven. Thunder was her laughter. **Shu**—Wind god who holds up the heavens. **Tefnut**—Goddess of moisture. **The 7 Hathors**—One of them is called Sky-Storm. **Sopedu**—astral star-god of the east.
8. Locusts Exodus 10:1-20	*Locusts eat crops. Crops are symbolic of fertility.* **Min**—God of fertility, both human and crops. **Nepri**—A god of crops. **Set**—A god of crops. **Osiris**—A god of crops. **Renenutet**—Guardian of Pharaoh who also nurtures crops for harvest. **Sothis**—Star goddess associated with crops. **Ash**—God of the fertile oases.

9. Darkness Exodus 10:21-29	**Ra**—Sun god creator. **Pharaoh**—A son of Ra. **Aten**—A sun god. **Khepri**—Sun god manifest as a scarab beetle. **Horus**—God of the sun's rays. "Eye of Ra." **Horakhti**—A manifestation of Horus as solar deity. **Harmachis**—A manifestation of Horus as solar deity. **Atum**—Creator sun god of Heliopolis. **Tem**—God of the sunset. **Shu**—God of sunlight and air. **Sekhmet**—Solar goddess. **Serqet**—defended the solar boat (sun) of Ra. **Thoth**—Navigated the solar boat (sun) of Ra. **Mehet-Weret**—Goddess waterway in heaven for Ra's solar boat. **Mehen**—Serpent deity that protects Ra's solar boat.

10. Firstborn Exodus 11:1-10	**Pharaoh**—Considered to be a god of Egypt. "The living Horus." Firstborn "Son of Ra." His firstborn son would become Pharaoh. **Horus**—Pharaoh is considered the Horus god. **Amun**—Creator god, protector of Pharaoh, gives him a "strong right arm." **Ma'at**—Goddess who personifies the cosmic order of the Pharaoh. **Osiris**—God of the underworld who Pharaoh becomes at death. Judge of the dead, god of rebirth in the afterlife **Apis**—Pharaoh identifies closely with the sacred bull. **Hathor**—Cow goddess mother of Pharaoh. Nurtures king **Two Ladies—Nekhbet and Wadjet**. Goddess guardians of Pharaoh. **Two Lords—Horus and Seth**. Guardian gods of Pharaoh. **Wepwawet**—Jackal god champion of Pharaoh as firstborn god. **Haurun**—Falcon god protector of Pharaoh. **Weret-Hakau**—Cobra or lion goddess guardian of Pharaoh. **Bastet**—Cat goddess closely linked to Pharaoh. **Meskhenet**—Goddess of childbirth. **The 7 Hathors**—7 who protect childbirth and determine destiny. **Min**—God of fertility and regeneration. **Isis**—Goddess of fertility. **Selket**—Guardian of life. **Andjety**—A manifestation of Osiris, giver of afterlife. **Renenutet**—Cobra goddess guardian of Pharaoh and motherhood. **Wadj Wer**—Fertility god. **Amun**—Creator god who could give new life to the dead.

	Anubis—Jackal-headed deity who protected Pharaonic mummies for the afterlife.
	Bes—Dwarf deity, protector of childbirth.
	Hekhet—Frog goddess of birth.
	Taweret—Goddess of birth.

Rather than laboring over an encyclopedic listing and description of each deity, this chart lays out in bullet form the basic picture of a pantheon of gods working together in a complex, integrated system that represents the natural world cosmos of the Egyptians. Now let's look at Yahweh's deconstruction of that system.

Plagues as De-creation

The third option that Zevit explores is that the plagues were a form of literary de-creation. God was breaking down the cosmos of the Egyptians because he was about to create a new one for Israel. It's as if Yahweh is returning the world to its chaotic state of Genesis 1:2—formless and void—in order to establish his new covenant order with Israel in the desert. A new creation, so to speak. This option actually works with the second option as well, since the cosmos of nature was allegedly created and sustained by the gods. Yahweh was undoing their claimed cosmos.

Zevit makes a profound connection between the Genesis story of creation and the destructive "de-creation" of the plagues. The question had always been, why the number of ten plagues? We have already dismissed the possibilities of it representing specific gods directly. Was it arbitrary?

Zevit gives the answer. "The number of plagues in Exodus was meant to correspond to the *ten divine utterances by which the world was created and ordered* (Genesis 1:3, 6, 9, 11, 14, 20, 24, 26, 28, 29)."[10] "And God said," was used to introduce his creative acts ten times in Genesis 1.

A closer look at Exodus 7-11 reveals a literary parallelism reflecting the reverse of Genesis 1, an undoing of that creation. When he calls forth the plagues, he is undoing those ten utterances and returning the cosmos to chaos.

To the Egyptians, this de-creation was a destruction of what they called *ma'at*. John Currid defines *ma'at* as "'the equilibrium of the whole universe,

---

[10] Ziony Zevit, "Three Ways to Look at the Ten Plagues," *Bible Review* 6:3, June 1990 online: https://www.baslibrary.org/bible-review/6/3/13

the harmonious co-existence of its elements, and the essential cohesion, indispensable for maintaining the created forms.' *ma'at* was the 'cosmic force of harmony, order, stability, and security…and the organizing quality of created phenomena.' It may be simply defined as universal order."[11] As explained earlier, the gods established ma'at, and Pharaoh's main responsibility was to maintain that cosmic order of Egypt. The plagues were a negation of Pharaoh's divinity through an undoing of ma'at and returning Egypt to a state of chaos.

For the first plague, God tells Aaron, "Take thy rod, and stretch out thy hand against the waters of Egypt, against their streams, against their rivers, and against their ponds, and against all their collections of waters; and they are blood" (Exodus 7:19 - YLT). The Hebrew word for "collection" of waters is *mikveh*, the same word used in Genesis 1:10: "and to the collection (*mikveh*) of the waters He hath called 'Seas'." Turning the collection of waters to blood killed the living things in them and made the water death instead of life for the Egyptians. "Let them become blood" of Exodus 7:19 echoes the use of "Let there be" in the creation story.

The next three plagues form a triad, addressing creatures in the water (frogs), earth (lice), and sky (flies), that replicates the Genesis tri-level creation of creatures—but with a negative chaos result instead of order. Frogs become a second plague of negative life swarming from the water, a degenerate version of "Let the waters swarm with swarms of living creatures" that was "good" (Genesis 1:20). The creepy-crawling lice (plague three) come from the "dust of the earth" (Exodus 8:12-13) and are a negative version of the "crawling things" on the earth created as "good" in Genesis 1:24. The swarming multiplication of disgusting flies (or insects) of the fourth plague, becomes a chaotic reversal of the "good" flying creatures multiplying on the earth in Genesis 1:22.

Genesis 1:26 speaks of God creating livestock for man to have dominion over. Exodus 9:3-7 describes the fifth plague as a pestilence on that livestock, but one that only affects the Egyptians, not the Hebrew herds and animals.

The sixth plague, boils, is not as obvious a fit for this argument. But Zevit points out that boils, as part of infectious diseases, were considered by both Egyptians and Hebrews to make people unclean. Particularly for the religious priests of the Egyptian gods. The creation element of "separation" so prevalent

[11] Quoting Georges Posener in John D. Currid, *Ancient Egypt and the Old Testament* (Grand Rapids, MI: Baker Books, 1997), 118.

in Genesis 1 is a reflection of the separation of holiness so elemental to Torah. Boils would violate that holy separation.

The next two plagues, hail and locusts, were an undoing of the vegetation of the land, returning the earth to its barren state before creation. As Zevit explains, Genesis 1:12 says, "The land brought forth vegetation: seed bearing fruit with seed in it." By contrast, in Exodus 10:15 we are told that "nothing green was left of tree or grass of the field in all the land of Egypt."

The ninth plague of darkness is a reversal of the first creative utterance, "Let there be light" (Genesis 1:3). It is described as "a thick darkness…that could be felt" (Exodus 10:21-22). This was more than merely blotting out the sun with cloudy skies. It seems to be describing, at least literarily, the kind of darkness of Genesis 1:2: "darkness over the face of the deep." It's as if Yahweh was returning their world to the primeval waters before the creation of any light.

The tenth plague against the firstborn of Egypt is an undoing of God's pinnacle of creation, mankind. (Genesis 1:26). Instead of breathing life into man's nostrils as God's imagers, God takes life away, replacing the miracle of life with a miracle of death.

So the ten utterances, "Let there be," of Yahweh's creation in Genesis 1 have been undone in a kind of de-creation, a reversion of the Egyptian cosmos back to its pre-created state of chaos and a humiliating subjugation of that pantheon of deities who supposedly controlled that cosmos.

But there is more meaning to this "de-creation story" than mere natural and supernatural phenomena. God was about to establish a covenant with Israel that would be described as a creation of heavens and earth.

Which is covered in the next chapter.

Genesis 1 Utterance of Creation	Corresponding Plague of Chaos/Decreation
Let there be light. (1:3)	Darkness
Let there be a firmament called heaven (1:6)	Hail (chaos from the heavens)
Let waters be gathered. (1:9)	Blood Nile (waters polluted)
Let the land appear. (1:9)	Lice/gnats (out of the earth)
Let the earth bring forth vegetation. (1:11)	Locusts (destroy all vegetation)
Let there be heavenly lights (seasons/festivals/holiness). (1:14)	Boils (unclean)
Let the waters swarm with creatures. (1:20)	Frogs
Let the air swarm with birds. (1:20)	Flies/Insects
Let the earth bring forth living creatures. (1:24)	Livestock
Let us make man in our image/dominion. (1:26)	Firstborn

Chapter 6
From Chaos to Creation

Leviathan, Chaos, and Creation

(Note: There is some new information in this section not addressed in previous versions)

Leviathan is a crucial character in the Chronicles universe. It shows up in all three series, Chronicles of the Nephilim, Apocalypse and Watchers. It is drawn from the ancient Near Eastern worldview that permeates the Bible, and it is sometimes connected to the notion of creation.

Contrary to what some hyper-literalists may think, Leviathan is not a real-world dinosaur or even an extinct sea monster. It is a spiritual image used by ancient Near Eastern religions to symbolize the chaos of the cosmos that their god fought to bring about his rule and order. The Babylonians called it Tiamat. The Canaanites called it Lotan. Hebrews called it Leviathan and sometimes Rahab, another name for the same kind of sea monster.[1]

The battle of divinity to create order out of chaos is called "chaoskampf" by theologians.[2] In Mesopotamian religion, Marduk fought and defeated Tiamat the sea dragon and split her in half to create the heavens and earth, which symbolized the establishment of Babylonian world power.[3] The Canaanite Baal fought and defeated Sea (Yam), River (Nahar), and Leviathan (Lotan) in order to establish his most-high rulership of the Canaanite pantheon.[4]

---

[1] Leviathan: Job 3:8; 41; Psalm 74:13-14; Psalm 104:26; Isa 27:1. Leviathan is said to dwell in the Abyss in Job 41:24 (LXX). "[Leviathan] regards the netherworld [Tartauros] of the deep [Abyss] like a prisoner. He regards the deep [Abyss] as a walk." Job 41:34, Tan, Randall, David A. deSilva, and Logos Bible Software. The Lexham Greek-English Interlinear Septuagint. Logos Bible Software, 2009.

For Rahab, see: Isaiah 51:9; Job 9:13; 26:12-13; Ps 87:4; Psalm 89:9-10.

[2] For Chaoskampf in the Bible, see: Psalm 89:9-10; Isaiah 51:9-10; Job 26:12-13. Psalms 18, 29, 24, 29, 65, 74, 77, 89, 93, and 104. Also, Exodus 15, Job 9, 26, 38, and Isaiah 51:14-16; 2 Samuel 22.

[3] *Enuma Elish*, Tablet IV, lines 104-105, 137-138, 144.

[4] See KTU 1.3:3.38-41.

As described previously, creation in these stories is not so much about the origin of the physical universe as it is an expression of deity establishing covenantal (cosmic) order out of chaos.

Psalm 74

Egypt is connected with Leviathan in Psalm 74 and outright called Rahab, another name for Leviathan, in Isaiah 30. And Pharaoh is called a dragon in Ezekiel 29:3-6.

> Isaiah 30:7
> Egypt's help is worthless and empty; therefore I have called
> her "Rahab who sits still [in the waters]."

But this is not a one-to-one equivalence of Leviathan with Egypt. Other pagan rulers and nations are also described as Leviathan or dragons. King Nebuchadnezzar of Babylon is called a dragon in Jeremiah 51:34. The spiritual powers of the first century are called Leviathan in Isaiah 27:1. The Roman empire is called a dragon in Revelation 12:3.

But let's take a look at the particular correspondence of Egypt with Leviathan. In Psalm 74, Yahweh is depicted as fighting and defeating Leviathan to establish his covenantal order with Israel at Sinai.

> Psalm 74:13–17:
> You [Yahweh] divided the sea by your might;
> you broke the heads of the <u>sea monsters [*tannim*]</u> on the waters.
> You crushed the heads of Leviathan;
> you gave him as food for the creatures of the wilderness.
> You split open springs and brooks;
> you dried up ever-flowing streams.
> Yours is the day, yours also the night;
> you have established the heavenly lights and the sun.
> You have fixed all the boundaries of the earth;
> you have made summer and winter.

In Psalm 74, the Yam Suph deliverance of the Israelites ("dividing the sea") was the metaphor of God taking them out of the chaos of pagan Egypt. As in other ancient religions, Yahweh is depicted as defeating the sea, which also represented chaos to land dwellers. Leviathan is in that sea as its instrument of power. But Yahweh crushes the heads of the sea dragon of chaos, and the creatures of the desert feast on his body. This banquet of eating the flesh of Leviathan symbolizes Yahweh's victory and is a common theme that appears in both biblical and extrabiblical Jewish poetry.[5]

For instance, 1 Enoch describes the Final Judgment symbolically as a final defeat of the chaos monsters, Leviathan and Behemoth.

> 1 Enoch 60:7-8, 27
> On that day, two monsters will be parted—one monster, a female named Leviathan, in order to dwell in the abyss of the ocean over the fountains of water; and (the other), a male called Behemoth…These two monsters are prepared for the great day of the Lord (when) they shall turn into food.[6]

The book of Revelation describes the victory of Christ over his enemies in chapter 19 as the "great supper of God" where the birds of prey eat the flesh of his defeated foes (19:17). While Leviathan is not included in this Revelation passage, it is the same kind of nature banquet motif as described in Psalm 74 with creatures feasting on the flesh of the enemies of God. The banquet of flesh was a common way of symbolizing deliverance from and victory over one's enemies.

Leviathan does show up in Revelation as the seven-headed sea dragon who is the satanic enemy of chaos against God's people.[7] Once again, the sea dragon's defeat is symbolically linked to God establishing a new order, namely the new covenant kingdom of God in Christ's blood (Revelation 12:9-11).

But back to Psalm 74, we see a strange thing in verse 14. It says that Yahweh crushes the *heads* of Leviathan. The Hebrew word there is "heads" plural, not "head" singular. Leviathan in the Old Testament is a multi-headed sea monster just like the seven-headed sea dragon of Revelation. And it is no coincidence that the Leviathan of the Canaanite Baal epic also has multiple heads (seven).[8]

The last component of Psalm 74 above is the creation language that reminds the reader of Genesis 1. God separates day and night, establishes the heavenly host, and makes the seasons (v. 15-17). This is not some unconnected jump back to the creation of the universe. It is another cosmic metaphor of the

---

[5] For 2nd Temple examples of the feast of Leviathan and Behemoth, see 4Ezra 6:47-52; 2Apoc. Bar. 29:4; 1 Enoch 60: 7-9, 24.

[6] James H. Charlesworth, *The Old Testament Pseudepigrapha,* vol. 1 (New York; London: Yale University Press, 1983), 40–42.

[7] See Rev 12:3-13:4; 16:13-16; 20:2-3.

[8] KTU 1.5:1:30

covenant in terms of a "heaven and earth." Right after Yahweh delivers the Israelites through the sea, he brings them to Sinai, where he establishes his covenant order. The Mosaic covenant was a spiritual cosmos, a heaven and earth of God's operations with his people. Yahweh delivers his people, destroys the dragon of chaos with victory, and creates his covenantal order with Israel, a new "cosmos."

Hyper-literalist assumptions may cause distress in the believer who thinks this would mean that the Yam Suph deliverance was "just a myth" or a spiritual symbol that didn't really happen in history. But this is simply a misunderstanding of the nature of ancient storytelling. Everything is not all "literal" or all "symbolic." It is very common for biblical writers to describe historic events with poetic or symbolic flair. So the Yam Suph deliverance connected to the Sinai covenant was an historic event. But it also had spiritual ramifications so important they had to be described using symbolic terms of Leviathan and creation.

Leviathan cannot be a literal physical creature because it is destroyed and eaten here in Psalm 74, yet is described by Isaiah as being alive and then slain *in the future* at another victory of God, namely, the coming of Messiah (Isaiah 27:6, 9).

> Isaiah 27:1:
> In that day the LORD with his hard and great and strong sword will punish Leviathan the fleeing serpent, Leviathan the twisting serpent, and he will slay the dragon that is in the sea.

So, it's actually most biblical to understand Leviathan not as a literal monster but as a symbolic one. More precisely, a covenantally symbolic one that is a reference to the chaos at enmity with the heavenly order of God's Kingdom.

Isaiah 51

Another passage that likens Egypt to the dragon Rahab/Leviathan during the days of the Exodus is Isaiah 50. In it, Isaiah calls to remembrance Yahweh's deliverance of Israel in days of old as a request for current redemption. Notice how Yahweh's "piercing of the dragon" occurs at the Yam Suph sea crossing. Like Psalm 74, that crossing of the sea is described using the creation language of Genesis:

> Isaiah 51:9–16
> Awake, awake, put on strength,

O arm of the Lord;
awake, as in days of old,
the generations of long ago.
Was it not you who cut Rahab in pieces,
who pierced the dragon?
Was it not you who dried up the sea,
the waters of the great deep,
who made the depths of the sea a way
for the redeemed to pass over?...
And the ransomed of the LORD shall return
and come to Zion with singing;
everlasting joy shall be upon their heads…
You have forgotten the Lord, your Maker,
who stretched out the heavens
and laid the foundations of the earth…
I am the Lord your God,
who stirs up the sea so that its waves roar—
the Lord of hosts is his name.
And I have put my words in your mouth
and covered you in the shadow of my hand,
establishing the heavens
and laying the foundations of the earth,
and saying to Zion, "You are my people."

The crossing of Yam Suph was the beginning of Yahweh establishing his covenant order with Israel. He "dries up" the sea, which represents the chaos they were leaving in Egypt. He pierces the sea dragon of chaos (Egypt?) in those waves so that he can lead the redeemed to "pass over" through the dry depths of the sea to their new world, free from slavery. God has "de-created" Egypt and will now lead Israel to Sinai, where he will establish his new creation, his covenant order that is so cosmically important he likens it to the "establishment of the heavens and foundations of the earth." Yahweh pushes back the chaos to create his new order at Sinai—the Mosaic covenant or Torah. This was when he "created" his people with the mere spoken words of his mouth: "You are my people." Of course Israel already existed as God's chosen people, but the giving of the Law at Sinai was the official legal documentation of legitimacy.[9]

---

[9] Psalm 77:17-21 describes the sea crossing in similar terms, but as Yahweh vs. the sea of chaos, without reference to Leviathan. Exodus 15:1-18, famously known as the Song of the Sea, describes the sea crossing and drowning of Pharaoh's army without reference to Leviathan or direct battle with sea, but scholar John Day concludes, "Nevertheless, it is very clear that the description has been shaped and influenced by motifs deriving from the myth of

Bible scholar John Day concludes of this passage: "In this passage, we have a blending of God's victory over chaos at the creation, at the Exodus, and in the coming deliverance from the Babylonian exile. Rahab is both the monster defeated at creation and Egypt at the time of the Exodus and also, by implication, it may be argued, the thought is extended to Babylon at the time of the prophet himself. The return from exile in Babylon is both a new creation and a new Exodus."[10]

Jeremiah 31

Jeremiah 31 is another text that expresses this same creation language at the Yam Suph crossing. It begins by prophesying the coming new covenant and compares it to the Mosaic covenant (Torah) made with the Hebrews.

> Jeremiah 31:31–33
> "Behold, the days are coming," declares the LORD, "when I will make a new covenant with the house of Israel and the house of Judah, <u>not like the covenant that I made with their fathers on the day when I took them by the hand to bring them out of the land of Egypt</u>."

That covenant, created out of the chaos of the parted sea, is described with the language of Genesis 1.

> Jeremiah 31:35–36
> Thus says the LORD, who gives the sun for light by day and the fixed order of the moon and the stars for light by night, <u>who stirs up the sea so that its waves roar</u>— the LORD of hosts is his name: "If this fixed order departs from before me, declares the LORD, then shall the offspring of Israel cease from being a nation before me forever."

Creation language here is a metaphor for covenant creation. Yahweh's establishment of his covenant in the Exodus, was an establishment of the "fixed order" of the foundations of the heavens and earth (Isaiah 51:13, 16), a creation of day and night, heavenly host, and seasons (Psalm 74:17; Jeremiah 31:35), after pushing back the chaos of the sea and defeating the dragon of chaos, Leviathan (Psalm 74, Isaiah 51). Though Leviathan is not described in

---

the divine conflict with the waters." John Day, *God's Conflict with the Dragon and the Sea: Echoes of a Canaanite Myth in the Old Testament* (Cambridge University Press, 1985), 98.

[10] John Day, *God's Conflict with the Dragon and the Sea: Echoes of a Canaanite Myth in the Old Testament* (Cambridge University Press, 1985), 91-92.

Jeremiah 31, the careful exegete can see that the narrative thread is a complete package of interconnected imagery. It's all saying the same thing.

Pharaoh as Leviathan

An Egyptian parallel to Leviathan is found in Apophis (or Apep), the underworld serpent of darkness, as well as Sobek, the crocodile god of the Nile. Though Apophis is not a part of a creation story per se, he does represent the chaos that seeks to capture and kill the sun god Ra every day as he sets out on the horizon in his solar boat called a "barque." At the end of every day, Ra must go through the underworld, called *Duat*, in order to rise in the east again in his barque to bring the rays of sunlight back upon the world. When he does, Apophis lies in wait to swallow him. He hypnotizes Ra's fellow travelers except for Set, who in turn charms Apophis with a spell so Ra can complete his journey through the Duat. Although this is not a creation story, Apophis does find simile with Leviathan as the serpent of primeval chaos and darkness that continues its fight against the *ma'at*, or order of the Egyptian cosmos.

By the time of the New Kingdom, Apophis had become known as a fleeing serpent, much like Leviathan in the Bible (Isaiah 27:1). He would flee the many curses cast upon him by those protecting Ra and his barque. And in New Kingdom texts, concurrent with the rise of Canaanite mythology in the north, Apophis was also sometimes described as having multiple heads, just like Leviathan (Psalm 74:14).[11]

Like the feast of Leviathan's flesh in the wilderness, so there are images of cutting up Apophis in victory as well. As *The Routledge Dictionary of Egyptian Gods and Goddesses* details: "In a papyrus in the British Museum, which dates to c.300 BC but contains linguistic styles of 2,000 years earlier, there is an account of the overthrow of Apophis and victory of Ra. Apophis is hacked up and burnt."[12]

The Bible itself makes an unsympathetic connection of Leviathan possibly with Sobek the crocodile god. Sobek could be depicted as a crocodile or as partly human with a crocodile head. But he was a representation of Pharaoh and his power as denizen guardian of the Nile river, the lifeline of Egypt. In another Egyptian manuscript, "The god Amon-Re declares to the victorious Thutmose III (1490–1436 B.C.): 'I cause [the enemy] to see thy

---

[11] William D. Barker, *Isaiah's Kingship Polemic: An Exegetical Study in Isaiah 24-27* (Mohr Siebeck, 2014), 148-149, 163-164. See the *Egyptian Book of the Dead*, Spell 108.

[12] George Hart, *The Routledge Dictionary of Egyptian Gods and Goddesses* (New York, NY: Routledge, 1986, 2005), 32.

majesty as a crocodile, the lord of fear in the water, who cannot be approached.'"[13]

As we saw earlier, the prophet Ezekiel ties the imagery of Leviathan/Rahab to Pharaoh Hophra (6th century B.C.) by describing him in a prophecy using the Hebrew word *tannin* for "dragon."[14] The imagery mocks the Egyptian identification of Pharaoh with the crocodile god Sobek or maybe Apophis, the reptile of chaos sometimes manifested as a crocodile.[15] The prophecy describes Yahweh's easy capture of him, followed by that recurring metaphor, the victory feast on the flesh of the enemy in the wilderness.

> Ezekiel 29:3–6
> Thus says the Lord GOD: "Behold, I am against you, Pharaoh king of Egypt, the great dragon that lies in the midst of his streams, that says, 'My Nile is my own; I made it for myself.' I will put hooks in your jaws…and I will draw you up out of the midst of your streams.…And I will cast you out into the wilderness...To the beasts of the earth and to the birds of the heavens I give you as food. Then all the inhabitants of Egypt shall know that I am the LORD."

I hear crocodile tastes just like chicken but a bit fishy. Be that as it may, destruction of the sea dragon of chaos called Leviathan or Rahab is a common symbolic motif for Yahweh's victory over chaos and the establishment and maintenance of his covenant order.z

Genesis Subversion

Leviathan is a spiritual symbol of the chaos that battles against order. But this *chaoskampf* in the Bible is not the same as pagan versions of it, where there is a dualist equivalence between the combatants and either one might win. God's only efforts described in the prophecies and poetry of his "battles" with Leviathan are described in terms of how Yahweh pierces, crushes, or captures the dragon of chaos. Leviathan is never depicted as capable of fighting back against Yahweh. It's almost like watching an old Monty Python skit of a brawny professional boxer pummeling a dainty little 8-year old girl in the ring. She never had a chance.

---

[13] John H Walton, *Zondervan Illustrated Bible Backgrounds Commentary (Old Testament): Isaiah, Jeremiah, Lamentations, Ezekiel, Daniel,* vol. 4 (Grand Rapids, MI: Zondervan, 2009), 467.

[14] Day, *God's Conflict with the Dragon*, 94-95.

[15] E.A. Wallis Budge, *The Gods of the Egyptians: Or Studies in Egyptian Mythology* (London, Methuen and Co., 1904), 325.

But this chaoskampf is not a universal interpretation in Scripture. Genesis 1 depicts Leviathan very differently than chaoskampf for its theological purposes. We read of God's Spirit hovering over the dark "face of the deep" (v. 2), which is "without form and void," or "an unfilled wasteland" (Hebrew: *tohu wa-bohu*), an expression of that chaos which the sea tends to represent to the ancient world. The Hebrew word behind "deep" is *tehom*, which some scholars argue is a linguistic connection to that Babylonian sea dragon Tiamat. But in this context, there is no *chaoskampf* battle depicted. God simply speaks, and order is established through the separation of things.

When a sea dragon does appear, it is simply one of many sea creatures God created to swarm in the sea.

> Genesis 1:21:
> So God created the great sea creatures [*tannim*] and every living creature that moves, with which the waters swarm...And God saw that it was good.

The Hebrew word for "sea creatures" (*tannim*) is a word that is translated elsewhere as *dragons*.[16] Though Leviathan is not used here, the intent of the chapter is to demythologize the elements of the natural world that pagan cultures had divinized, including not only the sun, moon, and stars, but the sea (chaos) and the dragons that resided there.

The imagery of *chaoskampf*, sea, and dragon are used poetically in some Bible passages to communicate the notion of God's creation of order out of chaos. In other passages, those mythopoeic symbols are tamed with ease and without a dualistic struggle because they are, after all, symbols in the service of their creator.[17] In the Bible, Leviathan has no chance of winning as he does in pagan mythology. All things are subject to the sovereign control of Yahweh, even chaos and evil.

See my book *When Giants Were Upon the Earth (affiliate link)* for more on the theological meaning of Leviathan and its interaction with other fantastical motifs in the Bible.

---

[16] Isaiah 51:9. "Serpent, dragon, sea-monster" Francis Brown, Samuel Rolles Driver, and Charles Augustus Briggs, *Enhanced Brown-Driver-Briggs Hebrew and English Lexicon* (Oxford: Clarendon Press, 1977), 1072.

[17] In Job 41, God's questions to Job about being able to make Leviathan a servant or "play with him as with a bird" are obvious implications that God does so with Leviathan as a domesticated pet. See also Psalm 104:26. See also "sea creatures" (tannim: dragons) Psalm 148:7; Psalm 74:13; Isaiah 51:9.

Genesis 1 Creation in its Egyptian Context

Ever since the 19th century, much critical scholarship has argued that the Pentateuch was not written by Moses, but rather by multiple sources edited together, probably sometime after the Babylonian exile. This critical theory was called the JEDP Theory or Documentary Hypothesis.[18] Based on speculative theorizing of the text, and without external factual evidence, this theory suggested that Genesis 1-2 was drawn from the Babylonian creation myth, most notably, the Enuma Elish.

It is certainly true that if the Hebrews were in subjection to Babylonian civilization for seventy years, their culture and literature would reflect some influence of their captors. And there is such textual evidence. This is not the place to rehearse the arguments of such Babylonian influence, but in recent years it has come into much doubt because of new evidence and scholarship.[19]

One of those fields previously ignored by many as having influence on the Old Testament was Egyptology. Newer studies have revealed that there are far more substantial connections between Genesis 1 and Egyptian creation stories than between Genesis 1 and the Babylonian creation story. This would be predictable if Moses had been the primary author of Genesis sometime after the Hebrew Exodus from Egypt. As a member of Pharaoh's family, he would have been educated in the known creation stories of both Egypt and Babylonia, since Egypt had much economic and cultural interaction with Mesopotamia at the time. This would account for the Babylonian accents one finds in the text. But Egyptian would be Moses's native tongue and culture. If the Hebrews had been in bondage to Egypt for 400 years (a bit more than 70 in Babylon), it would make sense that the Hebrew creation story would reflect the motifs of Egyptian stories more than Mesopotamian ones.[20]

---

[18] Each letter stands for a writer/editor who contributed to the text in succeeding generations. J stands for the earliest writer, the Yahwhist (Jehovah), E stands for the Elohist, D stands for the Deuteronomist, one more focused on Law and P stands for the Priestly author who was fixated on holiness.

[19] For details on the JEDP theory and its demise see Umberto Cassuto, *The Documentary Hypothesis and the Composition of the Pentateuch* (Skokie, IL: Varda Books, 1941, 2005); Duane A. Garrett, *Rethinking Genesis: The Sources and Authorship of the First Book of the Pentateuch* (Grand Rapids, MI: Baker Book House, 1991; Isaac M. Kikawada and Arthur Quinn, *Before Abraham Was: The Unity of Genesis 1-11* (Nashville, TN: Abingdon Press, 1985); Gleason Archer Jr., *A Survey of Old Testament Introduction*, 3rd. ed. (Chicago: Moody Press, 1994), 99–112.

[20] For details of Egyptian influence on Genesis, see Gordon H. Johnston, "Context and Contextualization of Ancient Israelite Creation Theology: Genesis 1:1-2:3 in the Light of Ancient Egyptian Creation Myths," (paper presented to the Annual Meeting of the Evangelical Theological Society 15 November 2006 (Washington, D.C.); Johnny V. Miller and John M. Soden, *In the Beginning ... We Misunderstood: Interpreting Genesis 1 in Its Original Context* (Grand Rapids, MI: Kregel Publications, 2012); James K. Hoffmeier, "Some Thoughts on Genesis 1 & 2 and Egyptian Cosmology," *Journal of the Ancient Near Eastern Society* 15 (1983): 39-49; John D. Currid, "An Examination of the Egyptian Background of the Genesis Cosmogony," *Biblische Zeitschrift* 35 (1991) 18-40; Richard J. Clifford, "Egyptian Creation Accounts," *Creation Accounts in the Ancient Near East and in the Bible*, The Catholic Biblical

Before I take a look at some of the similarities between these creation stories, I want to address a common problem in discussions about Genesis 1 as a creation account. There are many who feel that the Genesis creation narrative is a scientific description of the material physics of creation. They tend to assume that the Bible must be in accord with modern scientific processes or it would be false. They feel that if Moses drew from pagan myths, then the text is somehow not the Word of God.

This is to misunderstand the nature and purpose of the biblical text and to impose our own modern western bias upon the ancient author, which amounts to a kind of hermeneutical colonialism, the reshaping of a different culture into our own image through imposing our alien worldview upon the author's intentions.

Moses lived in a pre-scientific world that simply did not think of creation in the same way that we moderns do. Both secularists and Christians have been heavily influenced by the scientific method and a materialist worldview that reduces reality to matter and impersonal "laws of nature." Christians may add the supernatural element to this context, but we would still expect our creation stories to be narratives of the scientific method. We think in terms of natural laws and physics, of forces and matter. But the ancient mind like Moses's simply didn't think in those categories. To say that God somehow revealed 21st century concepts of science to pre-scientific authors like Moses or hid them in the text like Gnostic secret knowledge would be to render the Bible meaningless in its original context.

Gordon Johnston explains that Genesis 1 is not a scientific description of physics, but a pre-scientific description of meaning using the mythopoeic concepts available to the ancient Near Eastern mind. God did not give dictation to Moses about his creation events using alien scientific concepts. Rather, God used Moses providentially within his Egyptian world and sources to argue against the Egyptian creation story while using the imagery and concepts of that ancient world.

> Genesis 1 talks about creation in a way that would have been meaningful to ancient Near Eastern people. It uses pre-scientific imagery that they would have understood and that they themselves had even used in their own creation myths. This is a case of contextualization—God meeting ancient people where they were at in their pre-scientific worldview,

---

Quarterly Monograph Series (Washington DC: The Catholic Biblical Association of America, 1994) 101-07; James E. Atwell, "An Egyptian Source for Genesis 1," *Journal of Theological Studies* 51 (2000) 441-77.

> and accommodating—dare we say—their mythical way of speaking about origin. To take this approach does not give ground to liberalism or loose hold of biblical inerrancy. Rather, it recognizes Genesis 1 was originally written in an ancient context within which it was first understood. That ancient context was not the modern scientific world but the ancient Near East where people thought about creation in prescientific terms and talked about it using mythological symbolism. To be sure, mythological symbolism is not scientific, but that does not mean it is untrue.[21]

Ancient creation stories (such as Enuma Elish or Genesis 1) are stories about *the origin and meaning* of creation, not about the empirical science of it. Therefore all debate about the literal or figurative nature of the "days" or order of Genesis or why light existed before the sun is asking all the wrong questions. The genre of the literature is not scientific and empirical categorization of laws of physics. It is mythopoeic and teleological, a story about the meaning and purpose behind the natural order, and that was clearly religious or theological.

"Myth" or "mythopoeic" need not be words that strike fear into the hearts and minds of believers in the Bible. They are not words of "untruth" or fictional falsehood but of truth and meaning behind the observable world. Myths embody the worldview and values of a culture. There are false myths, but there are also true myths. This is a reference to the genre of a piece of literature. Genres have different purposes, and there are many different genres in the Bible. There is non-fiction, history, and biography, but there is also fiction, parable, poetry, and myth. A discerning reader can then accept ancient creation stories on their own terms instead of trying to force them into being something they are not—i.e., science textbooks.

With that said, let us look at Genesis 1 to see its similarities and differences with Egyptian creation stories of Moses's time. As I wrote in my book *God Against the gods* (Affiliate link), we will see that these similarities are not a syncretism or mixing of biblical narrative with paganism, but a subversion of paganism with biblical narrative.

Egyptologist John Currid defines the nature of this polemical theology.

> *Polemical theology* is the use by biblical writers of the thought forms and stories that were common in ancient Near Eastern culture while filling them with radically new

---

21 Johnston, "Context and Contextualization," 33.

> meaning. The biblical authors take well-known expressions and motifs from the ancient Near Eastern milieu and apply them to the person and work of Yahweh, and not to the other gods of the ancient world. Polemical theology rejects any encroachment of false gods into orthodox belief; there is an absolute intolerance of polytheism. Polemical theology is monotheistic to the very core.[22]

The first and most important element of this polemical approach is that the author of Genesis is monotheist against the polytheism of the Egyptians. As we will see below, the Egyptian cosmos depicts a multitude of gods behind the natural world of earth, air, seas, sky, and stars. The Genesis account is a marked desacralization of nature. Where the Egyptian sees the God Nun as the primeval ocean, Moses only sees a watery deep. Where the Egyptian sees a sun god, Ra, Moses describes only a "greater light" in the heavens created by Yahweh. So the Genesis account broke with millennia of pagan polytheism by redefining the natural world in terms of creation by Yahweh rather than incarnations of deity. The world is not a sacred system of multiple deities, but rather a useful creation of one sole God, Yahweh.

Before exploring Egyptian parallels with the Hebrew creation story, it is important to know that there was no single monolithic sacred narrative for the Egyptians. There are actually four reputed traditions of the mythic cycle of creation that were based on centers of power throughout Egypt's history. These come from rival sanctuaries and different time periods rooted in Heliopolis, Hermopolis, Memphis, and Thebes. Despite some differences, all four follow a similar basic storyline. The primeval waters (Nun) evolve out of ultimate oneness. Atum, a self-generated creator god, emerges from the waters on a primeval hillock of land separated from the waters and accompanied by light. Atum creates the Ennead (eight deities), who incarnate the physical world. The climax of this creation is Ra, or Ra-Atum, the sun god whose birth is represented in the first sunrise. The daily sunrise then re-enacts this one-day creation every day as the sun rises and sets. Creation of humans is almost an after-thought, an accident springing forth from the tears of the creator god. At the end of this creation day, Atum rests in satisfaction of his work. The creation cycle is then completed with the birth of Pharaoh as the god Horus, first-born son of Ra, whose earthly rule corresponds with the heavenly rule of the sun god.[23]

---

[22] John D. Currid, *Against the Gods: The Polemical Theology of the Old Testament* (Wheaton, IL: Crossway, 2013), 25.

[23] Johnston, "Context and Contextualization," 2.

Both Hebrew and Egyptian creation stories start with the beginning of time. "In the beginning" of Genesis 1:1 corresponds to the "first occasion" in Egyptian texts of creation. James Hoffmeier confirms the growing scholarly awareness of the four forces of the Hermopolitan Ogdoad matching up with the four elements of Genesis 1:2.[24] The Ogdoad were four pairs of gods and goddesses who represented the primeval forces together, referenced by the singular male deity names of Hehu, Keku, Nun, and Amun.

Let's look first at Genesis.

> Genesis 1:2 (LEB)
> Now the earth was formless and empty, and darkness was over the face of the deep. And the Spirit of God was hovering over the surface of the waters.

Comparing this passage with the Egyptian Ogdoad of gods, we see four striking correlations.

• The Hebrew "formless and empty" is remarkably similar to the "boundless imperceptibility" of the Egyptian god Hehu.

• The Hebrew "darkness" corresponds to the "darkness and obscurity" of the Egyptian god Keku.

• "Watery deep" matches perfectly with the primeval waters of the Egyptian god Nun.

• The "Spirit of God," also translated as "Wind of God," has a common motif in the Egyptian god of wind Amun.

It is no coincidence that these four deities align with the four elements of the primeval state of Hebrew creation. Again, these were deities that Genesis "depersonalizes" and interprets as natural elements under Yahweh's control. Another word for this is "demythologizing." Yahweh demythologizes nature into physical creation that obeys him rather than a nature that embodies the mythical gods of Egypt.

Though the Babylonian Enuma Elish also contains some of these concepts in its creation story, it lacks the "darkness" that the Egyptian and Hebrew accounts share.[25] Another disconnect lies in the fact that though the Babylonian version has a deity, Tiamat, that corresponds to the watery deep of Hebrew and Egyptian, the Enuma Elish tells a story of Chaoskampf, or

---

[24] These are drawn from the Coffin Texts and explored by James K. Hoffmeier, "Some Thoughts on Genesis 1 & 2 and Egyptian Cosmology," *Journal of the Ancient Near Eastern Society* 15 (1983): 42-45.

[25] Hoffmeier, "Some Thoughts," 45.

conflict between the sea dragon Tiamat and the god Marduk, that is entirely absent in the Genesis and Egyptian stories.

Hoffmeier also draws out a most significant parallel between Genesis and the Egyptian Memphite Theology. Yahweh in Genesis 1 (*Logos* in John 1) spoke creation into being with the words, "Let there be…" The primeval Egyptian gods Nun, Atum, and Ptah also create using the spoken word. As one text quotes Ptah: "One says in his mind (lit., heart), 'Look, may they come into being'." There is no creation through spoken word in the Babylonian creation story.[26]

Other ancient Near Eastern creation stories depict mankind being created from the earth or clay. But none are so similar to Genesis as the Egyptian accounts that include deity breathing life into the first humans just like Genesis 2:7. The god Hekhat pronounces, "My life is in their nostrils, I guide their breath into their throats."[27] At Thebes, the "hidden" god Amon was considered the "breath of life" in all things. In the Luxor temple an image shows Amon holding the sign of life toward Pharaoh Amenhotep III with the words: "My beloved son, receive my likeness in thy nose."[28]

There is actually a profound difference between the Hebrew and Egyptian accounts of human creation as it relates to the image of god in humankind. A statue or image of a god represented the presence of that deity on earth and embodied that presence through an "opening of the mouth" ritual that represented the receiving of breath into the image.[29] In this same way, Pharaoh was considered to be the image of Horus or Ra on earth, who received that divine breath as the god's representative. This *imago dei* was a religious justification of the king's rule over the land and people of Egypt. In Egyptian texts, the concept of a human being created in the image of a god, is used, with rare exception, exclusively of the king.[30]

The Genesis account is therefore revolutionary and defiant of this royal ideology, for its claim is that *all of humanity*, male and female, royal and commoner, are created in the image of God, for that royal dominion over all the earth and its creatures (Genesis 1:26-27). Moses was making the polemical

---

[26] Hoffmeier, "Some Thoughts," 45.

[27] Hoffmeier, "Some Thoughts," 47.

[28] As quoted in Henri Frankfort, *Kingship and the Gods: A Study of Ancient Near Eastern Religion as the Integration of Society & Nature* (Chicago, IL: University of Chicago Press, 1948, 1978), 160-161.

[29] Edward Mason Curtis, *Man as the Image of God in Genesis in the Light of Ancient Near Eastern Parallels* (Dissertation, University of Pennsylvania, 1984), 100-102.

[30] Curtis, *Man as the Image of God*, 86-96.

point that Pharaoh was no more special than any other person, because Yahweh alone was the one true God and king.

But back to similarities, both Hebrew and Egyptian creation is performed through separation of the waters in the heaven from the waters on the earth (Genesis 1:6) and the dry land from the waters (Genesis 1:9).

On the Shabaka stone, the Memphite theology declares at the end of creation, "So Ptah rested after he had made all things and all the words of god," just like Yahweh "rested from all his work that he had done in creation" (Genesis 2:1).[31]

One additional interesting problem has been the undeniable evidence of two creation stories in Genesis 1 and 2. They are not necessarily contradictory, but they focus on different things. Why? Though there are many attempts to address this biblical oddity, Tony Shetter provides one of the most compelling answers in light of Egyptian parallels. He explains that it may likely be a way of addressing the fact that the Egyptians had two traditions that separated their creation stories into that of the gods and nature and secondly of mankind. He writes, "One creation story would not suffice to argue against the views in Egypt since the Egyptians saw the creation of the universe and the creation of humans in two distinct ways, namely, creation by divine word and creation by forming. In order to sufficiently argue against both, two creation accounts were needed."[32]

There are certainly parallels between Genesis 1 and the Babylonian creation story in Enuma Elish. These include primordial waters, a separation of heaven from earth, and man formed from the earth among others. But many of these are parallels with other creation stories in the ancient Near East as well. It would make sense that Moses, being highly educated as an Egyptian royal, would have been familiar with foreign literature as recorded by Egyptian scribes for their own libraries. Johnston explains that the parallels with Egyptian creation stories is a much stronger connection of interaction because Genesis not only uses concepts and words in common with the Egyptian creation accounts, but most importantly *it follows the basic structure and sequence* of Egyptian creation.

---

31 Johnston, "Context and Contextualization," 3.

32 Tony L. Shetter, "Genesis 1-2 In Light Of Ancient Egyptian Creation Myths" (paper presented at the Student Academic Conference held at Dallas Theological Seminary in April 18, 2005) https://bible.org/article/genesis-1-2-light-ancient-egyptian-creation-myths#P107_27442

Johnston displays this amazing correspondence in a table, recreated here from his text.[33]

Memphis: Shabaka Stone	Genesis 1:1-2:3
1. Pre-creation condition: lifeless chaotic watery deep.	1. Pre-creation condition: lifeless chaotic watery deep.
2. Breath/wind (Amun) moves upon the waters.	2. Breath/wind of Elohim moves on the waters.
3. Thought and word of Ptah creates Atum (light).	3. Word of God creates light.
4. Emergence of primordial hill "in midst of Nun."	4. Creation of firmament "in midst of the waters."
5. Procreation of sky (Shu) when Nun is raised over earth.	5. Creation of sky when waters are raised above firmament.
6. Formation of heavenly ocean (Nut) by separation.	6. Formation of heavenly ocean when waters are separated.
7. Formation of dry ground (Geb) by separation.	7. Formation of dry ground when waters are gathered.
8. Sun created to rule world as image of Rê.	8. Creation of plants…later fish, birds, reptiles, animals.
9. Earth sprouts plants, fish, birds, reptiles, animals.	9. Sun and moon created to rule day and night.

[33] Johnston, "Context and Contextualization," 3.

10. Creation of god's statues, cult sites, food offerings.	10. Creation of man as divine image, food to eat, dominion.
11. Ptah completes activity and "rests" in satisfaction.	11. God completes activity and "rests" (in satisfaction).

The conclusion of this examination of creation stories is not that Moses is simply copying pagan narratives, but that he is using the categories of thought of his day to express Yahweh's identity as creator. He was not recounting what a physical eye would have seen had it been present at creation. He was describing the philosophical or theological meaning behind their cosmos in terms familiar to ancient Near Eastern people brought up to think like Egyptians as they sought to hold onto their identity as God's people.

And one of those meanings was tied to the idea of a temple.

Temple as Creation

One of the most fascinating discoveries in studying the nature of ancient temples is their connection to creation stories. The idea is that the temple incarnates the cosmos as a god's dwelling. Old Testament scholar John Walton explains that accounts of origins in the ancient world of the Near East often included accounts of temple building that are often at the climax of the stories or serving as the purpose of the creation. "[Jan] Assman goes so far as to assert that 'each temple was not only the center, but also the origin of the world.' Clifford similarly declares that the temple is 'the concrete expression of the finality of creation.'"[34] In Egypt, each temple was believed to be a "temple of the entire world" that was built upon the "primeval hillock" that emerged from "the primeval waters."[35]

Walton argues for the Genesis 1 creation account as being a temple dedication hymn. What this means is that the sacred story of creation of the universe is an analogy for the building of the temple and was written to be performed at the ritual dedication of the temple. The temple is a microcosm of the macrocosm of heavens and earth. This is true for Egypt as much as Mesopotamia and Canaan.

---

[34] John H. Walton, *Genesis 1 as Ancient Cosmology* (Winona Lake, IN: Eisenbrauns, 2011), 107.

[35] Jan Assman, *The Search for God in Egypt* (Ithaca, NY: Cornell Press, 1984, 2001), 27.

> In most temple-building texts, the temple becomes functional by means of a dedication ceremony. Prior to the dedication, it is nothing but timber, masonry, cloth, precious metals, and so on, that craftsmen have prepared. The temple becomes operational at the time of dedication by virtue of the fact that its functions are named (and thus come into existence), its accessories (functional furniture and trappings) are put in place, the priests are vested and commissioned (installed to begin the rituals), and, most importantly, at the climax, the deity is brought into his/her residence in the central cella. Only then is the temple functional; only then is it real; only then is it a temple. It is at this point that the deity is able to settle into his/her new home and is able to begin the job of ruling the cosmos and maintaining order.[36]

Yahweh's temple in Jerusalem was not built until King Solomon's day. But that structure was a permanent replacement for the tabernacle built in the wilderness wanderings of the Exodus.[37] God was on the move, so the tabernacle was effectively his mobile temple. All the elements of temple worship are embodied in the tabernacle along with all the elements of a picture of the heavens and earth.

God's blueprint for the tabernacle and its elements of worship can be found in Exodus 25–30. Later when Israel had settled in Canaan and established a Davidic monarchy, King Solomon built the temple as an expanded and updated version of the tabernacle. Because the tabernacle was intended to be a temporary mobile structure, it did not carry all the details that the temple would eventually have, but their structures were very similar in design.

---

36 John H. Walton, *Genesis 1 as Ancient Cosmology* (Winona Lake, IN: Eisenbrauns, 2011), 117.

37 Technically, the temple was an accommodation by Yahweh to David, who reasoned that if the king had a house, surely God deserved his own special house as well. But Yahweh questioned this decision by saying through the prophet Nathan, "I have not lived in a house since the day I brought up the people of Israel from Egypt to this day, but I have been moving about in a tent for my dwelling. In all places where I have moved with all the people of Israel, did I speak a word with any of the judges of Israel, whom I commanded to shepherd my people Israel, saying, "Why have you not built me a house of cedar?"' (2 Samuel 7:6–7) But Yawheh accommodated to David's desire and allowed the temple to be built by Solomon, tying it to the coming Messiah (2 Samuel 7:12-16). Those who say that the temple is not holy because it was not Yahweh's idea completely miss the fact that God DID order it to be made. So it certainly has Yahweh's stamp of approval.

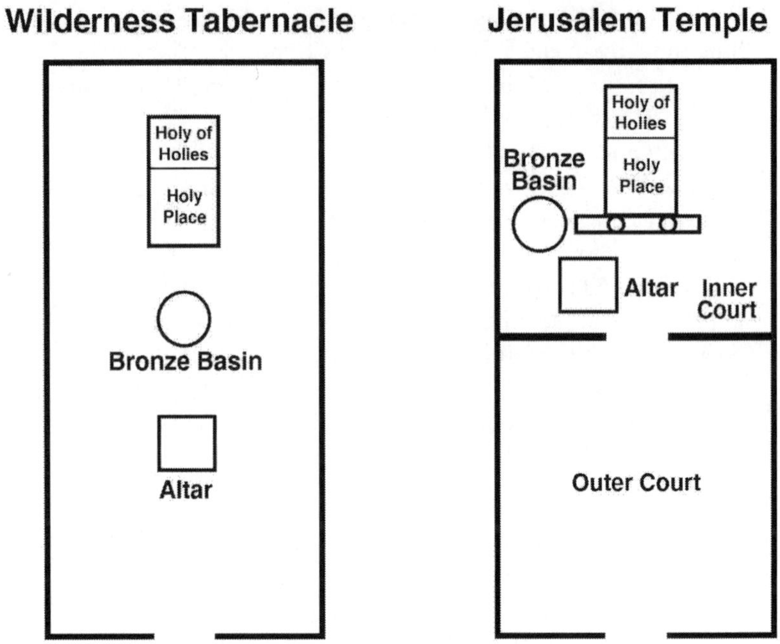

These are not to scale

Both tabernacle and temple had a walled enclosure around them with an inner temple or sanctuary, made of stone for the temple and a tent for the tabernacle. Both also had an altar of sacrifice and a bronze basin in front of the inner sanctuary. That altar hearth was a representation of the earth. In Ezekiel 43, the Hebrew words used for "altar hearth" meant "mountain of El" and "bosom of the earth."[38] Eden was described as being on a mountain (Ezekiel 28:14, 16), and the temple in Jerusalem was on "Mount Zion." The Song of Moses in the Exodus already looked forward to this future sanctuary as being Yahweh's own mountain.

> Exodus 15:17
> You will bring them in and plant them on your own mountain, the place, O LORD, which you have made for your abode, the sanctuary, O Lord, which your hands have established.

[38] Bible scholar Michael Heiser talks of this phrase altar hearth (*ha ari-el*)in Ezekiel 43 as meaning "mountain of El" and "bosom of the earth," in The Naked Bible Podcast #157 Ezekiel 40-48 Part 2 https://www.nakedbiblepodcast.com/naked-bible-157-ezekiel-40-48-part-2/

The eschatological temple was to be located on a mountain as well (Ezekiel 40:2; 43:12; Revelation 21:10).[39] So the altar hearth in the tabernacle/temple served to symbolize that earth mountain of Eden brought right into the very temple.

The large bronze basin was crafted with more detail in the temple as 12 bronze oxen holding up a "molten sea" with a rim "like a lily blossom" (1 Kings 7:23-26; 2 Chronicles 4:2-5). But in both temple and tabernacle, the basin represented the seas.

This imagery of earth and seas was complimented by the veil in the holy of holies that represented the heavens with images of cherubim, the guardians of Yahweh's throne in heaven (Exodus 26:31). The Jewish historian Josephus described the most-holy-place curtain as it appeared by the first century.

> …embroidered with blue, and fine linen, and scarlet, and purple, and of a contexture that was truly wonderful. Nor was this mixture of colors without its mystical interpretation, but was a kind of image of the universe; for by the scarlet there seemed to be enigmatically signified fire, by the fine flax the earth, by the blue the air, and by the purple the sea...This curtain had also embroidered upon it all that was mystical in the heavens.[40]

The tabernacle had the added element of its sanctuary being a tent, also embroidered with the same blue, purple, and red curtains and the same images of cherubim on them as the inner veil (Exodus 26:1). The heavens and earth and seas, three major tiers of creation, were symbolized like this in both tabernacle and temple.

But there were more images that likened the holy place sanctuary to the Garden of Eden.

Yahweh told Moses to create a golden lampstand for the holy place that would look like a symbolic almond tree with six branches, flowers, and almond blossoms (Exodus 3:31-40). As Gregory Beale notes, the Tree of Life in the Garden was probably the model for this lampstand in the garden-like environment of sacred space.[41]

---

[39] Gregory Beale, "The Final Vision of the Apocalypse and Its Implications for a Biblical Theology of the Temple," in *Heaven on Earth*, ed. T. Desmond Alexander and Simon Gathercole (Carlisle [England: Paternoster Press, 2004), 195, 197–199.

[40] Flavius Josephus, *The Wars of the Jews*, 5.5.4 §212-214. Flavius Josephus and William Whiston, *The Works of Josephus: Complete and Unabridged* (Peabody: Hendrickson, 1987), 707.

[41] Beale, "The Final Vision of the Apocalypse, 195, 197–199.

Pillars adorned both tabernacle and temple. The two massive pillars of the temple were adorned with lily capitals (tops) and pomegranates (1 Kings 7:15-20). The doors and walls of the Jerusalem temple also included images of gourds, flowers, cherubim, palm trees, open flowers, and pomegranates (1 Kings 6:18, 29, 32, 35; 1 Kings 7:18-20). Again, all imagery of the vegetation of creation that filled the earth as well as symbols of the Garden.

The pillars of the tabernacle were far fewer and simpler, no doubt for practical reasons of mobility (Exodus 27:9-17). But their plant and tree symbolism would also no doubt be the same in the minds of the Israelites. They had just come from an Egyptian culture where pillars in temples were all symbols of trees and plants. Their varieties of columns and pillars included fluted shafts that symbolized bundles of reeds with a diversity of capitals that represented palm trees, lotuses, papyrus plants, conifer trees, and other flower and foliage combinations.[42] To be in the tabernacle was to be in an image of the heavens and earth, and to be in the holy place was to be in the Garden of Eden of God's dwelling.

Beale even uncovers the symbolism connecting the priests of the holy place with Adam caring for the Garden.

> The same Hebrew verbal form (*hithpael*), *hithallek*, used for God's "walking back and forth" in the Garden (Gen. 3:8), describes God's presence in the Tabernacle (Lev. 26:12; Deut. 23:14 [15]; 2 Sam. 7:6–7).
> Secondly, Genesis 2:15 says God placed Adam in the Garden "to cultivate [work] it and to keep it." The two Hebrew words for "cultivate and keep" are usually translated "serve and guard" elsewhere in the Old Testament. When these two words occur together in the Old Testament (within an approximately fifteen-word range), they sometimes have this meaning and refer either to Israelites "serving" God and "guarding [keeping]" God's word or to priests who "keep" the "service" (or "charge") of the Tabernacle (see Num. 3:7–8; 8:25–26; 18:5–6; 1 Chr. 23:32; Ezek. 44:14).[43]

The holy of holies represented the heart of Eden, for it was here that the ark of the covenant rested, separated by that large, blue curtain veil of the heavens above. The ark is described as the footstool of God's throne from

---

[42] Richard H. Wilkinson, *The Complete Temples of Egypt* (New York, NY: Thames and Hudson, 2000), 66-67.

[43] Beale, "The Final Vision of the Apocalypse, 197.

where he "rests" with his rule (1 Chronicles 28:2), and in the temple there were two large statues of cherubim representing the cherubim who guarded the way to the tree of life (Genesis 3:24; with 1 Kings 6:23-27).

There is far more that can be said, but I want to make this last connection to the tabernacle/temple with the creation of heavens and earth. When Moses is described as erecting the tabernacle tent, the text uses the same creation language of God erecting creation like a tent.

> Exodus 40:17–19
> In the first month in the second year, on the first day of the month, the tabernacle was erected. Moses erected the tabernacle. He laid its bases, and set up its frames, and put in its poles, and raised up its pillars. And he spread the tent over the tabernacle.

"In the first…on the first" harkens back to "in the beginning." "Laying its bases," "setting up its frames," and "raising its pillars" are all echoed in Yahweh's own description to Job about his creation of heavens and earth.

> Job 38:4–6
> "Where were you when I laid the foundation of the earth?...Or who stretched the line upon it? On what were its bases sunk, or who laid its cornerstone [foundation]…"

God often used the description of creation of the heavens and earth in terms of spreading a tent.

> Psa. 104:2-3
> Stretching out the heavens like a tent. He lays the beams of his chambers on the waters.

> Isaiah 51:13
> …the LORD, your Maker, who stretched out the heavens and laid the foundations of the earth.

> Zech. 12:1
> Thus declares the LORD who stretches out the heavens, and founded the earth.

> Psa. 19:4
> He has set a tent for the sun.

So, what is the tabernacle/temple? It is a microcosm of the heavens and earth as well as a symbol of the Garden of Eden. But it is most finally the incarnation of the Mosaic covenant. All the Torah and its laws were focused on the sacred space of temple and priesthood created to perform the religious cult required by Yahweh. This would lead to the analogy of the heavens and earth with the covenant. The tabernacle/temple was the incarnation of the covenant and also the heavens and earth because God's establishment of his covenant with his people was seen as the establishment of the heavens and earth, their cosmos of existence.

We already looked at creation/covenant language in the chapter on Leviathan and the Yam Suph crossing. There and in other scriptures, the language of creation is linked to the Exodus and establishment of Yahweh's covenant. In this sense, Genesis 1 is a description of the creation of Yahweh's covenant with Israel as the creation of a cosmos. Those seven days of creation become meaningful in this covenantal context.

Biblical scholar Jon Levinson concludes at length:

> I should like to draw attention to two texts that connect the creation of the world and the construction of the Temple which have not been remarked before. 1 Kings 6:38b tells us that it took Solomon seven years to build his Temple. According to 1 Kings 8, he dedicated it during the Feast of Booths (Sukkot), which occurs in the seventh month (verse 2) and which, in Deuteronomic tradition, is a festival of seven days' duration (Deut. 16:13-15). Moreover, the speech in which Solomon dedicates his shrine, just completed, is structured around seven petitions (1 Kings 8:31-55). Can the significance of the number seven in this Temple dedication be coincidence?...It is more likely that the construction of the Temple is presented here as a parallel to the construction of the world in seven days (Gen. 1:1-2:4).[44]

Scholar Angel Manuel Rodriguez points to obvious parallels between Moses receiving instructions for the tabernacle at Mount Sinai and the creation days of Genesis 1.[45] When Yahweh gives Moses the instructions for building the tabernacle, he does so with seven speeches headed by "the Lord said to Moses" (Exodus 25:1; 30:11, 17, 22, 34; 31:1, 12). This corresponds to the six plus one days of Genesis 1 because in the seventh speech of Exodus, God concludes with a call to keep the Sabbath (31:13, 17), just like the seventh day of creation (Genesis 2:1-3).

---

[44] Jon Levenson, "The Temple and the World," *The Journal of Religion*, Vol. 64, No. 3 (Jul., 1984), pp. 289.

[45] Angel Manuel Rodríguez, "Genesis 1 and the Building of the Israelite Sanctuary" https://adventistbiblicalresearch.org/materials/genesis-1-and-the-building-of-the-israelite-sanctuary/

Even the language of Genesis creation is echoed in Exodus when after creating the tabernacle, Exodus 39:43 states, "Moses saw all the work, and behold, they had done it," reflecting Genesis 1:31, "God saw everything that he had made, and behold, it was very good."

Separation plays a significant part in Genesis. Light is separated from darkness, day from night, sky from earth, earth from water, creatures from other creatures of different "kinds." Separation was the essence of the holiness code, where the priests were to keep separation between the holy and the profane (Leviticus 10:10). The sacred space of the tabernacle, such as the holy place from the most holy place (Exodus 26:33), also reinforced the theological concept of separation.

Rodriguez draws from these obvious parallels between creation and tabernacle a picture of God's presence in his covenant temple with the intent of filling the earth as well. He concludes that the sanctuary is a cosmic symbol, "a realization of God's created order in history." And "within that theological frame of reference, the sacrificial system served the purpose of initiating, preserving, and restoring the state of order and harmony recreated by God in the tabernacle."[46] The tabernacle/temple/sanctuary was the heavens and earth of God's covenant with his people, his created order out of the chaos of the world around them.

This is why I think John Walton's suggestion that Genesis 1 is a temple dedication hymn is accurate. The creation story is not so much a scientific description of the creation of material and natural laws but rather a homologous description of God's covenant with his people as a creation of heavens and earth that they were about to enter into. The Promised Land would be their new world, which the tabernacle/temple would symbolize as a new heavens and earth, a new cosmos.

This was the temple theology I used to depict Moses's writing of Genesis 1 in the novel *Moses: Against the Gods of Egypt.*

---

[46] Rodríguez, "Genesis 1 and the Building, 3-4.

The Spiritual World of Jezebel and Elijah

Biblical Background to the Novel

Jezebel: Harlot Queen of Israel

By Brian Godawa

The Spiritual World of Jezebel and Elijah: Biblical Background to the Novel Jezebel: Harlot Queen of Israel
1st Edition

Warrior Poet Publishing
www.warriorpoetpublishing.com

ISBN: 978-1-942858-46-1 (paperback)
ISBN: 978-1-942858-47-8 (ebook)

Scripture quotations taken from *The Holy Bible: English Standard Version.* Wheaton: Standard Bible Society, 2001.

Chapter 1: The Characters

The Story First

Many of my readers like to learn about the biblical and historical research behind my novels after they've read them. The fact behind the fiction. It helps bring context and explains some of the "stranger things" of the novels to those who are intellectually and spiritually curious. This book is a presentation of the research behind my novel *Jezebel: Harlot Queen of Israel*. The truth is that the material in this book is so fascinating it can be read on its own by those who hunger as I do to uncover the ancient Near Eastern background of the biblical text.

The novel retells the biblical story centered around Queen Jezebel of Israel that can be found in 1 Kings 16 through 2 Kings 11. Jezebel, a daughter of the king of Tyre, marries King Ahab of Israel in the ninth century B.C. The marriage is a political one for the purposes of uniting in defense against the hostile Aramean kingdom in the north. Despite the pragmatism, king and queen find themselves falling in love.

Tyre, a Phoenician coastal city, is cosmopolitan and Canaanite. So Jezebel brings wealth, sophistication, and culture to a less advanced agrarian Israel. Unfortunately, she also brings the worship of Baal, the storm god of Canaan, and even builds a temple to him in Samaria, the heart of Israel.

Since Israel is supposed to be monotheist in its worship of Yahweh alone, the prophet Elijah the Tishbite and his students at the School of Prophets rise up to condemn Jezebel and call Ahab and Israel back to Yahweh from their spiritual adultery with Baal. This leads to a series of confrontations between the two worldviews that play out in the narrative, the most famous of which is the Mount Carmel episode of calling fire down from heaven.

But Jezebel doesn't give up. She fights back to gain more power and even trains Ahab's sister Athaliah to emulate her ways as future queen down in Judah. Jezebel's ruthless ambition forces a climactic battle that jeopardizes an entire family dynasty of kings.

The story of the novel is told through the eyes of Jehu son of Nimshi, who is the commander of the army of Israel. Jehu is a man who struggles with dual loyalty to both God and King. His dilemma becomes more pressing as the king whom Yahweh anointed strays from his God. As Jezebel's power grows, Jehu must rise up to do what is right, facing the loss of everything he holds dear, or suffer the damning consequences of doing nothing.

Another unique aspect of the novel is the depiction of the spiritual world. As I will explain in Chapter 2, the novel pulls back the curtain of the unseen realm. It depicts the "spiritual principalities and powers" that reign behind pagan Gentile nations and how they have influence on the course of history. Baal, Asherah, Molech, and others are not mere myths without bite. They are actual names of demonic powers that are real and have their own agenda.

Though this is obviously speculative, the principle is biblical. This is not simplistic "spiritual warfare" of demons of lust and gossip clinging to us like bacterial ghosts of influence. This is the bigger picture of higher entities of power ruling over Gentile nations as depicted in Deuteronomy 32:8-10 and Psalm 82. Nevertheless, the storyline of these spiritual powers is intended to reflect the mythology of pagans and how it reflects spiritual reality within a biblical worldview.

Thus, as Jezebel seeks to implant Baal worship in Israel, we see the spiritual entity named Baal and his allies, Astarte, Asherah, Anat, and others maneuver for power in the spiritual territories of Israel and Judah, much like human mobsters might maneuver for power over their regions in a city under their control.

But Yahweh and his archangels have other plans to protect the seed of David from the Seed of the Serpent. That is the basic storyline of the novel *Jezebel: Harlot Queen of Israel*. Now enjoy learning about the historical and biblical research behind it all.

Jezebel

The story of Jezebel and Elijah is one of the most exciting and iconic narratives in all the Bible. One of the most well-known biblical miracles was Elijah's showdown with Jezebel's prophets of Baal on Mount Carmel. Considered the most wicked queen in Israel's history, Jezebel has become a symbol for some in the modern church of women who embrace feminism. Feminists have sought to rehabilitate her image by revising it into one of a strong female misunderstood and oppressed by the "patriarchy." Some prophecy pundits even believe we are currently reliving her storyline as end times prophecy.

Regardless of what you think of these various reactions, Queen Jezebel and the prophet Elijah remain as relevant to us today as they were 2,900 years ago.

In the novel, I have sought to depict Jezebel fairly and faithfully within her original ancient Near Eastern context. That context included both the volatile world of the divided kingdoms of ninth-century Israel and Judah—the prophet Elijah's people as well as the culturally influential cosmopolitan spirit of Phoenicia—Jezebel's homeland. My research involved fascinating Bible scholarship, archaeology, and Canaanite mythology that I just had to share with my readers.

Let's start with the queen bee, herself.

One of the first things the reader will notice is that the name of Jezebel in the story is actually Izabel, an anglicized version of her real Sidonian name, Ai-zebul. The Hebrew name change from Izabel to Jezebel is not merely a matter of dialect difference but a form of ancient prophetic insult. Ai-zebul (Izabel) translated most likely meant "Where is the Prince?"[1] This was the phrase Baal worshippers would utter every harvest as they waited for their crops to arrive. It was symbolized in their myth of Baal, the god of storm and vegetation, being rescued from death in the underworld, who would then bring life back to their fields. Hillel Millgram explains,

> This myth, the centerpiece of Canaanite religion, found expression in Canaanite liturgy. During summer, the time of Baal's long absence, the worshipers of Baal would go out in procession "seeking Baal," chanting: "Where is Baal the Conqueror? Where is the Prince, the Lord of the Earth?" With the coming of the rains in the autumn, the cry would go up: "Baal the Conqueror lives! The Prince of the Earth has revived!" By their very names, Ethbaal and his daughter Jezebel proclaim the central beliefs of their religion. Ethbaal (its Phoenician form is Ittobaal) means "Baal Exists!" It is a proclamation of faith.[2]

Though Ethbaal and his daughter were priests of Astarte, their names carried the name of their most high god, Baal, a common naming technique of the ancient Near East, including Israel. In that world, names were also believed to assign destinies and even became expressions of authority by the namer

---

[1] G. Mussies, "Jezebel," ed. Karel van der Toorn, Bob Becking, and Pieter W. van der Horst, *Dictionary of Deities and Demons in the Bible* (Leiden; Boston; Köln; Grand Rapids, MI; Cambridge: Brill; Eerdmans, 1999), 473.

[2] Millgram, Hillel I., *The Elijah Enigma* (K Locations 1106-1117). McFarland & Company, Inc., Publishers. K Edition.

over the named.[3] Thus Abram's name, which meant "exalted father," was changed by God to Abraham, which meant "father of many nations" (Genesis 17:5) because that is what God would make him in his future.

In Jezebel's case, the text of 1 and 2 Kings renames Ai-zebul to Ee-zebel (Jezebel in English), which linguistically in Hebrew turns her name into a profanity of excrement. Millgram again explains,

> First *Ai* (where) was changed to *Ee*, a negative (none); thus Ai-Zebul (Where is the Prince? Where is the Exalted One?) becomes Ee-Zebul, "There is no Prince," or "Unexalted." Then Zebul (Prince, Exalted One) was altered to Zebel (feces, excrement).[4]

This named future of Jezebel is expressed in 2 Kings 9:37, which reduces the powerful queen to pathos with a double entendre of her future demise: "And the corpse of Jezebel shall be as dung on the face of the field in the territory of Jezreel, so that no one can say, 'This is Jezebel.'" The question her name was based upon, "Where is the prince (Baal)?" is related to his return from death to bring the rains and harvest. Just like no one can say, "Here is Baal," because he is not the true storm god, so no one will be able to say "here is Jezebel." Like her humbled god, she will be permanently shamefully reduced to dung on the field that awaits the rains from the true storm god, Yahweh.

This same technique of renaming is used elsewhere in the Bible. Another example I used in the novel was that of Ashtoreth, a goddess who shows up often in the Old Testament.[5] The name refers to the infamous Astarte (Phoenician: Ashtart) of Canaan and was in fact the goddess whom Jezebel's father served as high priest.[6]

It is said that ignoring someone is the most vicious way to hurt them. False gods were bad enough to the ancient Hebrew, but female goddesses were so offensive that the Bible writers didn't use a word for goddess. They simply used their names (Asherah, Ashtoreth, Lilith).[7] But it has long been noted that the name Ashtoreth was a deliberate diabolical distortion of Astarte by using the vowels of the Hebrew word for "shame" (*bosheth*) between the consonants

---

[3] John H Walton, Zondervan *Illustrated Bible Backgrounds Commentary (Old Testament): Genesis, Exodus, Leviticus, Numbers, Deuteronomy, vol. 1* (Grand Rapids, MI: Zondervan, 2009), 31–32.

[4] Millgram, Hillel I., *The Elijah Enigma* (K Locations 1266-1273). McFarland & Company, Inc., Publishers. K Edition.

[5] See 1King 11:15, 33; 2King 23:13; 1Sam 31:10.

[6] Josephus, *Against Apion* 1.18.

[7] In all my Chronicles series of novels, I make the fallen Watchers pose as the gods of the nations. Since angelic beings in the Bible are all male in gender, I have the Watchers masquerading as women goddesses.

of Astarte.[8] The goddess was too shameful or profane for Hebrews to use her real name.

Names and language are powerful tools for altering our interpretation of reality. I've explained more extensively how God and the writers of the Bible altered, subverted, reimagined, and deconstructed pagan imagination and concepts in my book *God Against the gods: Storytelling, Imagination, and Apologetics in the Bible.* (Affiliate link)

But this doesn't exhaust the biblical usage of Jezebel's name for theological purposes. In the New Testament book of Revelation, Jezebel shows up as a metaphor for spiritual apostasy among God's people. In Christ's message to the seven churches of Asia Minor, he warns the church at Thyatira of a "Jezebel."

> Revelation 2:18–23:
> But I have this against you, that you tolerate that woman Jezebel, who calls herself a prophetess and is teaching and seducing my servants to practice sexual immorality and to eat food sacrificed to idols. I gave her time to repent, but she refuses to repent of her sexual immorality. Behold, I will throw her onto a sickbed, and those who commit adultery with her I will throw into great tribulation, unless they repent of her works, and I will strike her children dead.

This condemnation has led to the common image of Jezebel as a harlot or sexually immoral woman. Some modern Christians call women who are sexually active outside of marriage "Jezebels." But a closer look at the context reveals that this is not really the apostolic intent of the imagery.

While it is possible the false teaching in Thyatira may have included sexual rituals, since pagan religions often did, it isn't likely this is the import of the text here. Christ was drawing from the books of 1 and 2 Kings as an analogy for what was going on in the Church. Jezebel wasn't criticized in the Old Testament for engaging in sexual immorality. She was damned for bringing Baal worship to Israel.

When Jezebel is first introduced in 1 Kings 16:31-33, she is described as the wife of Ahab who influenced him to build a temple of Baal and worship the Canaanite god, along with Asherah. And in Ahab's obituary in 1 Kings 21:25-26, it was said of him that "there was none who sold himself to do what

---

8 John Day, *Yahweh and the Gods and Goddesses of Canaan (The Library of Hebrew Bible/Old Testament Studies)* (Bloomsbury T&T Clark, 2002), 214.

was evil in the sight of the LORD like Ahab, whom Jezebel his wife incited" to go after abominable idols. But there is no mention of any sexual sin against her husband.

Jezebel could very likely have been a faithful, loving wife to Ahab. That is why she is portrayed as such in the novel. At least, she starts out that way. Her evil was not sexual immorality. Rather, sexual immorality was a metaphor for her spiritual evil of making Baal worship more popular in Israel.

Israel was called Yahweh's bride throughout the Old Testament.[9] His relationship with his people was so sacred and intimate that it was covenanted like a marriage. So when Israel worshipped other gods like Baal, Asherah, Molech, and others, the prophets all likened that apostasy to marital unfaithfulness to her husband Yahweh. The most recurring image used of Israel in prophetic denunciations by God was that of an unfaithful wife, described as a harlot, adulteress, or prostitute.[10]

Israel's spiritual infidelity was so prevalent that the prophets Isaiah and Jeremiah described her as "playing the whore," having sex with idols from the nations, "on every high hill and under every green tree" (Isaiah 57:5; Jeremiah 2:20; 3:6-9), which were the locations of the forbidden high places of idol worship. Ezekiel likened Judah's polytheism to a spiritual prostitute "offering herself" sexually "to any passerby," the gods of the Egyptians, Philistines, Assyrians, and Babylonians (Ezekiel 16:24-29, 35-36).

The Jezebel of Revelation was a *religious and spiritual* "whore" because of her apostate teachings as a so-called prophetess. Christians following those teachings were likened to "committing adultery with her." There is even reason to believe that the Jezebel of Revelation 2 is poetically linked to the "Great Harlot" who rides the scarlet Beast of Revelation 17.

The first step in understanding this connection is to realize that of the seven churches in Revelation 2-3, Thyatira is the fourth, which places it exactly in the middle of the seven. A well-known and oft-used literary device of many biblical writers is the poetic structure called "chiasm." In short, chiasm is the structuring of a narrative where the first half of the story builds to a midpoint climax, which represents the most important thematic focus.

---

9 Israel as married to Yahweh: Jeremiah 2.2; 31.32; Hosea 2:14–15; cf. 13.4–5.

10 Israel's unfaithfulness to Yahweh described as sexual infidelity and prostitution: Hosea 2:2; Jeremiah 3:6; Exodus 34:15–16; Leviticus 17:7; Numbers 15:39; 25:1; Deuteronomy 31:16; Judges 2:17; 8:27, 33; 1Chronicles 5:25; 2Chronicles 21:11, 13; Psalm 106:39; Isaiah 1:21; Jeremiah 2:20; 3:1–9; 5:7; Ezekiel 6:9; 16:15–17, 20, 22, 25–36, 41; 23:5–8, 11, 14, 19–19, 27–30, 35, 44; 43:7, 9; Hosea 1:2, 2:2, 4–5; 3:3; 4:10–15, 18; 5:3–4; 6:10; 9:1; Joel 3:3; Amos 7:17; Micah 1:7; Nahum 3:4.

Then the last half of the story mirrors the first half but in reverse, as if it is undoing the tension built up to the middle.

If the seven churches sequence of Revelation is understood as a chiasm, then that spiritual prophetess and harlot Jezebel is the midpoint focal theme. And it is precisely that royal/priestly figure of the Great Harlot, Mystery Babylon, which is being judged in Revelation 17. In fact, the judgment of that spiritually important city seems to be a climactic center point for Revelation's series of judgments (for a complete narrative story of who Mystery Babylon was, see my novel series *Chronicles of the Apocalypse – affiliate link*).

In conclusion, both Old and New Testaments explain Jezebel's harlotry as a spiritual analogy of apostasy, not earthly sexual behavior.

Jezebel's father was a priest of Baal, but he also became king of Tyre. So Jezebel was most likely a high priestess of Astarte since it was Phoenician custom to appoint the king's daughter as the high priestess of the local gods.[11] Astarte was considered Baal's consort in the Phoenician pantheon of Tyre. The writer of 2 Kings makes a poetic connection of Jezebel with the shameful goddess Astarte. And he does so during the description of her death at the command of Jehu, thus linking her execution with the eradication of goddess worship.

After Jehu had killed the king of Israel, he entered Jezreel to eliminate all of Ahab's family. His first order of business was to kill Jezebel. Jezebel heard that Jehu was coming, so she prepared for his arrival. The text says, "She painted her eyes and adorned her head and looked out of the window" (2 Kings 9:30). This is a peculiar thing to draw attention to in such a story. Knowing how much Jezebel and Jehu despised each other, it would be foolish of Jezebel to think she could seduce the zealous warrior king. But Jezebel was no fool. The writer is making a deliberate artistic reference to a very common motif of Astarte worship in Canaan: the "woman in the window."

Multiple ivory reliefs from the Iron Age have been found throughout Mesopotamia and the Levant that depict a woman peering out of a window.[12] She is linked to the cult of Astarte as a fertility goddess.[13] The writer of 2 Kings describes Jezebel as painting herself with make-up, a common motif of

---

[11] David Noel Freedman, "Jezebel," *The Anchor Yale Bible Dictionary* (New York: Doubleday, 1996), 848.

[12] Ivories of the Woman in the Window have been found in Arslan-Tash, Khorsabad, Nimrud and Samaria, Jezebel's second home. Eleanor Ferris Beach, "The Samaria Ivories, Marzeah, and Biblical Text," *Biblical Archaeologist* 55:3 (1992), pp. 130-139.

[13] Nehama Aschkenasy, *Woman at the Window: Biblical Tales of Oppression and Escape* (Detroit, MI: Wayne State University Press), 12.

seduction (Jeremiah 4:30), in this case the spiritual seduction by false goddesses. Jezebel was about to be attacked and destroyed just as the goddess whom she had brought to Israel was about to be attacked.

As archaeologist Eleanor Ferris Beach puts it, "In Jezebel, the literary Jehu encounters the personified visual image from the marzeah couch [Woman at the Window], and he shatters her, quite physically, as the last obstacle to the throne. He thereby denies the necessary memorial rites to the murdered kings and queen mother and asserts his independent legitimacy."[14]

The "marzeah" mentioned in the previous quotation was a ritual banquet feast that was part of a hero-cult of the dead. The marzeah memorialized the death of one king and his living replacement, who was approved by previous kings now in the underworld (more on marzeah and the cult of the dead later in this book).

Installation of the High Priestess

In the novel, Jezebel's installation as high priestess to Baal in Tyre is depicted with liturgy and fanfare. This is based on an existing manuscript of rituals from ancient Emar called *The Installation of the Storm God's High Priestess*.[15] For the sake of story pacing, I've used creative license to draw elements from the text and telescope the ceremony from nine days into a mere one day.

In the original text, day one involved anointing the priestess's head with oil and sacrificing a sheep along with a jar of barley and jug of wine. Day two was the shaving of the priestess with another sacrifice of one ox and six sheep. Here we are told of the "divine weapon" as an axe that was used as a symbolic sacred implement. The priestess was shaved at the entrance to the temple.

Day three involved more sacrifices with singers in a procession, presentation of the sacred weapon, and the high priestess's entrance into the temple. She is described as wearing gold earrings and the gold ring of Baal while her head is wrapped with a red headdress. She is carried on the shoulders of her brothers to the house of her father, where the elders then bow before her and offer gifts of silver.

---

[14] Eleanor Ferris Beach, "The Samaria Ivories, Marzeaḥ, and Biblical Text." *The Biblical Archaeologist*, Vol. 56, No. 2 (Jun., 1993), 101.

[15] Translated by Daniel Fleming, Eds., William W. Hallo and K. Lawson Younger, *The Context of Scripture* (Leiden; New York: Brill, 1997–), 427.

The next six days are filled with daily sacrifices of sheep and offerings of loaves, cakes, and fruit, along with goblets of wine and barley beer presented to the storm god Baal.

On the final ninth day, the priestess leaves her father's house with a veiled face like a bride and is taken to the temple of Baal, where more sacrifices are made and she offers her own sacrifice of lamb and loaves.

A large feast by the elders is followed by placing on her a fine robe. Then she is shown to her bedroom. Her feet are washed, and she lies down to sleep.

Elijah

Elijah the Tishbite is one of the most fascinating characters in the whole of Scripture. He is the first of the line of major prophets used to call Israel and Judah back to Yahweh, and he becomes so symbolically important that he was prophesied to return before Messiah would come to bring the Day of the Lord.

> Malachi 4:5:
> Behold, I will send you Elijah the prophet before the great and awesome day of the LORD comes.

Jesus explained that John the Baptist was the fulfillment of this prophecy as a spiritual symbol rather than a physical reincarnation (Matthew 11:12-14; Mark 9:11-13, Luke 1:17). John the Baptist came "in the spirit and power of Elijah" to be the messenger announcing Messiah as well as the destruction of the old covenant temple that Messiah replaced with his new covenant (Malachi 3:1-3).

> Malachi 3:1–2:
> Behold, I send my messenger, and he will prepare the way before me. And the Lord whom you seek will suddenly come to his temple; and the messenger of the covenant in whom you delight, behold, he is coming, says the LORD of hosts. But who can endure the day of his coming, and who can stand when he appears?

At the Mount of Transfiguration, Elijah showed up with Moses to validate Jesus as Messiah (Matthew 17:1-17). The team of Moses and Elijah had become a symbolic expression of the "Law and the Prophets," or the whole of the Scriptures. So their presence at the transfiguration was another way of God saying that all the Scriptures point to the supremacy of Jesus.

Elijah was only one of two men in Scripture who never died but were taken away to heaven. Enoch was the other. (2 Kings 2:11-12. Genesis 5:24).

The story of Elijah's fiery chariot ascension is told in the novel *Jezebel: Harlot Queen of Israel*.

But perhaps one of the most endearing character traits of the prophet was his fear. I think this is why he is so relatable to most believers despite being given such a high calling and status in the family of God.

Here you have a man who does one of the most gutsy things anyone can do, call a contest of gods in the real world (1 Kings 18:17-41). He tells Ahab to bring his prophets of Baal and Asherah to Mount Carmel and to set up an altar sacrifice. And Elijah would do the same. Then they were to each call upon their gods respectively and see which god would answer with fire from heaven. The scene is emblazoned in the minds of believers as one of the most glorious miracles outside of the Red Sea deliverance and the resurrection of Christ.

So there is Elijah, having just won that contest and slaughtered four hundred prophets of Baal in a display of Yahweh's power and might. Then he gets a letter—a mere letter—from Jezebel threatening his life in return (1 Kings 19:2), and he runs like a scaredy-cat into the desert for forty days and forty nights all the way to Mount Horeb.

On the one hand, having your life threatened by a queen is no minor thing. But when it comes from the loser over whose god you've just won a major victory, you can't help but wonder how a person could fall from the heights of faith to the depths of fear so instantaneously. Or rather, how such a man of God who had experienced the power of God, unlike any of us, could be so weak in faith.

And therein lies Elijah's relatableness to us. For who hasn't wondered at their own pathetic lack of faith or easy fall into temptation? Who hasn't questioned their own relationship to God as fraudulent because of some besetting sin? It would be doubly tempting to conclude that holiness is just too difficult to achieve. That great people of God like the prophets are simply impossible examples of unattainable heroism.

But Elijah is an attainable model after all. He is one of the most important prophets in God's plan, and yet he is one of the most human—*the most like us*—precisely because he acts just like us even though he has experienced much more of God's power and glory than any of us likely ever will.

He is also similar to the Israelite nation, who after being delivered through the parting of the Red Sea, just a short time later cast and worshipped a golden calf. They just couldn't wait long enough for the ten commandments.

I find great comfort and hope in following the example of a man who, when he fled in fear, didn't just run away from evil but *ran toward his God*—at Mount Sinai in Horeb, the mountain of Yahweh's presence. It was faith that made Elijah run to God in his fear. We'll talk about cosmic mountains later. But my goal in exploring Elijah's character was a personal journey of struggling with trying to understand the nature of faith and fear in all of us.

Then Elijah has the experience at Sinai where he observes great miraculous spectacles of wind, earthquake, and fire and yet discerns that "God is not in" these traditionally understood means of theophany. God, it turns out, speaks to him instead in "a still small voice" (1 Kings 19:9-12). At least that is how some have translated it. But looking more closely at the Hebrew of the text, I found that the phrase isn't really about an audible voice at all. It's more like an oxymoron, like saying "the sound of silence." *The New Interpreter's Bible* explains it this way:

> The traditional translation of the phrase as "a still small voice" (so KJV) has been popularized in hymns, but it does not convey the oxymoron. The NRSV takes it to be "a sound of sheer silence," which is what the words mean, and yet Elijah is able to hear something (v. 13)… In any case, the structure of the text implies that it is in this stillness that Elijah somehow encounters the Lord.[16]

It wouldn't make sense to conclude that God speaks through soft whispers or internal feelings instead of external spectacle. In fact, that would contradict the Bible. After all, God had just spoken through the external spectacle of fire from heaven, not to mention previous spectacles of food multiplication and resurrection of the dead (1 Kings 17) with more spectacle to come (2 Kings 2). He couldn't be saying that he really didn't speak through those things.

Rather, I think the picture being painted here is more of an object lesson for Elijah's faith. Perhaps the point was more about walking by faith than by sight, for when we see spectacle, we believe. But as soon as we don't, our faith falters and we worship idols. We are a fickle lot, we humans. We tend to trust only what we can see or experience. But the Scripture's focus is on the life of faith as "the assurance of things hoped for, the conviction of things not seen" (Hebrews 11:1).

Perhaps God was using one instance where he was not in the usual theophany to draw Elijah to him through his seeming absence. It is the times in life when we are suffering or dry and don't feel God's presence, when we

---

[16] Choon-Leong Seow, "The First and Second Books of Kings," in *New Interpreter's Bible*, ed. Leander E. Keck, vol. 3 (Nashville: Abingdon Press, 1994–2004), 142.

don't "experience" him, that we start to wonder where he is because he appears silent. It isn't that we have to calm down and listen because he's whispering, but rather *that he is in the silence itself.* It is the silence that cuts through our distractions and self-delusions and forces us to long for eternity and for our Maker. And it is in that longing of silence that we find him.

The cliché "absence makes the heart grow fonder" is quite relevant here for our character growth, even if not something some modern believers want to hear, especially those who may highly value "spiritual experiences."

Perhaps there is some truth to the mystic's claim that God's presence can be found in his "absence." Of course as infinite Creator, God is always everywhere present, so this isn't a theological proposition of God being literally absent, but more an expression of our own lack of experiencing that presence. When we have that realization, we connect with God whether there is spectacle or not, in pleasure or in pain, in presence or in absence, in joy or in suffering. My attempt at translating that biblical event at Sinai in the novel was another journey of attempting to make sense of a truth through narrative that couldn't really be as effectively expressed through systematic theology.

Forgive me for quoting pop culture to conclude, but I think I now have a stronger appreciation for the words of a famous song whose lyrics many may have listened to without ever hearing the echoes of Scripture within *The Sounds of Silence* by Simon and Garfunkle.

> And the people bowed and prayed
> To the neon God they made,
> And the sign flashed out its warning
> In the words that it was forming,
> And the signs said, "The words of the prophets
> Are written on the subway walls and tenement halls,"
> And whispered in the sounds of silence.

Jehu

Jehu, son of Nimshi, is the protagonist in the novel *Jezebel: Harlot Queen of Israel.* Jehu had a peculiar relationship to heroism. Because of his extremely violent actions of killing Jezebel, killing all the house of Ahab, and deceiving the Baal priests into a trap of death, he is criticized by some scholars as being a flawed hero who went too far with his pursuit of justice. As one commentator put it: "The activities of Jehu, however, are characterized by a brutality that goes beyond reason and a religious zeal which in its results has little to commend it."[17]

This negative interpretation seems supported by one prophecy in Hosea where God tells the prophet to marry a harlot and name her first child Jezreel as a prelude to the punishment of exile that is about to happen.

> Hosea 1:4:
> And the LORD said to him, "Call his name Jezreel, for in just a little while I will punish the house of Jehu for the blood of Jezreel, and I will put an end to the kingdom of the house of Israel."

So the idea here is that Jehu was in some way guilty for the blood he spilled when he killed Jezebel and the kings of both Judah and Israel in Jezreel (2 Kings 9). While in Jezreel, Jehu wrote to the elders of Samaria and told them to bring him the heads of the sons of Ahab residing in the city (2 Kings 10). Then Jehu called all the worshippers of Baal throughout Samaria to come to the temple of Baal because Jehu was going to perform a sacrifice to Baal. Jehu said he wanted to prove that he was going to have greater devotion to the deity than even Ahab had expressed. But this was just a deception to bring all the Baal worshippers together so he could kill them all and destroy the temple of Baal (2 Kings 10:18-28).

But there is a problem here, because these very actions of Jehu were commanded by Yahweh and predicted favorably by Yahweh's prophets, so why would Jehu be condemned for doing what God told him to do?

Elijah the prophet gave the word of the Lord to Ahab himself.

> 1 Kings 21:21–24:
> Behold, I will bring disaster upon you [Ahab]. I will utterly burn you up, and will cut off from Ahab every male, bond or free, in Israel. …because you have made Israel to sin. And of Jezebel the LORD also said, "The dogs shall eat Jezebel within the walls of Jezreel." Anyone belonging to Ahab who dies in the city the dogs shall eat, and anyone of his who dies in the open country the birds of the heavens shall eat."

In this passage, it is very clear from the words of God's own mouthpiece, Elijah, that Yahweh was not merely predicting Jehu's slaughter of the house of Ahab and Jezebel, but that God's own hand was in it. "I will burn you up

[17] T. R. Hobbs, *2 Kings, vol. 13, Word Biblical Commentary* (Dallas: Word, Incorporated, 1998), 119.

and cut you off . . . I will make your house barren" is all language of God's own providential involvement in the killings. In this sense, Jehu's actions were Yahweh's own actions. Later, Elisha repeats the prophecy to Jehu with its justification, "so that I may avenge on Jezebel the blood of my servants the prophets, and the blood of all the servants of the LORD" (2 Kings 9:6-10). God was using Jehu *as his own hand of vengeance* to destroy the line of Ahab.

But what about the deception that Jehu used to trap and kill the Baal worshippers, what about Jehu's execution of Ahaziah, king of Judah? Those weren't mentioned in the prophecies. Were they excessive overreach by Jehu's own violent character?

The deception of Jehu bringing in the Baal worshippers is surely not an evil, since all warfare and trapping evildoers requires deception in order to lure them to justice. That kind of "deception" is universally accepted as morally justifiable. The Baal worshippers would hardly have come of their own accord to their judgment. Regarding their slaughter, it isn't inconsistent with Elijah's commands to kill the prophets of Baal on Mount Carmel (1 Kings 18:40). But God had also decreed that Jehu would be anointed by Elijah to be king of Israel whose sword would bring God's judgment upon many.

> 1 Kings 19:16–18:
> And the one who escapes from the sword of Hazael [king of Syria] shall Jehu put to death, and the one who escapes from the sword of Jehu shall Elisha put to death. Yet I will leave seven thousand in Israel, all the knees that have not bowed to Baal, and every mouth that has not kissed him.

King Hazael was the king of Syria who fought against Israel and killed many of his people. While this prophecy is not necessarily a prescriptive command, it certainly is a justification since Elisha the righteous prophet was described as killing those who escaped Jehu's sword. And the context given here is the worship of Baal, which implicates the bloodguilt of Baal worshippers.

The only other death in need of explanation is Jehu's execution of Ahaziah, king of Judah. Though this was not commanded by Yahweh, its justification is found in the scriptural connection of Ahaziah to that house of Ahab that Jehu was justified in destroying: "[Ahaziah] also walked in the way of the house of Ahab and did what was evil in the sight of the LORD, as the house of Ahab had done, for he was son-in-law to the house of Ahab" (2 Kings 9:27).

After the text describes Jehu's actions positively as wiping out Baal from Israel, Yahweh himself gives his blessing on Jehu for "carrying out what is right in my eyes, and have done to the house of Ahab according to all that was in my heart" (2 Kings 10:30). No better approval than from God's own heart.

So, if Jehu was justified in all the blood he shed, why would Hosea speak of Jehu's bloodguilt in Jezreel? Perhaps the answer lies in the qualification right after the blessing:

> 2 Kings 10:31:
> But Jehu was not careful to walk in the law of the LORD, the God of Israel, with all his heart. He did not turn from the sins of Jeroboam, which he made Israel to sin.

Bible commentator Stuart Douglas explains that Hosea was not "condemning Jehu for fulfilling God's command. Instead, Yahweh now announces that he will turn the tables on the house of Jehu because of the real issue, i.e., *what has happened in the meantime*. In the same way that Jehu in 842 [B.C.] had annihilated a dynasty famed for its long history of oppression and apostasy, so Yahweh himself will now put an end to the Jehu dynasty because it, in turn, has grown hopelessly corrupt."[18]

Jehu has an additional historical interest because he is one of the few biblical characters who have been found on archaeological inscriptions unearthed in Israel. The Black Obelisk of Shalmaneser III contains the only known possible image of an Israelite king, and that king is Jehu. Discovered in modern day Nimrud in northern Iraq, the location of ancient Assyria of the ninth century B.C., the obelisk is about seven feet tall and is inscribed with both text and relief sculptures depicting events from Shalmaneser's reign in Assyria. As the Zondervan Illustrated Bible Backgrounds Commentary describes it:

> Among the reliefs is one that shows Jehu kneeling before the Assyrian emperor in the course of his western campaign of 841 B.C.—the only contemporary portrait in existence of an Israelite king. The relief is accompanied by the following caption: "The tribute of Jehu, son of Omri: I received from him silver, gold, a golden bowl, a golden vase with pointed bottom, golden tumblers, golden buckets, tin, a staff for a king, and javelins."[19]

---

[18] Douglas Stuart, *Hosea–Jonah*, vol. 31, *Word Biblical Commentary* (Dallas: Word, Incorporated, 2002), 29.

[19] John H Walton, *Zondervan Illustrated Bible Backgrounds Commentary (Old Testament): 1 & 2 Kings, 1 & 2 Chronicles, Ezra, Nehemiah, Esther*, vol. 3 (Grand Rapids, MI: Zondervan, 2009), 149.

The following image is by Steven G. Johnson and is licensed under the Creative Commons Attribution-Share Alike 3.0 Unported license.

Possible depiction of Jehu King of Israel giving tribute to King Shalmaneser III of Assyria, on the Black Obelisk of Shalmaneser III from Nimrud (circa 827 BC) in the British Museum (London).

Athaliah

In the novel, Athaliah is depicted as a young sister of Ahab whom Jezebel takes under her wing to prepare her for marrying the prince of Judah for political diplomacy. In the Bible, she was in fact married this way for that very purpose. But some believe she was the daughter of Ahab because the Bible seems to indicate she was.

Unfortunately, there are a couple problems with that theory. First, 2 Kings 8:18 describes Athaliah as the "daughter of Ahab." But just a few lines down in verse 26 of that same chapter, Athaliah is called the "daughter of Omri." I don't believe this is a contradiction because phrases about offspring like "son of" or "daughter of" are known to be very elastic in meaning. They can mean the immediate offspring of someone or the distant ancestor of that same person. This is most notable in the declaration of Jesus Christ to be the "Son of David." He was in the lineage of David and as such is described as a son in a distant sense. In the same way, "daughter of" could be a reference to daughter, granddaughter, or a distant ancestral designation as in "the lineage of."

So if Athaliah was the immediate daughter of Ahab, she could be considered in the household lineage of ("daughter of") Omri, her actual grandfather. Or if she was the immediate daughter of Omri, now dead, and she was taken in by her brother Ahab and his wife Jezebel, then she could be referred to as both a daughter of Omri and of Ahab. So is she the immediate daughter of Ahab or Omri?

Scholar H.J. Katzenstein has provided a solution. In his aptly titled article "Who Were the Parents of Athaliah?", he writes that by synchronizing with known dates of Assyrian kings and other scholarly references, we are able to establish the following chronology of events with reasonable accuracy:

887 BC – Ethbaal (father of Jezebel) becomes king of Tyre (age 16)
880 BC – Omri (father of Ahab) becomes king of Israel
880 BC – Athaliah is born
874 BC – Ahab becomes king of Israel
874/3 BC – Ahab marries Jezebel (age 16?)
865 BC – Athaliah (age 15) marries Jehoram of Judah
864 BC – Athaliah gives birth to Ahaziah[20]

It is clear from these strongly attested dates that Athaliah couldn't have been Jezebel's child because she was born about six years before Jezebel married Ahab. Athaliah could technically have been a child of Ahab by another wife, but that becomes more problematic because no other wives of Ahab are mentioned with royal claims for their children.

So Katzenstein concludes that Athaliah must have been the immediate daughter of Omri and therefore a very young sister of Ahab. When Omri died, she grew up as a young orphan in the court of Ahab ("daughter of Ahab") in order to represent his house in marriage to Judah. "She was educated under the supervision of Queen Jezebel and so influenced by that Tyrian princess. This makes plausible the character of Athaliah and her leanings to the Tyrian worship, which she witnessed daily in Samaria and later tried to introduce in Jerusalem."[21]

---

[20] H.J. Katzenstein, "Who Were the Parents of Athaliah?," *Israel Exploration Journal*, Vol. 5, No. 3 (1955), 194-197.

[21] Katzenstein, "Who Were the Parents," 197.

The Rechabites

One of the enigmatic groups of characters that arise in the story of Jezebel in 1 and 2 Kings is the Rechabites. There is very little about them in the Bible, but they end up playing a significant role in the end of the Omride rule over Israel and the establishment of Jehu's kingdom. So they make an appearance in the novel *Jezebel* within the context of another important background concept in the Old Testament: the Remnant.

We only read about the Rechabites at the end of 2 Kings 10 after Jehu has already killed Jezebel, Jehoram (Joram) of Israel, Ahaziah of Judah, and the seventy sons of Ahab. Then on the way to Samaria, Jehu runs into Jehonadab (or Jonadab) son of Rechab.

> 2 Kings 10:15–17:
> And when [Jehu] departed from there, he met Jehonadab the son of Rechab coming to meet him. And he greeted him and said to him, "Is your heart true to my heart as mine is to yours?" And Jehonadab answered, "It is." Jehu said, "If it is, give me your hand." So he gave him his hand. And Jehu took him up with him into the chariot. And he said, "Come with me, and see my zeal for the LORD." So he had him ride in his chariot. And when he came to Samaria, he struck down all who remained to Ahab in Samaria, till he had wiped them out, according to the word of the LORD that he spoke to Elijah.

So Jehonadab has some apparent prior connection to Jehu because the new king speaks as if he already knew Jehonadab's heart. The ancient Jewish historian Josephus explains that Jehonadab was a "good and righteous man" who "had been his [Jehu's] friend of old."[22]

Jehonadab helped Jehu finish killing the surviving members of the house of Ahab. Later, Jehonadab went with Jehu to the temple of Baal to presumably take part in putting the priests of Baal to the sword (2 Kings 10:23-27). These two were warrior friends.

While there is no specific mention of Rechabites in 2 Kings, Jehonadab is referenced both times as "son of Rechab." The idea that Jehonadab had founded a community called the Rechabites actually comes from Jeremiah's prophecy that describes this community years after Jehu's story.

---

[22] Flavius Josephus, *Antiquities of the Jews* 9.132.

The word of the Lord comes to Jeremiah, telling him to "go to the house of the Rechabites and speak with them" (Jeremiah 35:2). Jeremiah orders the Rechabites to drink some wine, but the Rechabites refuse.

> Jeremiah 35:6–8:
> But they answered, "We will drink no wine, for Jonadab the son of Rechab, our father, commanded us, "You shall not drink wine, neither you nor your sons forever. You shall not build a house; you shall not sow seed; you shall not plant or have a vineyard; but you shall live in tents all your days, that you may live many days in the land where you sojourn." We have obeyed the voice of Jonadab the son of Rechab, our father, in all that he commanded us.

Yahweh uses the Rechabites as an example of faithfulness to vows as a rebuke against Israel's unfaithfulness. But notice that their vows were based on Jonadab (alternate spelling of Jehonadab), son of Rechab. That's our man, the friend of Jehu.

Their peculiar vows of not drinking wine, and not living in built homes, or engaging in agriculture have been compared with holy Nazirite vows. Scholars have brought some historical interpretation to light that I incorporated into the novel *Jezebel*.

Herbert Huffman links the Rechabites to the tent-dwelling, metal-working Kenites descended from Tubal-Cain. He explains that their primitivist lifestyle was …

> … probably an attempt to reenact a notion of life patterned on the wilderness period, or a kind of counter-cultural reaction to the excesses of the prosperous, indulgent life in the Omride period in Israel…The wilderness period was a time without the comforts of established cities or fields and without sacrifices or oblations, and it was a time of special faithfulness… God will show Israel favor by letting them dwell in tents again as in the days of old… By renouncing a settled lifestyle, the Rechabites resemble the prophets, and they perhaps serve even as an intercessory group standing before God. [23]

Another oft-quoted commentator, Frick, explains, "The Hebrew name [Rechab] also can be the basis for the word "chariot." A guild of artisans

---

[23] Herbert B. Huffmon, "Rechab, Rechabites," ed. Katharine Doob Sakenfeld, *The New Interpreter's Dictionary of the Bible* (Nashville, TN: Abingdon Press, 2006–2009), 744.

would of necessity be somewhat nomadic in lifestyle, moving to ply their trade. The prohibition against wine becomes a possible caution against… the "loose lips sink ships" syndrome in this munitions craft, for chariots were certainly major elements in defense arsenals of the day."[24]

In his commentary on 2 Kings, T.R. Hobbs further adds, "that Jehonadab was associated with chariotry in some way, either as a rider or as a member of the chariot-making guild, is most attractive. It would explain Jehu's interest in gaining the support of such a man, especially if he had access to vehicles of war. The question Jehu asks Jehonadab also echoes the establishment of military alliances." [25]

This became the foundation for my depiction of Jonadab and the Rechabites in *Jezebel* as the tent-dwelling chariot-makers as well as pure Yahwists in their religion who are protected by the archangels.

Within the context of a corrupt Israel full of idolatry, the Rechabites would be considered part of what the Scriptures call "the remnant." Remnant theology is rooted in the blessings and curses of Deuteronomy (Deuteronomy 4:25-27; 28:15-68), where Yahweh promised to destroy Israel and scatter her to the ends of the earth if she didn't obey Yahweh. And the only reason why Yahweh withheld his judgment for so long was for the sake of the remnant of true believers within the larger body of apostate Israel. God holds back punishment of the whole for the sake of the remnant of elect.

Isaiah wrote about the coming destruction and exile of apostate Israel and yet how a remnant would return to the land (Isaiah 6:11-13; 10:20-22) and that a remnant would also return from the Babylonian exile of Judah (Isaiah 46:3-4). Ezekiel too speaks of a remnant of God's spiritually chosen survivors (Ezekiel 6:7–9; 7:16; 14:22f.; 24:26). Isaiah predicts that another remnant would be saved when Messiah came (Isaiah 4:2-4; 11:11–16; 37:30–32). Micah echoes this return from exile (Micah 2:12; 4:6-8) at the incarnation of Jesus (Micah 5:2-5), as does Joel (Joel 2:32), Obadiah (Obadiah 17), and Zephaniah (Zephaniah 3:12). Jeremiah too writes of the remnant of a new heart and a new covenant (Jeremiah 23:3; 31:7-9, 31-34). And these are by no means an exhaustive list.

But the notion of the Remnant actually begins with the story of Elijah. The Apostle Paul explains Remnant theology from our very story of Elijah and Baalism. As in the Old Covenant, so in the New Covenant. The Jewish believers in Messiah in the first century were the true remnant of "God's

---

[24] Gerald L. Keown, *Jeremiah 26–52, vol. 27, Word Biblical Commentary* (Dallas: Word, Incorporated, 1995), 196.

[25] T. R. Hobbs, *2 Kings, vol. 13, Word Biblical Commentary* (Dallas: Word, Incorporated, 1985), 128–129.

people" in the midst of an apostate Israel that rejected Jesus and were ultimately judged.

> Romans 11:2–6:
> God has not rejected his people whom he foreknew. Do you not know what the Scripture says of Elijah, how he appeals to God against Israel? "Lord, they have killed your prophets, they have demolished your altars, and I alone am left, and they seek my life." But what is God's reply to him? "I have kept for myself seven thousand men who have not bowed the knee to Baal." So too at the present time there is a remnant, chosen by grace. But if it is by grace, it is no longer on the basis of works; otherwise grace would no longer be grace.

I carried this Remnant theology to its fruition in my novel series *Chronicles of the Apocalypse (affiliate link)*, which takes place in the time just after Paul wrote those words to the Romans. Christians were spared the destruction of Israel, Jerusalem, and the temple in AD 70 when they fled to the mountains in response to Jesus' warnings (Matthew 24:15-20). But it began with the story of Elijah and Yahweh's faithful followers as the true seed of Eve.

Chapter 2: The Spiritual World of Israel

Monotheist or Polytheist?

The story of the novel *Jezebel: Harlot Queen of Israel* takes place in the middle of the ninth century B.C., a key turning point in biblical history. Because of Solomon's disobedience to Yahweh, the monarchy was split into two kingdoms, Israel in the north and Judah in the south, which launches the narrative that is 1 and 2 Kings, a forensic argument that confirmed Samuel the prophet's warning that Israel shouldn't have sought to have a king like the other nations. It reads like a heavenly Most Wanted list of spiritual criminals against God.

In my research for this novel, I was surprised at how inaccurate my view of ancient Israel had been in previous years.

Like most Christians raised in Sunday School, I had known of the apostasy both Israel and Judah experienced in worshipping other gods. But I had always seen it as a kind of reflection of our modern day world of Christianity. When I read that the Jews worshipped Baal, Asherah, Molech, or Astarte, I thought of it as a Christian whose addiction or besetting sin haunted them like some alcoholic or porn addict who give in to their "inner demons" and fall off the wagon, only to confess and repent and get back up again. So the Jews were spiritual addicts who would fall off the monotheist wagon and worship other gods, only to confess and repent and get back up again.

But this isn't really how it was. The biblical text and archaeology confirms that the Jews were not monotheists with occasional polytheist episodes. They were more like polytheists with occasional monotheist episodes. For the most part, the king dictated the direction of the people's religious observances. At the split of the monarchy, the king of the northern ten tribes, Jeroboam, made two golden calves just like the one in the wilderness, for which God destroyed thousands of Hebrews. He placed one of those idols in the city of Dan in the far north of his territory and the other in the city of Bethel in the far south. He also built pagan temples on high places and appointed priests from among the people who were not Levites as God had commanded (1 Kings 12:28-32). This action virtually established a blasphemous religion of idolatry to which the ten northern tribes of Israel ascribed. Those golden calves were not destroyed until the Assyrian exile in 722 B.C. (Dan) and Josiah's reform in 621 B.C. (Bethel: 2 Kings 23:15–16). Those calves stood with their idolatrous cult in Israel for two hundred years.

The calves most likely represented Yahweh, not Baal or some other deity, which is technically not polytheism. But the prophetic narrative of 1 and 2 Kings considers that idolatry to be so crucial to the judgment of the exile that "the sins of Jeroboam" and "way of Jeroboam" are phrases used repeatedly of subsequent kings who never destroyed those golden calves.[1] One after another with a few exceptions, they would walk "in the sins of Jeroboam" by continuing the high places and golden calf worship.

Solomon promoted actual polytheism when he created sacred "high places," altars and temples built on hills for Molech the underworld god of the Ammonites, Chemosh, chief god of the Moabites, and Astarte, the Queen of heaven and goddess of the Sidonians (1 Kings 11:5-8). The very son of David who built the temple of Yahweh in Jerusalem also built high place temples *for other deities*. Let that sink in. It's both astonishing and disturbing.

And these gods, along with Baal and others, were worshipped by the Jews for hundreds of years until the Assyrian and Babylonian exiles. The prophets blamed the exile precisely on this fact (2 Kings 17:6–12). If one charts the forty kings of the divided monarchy as listed in 1 and 2 Kings, it becomes readily apparent that the one unifying factor between almost every one of them is some form of false worship of God or gods, described euphemistically as "doing evil in the sight of the Lord"[2] or "walking in the sins of his father."[3]

There were some righteous kings in those several hundred years who did remove some idols. But even those only removed them for a short time and never removed all of them—or the high places.[4] This means that for hundreds of years Israelites never failed to have some false gods they worshipped along with Yahweh. The good kings are sometimes described as mostly "doing right," *yet* not taking down the high places or the asherim idols.[5] The hero of the Jezebel story, Jehu, who wiped out Baal worship in Israel, nevertheless didn't take down the golden calves when he became king (2 Kings 10:28-29).

---

1 1Kings 14:16; 15:30; 16:19, 26, 3; 22:52; 2Kings 3:3; 10:28; 13:2; 14:24; 15:9, 24, 28.

2 1King 14:22; 15:34; 16:19, 25; 2King 8:27; 13:2, 11; 14:24; 15:18, 28; 16:2; 17:17; 21:20; 23:32, 37; 24:9, 19.

3 1 King 15:3, 25; 2 King 8:18. 27; 16:2; 21:20.

4 1 King 15:14; 22:43; 2King 13:6; 14:4; 15:4, 14, 35; 16:4;17:10-11; 21:3;

5 1King 15:11-14; 22:43; 2King 13:3-4; 15:3-4; 34-35.

Baal worship was brought to Judah by Jezebel's step-daughter Athaliah, thriving for another two hundred years.

The most well-known reformer was Josiah, who in 640 B.C. seemed to destroy every last vestige of idol worship in Judah like none before him. Unfortunately, even after him, new kings of Judah came in and restored those gods to the Jewish pantheon (2 Kings 23:31-24:19).

The Priesthood

The truth of the matter is that the ancient Jews of this time period were fundamentally polytheistic, not monotheistic. And it wasn't just the monarchy that was so. It was also the priesthood of the temple in Jerusalem. One would think that the priests of the very temple of God would promote monotheism. But according to Scripture, even they engaged in polytheistic cult rituals for most of the time that the temple was erect in Jerusalem. You read that correctly. The "holy" temple of Solomon was from its origin a temple used for idolatrous polytheism.

The author of 2 Kings tells us that the first great reformer, Hezekiah, removed the high places, broke the pillars, and cut down the asherah in the temple sometime around 716 B.C. But there was one other image in the temple that had been there from the beginning: the bronze serpent.

> 2 Kings 18:4:
> And [Hezekiah] broke in pieces the bronze serpent that Moses had made, for until those days the people of Israel had made offerings to it (it was called Nehushtan).

The bronze serpent had been made in the wilderness wandering by Yahweh's orders as a totem for healing. Israel had grumbled against God, so he sent fiery serpents among them as judgment. When they cried out in repentance, God had Moses cast the serpent as an image, and whoever looked upon it, would be healed (Numbers 21:4-9).[6]

But 2 Kings informs us that the Israelites had turned a temporary talisman of deliverance into an image of worship. We can't know for sure how long the Israelites made offerings to Nehushtan. Was it the two hundred-fifty years of the temple's existence, or was it the entire seven hundred years since the original event? In either case, it was hundreds of years of priest-led idolatry.

---

[6] Ironically, this bronze serpent on a pole idol has evolved into the caduceus, an icon of two serpents on a pole with angelic wings as a symbol for medical practice.

But the temple also had an idolatrous asherah pole in its walls for most of the three hundred and seventy years of its existence. Asherah poles, or *asherim*, will be explained later. But for now, they were carved wooden images that represented the goddess Asherah and bore her name. Scholar Raphael Patai explains this phenomenon:

> To sum up, we find that the worship of Asherah, which had been popular among the Hebrew tribes for three centuries, was introduced into the Jerusalem Temple by King Rehoboam, the son of Solomon, in or about 928 B.C.E. Her statue was worshiped in the Temple for 35 years, until King Asa removed it in 893 B.C.E. It was restored to the Temple by King Joash in 825 B.C.E. and remained there for a full century, until King Hezekiah removed it in 725 B.C.E. After an absence of 27 years, however, Asherah was back again in the Temple: This time it was King Manasseh who replaced her in 698 B.C.E. She remained in the Temple for 78 years, until the great reformer King Josiah removed her in 620 B.C.E. Upon Josiah's death eleven years later (609 B.C.E.), she was again brought back into the Temple, where she remained until its destruction 23 years later, in 586 B.C.E. Thus it appears that, of the 370 years during which the Solomonic Temple stood in Jerusalem, for no less than 236 years (or almost two-thirds of the time) the statue of Asherah was present in the Temple, and her worship was a part of the legitimate religion approved and led by the king, the court, and the priesthood and opposed by only a few prophetic voices crying out against it at relatively long intervals.[7]

We know that this Asherah pole was not merely a passive image sitting there in the temple complex because during the reforms of Josiah, 2 Kings states that Josiah took out sacred garments woven for the asherah in the temple as well as "vessels made for Baal, for Asherah, and for all the host of heaven" and burned them outside Jerusalem in the Kidron valley (2 Kings 23:4, 7). These sacred vessels in the temple were paraphernalia used in cultic practices of active polytheistic worship.

But I want to draw your attention to the fact that there were not merely cultic vessels for Asherah in the temple, but for Baal as well. This means that

---

[7] Raphael Patai, *The Hebrew Goddess Third Enlarged Edition* (Detroit MI: Wayne State University Press, 1967,1978, 1990), 50.

by the time of Josiah, Nehushtan, Asherah, and Baal had all been worshipped for years in the Jerusalem temple along with Yahweh.

Susan Ackerman goes so far as to say that "it was the norm in the southern kingdom in the ninth century, the eighth century, and the seventh century to worship both Yahweh and Asherah in the state temple in Jerusalem. The zeal of the reformer kings, Asa, Hezekiah, and Josiah, to remove the Asherah cult was the exception."[8]

It doesn't matter how much lip service one gives to Yahweh, if you have sacred images of an animal and a goddess along with cultic implements for three gods that you actively serve in your sole temple for decades, your priests are serving more than one god. It is fair to say that the Jewish priests were not monotheists with occasional polytheist episodes. Rather, they were polytheists with occasional monotheist episodes. It's easy to see why Yahweh grew so angry at them to the point of exiling them into the hands of their pagan lovers' gods. They were sharing Yahweh's house in Jerusalem with the goddess Asherah, as well as Baal, and Nehushtan.

The People

Much of the Old Testament was written by the educated scribal or royal class. So it tends to focus on the actions of rulers, judges, and kings. It doesn't really describe the life of common folk outside of those who make an important impact on the redemptive history of Israel. Archaeological finds in recent years have helped fill in the blanks of the common Jewish family in the Promised Land. And that common life was quite polytheistic indeed.

Archaeologist William Dever uncovers Israelite folk religion based on both the Bible and archaeological finds. He argues that the folk religion of the commoner "in the streets" was often very distinct from the religious cult of the ruling class in the palace or temple. This would make sense when you consider they didn't have mass communication. Uneducated farmers and shepherds out in the wilderness would carry on their folk religion with little distraction from directives by the priesthood miles away in Jerusalem.

I will address most of these elements in individual chapters as they arise. But here is Dever's brief summary list of the activities of Israelite folk religion:

---

[8] Susan Ackerman, "The Queen Mother and the Cult in Ancient Israel," *Journal of Biblical Literature 112* (1993): 391.

> A list of proscribed activities would be long and complex, mostly derived from the Deuteronomistic and prophetic writings, but it could be summed up as follows.
> 1. Frequenting local shrines (bâmôt)
> 2. Setting up standing stones (massëbôt)
> 3. Making of images of various deities
> 4. Venerating the goddesses
> 5. Burning incense
> 6. Baking cakes for the "Queen of Heaven" [Astarte]
> 7. Making vows
> 8. "Weeping for Tammuz" [a Babylonian deity]
> 9. Performing rituals having to do with childbirth and children
> 10. Holding marzëah feasts [cult of the dead]
> 11. Conducting funerary rites; "feeding the dead"
> 12. Making pilgrimages to holy places and saints' festivals
> 13. Engaging in various aspects of astral and solar worship
> 14. Divining and "magic," except by priests
> 15. Sacrificing children (?)
>
> All these things, mostly discussed above, are condemned by the male writers of the Hebrew Bible as "idolatrous," that is, non-Yahwistic. But their inclusion implies that the majority of people, not just an easily ignored minority, were doing them — and, I would argue, principally doing them in a family context where women played a highly significant role. I have also argued that all this was part of "Yahwism," at least until the 7th century B.C. attempts at reform.[9]

Dever is a critical scholar and an unbeliever. But he also avoids both extremes of Minimalism and Maximalism. Minimalism seeks only to cynically disprove the Bible with archaeology while Maximalism seeks only to naïvely prove the Bible with archaeology. Both extremes tend to be close-minded to counter-factual evidence. So despite his secular bias, Dever remains a respectable voice in biblical archaeology. And that archaeology has uncovered many examples of all these artifacts of folk religion in manifold locations throughout the land of ancient Israel.[10]

---

[9] William G. Dever, *Did God Have a Wife?: Archaeology and Folk Religion in Ancient Israel* (Grand Rapids, MI: Eerdmans Publishing, 2005), 237

[10] See William G. Dever, *The Lives of Ordinary People in Ancient Israel: Where Archaeology and the Bible Intersect* (Grand Rapids, MI; Cambridge, U.K.: William B. Eerdmans Publishing Company, 2012) and William G. Dever, *Did*

Here is where all the difference lies. Critical scholars, because of their presupposition of anti-supernaturalism (there is no supernatural), interpret these facts within an evolutionary framework constructed to conclude that the monotheist religion of Israel evolved out of polytheism. They refuse to allow the possibility that there is a God who speaks and interacts in history with humanity. Therefore, they conclude before even looking at the evidence that monotheism was artificially thrust upon the people by priests and rulers, not God. In other words, monotheism evolved out of polytheism. After all, if there is no God who speaks into history, then all claims of him doing so are by definition lies of those in power used to manipulate the masses or the common man. Natural evolution, not supernatural revolution is their interpretive paradigm.

Furthermore, they think that uncovering ubiquitous polytheism in Israel somehow debunks the Bible. This is another function of prejudicial bias. As scholar Benjamin Sommer points out,

> It is important to emphasize that the biblical texts largely portray the Israelites as polytheists, because many modern scholars somehow assume that the biblical texts must have said that Israelites were monotheists. A depressingly large amount of scholarly writing on this subject consists of an attempt to debunk the Bible by demonstrating something the Bible itself asserts – indeed, something the Bible repeatedly emphasizes: that Israelites before the exile worshipped many gods.[11]

On the other hand, some Maximalists get freaked out because the picture of such deeply-rooted widespread polytheism in Israel doesn't fit the paradigm of Jewish monotheism they've been taught to accept. It makes them fear that the secularists and Minimalists may be right with their revisionary history and therefore their faith is in vain. So these believers deny or try to ignore the facts to protect their own bias and presuppositions.

But this fear is unnecessary. There is a third way of understanding between these two extremes. We can acknowledge the fact that during these centuries, Israelites claimed monotheism of a kind (some scholars call it more accurately, *monolatry*), but were practical polytheists in disobedience to Yahweh. Kings, priests, and common men were all infected by this evil at different levels. And of course, there were no doubt many individuals or pockets of people who were true to Yahweh. In the story of Elijah and Jezebel,

---

God Have a Wife?: Archaeology and Folk Religion in Ancient Israel (Grand Rapids, MI: Eerdmans Publishing, 2005). Also, Ziony Zevit, *The Religions of Ancient Israel: A Synthesis of Parallactic Approaches* (London, Continuum, 2001).

[11] Benjamin Sommer, *The Bodies of God and the World of Ancient Israel* (NY: Cambridge University Press, 2009), 149.

we are told that there were seven thousand who did not bow the knee to Baal (1 Kings 19:18).

Acknowledging mass apostasy in Israel for centuries is not the same as claiming monotheism evolved out of polytheism. It simply reinforces the doctrine of Original Sin. Because of the Fall in the Garden, human nature is bent toward evil, not good. So of course if there is a God who is there and is not silent, then he would have to be constantly pulling his chosen people away from their inherent nature toward polytheism. That's supernatural revolution, not natural evolution.

This also makes the prophets and their extreme language of condemnation of Israel and Judah that much more spiritually meaningful. It means that God really was so frustrated with the depth of apostasy in his own people that he had to choose individual spokesmen to Israel (prophets) in order to get his message to them. And that polytheism was so ingrained in the people's nature that they wouldn't get rid of it and because of it, would ultimately be carried away into exile. The promises of Messiah drawing the twelve tribes back under Yahweh are for a distant future. For now, the Jews lived, moved, and breathed in idolatrous polytheism.

That is the picture I tried to capture in my *Jezebel* novel, an accurate portrayal of the kind of religious world in which kings, priests, and commoners lived and worshipped.

The Watchers

I explained in the Note to the Reader at the beginning of *Jezebel* that I employ the Deuteronomy 32 worldview, or divine council motif, as a fantasy element to tell the supernatural side of the story of Jezebel and Elijah. The basic premise is that there is a spiritual world of principalities and powers whose stories are linked to earthly rulers.

Deuteronomy 32 tells the story of Israel and how she had come to be God's chosen nation. Moses begins by glorifying God and then telling the Israelites to "remember the days of old."

> Deuteronomy 32:8–9:
> When the Most High gave to the nations their inheritance,
>   when he divided mankind,
> he fixed the borders of the peoples
>   according to the number of the sons of God.
> But the Lord's portion is his people,
>   Jacob his allotted heritage.

The context of this passage is the Tower of Babel incident in Genesis 11 when mankind was divided. Rebellious humanity sought divinity in unified rebellion, so God separated them by confusing their tongues, which divided them into the seventy nations (of Gentiles) described in Genesis 10 and their ownership of those bordered lands as the "inheritance" of those peoples.

But inheritance works in heaven as it is on earth. The people of Jacob (Israel) would become Yahweh's allotted inheritance while the other seventy Gentile nations were the allotted inheritance of the *Sons of God.*

So who were these Sons of God who ruled over the Gentile nations (Psalm 82:1-8)? Some believe they were human rulers. Others argue for their identities as supernatural principalities and powers. I am in the second camp. In my *Psalm 82* book, I prove why they can't be humans and must be heavenly creatures.

The phrase "Sons of God" is a technical term that means divine beings from God's heavenly throne court (Job 1:6; 38:7), and they are referred to with many different titles. They are sometimes called "heavenly host" (Isaiah 24:21-22[12]), sometimes called "holy ones" (Deuteronomy 33:2-3[13]), sometimes called "the divine council" (Psalm 82:1[14]), sometimes called "Watchers" (Daniel 4:13, 17, 23), and sometimes called "gods" or *elohim* in the Hebrew (Deuteronomy 32: 17, 43; Psalm 82:1; 58:1-2). Yes, you read that last one correctly. God's Word calls these beings *gods*.

But fear not. That isn't polytheism. The word "god" in this sense is a synonym for "heavenly being" or "divine being" whose realm is that of the spiritual. It doesn't mean uncreated beings who are all-powerful and all-knowing. Yahweh alone is that God. Yahweh is the God of gods (Deuteronomy 10:17; Psalm 136:2). He created the other *elohim* ("gods"). These "gods" are created angelic beings who are most precisely referred to as Sons of God.

The narrative is this. Before the Flood, some of these heavenly Sons of God rebelled against Yahweh and left their divine dwelling to come to earth (Jude 6), where they violated Yahweh's holy separation and mated with human women (Genesis 6:1-4). This was not a racial separation, but a spiritual one. Their corrupt hybrid seed were called "nephilim" (giants), and their effect on humanity included such corruption and violence on the earth that Yahweh sent the Flood to wipe everyone out and start over again with Noah and his family.

Unfortunately, after the Flood humanity once again united in evil while building the Tower of Babel, a symbol of idolatrous worship of false gods. So

---

[12] See also Deut 4:19 with Deut 32:8-9; 1 King 22:19-23.

[13] See also Psalm 89:5-7; Heb 2:2.

[14] See also Psalm 89:5-7.

Yahweh confused their tongues and divided them into the seventy nations. Since mankind wouldn't stop worshipping false gods, the living God gave them over to their lusts (Romans 1:24, 26, 28) and placed them under the authority of the fallen Sons of God whom they worshipped. Fallen spiritual rulers for fallen humanity (Psalm 82:1-7). It's as if God said to humanity, "Okay, if you refuse to stop worshipping false gods, then I will give you over to them and see how you like them ruling over you."

Deuteronomy 32 hints at a spiritual reality behind the false gods of the nations, calling them "demons" (Deuteronomy 32:17; also Psalm 106:37-38). The Apostle Paul later ascribes demonic reality to false gods as well (1 Corinthians 10:20; 8:4-6). The New Testament continues this ancient notion that spiritual principalities and powers lay behind earthly powers (Ephesians 6:12; 3:10). The two were inextricably linked in historic events. As Jesus indicated, whatever happened in heaven also happened on earth (Matthew 6:10). Earthly kingdoms in conflict are intimately connected to heavenly powers in conflict.[15]

When earthly rulers battle on earth, the Bible describes the host of heaven battling with them in spiritual unity. In Daniel 10, hostilities between Greece and Persia is accompanied by the battle of heavenly Watchers over those nations (described as spiritual "princes").

> Daniel 10:13, 20-21:
> The prince of the kingdom of Persia withstood me twenty-one days, but Michael, one of the chief princes, came to help me, for I was left there with the kings of Persia. …Then he said, "Do you know why I have come to you? But now I will return to fight against the prince of Persia; and when I go out, behold, the prince of Greece will come. But I will tell you what is inscribed in the book of truth: there is none who contends by my side against these except Michael, your prince."

When Sisera fought with Israel, the earthly kings and heavenly authorities (stars or host of heaven) are described interchangeably in unity.[16]

---

[15] Daniel10:12-13, 20-21; 2Kings 6:17; Judges 5:19-20.

[16] See also 2 Kings 6:15-17 where Elisha's servant has his spiritual eyes opened to see the myriad of heavenly warriors surrounding Israel preparing to battle Syria.

> Judges 5:19–20:
> "The kings came, they fought; then fought the kings of Canaan…From heaven the stars fought, from their courses they fought against Sisera.

When God punishes earthly rulers, he punishes them along with the heavenly rulers ("host of heaven") above and behind them.

> Isaiah 24:21–22:
> On that day the LORD will punish the host of heaven, in heaven, and the kings of the earth, on the earth. They will be gathered together as prisoners in a pit; they will be shut up in a prison, and after many days they will be punished.[17]

Jeremiah also affirms the connection between earthly authorities and their heavenly principalities when he prophesies Yahweh's judgment upon Egypt and her gods, including the high god Amon, who was the patron deity of Thebes.

> Jeremiah 46:25
> Yahweh of hosts, the God of Israel, said: "Behold, I am bringing punishment upon Amon of Thebes, and Pharaoh and Egypt and her gods and her kings.

Yahweh is not using punishment upon the gods as mere generic rhetoric. He is specifically naming a deity that he will be punishing as the spiritual prince of that territory. When Yahweh punishes heavenly rulers, he also punishes earthly rulers along with them and vice versa.

This notion of territorial archons or spiritual rulers is biblical and carries over into intertestamental literature such as the Book of Enoch and others.[18] It is one of the foundational storylines of this series, Chronicles of the Watchers, as well as Chronicles of the Nephilim and Chronicles of the Apocalypse.

In the Bible, the term "Watchers" only appears in Daniel 4, where a Watcher, also called a "holy one," came down from heaven to proclaim to Daniel the "decree of the Watchers" that Nebuchadnezzar would go mad like

---

[17] Interestingly, this passage of Isaiah is not clear about what judgment in history it is referring to. But the language earlier in the text is similar to the Flood when it says, "For the windows of heaven are opened, and the foundations of the earth tremble. 19 The earth is utterly broken, the earth is split apart, the earth is violently shaken. 20 The earth staggers like a drunken man; it sways like a hut; its transgression lies heavy upon it, and it falls, and will not rise again." So this may be another passage that uses a Flood reference tied in with the Watchers and their punishment.

[18] 1 En. 89:59, 62-63; 67; Jubilees 15:31-32; Targum Jonathan Deut. 32, Sect. LIII; 3Enoch 48C:9, DSS War Scroll 1Q33 Col. xvii:7, Targum Jonathan, Genesis 11, Section II.

a beast (Daniel 4:13-17, 23). Though the Watchers of Daniel 4 are not specifically equated with the "princes" over the kingdoms of the nations in Daniel 10, they are considered by ancient Jews to be synonyms. The Watchers over the nations were the princes or principalities of those nations.

Two examples of how the ancient Jews interpreted Deuteronomy 32:8-9 illustrate this notion of territorial principalities watching over nations.

> Jubilees 15:31-32:
> (There are) many nations and many people, and they all belong to [Yahweh], but over all of them he caused spirits to rule so that they might lead them astray from following him. But over Israel he did not cause any angel or spirit to rule because he alone is their ruler and he will protect them.
>
> Targum Jonathan, Deuteronomy 32, Section LIII:
> When the Most High made allotment of the world unto the nations which proceeded from the sons of Noach [Noah], in the separation of the writings and languages of the children of men at the time of the division, He cast the lot among the seventy angels, the princes of the nations with whom is the revelation to oversee the city.[19]

It is the book of 1 Enoch that uses the term "Watchers" most commonly of these territorial princes or angels or spirits or holy ones. The Sons of God of Genesis 6 are called Watchers all throughout 1 Enoch.[20] And those Sons of God are described in the Old Testament as Yahweh's heavenly host that surround him in his divine council.

Job describes the Sons of God as divine beings who were heavenly host present at the creation (Job 38:4-7) and who gathered around Yahweh, along with the satan, to council with him and perform his decrees (Job 1:6-7; 2:1-6). 1 Kings 22:19-23 depicts these same "host of heaven" as spirits surrounding Yahweh who do his bidding. Psalm 82 and 89 describes the assembly of heavenly host as his "divine council" of "gods," "holy ones," and "Sons of the Most High" (82:6), in other words, Sons of God.

---

[19] See also 1 Enoch 89:59; 90:25, 3Enoch 48C:9, DSS War Scroll 1Q33 Col. xvii:7, Targum Jonathan, Genesis 11, Section II; Philo, On the Posterity of Cain and His Exile 25.89; Concerning Noah's Work as a Planter 14.59; On the Migration of Abraham 36.202; 1 Clement 29; Origen, First Principles 1.5.1. Thanks to Don Enevoldsen for some of these passages. Walter Wink footnotes a plenitude of texts about the 70 angel "gods" over the 70 nations in the Targums in Walter Wink. *Naming the Powers: The Language of Power in the New Testament* (The Powers : Volume One) (Kindle Locations 2235-2242). Kindle Edition.

[20] 1 Enoch 10:9, 15; 12:2-6; 13:10; 14:1-3; 15:9; 16:1-2.

All these terms are used synonymously for the divine beings of God's heavenly host, the Sons of God to whom Deuteronomy 32:8 declared were allotted the nations for an inheritance to watch over (territorial powers).

So the Bible says that there is demonic reality to false gods. But since those Sons of God who were territorial authorities over the nations were spiritually fallen Watchers, that makes them demonic or evil in essence. So what if they were the actual demonic beings behind the false gods of the ancient world? What if the fallen Sons of God were masquerading as the gods of the nations in order to keep humanity enslaved in idolatry to their authority? That would affirm the biblical stories of earthly events with heavenly events occurring in synchronization.

That is the biblical premise of all three of my Chronicles series of novels, including *Chronicles of the Watchers*. The pagan gods like Isis, Horus, Set, Baal, Astarte, and others, are actually fallen Sons of God, Watchers of the nations, crafting false identities and narratives as gods of the nations that are connected with and reflected in the earthly events of human history and its rulers. For a detailed biblical defense of this interpretation, see my booklet *Psalm 82: The Divine Council of the Gods, the Judgment of the Watchers and the Inheritance of the Nations.* (affiliate link)

1 Kings 22

My favorite Bible passage about the divine council is the story of King Ahab asking for the prophet Micaiah's advice on attacking Ramoth-gilead. I've included this story in the novel as an example of God's angelic heavenly host versus the fallen heavenly host who are the demonic gods of the nations.

Micaiah describes a scenario so obviously supernatural that little explanation is required. Though the beings in the council here are not described as "gods" like elsewhere, they are described as the "host of heaven," which the Bible defines as divine beings or gods.[21]

> 1 Kings 22:19–23:
> And Micaiah said, "Therefore hear the word of the LORD: I saw the LORD sitting on his throne, and all the host of heaven standing beside him on his right hand and on his left; and the LORD said, 'Who will entice Ahab, that he may go up and fall at Ramoth-gilead?' And one said one thing, and another said another. Then a spirit came forward and stood

---

[21] Jeremiah19:13; Deut 4:19; 17:3; 29:26; 2 Chron 33:3-5; Acts 7:42-43.

> before the LORD, saying, 'I will entice him.' And the LORD said to him, 'By what means?' And he said, 'I will go out, and will be a lying spirit in the mouth of all his prophets.' And he said, 'You are to entice him, and you shall succeed; go out and do so.' Now therefore behold, the LORD has put a lying spirit in the mouth of all these your prophets; the LORD has declared disaster for you."

The fascinating thing about this vision is that we get a glimpse into the actual process of counseling that God takes from his heavenly host. We see them surrounding his throne in counsel. We see them suggesting different things. Then God chooses one and empowers the spirit to accomplish his task. Most shocking of all, God is shown to be sovereignly ordaining "a lying spirit" to achieve his holy purpose of judgment. God ordains whatsoever comes to pass, though without himself being guilty of sin.

This may all seem rather scandalous to those Christians who prefer a simple and uncomplicated spiritual world where God sits on his throne and declares the end from the beginning without anyone's input. But biblical facts are the facts. God uses a bureaucracy of intermediary divine agents called gods, Sons of God, heavenly host, or holy ones, with whom he interacts and engages counsel.

Or as Psalm 82:1 puts it:

> God has taken his place in the divine council;
> in the midst of the gods he holds judgment:

There are plenty of other passages that describe the divine council of heavenly beings around Yahweh who counsel with him and carry out his decisions with duly delegated legal responsibility. But this one shows it at work in our very story of Jezebel's husband Ahab.[22]

Leviathan

Leviathan is a crucial character in the Chronicles universe. It shows up in Chronicles of the Nephilim, Chronicles of the Apocalypse, as well as Chronicles of the Watchers. It is drawn from the ancient Near Eastern worldview that permeates the Bible.

---

[22] Deut 32:43 LXX; Zech 2:13-3:7; Jer 23:18-22. And there are other passages where the divine council is not mentioned, but scholars explain that the plural grammar of the speech and activity imply the heavenly court motif of God addressing the council (Gen 1:26; 11:3, 4, 7; Isaiah6:8; 40:1; 41:21-23).

Contrary to what some hyper-literalists may think, Leviathan is not a real world sea dinosaur or even an extinct sea monster. It is a spiritual image used by ancient Near Eastern religions to symbolize the chaos of the cosmos that their god fought to bring about his rule and order. The Babylonians called it Tiamat. The Canaanites called it Lotan, the Ugaritic translation for "Leviathan." Hebrews called it Leviathan and sometimes Rahab.[23]

The battle of divinity to create order out of chaos is called "chaoskampf" by theologians.[24] In Mesopotamian religion, Marduk fought and defeated Tiamat the sea dragon and split her in half to create the heavens and earth that symbolized the establishment of Babylonian world power.[25] The Canaanite Baal fought and defeated Sea (Yam), River (Nahar), and Leviathan (Lotan) in order to become the Most High ruler of the Canaanite pantheon.[26]

So, Yahweh is depicted as fighting and defeating Leviathan to establish his covenantal order with Israel at Sinai.

> Psalm 74:13–17:
> You [Yahweh] divided the sea by your might;
> you broke the heads of the sea monsters on the waters.
> You crushed the heads of Leviathan;
> you gave him as food for the creatures of the wilderness.
> You split open springs and brooks;
> you dried up ever-flowing streams.
> Yours is the day, yours also the night;
> you have established the heavenly lights and the sun.
> You have fixed all the boundaries of the earth;
> you have made summer and winter.

In the above psalm, the Red Sea deliverance of the Israelites ("dividing the sea") was the metaphor of God taking them out of the chaos of pagan Egypt. As in other ancient religions, Yahweh is depicted as defeating the sea, which also represented chaos to land dwellers. And Leviathan is in that sea as its instrument of power. But Yahweh crushes the heads of the sea dragon of

---

[23] Leviathan: Job 3:8; 41; Psalm 74:13-14; Psalm 104:26; Isa 27:1. Leviathan is said to dwell in the Abyss in Job 41:24 (LXX). "[Leviathan] regards the netherworld [Tartauros] of the deep [Abyss] like a prisoner. He regards the deep [Abyss] as a walk." Job 41:34, Tan, Randall, David A. deSilva, and Logos Bible Software. The Lexham Greek-English Interlinear Septuagint. Logos Bible Software, 2009.

For Rahab, see: Isaiah51:9; Job 9:13; 26:12-13; Ps 87:4; Psalm 89:9-10.

[24] For Chaoskampf in the Bible, see: Psalm 89:9-10; Isaiah 51:9-10; Job 26:12-13. Psalms 18, 29, 24, 29, 65, 74, 77, 89, 93, and 104. Also, Exodus 15, Job 9, 26, 38, and Isaiah 51:14-16; 2 Samuel 22.

[25] *Enuma Elish*, Tablet IV, lines 104-105, 137-138, 144.

[26] See KTU 1.3:3.38-41.

chaos, and the creatures of the desert feast on his body. This banquet of eating the flesh of Leviathan symbolizes Yahweh's victory and is a common theme that appears in both biblical and extrabiblical Jewish poetry.[27]

The book of Revelation describes the victory of Christ over his enemies in chapter 19 as the "great supper of God" where the birds of prey eat the flesh of his defeated foes (19:17). While Leviathan is not included in this Revelation passage, it is the same kind of nature banquet motif as described in Psalm 74 with creatures feasting on the flesh of the enemies of God. The banquet of flesh was a common way of symbolizing deliverance from and victory over one's enemies.

Leviathan does show up in Revelation as the seven-headed sea dragon who is the satanic enemy of chaos against God's people.[28] Once again, the sea dragon's defeat is symbolically linked to God establishing a new order, namely the new covenant kingdom of God in Christ's blood (Revelation 12:9-11).

But did the monster grow some new heads in this new incarnation? Not necessarily. If one looks closely at the fourteenth verse of Psalm 74 (especially in the Hebrew), it says that Leviathan has multiple *heads*, plural, not *head*, singular (Yahweh "crushed the *heads* of Leviathan"). And it is no coincidence that the Leviathan of the Canaanite Baal epic also has multiple heads (seven).[29]

But the last component of Psalm 74 above is the creation language that reminds the reader of Genesis 1. God separates day and night, establishes the heavenly host, and makes the seasons (v. 15-17). This is not some unconnected jump back to the creation of the universe. It is another cosmic metaphor of the covenant in terms of a "heaven and earth." Right after Yahweh delivers them through the sea, he brings them to Sinai, where he establishes his covenant order. The Mosaic covenant was a spiritual cosmos, a heaven and earth of God's operations with his people. Yahweh delivers his people, destroys the dragon of chaos with victory, and creates his covenantal order with Israel, a new "cosmos."

Hyper-literalist assumptions may cause distress in the believer who thinks this would mean that the Red Sea deliverance was "just a myth" or a spiritual symbol that didn't really happen in history. But this is simply a misunderstanding of the nature of ancient storytelling. Everything is not all "literal" or all "symbolic." It is very common for biblical writers to describe historic events with poetic or symbolic flair. So the Red Sea deliverance

---

27 For 2nd Temple examples of the feast of Leviathan and Behemoth, see 4Ezra 6:47-52; 2Apoc. Bar. 29:4; 1 Enoch 60: 7-9, 24.

28 See Rev 12:3-13:4; 16:13-16; 20:2-3.

29 KTU 1.5:1:30

connected to the Sinai covenant was an historic event. But it also had spiritual ramifications so important they had to be described using symbolic terms of Leviathan and creation.

Leviathan can't be a literal physical creature because it is destroyed and eaten here in Psalm 74, yet is described by Isaiah as being alive then slain *in the future* at another victory of God, namely, the coming of Messiah (Isaiah 27:6, 9).

> Isaiah 27:1:
> In that day the LORD with his hard and great and strong sword will punish Leviathan the fleeing serpent, Leviathan the twisting serpent, and he will slay the dragon that is in the sea.

Leviathan is a spiritual symbol of the chaos that battles against order. But this *chaoskampf* in the Bible is not the same as pagan versions of it, where there is a dualist equivalence between the combatants, and either one might win. For example, Genesis 1 depicts Leviathan very differently for its theological purpose. We read of God's Spirit hovering over the dark "face of the deep" (v. 2), which is "without form and void," or "an unfilled wasteland" (Hebrew: *tohu wa-bohu*), an expression of that chaos which the sea tends to represent to the ancient world. The Hebrew word behind "deep" is *tehom*, which scholars argue is a linguistic connection to that sea dragon Tiamat. But in this context, there is no *chaoskampf* battle depicted. God simply speaks, and order is established through the separation of things.

When a sea dragon does appear, it is simply one of many sea creatures God created to swarm in the sea.

> Genesis 1:21:
> So God created the great sea creatures [*tannim*] and every living creature that moves, with which the waters swarm...
> And God saw that it was good.

The Hebrew word for "sea creatures" (*tannim*) is a word that is translated elsewhere as *dragon*.[30] Though Leviathan is not used here, the intent of the chapter is to demythologize the elements of the natural world that pagan cultures had divinized, including not only the sun, moon, and stars, but the sea (chaos) and the dragons that resided there.

---

30 Isaiah 51:9. "Serpent, dragon, sea-monster" Francis Brown, Samuel Rolles Driver, and Charles Augustus Briggs, *Enhanced Brown-Driver-Briggs Hebrew and English Lexicon* (Oxford: Clarendon Press, 1977), 1072.

The imagery of *chaoskampf*, sea, and dragon are used poetically in some Bible passages to communicate the notion of God's creation of order out of chaos. In other passages, those mythopoeic symbols are tamed with ease and without a dualistic struggle because they are after all symbols in the service of their creator.[31] In the Bible, Leviathan has no chance of winning as he does in pagan mythology. All things are subject to the sovereign control of Yahweh, even chaos and evil.

One last element bears discussion related to Leviathan. In the novel *Jezebel: Harlot Queen of Israel*, Jezebel is portrayed as having a tattoo of Leviathan on her back. This connects her spiritually to both Leviathan *and* Asherah, a key figure in the story. Asherah was considered the mother of the gods in Canaanite mythology. She was the consort of the high god El, and as such was mother of Baal. Though Jezebel was a priestess of Astarte, there is some evidence that over time, Asherah, Astarte, and even Anat may have blended into one another as different names of one goddess.[32] One of the epithets of Asherah was "Lady of the Sea," or "Lady who Treads the Sea." Some scholars suggest that the epithet can be translated, "Lady who Treads the Sea Dragon."[33] The theological interconnections of all these images with the Asherah whom Israel embraced becomes readily apparent.

See my book *When Giants Were Upon the Earth (affiliate link)* for more on the theological meaning of Leviathan and its interaction with other fantastical motifs in the Bible.

---

31 In Job 41, God's questions to Job about being able to make Leviathan a servant or "play with him as with a bird" are obvious implications that God does so with Leviathan as a domesticated pet. See also Psalm 104:26. See also "sea creatures" (tannim: dragons) Psalm 148:7; Psalm 74:13; Isaiah51:9.

32 William G. Dever, *Did God Have a Wife?: Archaeology and Folk Religion in Ancient Israel* (Grand Rapids, MI: Eerdmans Publishing, 2005), 220.

33 John Day, "Asherah in the Hebrew Bible and Northwest Semitic Literature," *Journal of Biblical Literature* 105 (1986): 388.

Chapter 3:
The Gods of Canaan

Baal

In 1929, an archeological excavation at a mound in northern Syria called Ras Shamra unearthed the remains of a significant port city called Ugarit, whose developed culture reaches back as far as 3000 BC.[1] Among the important finds were literary tablets that opened the door to a deeper understanding of ancient Near Eastern culture and the Bible. Those tablets included Syro-Canaanite religious texts of pagan deities mentioned in the Old Testament. One of those deities was Baal (alternate spelling of Ba'al).

In the Bible, Baal is used both as the name of a specific deity[2] and as a generic term for multiple idols worshipped by apostate Israel.[3] It was also used in conjunction with city names and locations, such as Baal-Hermon and Baal-Zaphon, indicating manifestations of the one deity worshipped in a variety of different Canaanite situations.[4] Simply speaking, in Canaan, Baal was all over the place. He was the chief god of the land. One could say he was the spiritual prince of Canaan as the angel Michael was the prince of Israel who fought the spiritual princes of Persia and Greece (Daniel 10:13, 20-21).

Though the Semitic noun *baal* means lord or master, it was also used as the proper name of the Canaanite storm god.[5] In the Baal epic from Ugarit, El was the supreme father of the gods who lived on a cosmic mountain. A divine council of gods called Sons of El surrounded him, vying for position and power. When the god Sea (Yam) is coronated by El and given a palace, Baal rises up and kills Sea, taking Sea's place as Most High over the other gods

---

1 Avraham Negev, "Ugarit," *The Archaeological Encyclopedia of the Holy Land*, 3rd ed. (New York: Prentice Hall Press, 1996).

2 Judges 6; 1 Kings 18; 2 Kings 10.

3 Judges 2:13; 1 Samuel 12:10; Jeremiah 2:23.

4 "Baal," *DDD,* 136.

5 Karel van der Toorn, Bob Becking, and Pieter Willem van der Horst, *Dictionary of Deities and Demons in the Bible* (*DDD*), 2nd ext. rev. ed. (Grand Rapids: Eerdmans, 1999), 132.

(excepting El). A temple is built and a feast celebrated. Mot (Death) then insults Baal, who goes down to the underworld, only to be defeated by Mot. Anat, Baal's violent sister, seeks Death and cuts him up into pieces, then brings Baal's body back up to earth, where he is brought back to life, only to fight Mot to a stalemate.[6] This return of the storm and vegetation god is a common mythical representation of the annual death of winter and new life of spring and autumn.[7]

The temporary loss of Baal to the underworld is also reflected in Jezebel's name, which in Canaanite means "Where is the Prince?" a liturgical call that Canaanites proclaimed every harvest. It is also reflected in Elijah's taunt to the prophets of Baal on Mount Carmel when he wonders if their god is absent because he is asleep in the earth (1 Kings 18:27).

The reader will notice that I have depicted this mythical narrative in the novel as a real journey where Anat rescues Baal from Mot in Sheol. And it is spiritually connected to Elijah's drought and the confrontation on Mount Carmel, thus affirming the biblical notion of the connection between earthly events and heavenly principalities. I consider it biblical appropriation and subversion of pagan mythology by the Hebrew metanarrative.

In the novel, I depict the Baal that Jezebel brings to Israel as Baal-Hadad, the storm god. This is contrary to a commonly argued interpretation that the god referred to in the Mount Carmel confrontation is Melqart. The argument for the latter is that Melqart was the patron god of Tyre, his name meaning literally, "king of the city." Melqart was a Phoenician appropriation of Herakles, the Greek divinized warrior. When Elijah mocked the prophets of Baal, he said, "Cry aloud, for he is a god. Either he is musing, or he is relieving himself, or he is on a journey, or perhaps he is asleep and must be awakened." Herakles was known as a philosopher ("musing") and for having gone on a hero's journey into the underworld. There was also a ceremony of "awakening" the god Herakles from his winter sleep. The taunt of Elijah is considered an allusion to elements of musing, journey, and awakening.[8]

But biblical scholars John Day and Mark Smith explain that there are significant problems with this interpretation and argue convincingly that the Baal of Jezebel is Baal-Shamem (another name for Hadad; it gets confusing

---

6 N. Wyatt, *Religious Texts from Ugarit*, 2nd ed., The Biblical Seminar, vol. 53 (London: Sheffield Academic Press, 2002), 36-39.

7 "Baal," *DDD*, 134.

8 John Day, *Yahweh and the Gods and Goddesses of Canaan (The Library of Hebrew Bible/Old Testament Studies)* (Bloomsbury T&T Clark, 2002), 74.

sometimes with all the multiple names for one being!).[9] Baal-Shamem means "lord of the heavens." This Shamem/Hadad was a storm god who was also associated with the Greek god Zeus. The most significant element of the Mount Carmel episode was that it was a contest of whose god was the storm god, lord of the heavens, a result of the drought called by Elijah. Melqart was not a storm god while Shamem/Hadad was.

Smith points out that an ancient inscription on Carmel identifies the god of Carmel as Zeus Heliopolis, the namesake of Shamem/Hadad, not Melqart.[10] Day argues that there are no royal names in Tyre that incorporate Melqart into their nomenclature, a common ancient practice. But there are many Tyrian names that incorporate Baal (a common reference to Shamem/Hadad) into their names, not the least of which is Jezebel and her father Ethbaal.[11]

Regarding the taunt of Elijah, Smith writes that the notion of a sleeping god being awakened is common to deities throughout the Near East, including Yahweh (Psalm 44:24; 78:65). As illustrated above, the Baal epic depicts Hadad/Shamem as being held in the underworld by Mot and being brought back to life out of the "sleep of death" by Anat. Jezebel's name is a translation of the liturgical phrase Tyrians would chant to raise Baal from that sleep to bring the rains.

In fact, according to the Baal epic, it is Hadad (Shamem) who is captured by Mot (Death) and imprisoned in the underworld as dead, which represents the seasonal deadness of the weather and crops in winter. The question "Where is the Prince?" is given in the text as a call to the return of harvest rains.

> Parched are the furrows of the grand fields,
> May Baal restore the furrows of the ploughed land.
> Where is Mightiest Baal?
> Where is the Prince, Lord of the Earth?
> (KTU 1.6:4:1-5)[12]

So Elijah's taunt is a sarcastic answer to the Baal prophets' liturgical calling for their Lord. But rather than just the mockery of being awakened from the dead, Elijah adds other options of musing, going to the toilet, or being on a journey (perhaps a reference to Anat's journey to find Baal in the

---

9 John Day, *Yahweh and the Gods and Goddesses of Canaan (The Library of Hebrew Bible/Old Testament Studies)* (Bloomsbury T&T Clark, 2002), 74-77; Mark Smith, *The Early History of God: Yahweh and the Other Deities in Ancient Israel*, 2nd Edition (Grand Rapids, MI: Eerdmans, 1990, 2002), 68-71.

10 Smith, *The Early History of God,* 71.

11 Day, *Yahweh and the Gods,* 75.

12 Mark S. Smith and Simon B. Parker, *Ugaritic Narrative Poetry,* vol. 9, Writings from the Ancient World (Atlanta, GA: Scholars Press, 1997), 158–159.

underworld). The contest on Mount Carmel was ultimately about ending the death of drought and returning the rains of harvest season. It was a contest of storm gods. Baal (Shamem/Hadad) was a storm god, Melqart was not.

When the prophets of Baal "cut themselves after their custom with swords and lances until the blood gushed" (1 Kings 18:28), this was a liturgical mourning ritual to bring Baal-Hadad back from the underworld. The activity was sympathetic magic, replaying Anat's own activity in the Baal epic before freeing Baal to bring the rains.

> With a stone [Anat] scrapes her skin,
> Double-slits with a blade.
> She cuts cheeks and chin,
> Furrows the length of her arm.
> She plows her chest like a garden,
> Like a valley she furrows her back:
> "Baal is dead! What of the peoples?"
> (KTU 1.6:1:2-8)[13]

What appears upon a cursory reading of the biblical text to be a mockery of Baal and his prophets turns out to be a complex subversion of their entire Baal-Hadad narrative and mythology. Elijah's wit and wisdom made him the holy Oscar Wilde of the ancient world (for more on God's use of sarcasm in the Bible, see my book, *The Imagination of God* (affiliate link).

While Melqart was a patron god of Tyre, he was not the only one. Shamem/Hadad was not only the head of the Phoenician pantheon but also had a temple at Tyre along with Melqart and Astarte. Shamem's temple is most likely the oldest on the island.[14]

Day concludes,

> Since the Baal promoted by Jezebel was the same Baal who had been worshipped by the Canaanite population of Israel and syncretistic Israelites, it can readily be understood how he gained such a large following. This would not be the case with Melqart, the city god of Tyre, and, as MJ. Mulder has emphasized, Ahab would have committed political suicide had he attempted to promote such a foreign god.[15]

---

13 Smith and Parker, *Ugaritic Narrative Poetry,* 151.

14 H. Jacob Katzenstein, *The History of Tyre*, 2nd ed. (Beer Sheva, Israel: Negev Press, 1997), 89. Quoted in Jennifer Lynn Greig-Berens, *Jezebel: Religious Antagonist in Israel*, Masters Thesis (Oral Roberts University, 2011), 8.

15 Day, *Yahweh and the Gods,* 76.

The Image of Baal

I depicted the Baal temple idol in the novel as a seated bronze humanoid dressed in his conical Egyptian ateph headdress with horns of deity. His arms were outstretched for sacrifice over a pit of fire. Though we don't have any actual temple images as artifactual examples, I have drawn from the writings of the ancients who described such images in relation to human sacrifice, another component of Canaanite/Phoenician religion. Though these are much later in time than the ninth century B.C., it's the closest we can get. Here are two of them.

> Greek author Kleitarchos (4th century B.C.):
> Kleitarchos says that, out of reverence for Kronos [Baal], the Phoenicians, and especially the Carthaginians… There stands in their midst a bronze statue of Kronos [Baal], its hands extended over a bronze brazier, the flames of which engulf the child. When the flames fall upon the body, the limbs contract and the open mouth seems almost to be laughing, until the contracted (body) slips quietly into the brazier."[16]

> Historian Diodorus Siculus (1st century B.C.):
> There was in their city a bronze image of Cronus [Baal], extending its hands, palms up and sloping toward the ground, so that each of the children when placed thereon rolled down and fell into a sort of gaping pit filled with fire.[17]

The Temple of Baal

In the novel, Ahab builds the temple of Baal in Jezreel, the summer royal residence, rather than in Samaria, the royal capital of Israel. A common belief is that the Baal temple was built in the city of Samaria because 1 Kings 16:32 says Ahab "erected an altar for Baal in the house of Baal, which he built in Samaria."

But archaeologist Yigael Yadin has provided compelling evidence that the temple was actually built in the city of Jezreel rather than Samaria.[18] This is not to say the Bible is incorrect. The word "Samaria" is used in the text as

---

[16] Paul G. Mosca, Child Sacrifice in Canaanite and Israelite Religion: A study in Mulk, PhD Thesis, (Cambridge, MA, Harvard University, 1975), 22.

[17] Diodorus Siculus, *The Library of History*, Book 20, 14:4-7, Loeb Classical Library, 1954, 153, quoted in Henry B. Smith, Jr., "Canaanite Child Sacrifice, Abortion, and the Bible," *The Journal of Ministry and Theology*, 98.

[18] Yigael Yadin, "The 'House of Ba'al' of Ahab and Jezebel in Samaria, and that of Athalia in Judah," in *Archaeology in the Levant*, eds. Peter Roger Stuart Moorey and Peter Parr (Warminster, UK: Aris & Phillips, 1978).

both a reference to the city as well as the governmental state (1 Kings 13:32; 16:24: 2 Kings 21:1). The phrase in 1 Kings 16:32 doesn't stipulate the city or the region as the temple's location, so it could be either.

But tellingly, archaeological excavations haven't unearthed a temple in the city of Samaria. Writer Jennifer Greig-Berens concludes from the evidence:

> Due to Ahab's loyalty to a central Yahwist cult in the capital of Israel, it is unlikely he would have built a temple to Baal in that place and arouse the opposition of those loyal to monotheism in Israel. It may have been in Jezreel that Ahab set up a palace and temple in order for his new wife and her entourage to practice their Baal worship. Jezreel seems to be the center of Baalism in the biblical narratives and is in closer proximity to Mount Carmel, where the altar of Yahweh had been "torn down" and replaced with an altar to Baal (1 Kings 18:30). This is also the abode of Jezebel after the death of her husband and during the reign of her son, Joram.
>
> Furthermore, the area of Jezreel is the usual focal point of prophetic fulfillment throughout the narratives: the location of Naboth's ancestral property (1 Kings 21:1-4); the place where the dogs would devour Jezebel (1 Kings 21:23); the place where Joram is assassinated (2 Kings 9:21-26); as well as where the heads of Ahab's "seventy sons" are sent and piled up next to the gate of the city during Jehu's revolt (2 Kings 10:8-9). By all accounts, Jezreel appears to be the central hub of Jezebel's proliferation of the Baal cult in Israel.[19]

I've drawn my description of the temple of Baal from archaeology. The most popular Phoenician designs known from Ugarit, Byblos, and other sites commonly include a long tripartite rectangular building, a pillared entrance with steps, and a long hall with an elevated holy of holies at the back where the image of the deity resided.[20]

This explains why the Baal temples are the same design as the Yahweh temple in Jerusalem. King Hiram of Tyre was hired by Solomon to help build Yahweh's house with Phoenician craftsmanship (1 Chronicles 14:1).[21]

---

[19] Jennifer Lynn Greig-Berens, *Jezebel: Religious Antagonist in Israel*, Masters Thesis (Oral Roberts University, 2011), 45-46.

[20] John H Walton, *Zondervan Illustrated Bible Backgrounds Commentary (Old Testament): 1 & 2 Kings, 1 & 2 Chronicles, Ezra, Nehemiah, Esther, vol.* 3 (Grand Rapids, MI: Zondervan, 2009), 71.

[21] See also 2 Chron 2:3, 7, 13-14.

Some Bible readers may fear this reeks of syncretism, melding foreign pagan religions with biblical religion. It's not syncretism but subversion. Subversion is defined as the appropriation and repurposing of a foreign cultural element into one's own cultural meaning. I've argued extensively in my books *The Imagination of God* and *God Against the gods* (affiliate links) that God and his scriptural authors in both Old and New Testaments engage in extensive subversion of pagan imagination. The temple is but one example.

In ancient Near Eastern religion, the temple was considered the center of the cosmos. Its architecture and design was a microcosm that reflected the macrocosm of the universe. The temple was described as being situated on a "cosmic mountain," a holy hill where creation first began, along with a river that flowed out of the mountain as the source of eternal life.[22] So too in the Bible, God's temple was a designed microcosm of the universe (Psalm 78:68-69) on the holy hill, the cosmic Mount Zion (Psalm 43:3-4; Is 2), where an Edenic river of eternal life is symbolically described as flowing out of its gates (Ezekiel 47:1-12).

But whereas similarities help to illuminate similar meaning, differences change meaning and make all the difference in the world. Differences are where subversion rather than syncretism takes place. Whereas the image of the deity was housed in the holy of holies of pagan temples, there was no image of Yahweh in his temple because of his prohibition of images. But also, he wanted to make it clear that the temple was only a sacramental symbol of connection between heaven and earth. "Heaven is my throne, and the earth is my footstool; what is the house that you would build for me, and what is the place of my rest?" (Isaiah 66:1-2).

Yahweh Versus Baal

This subversion of pagan imagination was not only in archaeological artifacts but also in literary poetry and prose. What critical scholars interpret as syncretistic evolution of Canaanite religious ideas are actually polemical subversions of those ideas by biblical authors.

It has long been known that the Old Testament contains many allusions and reflections of Canaanite literature. Some of those similarities include language used by Canaanites of Baal that were also used by the Hebrews of

---

[22] John H. Walton, *Ancient Near Eastern Thought and the Old Testament: Introducing the Conceptual World of the Hebrew Bible* (Grand Rapids: Baker, 2006), 113-34.

Yahweh. A side-by-side sampling of Ugaritic texts with Scripture illustrates strong echoes of Canaanite imagery in the biblical storytelling (see below).

UGARITIC TEXTS[23]	OLD TESTAMENT
Baal sits… in the midst of his divine mountain, Saphon, in the midst of the mountain of victory. Seven lightning-flashes, eight bundles of thunder, a tree-of-lightning in his right hand. His head is magnificent, His brow is dew-drenched. his feet are eloquent in wrath. (KTU 1.101:1–6)[24] The season of his rains may Baal indeed appoint, the season of his storm-chariot. And the sound of his voice from the clouds, his hurling to the earth of lightning-flashes (KTU 1.4:5.5–9)	"Yahweh came from Sinai… At His right hand there was flashing lightning… There is none like the God of Jeshurun, Who rides the heavens to your help, And through the clouds in His majesty… And He drove out the enemy from before you, And said, 'Destroy!' So Israel dwells in security, The fountain of Jacob secluded, In a land of grain and new wine; His heavens also drop down dew." (Deuteronomy. 33:2, 26–28)
At his holy voice the earth quaked; at the issue of his lips the mountains were afraid. The ancient mountains were afraid; the hills of the earth tottered. (KTU 1.4:7.30–35) now your foe, Baal, now your foe the Sea you must smite; now you must destroy your adversary! Take your everlasting kingdom, your eternal dominion! (KTU 1.2:4.9–10) Then Baal returned to his house [temple]. 'Will either king or commoner establish for himself dominion in the earth? (KTU 1.4:7.30–35)	The voice of the LORD is over the waters; the God of glory thunders, the LORD, over many waters… The voice of the LORD breaks the cedars; the LORD breaks the cedars of Lebanon… The voice of the LORD flashes forth flames of fire [lightning]. The voice of the LORD shakes the wilderness… And in His temple everything says, "Glory!" Yahweh sits enthroned over the flood; Yahweh is enthroned as King forever. (Psalm 29:3–11)

23 The abbreviation *KTU* stands for "Keilalphabetische Texte aus Ugarit", the standard collection of this material from Ugarit.

24 All these Ugaritic texts can be found in N. Wyatt, *Religious Texts from Ugarit*, 2nd ed., The Biblical Seminar, vol. 53 (London: Sheffield Academic Press, 2002).

Critical scholars interpret these similarities as syncretistic evolution—i.e., that the Jews originally worshipped Baal and transformed him into Yahweh. But this ignores the more germane explanation of similarities as being a common usage of images in polemical arguments. Remember, the differences make all the difference in the world. And those differences in meaning are loud and clear. Yahweh inspires his authors to use water and storm language to reflect God's polemic against the so-called storm god Baal.

Comparing the texts yields identical words, memes, and metaphors that suggest God is engaging in polemics against Baal through scriptural imagery and storytelling. It isn't Baal who rides his cloud chariot from his divine mountain Saphon but Yahweh who rides the clouds from his divine Mount Sinai (and later, Mount Zion). It isn't Baal who hurls lightning flashes in wrath but Yahweh whose lightning flashes destroy his enemies. It isn't Baal whose dew-drenched brow waters the land of Canaan but Yahweh who drops dew from heaven to Canaan. It isn't Baal's voice that thunders and conquers the waters, resulting in his everlasting temple enthronement, but Yahweh whose voice thunders and conquers the waters, resulting in his everlasting temple enthronement.

Psalm 29 (quoted in part above) is so replete with poetry in common with Canaanite poetry that many Ancient Near East scholars have concluded it is a Canaanite hymn to Baal rewritten with the name Baal replaced by the name Yahweh.[25] God was not only *physically* dispossessing Canaan of its inhabitants but *literarily* dispossessing the Canaanite gods as well. Old Testament appropriation of Canaanite culture is a case of subversion, not syncretism — overthrowing cultural narratives as opposed to blending with them. See my book *God Against the gods (affiliate link)* for an in-depth examination of this biblical literary use of creative subversion.

Asherah

Another major deity who has an important role to play in the story of Jezebel's ninth century Israel is Asherah (Athirat in Canaanite). This goddess has a veiled yet significant presence in the Bible during this time period. In some ways, she may have had a more insidious effect on the Israelites than Baal ever had.

Scholar Raphael Patai introduces the Asherah of Canaanite mythology as a fertility goddess and the wife of El, the chief god.

---

25 Aloysius Fitzgerald, "A Note on Psalm 29," *Bulletin of the American Schools of Oriental Research*, no. 215 (October 1974), 62. A more conservative interpretation claims a common Semitic poetic discourse.

> Her full name was "Lady Asherah of the Sea"—apparently, her domain proper was the sea, just as that of her husband El was heaven. She was, however, also referred to simply as Elath or Goddess. She was the "Progenitress [Mother] of the Gods": all other gods, numbering seventy, were her children, including Baal, Anath [Anat], Mot, and the other chief protagonists of the Ugaritic pantheon... Asherah's relationship to her husband El was not unlike that of an Oriental queen to her master: when entering into his presence, she would prostrate herself, whereupon El would kindly inquire after her desire. When Baal wished to obtain permission from El to build a house, he sent his mother Asherah to intercede with El. Upon the death of Baal, El asked Asherah to name one of her sons to succeed him as king. Asherah was a motherly goddess and as such she, together with her daughter Anath, served as the wet-nurse of the gods.[26]

Canaanite writings speak of a shrine of Asherah in Tyre, "the goddess of the Sidonians."[27] Archaeologist William Dever adds that excavated imagery of Asherah often involve her wearing an Egyptian-style Hathor wig and standing on the back of a lion or escorted by two lions, thus giving the great Mother Goddess the additional epithet, "The Lion Lady."[28]

Patai examines the manifold ancient artifacts found all over Palestine of clay figurines of nude women with protruding breasts and explains how they conform to stereotypical representations of Asherah. He concludes that Asherah was very popular with the common folk women of Israel, probably because she promoted fertility and facilitated childbirth.[29]

Dever imagines an ancient cultural context of men spending "too much time with their noses stuck in the Torah" and the moral dilemmas of public life while being oblivious to their families' needs. Meanwhile, the women guided the family exercise of religious rituals and cult to safeguard their loved ones and therefore regarded themselves as morally superior to the men.[30] Depending on your presuppositions, one could see this as an anachronistic

---

[26] Raphael Patai, *The Hebrew Goddess 3rd Enlarged Edition* (Detroit, MI: Wayne State University Press, 1967, 1978, 1990), 37.

[27] N. Wyatt, "Asherah," ed. Karel van der Toorn, Bob Becking, and Pieter W. van der Horst, *Dictionary of Deities and Demons in the Bible* (Leiden; Boston; Köln; Grand Rapids, MI; Cambridge: Brill; Eerdmans, 1999), 99.

[28] William G. Dever, *Did God Have a Wife?: Archaeology and Folk Religion in Ancient Israel* (Grand Rapids, MI: Eerdmans Publishing, 2005), 219-220.

[29] Patai, *The Hebrew Goddess,* 39.

[30] Dever, *Did God Have a Wife?,* 250.

projection of modernity back upon the ancient world or as a reflection of the unchanging nature of gender weaknesses.

But Karel van der Toorn agrees that in the Bible Israelite women are often portrayed as displaying a greater religious sensibility than their husbands:

> All in all, then, ancient Israelite religion played a double role in the lives of women. While legitimating their subservient social position, it opened the possibility as well of an intense religious experience. In this way, it gave a compensation on one level for what it had taken on another. As it seems, Israelite women eagerly seized upon this possibility.[31]

As a goddess of fertility, Asherah was a predictable point of connective identity for Israelite women. Asherah appears in the Bible dozens of times. But the word (singular: *asherah*; plural: *asherim*) is used for both the goddess and the image used to represent the goddess.[32] Asherah was often depicted in Canaanite art as a tree of life.[33] The Septuagint (Greek translation of the Old Testament) translated the word "asherim" as "sacred groves," and the high places with asherim were often referred to as "every high hill and green tree" (1 Kings 14:23). Because of these connections with trees, Dever concludes, "Thus it seems clear that originally in ancient Israel there was a goddess named Asherah, who was associated with living trees and hilltop forest sanctuaries, and who could sometimes be symbolized by a wooden pole or an image of a tree."[34]

Though it isn't clear exactly what these asherim poles looked like, a perusal of the Old Testament passages gives the reader some clues. They are wooden (Judges 6:26), probably tree-like in symbolism (Deuteronomy 16:21), that were "made" (2 Kings 21:3), "carved" (2 King 21:7), could be "chopped down" (Deuteronomy 7:5), "cut down" (2 Kings 18:4), and "burned with fire" (1 King 15:13). They were often "planted" beside altars of Baal (Deuteronomy 16:21; Judges 6:28) or altars of Yahweh (2 Kings 23:6) and often spoken of together with Baal (Judges 3:7). Whatever they looked like, they represented the presence of the mother goddess, most likely as a consort to both Baal and Yahweh.

---

31 Karel Van Der Toorn, "Female Prostitution in Payment of Vows in Ancient Israel," *Journal of Biblical Literature* 108 (1989): 195.

32 Raphael Patai, *The Hebrew Goddess 3rd Enlarged Edition* (Detroit, MI: Wayne State University Press, 1967, 1978, 1990), 38.

33 The most famous of these references is the Ta'anach cult stand that depicts Asherah as both a naked mistress of animals and a tree of life. See Dever, *Did God Have a Wife*, 219-220.

34 William G. Dever, *Did God Have a Wife?: Archaeology and Folk Religion in Ancient Israel* (Grand Rapids, MI: Eerdmans Publishing, 2005), 102.

In more recent years, discoveries of inscriptions at Kuntillet ʿAjrûd in the Sinai and Khirbet El-Qom near Lachish have supported the idea that it was common for Israelites to consider Asherah as a wife or consort of Yahweh. Though interpretations are varied, some scholars argue the inscriptions may be translated as in the following examples:

- I bless you before Yahweh of Samaria and his Asherah.
- Yahweh of Teman and his Asherah.
- Blessed by Uriyahu by Yahweh.
- By his Asherah, he has saved him.[35]

They all reflect the common localization of a deity with a city (Yahweh of Samaria), but there is disagreement over whether Asherah refers to the distinct deity or to the images that represent her. In either case, there is an intimate pairing of Yahweh with the goddess Asherah.

I've already examined the fact that there was an asherah in the Jerusalem temple for most of its existence (236 out of 370 years). As indicated in the texts, asherim were usually "planted beside altars" (Deuteronomy 16:21; Judges 6:28), so the asherah in Jerusalem was most likely beside the stone altar in the inner court of Yahweh's temple. All the evidence seems to affirm that the norm of the official Judahite religion included Asherah as Yahweh's consort. The reformers such as Hezekiah and Josiah were the anomaly (righteous though they were). When Josiah eliminated the asherah and other idolatrous elements of worship from the temple in the seventh century, he included rooms for male cult prostitutes "where the women wove garments for the asherah" (2 Kings 23:7). These were apparently garments that were used to clothe the asherah in some ritualistic manner.[36]

Strangely, Asherah was not always treated with the same level of condemnation as was Baal in the Scriptures. In our particular story of Jezebel, Elijah calls upon Ahab to send his 450 prophets of Baal and Jezebel's 400 prophets of Asherah to Mount Carmel (1 Kings 18:19). But in the showdown, only the prophets of Baal are ever mentioned as being there and as being slaughtered. Either the prophets of Asherah didn't show up and were spared, or they *did* show up and were spared. Either way, they don't appear to have

---

35 Othmar Keel, Chirstoph Uehlinger, *Gods, Goddesses, and Images of God in Ancient Israel* (Minneapolis: MN, Fortress Press, 1998), 229-239. Ziony Zevit translates the phrases without the possessive, "his," thus indicating "Yahweh and Asherah," still as consorting deities. Ziony Zevit, *The Religions of Ancient Israel: A Synthesis of Parallactic Approaches* (London, Continuum, 2001), 361, 373.

36 "The word here rendered "garments" is Hebrew bāttîm, which surely cannot have its usual meaning "houses" but rather, as originally suggested by A. Šanda, is probably cognate with Arabic batt "woven garment." John Day, "Asherah in the Hebrew Bible and Northwest Semitic Literature," *Journal of Biblical Literature 105* (1986): 406–407.

been killed along with the Baal prophets. If they had been, the writer of Kings would have certainly exulted in it. After executing Jezebel, Jehu is described as "wiping out Baal" from Israel, and "demolishing" his temple. But no word is written of Asherah. As already noted above, the priesthood of Jerusalem had kept an asherah in Solomon's temple for 236 out of its 370 years, two-thirds of its existence. It seems that worship of the goddess had a more entrenched grip on Israelites and Jews than did Baal or other deities.

Who says there wasn't female privilege in the ancient patriarchy?

Critical scholars interpret all this polytheistic polyamory as evidence that Asherah worship was a normal part of Israel's religion, claiming Asherah as Yahweh's wife, and that only later "fundamentalist" priests got rid of the other gods for the sake of their own religious bias. Confessional scholars agree with Yahweh and the prophets that it only showed God's wife Israel was committing spiritual adultery for most of their spiritual marriage, thus deserving exile (Jeremiah 3:1-9).[37]

My interpretation then of asherim in the novel as large poles with stylized tree branches of gold on the top and carved Asherah stories on the bottom is based on these hints of ancient totemic imagery. And my depiction of the Watcher known as Asherah reflects her influence on Israelites as a fertility goddess and "Mother of the gods," despite her subordination to Baal.

Astarte

Two other goddesses who show up in the novel of Jezebel are Astarte and Anat. They are depicted as being in competition for Baal's favor. Astarte is sent to Jerusalem because of their worship of her, while Anat is Baal's sister who journeys into Sheol to try to rescue him from Mot's death grip. These elements are all present in the Bible and in Canaanite lore. I've integrated them into the novel's storyline, giving them new meaning in a biblical context.

In Canaan, Astarte ("Ashtart" in Phoenician) was a goddess of fertility and war as well as a consort of Baal.[38] She had an astral identification with the planet Venus, thus earning her the epithet "Astarte of the Highest Heavens,"

---

[37] See also: Hosea 2:2; Jeremiah 3:6; Exodus 34:15–16; Leviticus 17:7; Numbers 15:39; 25:1; Deuteronomy 31:16; Judges 2:17; 8:27, 33; 1 Chronicles 5:25; 2 Chronicles 21:11, 13; Psalm 106:39; Isaiah 1:21; Jeremiah 2:20; 3:1–9; 5:7; Ezekiel 6:9; 16:15–17, 20, 22, 25–36, 41; 23:5–8, 11, 14, 19–19, 27–30, 35, 44; 43:7, 9; Hosea 1:2, 2:2, 4–5; 3:3; 4:10–15, 18; 5:3–4; 6:10; 9:1; Joel 3:3; Amos 7:17; Micah 1:7; Nahum 3:4.

[38] N. Wyatt, "Astarte," ed. Karel van der Toorn, Bob Becking, and Pieter W. van der Horst, *Dictionary of Deities and Demons in the Bible* (Leiden; Boston; Köln; Grand Rapids, MI; Cambridge: Brill; Eerdmans, 1999), 110.

and "Queen of Heaven,"[39] linking her to the Mesopotamian goddess Ishtar. Jezebel's father Ethbaal was originally a high priest of Astarte from Sidon who became king of Tyre.[40]

In the Bible, Astarte is referred to in Hebrew as Ashtaroth or Ashtoreth, goddess "of the Sidonians" (1 Kings 11:5; 1 Samuel 12:10). Like Jezebel's name in the text, Ashtoreth is most likely a deliberate mockery of her name by using the vowels of the Hebrew word for shame, *bosheth,* with the consonants of Astarte.[41] The word "shame" was already used explicitly to refer to Baal in Jeremiah 11:13 and Hosea 9:10.

> Jeremiah 11:13:
> For your gods have become as many as your cities, O Judah,
> and as many as the streets of Jerusalem are the altars you
> have set up to shame, altars to make offerings to Baal.

Though the prophets and Deuteronomist authors of Kings may have had contempt for the goddess, the Hebrew populace at large surely did not. The Israelites had worshipped her along with Baal since the days of the judges hundreds of years earlier (Judges 2:13).[42] While she is absent in the text during the reign of David (1 Samuel 12:10-11), Astarte seems to have returned with a particularly strong hold on Judah when Solomon built high places for her in Jerusalem (1 Kings 11:5, 33).

Astarte appears to be the "Queen of Heaven" that Jeremiah condemns with much rigor in Judah long after Israel is gone into the Assyrian exile (Jeremiah 44:15-23). The rituals of Astarte worship described by Jeremiah involve the whole household, but are apparently led by the wives, who are depicted as making offerings to the Queen of Heaven proudly without their husband's approval (44:19) and to whom they attribute their food and prosperity (v.17-18).

As biblical scholar Susan Ackerman conveys, Jeremiah reveals that the whole family was involved in the goddess worship, which included pouring libations, burning incense, and baking cakes.

---

39 John Day, *Yahweh and the Gods and Goddesses of Canaan (The Library of Hebrew Bible/Old Testament Studies)* (Bloomsbury T&T Clark, 2002), 149. Susan Ackerman, "At Home with the Goddess," in *Symbiosis, Symbolism, and the Power of the Past: Canaan, Ancient Israel, and Their Neighbors from the Late Bronze Age through Roman Palaestina*, ed. William G. Dever and Seymour Gitin (Winona Lake, IN: Eisenbrauns, 2003), 461.

40 Josephus, *Antiquities of the Jews* 8.13.2.

41 John Day, *Yahweh and the Gods and Goddesses of Canaan (The Library of Hebrew Bible/Old Testament Studies)* (Bloomsbury T&T Clark, 2002), 214.

42 See also Judges 10:6; 1 Sam 7:3-4; 12:10.

> The *children* gather wood, the *fathers* kindle fire, and the *women* knead dough to make cakes for the Queen of Heaven (Jeremiah 7:18). Still, despite this depiction of the whole family's involvement, I think that it is fair to say that the women's contribution—the actual making of the offering cakes—is the most religiously significant, and thus it is reasonable to see these women as somehow *especially* involved in the goddess's worship. Indeed, in the polemic against the Queen of Heaven cult in Jeremiah 44, Jeremiah seems to make exactly this point, since it is *women* who are specifically identified in Jeremiah 44:19 as those who have "burned incense to the Queen of Heaven and poured out libations to her… and made for her cakes in her image," and it is thus *women*, in the culmination of Jeremiah's fulminations (44:25), who are singled out for the prophet's special scorn.[43]

Perhaps Dever's claim of female-led folk religion is not so anachronistic after all.

Anat

Another goddess who plays significantly into the plot of the novel *Jezebel* is Anat. In the Ugaritic texts, Anat is a fertility goddess, the sister of Baal as well as his consort. *The Dictionary of Deities and Demons* (*DDD*) describes her as a "volatile, independent, adolescent warrior and hunter." Her epithet, Virgin Anat, is more a commentary on her age than her actual sexual status since she is considered sexually active with Baal. One passage in the Baal epic most likely describes her in the form of a heifer having sex with Baal eighty-eight times.[44] But her ability to remain active in the male realms of war and hunting is due to her failure to "grow up" to be a marriageable female.[45]

Susan Ackerman describes Anat's lust for violence from the pages of the Baal epic:

---

[43] Susan Ackerman, "At Home with the Goddess," in Symbiosis, Symbolism, and the Power of the Past: Canaan, Ancient Israel, and Their Neighbors from the Late Bronze Age through Roman Palaestina, ed. William G. Dever and Seymour Gitin (Winona Lake, IN: Eisenbrauns, 2003), 464.

[44] KTU 1.5.20; 1.10.

[45] P. L. Day, "Anat," ed. Karel van der Toorn, Bob Becking, and Pieter W. van der Horst, *Dictionary of Deities and Demons in the Bible* (Leiden; Boston; Köln; Grand Rapids, MI; Cambridge: Brill; Eerdmans, 1999), 37–38.

> The goddess adorns herself with a necklace of skulls and a girdle of hands (CTA 3.2.11-13). Her joy in battle is vividly described in this passage (CTA 3.2.23-28):
>
> She fought hard and looked,
> Anat battled and saw:
> Her liver swelled with laughter,
> Her heart was filled with joy,
> The liver of Anat was exultant,
> As she plunged knee-deep in the blood of the mighty,
> Up to her hips in the gore of warriors.
>
> Anat's violent and ruthless behavior is further evident in the epic of Aqhat, where she schemes against Aqhat and eventually kills him in order to gain possession of his magnificent bow and arrows (CTA 17.6; 18.4).[46]

In the novel, Anat with her special bow of Aqhat in hand seeks Baal in the underworld. According to the Baal epic, when she finds him…

> …She grabs Mot by the hem of his garment,
> She seizes him by the edge of his cloak.
> She raises her voice and cries:
> "You, O Mot, give up my brother."
> And Divine Mot answers:
> "What do you desire, [Virgin] Anat?...[47]
> She seizes Divine Mot,
> With a sword she splits him,
> With a sieve she winnows him.
> With a fire she burns him,
> With millstones she grinds him,
> In a field she sows him.
> The birds eat his flesh,
> Fowl devour his parts,
> Flesh to flesh cries out.[48]

Baal returns to the earth above, is seated on his royal throne once again, and the father god El rejoices…

> …For Mightiest Baal lives,

46 Susan Ackerman, *Under Every Green Tree: Popular Religion in Sixth-Century Judah*, (Atlanta: GA, Scholars Press, 1992), 51.

47 KTU 1.6:2:6-9.

48 KTU 1.6:2:30-37. Smith and Parker, *Ugaritic Narrative Poetry*, 155-156.

The Prince, Lord of the Earth is alive.[49]

Anat was not to be trifled with. And her pride is displayed not merely in her defeat of Mot but in her claim to have defeated Leviathan (Lotan) and Sea (Yam), "a conquest elsewhere attributed to Baal and a necessary step towards Baal's acquisition of kingship."[50] As the saying goes, behind every successful god there stands a supportive goddess—or in this case, a usurping one.

The depiction in the novel of Sheol, through which Anat travels to find Mot's city, is based upon the Jewish cosmic geography mostly found in 1 Enoch. For details of that picture of the underworld, see below Chapter 4: Cosmic Geography, Sheol.

Though Anat is not referenced directly in the Old Testament, she is most likely alluded to in some passages relevant to her character as a patron of warriors.

The place-name of the city Beth-Anat (House of Anat) in the Bible indicates the presence of a temple of Anat in the city.[51] 1 Samuel 31:10 describes the Philistines as placing the slain King Saul's armor in "the temple of Ashtaroth" in Beth Shan. Recent discoveries of a temple of Anat in Beth Shan, coupled with the possibility of the term "Ashtaroth" being used as a generic Akkadian language reference to a goddess without dignifying her name, point to a strong possibility that this was the temple of Anat. As the *DDD* writes, "Given Anat's clear portrayal as a warrior and a patron or guardian of warriors and royalty in extrabiblical sources, and given that we know she had a temple in Beth Shan, it makes good sense to suggest that the armor of a vanquished warrior-king would be brought to her temple by the grateful victors."[52]

The other biblical allusion to Anat can be found in the name of Shamgar ben Anat, a warrior who had killed six hundred Philistines with an ox goad (Judges 3:31; 5:6). Keep in mind that names in the ancient world and the

---

[49] KTU 1.6:3:20-21. Smith and Parker, *Ugaritic Narrative Poetry*, 158.

[50] For Baal's defeat of Leviathan, see: (KTU 1.2 iv; 1.5 i:1–3) P. L. Day, "Anat,_" ed. Karel van der Toorn, Bob Becking, and Pieter W. van der Horst, *Dictionary of Deities and Demons in the Bible* (Leiden; Boston; Köln; Grand Rapids, MI; Cambridge: Brill; Eerdmans, 1999), 37–38.

[51] "Beth-Anat (bet-'andt) in Naphtali (Josh. 19.38; Judg. 1.33); Beth-Anot (bet-'anot) in Judah (Josh. 15.59), and Anathoth in Benjamin ('anatdt, in Josh. 21.18; 1 Kings 2.26 and '"natotin 1 Kings 2.26; Isa. 10.30; Jer. 1.1,11.21, 23, 32.7, 8, 9; 1 Chron. 6.45; Ezra 2.23; Neh. 7.27; cf. also the adjective 'the Anathothite', ha'annetoti in 2 Sam. 23.27, 1 Chron. 12.3 and Jer. 29.27; and hd'annetdtim 1 Chron. 11.28, 27.12)." John Day, *Yahweh and the Gods and Goddesses of Canaan (The Library of Hebrew Bible/Old Testament Studies)* (Bloomsbury T&T Clark, 2002), 132-133.

[52] P. L. Day, "Anat," ed. Karel van der Toorn, Bob Becking, and Pieter W. van der Horst, *Dictionary of Deities and Demons in the Bible* (Leiden; Boston; Köln; Grand Rapids, MI; Cambridge: Brill; Eerdmans, 1999), 42.

biblical text often reflected character, origins, or destinies. The word "ben" means "son of." But since patronyms refer to male lineage, not females such as Anat, it is better seen as a metaphorical reference. Day argues it is most likely an honorific military title for a warrior, Shamgar, as a son of the goddess Anat, a not uncommon title in Canaan.[53] Is it a coincidence this mighty warrior of mass slaughter carries the name of a mighty deity of mass slaughter?

In the Ugaritic texts, Anat is a consort of Baal as is Astarte, thus placing them somewhat at odds, as portrayed in the novel. Though Astarte is more prominent in the Old Testament than her competitor Anat.[54]

Mot

Mot ("Death") is considered the supreme god of the underworld in Canaanite mythology. The Bible draws on imagery and language that echoes that narrative and subverts it into the biblical worldview, a subversion that the novel *Jezebel: Harlot Queen of Israel* continues in like manner.

The story of Mot and Baal in the Baal epic shows Mot addressing Baal, the one who "killed Litan [Leviathan], the fleeing serpent, the twisting serpent with seven heads."[55] Mot does this as a way of building up Baal in order to show Mot's greater power when he captures him.

> Surely [Baal] will descend into Divine Mot's throat,
> Into the gullet of El's Beloved, the Hero. [56]

Mot's (Death's) boundless appetite is described as a gaping jaw that swallows his victims into the underworld. His mouth is:

> One lip to Earth, one lip to Heaven,
> a tongue to the Stars.[57]

In the novel, Baal is captured by being swallowed up into "Mot's jaws" in the Hinnom Valley outside Jerusalem, which leads down to Sheol.

---

[53] Day, *Yahweh and the Gods,* 134.

[54] Day, *Yahweh and the Gods,* 131.

[55] KTU 1.5:1:1-4.

[56] KTU 1.5:1:4-8. Mark S. Smith and Simon B. Parker, *Ugaritic Narrative Poetry,* vol. 9, Writings from the Ancient World (Atlanta, GA: Scholars Press, 1997), 141.

[57] KTU 1.5:2:2-6. Smith and Parker, *Ugaritic Narrative Poetry,* 143. See also N. Wyatt, *Religious Texts from Ugarit, 2nd ed.,* Biblical Seminar, 53 (London; New York: Sheffield Academic Press, 2002), 120.

In the Ugaritic literature, Baal is brought to Mot's underworld city, translated alternatively the Swamp, the Pit, his royal house, Filth, or the land of his inheritance.[58]

Hearing that Baal is dead, Anat journeys into the underworld to hunt down Mot. When she finds him, as described earlier, she cuts him into pieces, winnows him, burns him, grinds him, and sows him in the field for the birds to eat his flesh.[59] Baal returns to life on the earth above and is seated once again on his royal throne.[60] Later, Mot returns to argue with Baal and fight him, but he eventually acknowledges the storm god's rule on his throne.[61]

Sheol was the Hebrew word for the underworld of the dead.[62] I will discuss the geography of Sheol as a location in Chapter 4 on Cosmic Geography. For now, I will focus on the biblical use of the term as a metaphor for death and as an analogy of the Canaanite Mot.

The Old Testament uses personified descriptions of Sheol that are very similar to those of Mot. But the Hebrew writers don't treat Sheol as a personal god like Mot. In this way, the biblical text demythologizes and subverts the pagan god of death into a demonic phenomenon with real spiritual impact.

The Canaanite language of Death's (Sheol's) ravishing appetite and wide throat swallowing up life shows up in Old Testament texts:

> Isaiah 5:14:
> Therefore Sheol has enlarged its appetite and opened its mouth beyond measure, and the nobility of Jerusalem and her multitude will go down...
>
> Habakkuk 2:5 (NASB95):
> [The haughty man] enlarges his appetite like Sheol, And he is like death, never satisfied. He also gathers to himself all nations And collects to himself all peoples.
>
> Proverbs 1:12:
> Like Sheol let us swallow them alive,
> and whole, like those who go down to the pit.

---

58 KTU 1.5:2:13-16. Coogan, Michael D.; Mark S. Smith. *Stories from Ancient Canaan, Second Edition* (Kindle Locations 5072-5073). Westminster John Knox Press. Kindle Edition.

59 KTU 1.6:2:30-37.

60 KTU 1.6:3:20-21.

61 KTU 1.6:5:5-6:38.

62 "Sheol," *DDD*, p 768.

Bible scholar John Day writes about these parallels of Sheol and Mot.

> Sheol is also referred to as swallowing people up in Proverbs 1.12, and its insatiable appetite is alluded to in Proverbs 27.20 and 30.15b-16. In Psalm. 49.15 (ET 14) death is a shepherd and those who go to Sheol are like sheep, "Like sheep they are appointed for Sheol; Death shall be their shepherd..." Although this is only poetic language, it recalls what is said of the god Mot in the Baal text, KTU 1.6.II.21-23, "I myself came upon the victor Baal, I myself made him as lamb in my mouth; he himself like a kid in my jaws was carried away." The same word "mouth" (pi) is used of Sheol in Psalm 141.7.

It seems clear that the Hebrews used the same kind of terminology for Sheol that Canaanites used of Mot. But in some cases, they go out of their way to seemingly subvert the pagan deity like this passage in Isaiah's "little apocalypse."

> Isaiah 25:8:
> He will swallow up death [Mot] forever; and the Lord GOD will wipe away tears from all faces, and the reproach of his people he will take away from all the earth.

As Day points out, in this case, Isaiah is positing an ironic power of Yahweh over Death (Mot). Whereas it is usually Death or Mot who does the swallowing, in this case it is the swallower that is to be swallowed up.[63] There are no gods who compare to Yahweh, the creator and sustainer of all things, Death included.

In Isaiah 28, the phrase "covenant with death" is used of Jerusalem's intermixing with foreign peoples and their gods (v. 11; 27:9). Spiritual apostasy is likened to a covenant with Mot.

> Isaiah 28:15:
> Because you have said, "We have made a covenant with death [Mot], and with Sheol we have an agreement, when the overwhelming whip [scourge] passes through it will not come to us, for we have made lies our refuge, and in falsehood we have taken shelter."

---

[63] Day, *Yahweh and the Gods,* 186.

The first thing to notice in this passage is that covenants were only made with persons, usually a tribe or nation with a ruler or god. Making a covenant with Mot was not merely a metaphorical covenant with death as an abstraction. The covenantal language represented the spiritual unfaithfulness that Judah displayed toward Yahweh in going after other gods. Isaiah was saying that they thought they were covenanting with the gods Baal, Asherah, Astarte, Molech, and Chemosh, but they were actually covenanting with the god Mot, which represented their spiritual Death.

God's judgment is described as a strong wind like a scourge upon them. As scholar Mark Smith argues, "Biblical descriptions of the east wind as an instrument of divine destruction may have derived from the imagery of Mot in Canaanite tradition...The juxtaposition of the east wind and personified Death in Hosea 13:14-15 may presuppose the mythological background of Mot as manifest in the sirocco."[64]

Speaking of Hosea 13, let's look closer at that passage. It addresses more than one deity in its reference.

> Hosea 13:14-15 (NRSV):
> Shall I ransom them from the power of Sheol?
> Shall I redeem them from Death [*Mot*]?
> O Death [*Mot*], where are your plagues [*Deber*]?
> O Sheol, where is your destruction [*Qeteb*]?
> Compassion is hidden from my eyes…
> the east wind shall come, a blast from the LORD,
> rising from the wilderness; and his fountain shall dry up,
> his spring shall be parched.
> It shall strip his treasury of every precious thing.

Death here is a strong allusion to the Canaanite Mot because of the reference to the east wind and the other two Hebrew words used of Death's power: "plagues" (*deber*) and "destruction" (*qeteb*). These two words are considered literary references to two Canaanite underworld deities as demons.[65]

---

[64] Mark Smith, *The Early History of God: Yahweh and the Other Deities in Ancient Israel*, 2nd Edition (Grand Rapids, MI: Eerdmans, 1990, 2002), 88.

[65] "The eschatological hymn in Hab 3 presents Deber and Resheph marching at Yahweh's side as His helpers. This follows the ancient Mesopotamian tradition according to which 'plague' and 'pestilence' are present in the entourage of the great god Marduk... On the other hand, in Ps 91:6 it is Yahweh who liberates his faithful from the fear of this nocturnal demon Deber, in parallel this time with Qeteb, another awesome destructive demon." del Olmo G. Lete, "Deber," ed. Karel van der Toorn, Bob Becking, and Pieter W. van der Horst, *Dictionary of Deities and Demons in the Bible* (Leiden; Boston; Köln; Grand Rapids, MI; Cambridge: Brill; Eerdmans, 1999), 232.

In the Ugaritic Baal epic, the plague god Qeteb appears to be a kinsman of Mot. In the four places *qeteb* occurs in the Old Testament (Deuteronomy 32:24; Psalm 91:5-6; Hosea 13:14; Isaiah 28:2), it is translated in English as "pestilence" or "destruction," and is paralleled with Mot, Deber, or Resheph (another Canaanite underworld deity of plague[66]). The *DDD* concludes, "Qeṭeb is more than a literary figure, living as a spiritual and highly dangerous reality in the minds of poets and readers."[67] Deber "seems to be used a number of times in a personified sense as a demon or evil deity (Hab 3:5; Ps 91:3, 6; cf. Hos 13:14),"[68] and Resheph "is a demonized version of an ancient Canaanite god, now submitted to Yahweh."[69]

In the Bible, Qeteb (*destruction*), Deber (*plague*), Resheph (*pestilence*), and Mot (*death*) are all demonic realities.

Molech

Molech is a Canaanite god of the underworld. Though he only appears briefly in *Jezebel: Harlot Queen of Israel*, he is certainly significant in the big picture of the spiritual world of Judah at this time, as well as a prominent player in the storyline of my other series *Chronicles of the Nephilim.*

Until 1935, all scholars believed that the name Molech in the Old Testament referred to a god. Then new views came out of the academic community that the Hebrew word translated "Molech" or "Moloch," (*mlk*) was a kind of sacrifice rather than the name of a divinity. They argued that it was linguistically influenced by the Phoenician term *molk*, found in many sacrificial inscriptions in the Mediterranean world.[70]

But this problem has been put to rest in a way that reveals just who this Molech really is. John Day provides the answers in his excellent primer, *Yahweh and the Gods and Goddesses of Canaan*. Leviticus 20:5 declares Israel as "whoring after Molech." This phrase of "whoring after" a god is used

---

66 *KTU* 1.82:3. "[Resheph] appears as a cosmic force, whose powers are great and terrible: he is particularly conceived of as bringing epidemics and death. The Hebrew Bible shows different levels of demythologization: sometimes it describes Resheph as a personalized figure, more or less faded, sometimes the name is used as a pure metaphor. At any rate it is possible to perceive aspects of the personality of an ancient chthonic god, whichs fits the image of Resheph found in the other Semitic cultures."

van der Toorn, Becking van der Horst, *DDD*, 703-704.

67 N. Wyatt, "Qeteb," ed. Karel van der Toorn, Bob Becking, and Pieter W. van der Horst, *DDD*, 674.

68 del Olmo G. Lete, "Deber," ed. Karel van der Toorn, Bob Becking, and Pieter W. van der Horst, *DDD*, 231–232.

69 P. Xella, "Resheph," ed. Karel van der Toorn, Bob Becking, and Pieter W. van der Horst, *DDD*, 703.

70 John Day, *Yahweh and the Gods and Goddesses of Canaan* (The Library of Hebrew Bible/Old Testament Studies) (Bloomsbury T&T Clark, 2002), 209

throughout the Bible in reference to many different deities of Canaan.[71] It is never used of people "whoring after a sacrifice." And all the verbs employed in connection with the Molech cult, "offering to," "giving to," "burning as an offering to," are actions toward a divine being, not toward a cultic ritual itself.[72]

The Old Testament is clear that Molech is a Canaanite deity, not a Phoenician one. His cult is described as a Canaanite abomination (Leviticus 18:21; 20:2-5). The Hebrew word for king is "melek," which uses the same consonants as Molech, so there is some kingly context inherent in the divine name. But as with the names Jezebel, Ashtoreth, and others, it is possible that the scribes of the later Hebrew text used the vowels of the Hebrew word for "shame" (*bosheth*) and inserted them in the consonants of Molech's name.

Day explains the external evidence for Molech as an underworld deity in Canaan:

> That there was such a deity [Molech] is shown by two Ugaritic serpent charms which mention him (KTU2 1.100.41 [Ugaritica V.I, RS 24.244] and KTU2 1.107.17 [Ugaritica V.8, RS 24.251]). In both places it is associated with the place name Ashtaroth in Transjordan, a place elsewhere connected in the Ugaritic texts with rp'u [Rephaim] (KTU2 1.108.1-2), indicating an underworld association. He also appears as Malik in various god lists and in personal names from Ebla, Mari, and Ugarit. Significantly, Malik is twice equated with Nergal, the Mesopotamian underworld god, once in an Old Babylonian god-list where we read Ma-lik = Nergal, and again in a later god-list from Ashur, which likewise has Ma-lik = Nergal. This clearly indicates an underworld deity.

In the Bible, Molech is connected with the underworld in key ways. First, Isaiah 57 describes child sacrifices "in the valleys, under the clefts of the rocks" (57:5), the activity most connected to the Molech cult. The text describes the journey to that abominable altar as an adulterer seeking the bed of a foreign god.

---

[71] Exod. 34.15, 16; Lev. 17.7; Deut. 31.16; Judg. 2.17, 8.33.

[72] Day, *Yahweh and the Gods*, 210.

> Isaiah 57:9:
> You journeyed to the king (*melek*) with oil and multiplied your perfumes; you sent your envoys far off, and sent down even to Sheol.

In this case, "king" (*mlk*) is most likely a double entendre of Molech (*mlk*). Notice that the king resides in Sheol, the underworld. And that underworld was connected to the valley location of Molech's cult in Jerusalem.[73]

The Molech cult was known for its child sacrifice, or "passing one's children through the fire" (2 Kings 23:10). The altar of this sacrifice was called a Tophet or Topheth, a place of burning, which once again used the vowels of "shame" (*bosheth*) inserted into the consonants of the Aramaic word for "burning place" (*tepat*).[74] We will discuss the details of human sacrifice later in Chapter 5. But this shameful and atrocious activity was infamously popular in the Valley of Hinnom just outside the southwest walls of Jerusalem. Yahweh condemned this infernal location through the prophet Jeremiah for their "high places of Tophets" where they "burned their sons and daughters in the fire" (Jeremiah 7:31). He then proclaimed the name of the valley would be changed from "Valley of the Sons of Hinnom" to "Valley of Slaughter" (7:32), a term that would come to refer to Gehenna or hellfire in later years of Second Temple Judaism. Molech was an underworld god of fire sacrifice of children. This is why I portrayed him in my novels as mole-like with a maze of underground tunnels beneath the Hinnom Valley of the Tophet outside Jerusalem.

In chapter 4, we'll look more closely at that underworld and the rest of the cosmic geography that fills the pages of Scripture and the novel of *Jezebel*.

The Archangels

One of the ongoing series of characters that appear in all the Chronicles series of novels is the archangels. In the *Jezebel* novel, they are depicted as they are in previous stories as protecting God's people, most specifically the Remnant. Mikael (Michael) in particular is tasked with the protection of the bloodline of Messiah in Judah as he is considered the "prince of Israel," or the principality of the Hebrew nation, in the same way that gods like Baal are considered the principalities of the pagan nations. This is rooted in a biblical tradition.

---

[73] Day, *Yahweh and the Gods,* 215.

[74] J. F. Prewitt, "Topheth," ed. Geoffrey W. Bromiley, *The International Standard Bible Encyclopedia*, Revised (Wm. B. Eerdmans, 1979–1988), 876.

The only archangels named explicitly in the Bible are Michael and Gabriel. Gabriel is well known in the New Testament as the angel who comes to herald the births of both John the Baptist (Luke 1:11-20) and Jesus the Messiah (Luke 1:26-35).

The angel Gabriel is described as "one having the appearance of a man" who explains visions to Daniel the prophet in Daniel 8:16 and 9:21. Though it isn't explicitly stated, some scholars believe Gabriel is also the unidentified angelic man who explains Daniel's vision of the spiritual principalities of the nations in Daniel 10.

In that vision, we hear about Michael, who is described as "one of the chief princes" (Daniel 10:13) and the spiritual prince of Daniel's people Judah (10:21; 12:1), who fights with Gabriel against the spiritual "princes" (principalities) of Persia and Greece.

> Daniel 10:12–13:
> Then [Gabriel] said to me… I have come because of your words. 13 The prince of the kingdom of Persia withstood me twenty-one days, but Michael, one of the chief princes, came to help me, for I was left there with the [human] kings of Persia.
>
> Daniel 10:20–21:
> Then he said… "But now I will return to fight against the prince of Persia; and when I go out, behold, the prince of Greece will come.…there is none who contends by my side against these except Michael, your prince.
>
> Daniel 12:1:
> "At that time shall arise Michael, the great prince who has charge of your people. And there shall be a time of trouble, such as never has been since there was a nation till that time. But at that time your people shall be delivered.

The underlying Hebrew word for "prince" (*sar*) in these passages can be used of human as well as spiritual rulers. But most scholars acknowledge that the context of these passages dictates a spiritual principality over earthly powers. As Bible scholar John Collins explains,

> The title "prince" does not necessarily imply less than divine status. The "prince of the host" in Daniel 8:11 is apparently the God of Israel. A precedent for the title "prince" being applied to an angel can be found in the [commander of the army of Yahweh] who appears in Josh 5:14. The title is used for the chief angelic powers at Qumran, for example, the

> "prince of lights" (1QS 3:20; CD 5:18) and the "prince of the dominion of wickedness" (1QM 17:5–6).[75]

This vision reveals the Deuteronomy 32 worldview played out in the unseen realm. The earthly kingdom of Persia was in battle with earthly Babylon, who held Judah captive, and so the spiritual prince of Persia was at war with the spiritual princes Michael and Gabriel, who were protecting Judah. When earthly Greece would come after Persia, their spiritual principalities too would fight in connection with the earthly battles of history (Deuteronomy 32:8-10; Judges 5:19-20; Isaiah 24:21-22; Ecclesiastes 17:17; Jubilees 15:31–32).[76]

The concept of *archangel* is drawn from the reference to Michael as one of the "chief princes" (Daniel 10:13). He is also called an archangel in Jude 9, and he is described in the Daniel passages above as the prince in charge of Israel who protects and delivers her (12:1).

There are two other places where Michael is described in his archangel capacity or leading the heavenly host. The first is in Jude, where a strange event is referenced that has no evidence in the Old Testament. Michael was said to have disputed with the devil over the body of Moses.

> Jude 9:
> But when the archangel Michael, contending with the devil, was disputing about the body of Moses, he did not presume to pronounce a blasphemous judgment, but said, "The Lord rebuke you."

The context of this passage is that Jude is talking about the false teachers of his time who "defile the flesh, reject authority, and blaspheme the glorious ones" (v. 8). This raises all kind of questions. If this story was not in the Old Testament, where did Jude get it? What did it mean to "dispute about the body of Moses"? And who are the glorious ones?

The story, though not available to us in any known manuscripts, was claimed by various early church fathers to have been taken from a book they had access to called by some *The Assumption of Moses* and by others *The Testament of Moses*. In either case, we no longer have the text. But it certainly opens the door to understanding how New Testament writers used Second Temple Jewish texts as sources in their canonical writing.

---

[75] John Joseph Collins and Adela Yarbro Collins, *Daniel: A Commentary on the Book of Daniel*, ed. Frank Moore Cross, Hermeneia—a Critical and Historical Commentary on the Bible (Minneapolis, MN: Fortress Press, 1993), 375.

[76] Daniel L. Smith-Christopher, "The Book of Daniel," in *New Interpreter's Bible*, ed. Leander E. Keck, vol. 7 (Nashville: Abingdon Press, 1994–2004), 137.

I try to make some sense out of the strange disputation over Moses's body in my novel Caleb Vigilant (affiliate link). I believe it might have something to do with the fact that Moses's body had been transformed in some way by being in the presence of God. He was "shining," not unlike those heavenly host around God's throne (Exodus 34:29). Perhaps, the more time Moses spent in God's presence, the more his physical body transformed to be more like those Sons of God around the throne.

So, the "glorious ones" in Jude 8 are contextually the shining angels from God's throne. They are referred to earlier in the text when Jude writes of the angels who left their heavenly habitations in primeval days. "Blaspheming the glorious ones" is then likened to those humans of Sodom and Gomorrah who sexually "pursued strange flesh" by trying to copulate with angels (v.7). Divine beings are often described as shining with brilliance and glory in both the Old Testament (Ezekiel 1:4–7, 27–28; Daniel 10:6) as well as the New Testament (Matthew 28:3; Luke 24:4).

Lastly, Michael is referenced again as the archangel who fights with his angels against the satanic dragon and his angels in Revelation 12.

> Revelation 12:7–8:
> Now war arose in heaven, Michael and his angels fighting against the dragon. And the dragon and his angels fought back, but he was defeated, and there was no longer any place for them in heaven.

I write about this momentous spiritual event in my series Chronicles of the Apocalypse (affiliate link).

Though both Old and New Testament only names Michael as the Watcher, or guardian angel, of God's people and Gabriel as his "wingman," Second Temple Jewish apocalypticism maintained a strong tradition that there are seven named archangels, four of whom stand in God's presence: Michael, Gabriel, Raphael, and Uriel (sometimes called Phanuel). The other three are named Raguel, Saraqael, and Remiel (1 Enoch 20:1-7; Tobit 12:15).

Though not as explicit, Revelation 8:2 mentions "seven angels who stand before God," and Gabriel describes himself also as "standing before God" (Luke 1:19), the same phrase used of the archangels in the Second Temple tradition (1 Enoch 40:3; Tobit 12:15).

Thus, I followed this archangelic tradition throughout all my Chronicles series, including Chronicles of the Watchers.

Chapter 4:
Cosmic Geography

Underworld Valleys

In the novel *Jezebel: Harlot Queen of Israel*, there is a sequence where Baal travels to Jerusalem but is trapped by the archangels in the Valley of Hinnom just outside the city walls. It is here at the infamous location of the tophet of Molech where Baal is swallowed up in a sinkhole as the jaws of Mot takes him down into the underworld of Sheol. While we have already discussed Mot above and will further discuss Sheol below, let's take a look at the notion of valleys as connections to the underworld in the Bible and in the ancient Near East.[1]

Critical Bible scholar Francesca Stavrakopoulou explains that, as the holy city, Jerusalem's sacred topography is mapped onto the biblical cosmos of a three-tiered universe: the heavens above where divinity resides, the earth below for humankind, and the underworld of the dead beneath it all. The mountain is the transition between heaven and earth. It's where temples of the gods reside like the temple of Yahweh on Mount Zion. The valleys, therefore, operate in a similar manner as the transition or points of entry from the earth into the underworld—like the Valley of Hinnom on the southwest side of Jerusalem.

> As sites of transition, the valleys surrounding Jerusalem are thus imbued with a potent mytho-symbolic character; they are liminal locations marking at once three interrelated places: the transitional place between the ordered city and the uncultivated wilderness, the roots of the holy hill upon which the heavenly and earthly realms meet, and the intersection of the earthly realm and the underworld.[2]

The Second-Temple Jewish text of 1 Enoch uses this image of the valley as a place of judgment that ends in the underworld.

---

[1] Special thanks to Robert Cruickshank for finding some of the scholarship presented here on Underworld valleys.

[2] Francesca Stavrakopoulou, "The Jerusalem Tophet: Ideological Dispute and Religious Transformation," *Studi Epigrafici e Linguistici* 29-30, 2012-2013: 141.

> 1 Enoch 53:1-3:
> My eyes saw there a valley with a wide and deep mouth. And all those who dwell upon the earth, the sea, and the islands shall bring to it gifts, presents, and tributes; yet this deep valley shall not become full… Sinners shall be destroyed from before the face of the Lord of the Spirits—they shall perish eternally, standing before the face of his earth.[3]

The first sentence about the valley of judgment uses the language of Mot (Death) as the wide and deep mouth that is never satisfied ("shall not become full"). The idea here is that the valley is a place of judgment where sinners meet their destruction ("perish"). In 1 Enoch, valleys are places of judgment that lead to Sheol, like the mouth of Mot.

Then Enoch sees another valley of judgment where kings are judged in connection with the angelic Watchers who rule over them.

> 1 Enoch 54:1-2:
>
> Then I looked and turned to another face of the earth and saw there a valley, deep and burning with fire. And they were bringing kings and potentates and were throwing them into this deep valley. And my eyes saw there their chains while they were making them into iron fetters of immense weight. And I asked the angel of peace, who was going with me, saying, "For whom are these imprisonment chains being prepared?" And he said unto me, "These are being prepared for the armies of Azaz'el [the Watchers], in order that they may take them and cast them into the abyss of complete condemnation.[45]

So the valley of judgment leads to the Abyss of Sheol where earthly and heavenly rulers and powers are cast down for judgment to be imprisoned and punished later. Another linking of valleys with the underworld.

In the Old Testament, several texts point to this same idea of valleys as portals to the underworld. The first one is a prophecy by Isaiah that reflects the same concept as the 1 Enoch passages above.

---

[3] James H. Charlesworth, *The Old Testament Pseudepigrapha, vol. 1* (New York; London: Yale University Press, 1983), 37. Thanks to Robert Cruickshank for finding this passage.

[4] James H. Charlesworth, *The Old Testament Pseudepigrapha,* vol. 1 (New York; London: Yale University Press, 1983), 38.

[5] Charlesworth, *Old Testament Pseudepigrapha,* vol. 1, 38.

> Isaiah 24:21–22:
> On that day the LORD will punish the host of heaven, in heaven, and the kings of the earth, on the earth. They will be gathered together as prisoners in a pit; they will be shut up in a prison, and after many days they will be punished.

Though the word "valley" is not used here, the prophetic picture is almost a mirror description of Enoch's prophecy of earthly and heavenly rulers and powers being cast down into a pit to be imprisoned and punished later.

Secondly, there is a valley just outside of Jerusalem called Valley of the Rephaim (2 Samuel 5:22).[6] In Canaanite mythology, the Rephaim were divinized dead warrior kings, heroes of the past, who were called up from the underworld to legitimize current rulers.[7] Another valley linked with the underworld. We'll explore the Rephaim in more detail under Chapter 5, the "marzeah feast."

The third example of underworld valleys is the Valley of Hinnom at the southwest walls of Jerusalem. As shown in the novel, this valley was the location of a Tophet altar of Molech where children were sacrificed by being "burned with fire" (Jeremiah 7:31). Because this idolatrous practice was so abominable to Yahweh, Jeremiah prophesied destruction upon Jerusalem so devastating it would fill the valley with dead corpses and lead to the Babylonian exile of death (7:33). The name of the Valley of Hinnom would be changed to the Valley of Slaughter (7:32).

> Jeremiah 7:32–33:
> Behold, the days are coming, declares the LORD, when it will no more be called Topheth, or the Valley of the Son of Hinnom, but the Valley of Slaughter; for they will bury in Topheth, because there is no room elsewhere. And the dead bodies of this people will be food for the birds of the air, and for the beasts of the earth.

During the Hellenistic development of the Second Temple period, "the Valley of Hinnom, often referred to simply as 'the accursed valley' or 'abyss,' then came to represent the place of eschatological judgment of wicked Jews

---

6 See also Josh 15:8; 2 Sam 23:13; 1 Chron 11:15; 14:9: Isaiah17:5.

7 Nick Wyatt, "À la recherche des Rephaïm perdus", *The Archaeology of Myth*, ed. Nick Wyatt, (London: Equinox, 2010) , 587-588.

by fire (1 Enoch. 26–27; 54:1–6; 56:1–4; 90:24–27)… Gehenna had become hell itself."[8]

When Ezekiel predicted the destruction of Gog in his major eschatological prophecy, he declared that it would occur in a valley that is tied to the underworld:

> Ezekiel 39:11:
> "On that day I will give to Gog a place for burial in Israel, the Valley of the Travelers, east of the sea. It will block the travelers, for there Gog and all his multitude will be buried. It will be called the Valley of Hamon-gog.

"Valley of the Travelers" in Hebrew is *Valley of the Oberim.* That name is not about mere travelers on the roads and valleys. Bible commentator Daniel Block explains the underworld valley connection best as a designation for "those who have passed on," in other words, deceased heroes that are referred to elsewhere as Rephaim.

> This netherworldly connection may hold the key to this frame as a whole. Gog and his warriors have imagined themselves to be like the nobles of old, but Yahweh hereby declares their doom. They are sentenced to death just as Egypt and all his companions in ch. 32…When the corpses of Gog and his horde are gathered, the pile in the "valley of those who have passed on" will be completely blocked off, that is, filled, so it will hold no more bodies. Sixth, because of its new usage, the site will receive a new name, *gê' hămôn gôg*, "the Valley of Hamon-Gog," which appears to play on *gê' hinnōm*, "the valley of Hinnom." Earlier this was the site of Molech worship and child sacrifice (e.g., Jeremiah 2:23), and the place where the bodies of animals and criminals were burned.[9]

Block also points out that "east of the sea" presumably meant the Mediterranean Sea and that the mass burial was suggestive of this important locale being reduced to a common cemetery. Notice also the linguistic connection to that other underworld Valley of Hinnom, which would become the ultimate symbol of judgment.

---

[8] Duane F. Watson, "Gehenna (Place)," ed. David Noel Freedman, *The Anchor Yale Bible Dictionary* (New York: Doubleday, 1992), 927.

[9] Daniel Isaac Block, *The Book of Ezekiel, Chapters 25–48, The New International Commentary on the Old Testament* (Grand Rapids, MI: Wm. B. Eerdmans Publishing Co., 1997–), 468–470.

You might remember those victory feasts we mentioned earlier of eating Leviathan in the desert of Sinai (Psalm 74:14), birds consuming the enemies of Jesus in the marriage supper of the Lamb (Revelations 19:17-18), and Jeremiah's slaughter (Jeremiah 7:33). Ezekiel's prophecy has such a feast as well.

> Ezekiel 39:17–18:
> Thus says the Lord GOD: "Speak to the birds of every sort and to all beasts of the field: 'Assemble and come, gather from all around to the sacrificial feast that I am preparing for you, a great sacrificial feast on the mountains of Israel, and you shall eat flesh and drink blood. You shall eat the flesh of the mighty, and drink the blood of the princes of the earth—of rams, of lambs, and of he-goats, of bulls, all of them fat beasts of Bashan.'"

The birds would feast on Gog as a memorial of God's destruction of his enemies. The valley would be a valley of death—in Israel. But notice that last word. The beasts being eaten would be "fat beasts of Bashan." Bashan was a deeply significant spiritual location to the Canaanites and the Hebrews. As the *DDD* puts it, biblical geographical tradition agrees with the mythological and cultic data of the Canaanites of Ugarit that "the Bashan region, or a part of it, clearly represented 'Hell', the celestial and infernal abode of their deified dead kings," i.e., the Rephaim.[10]

Mount Hermon was in Bashan, and Mount Hermon was a location in the Bible linked to the Rephaim and ruled over by Og (Joshua 12:1–5). But it was also the legendary location where the heavenly Sons of God were considered to have come to earth in rebellion before the Flood.[11]

The underworld connections just keep growing. But we'll stop there and jump into the abyss of that underworld, which is the next cosmic geographical location: Sheol.

---

[10] "Bashan," *DDD*, p 161-162. "According to *KTU* 1.108:1–3, the abode of the dead and deified king, and his place of enthronement as *[Rephaim]* was in *[Ashtarot and Edrei]*, in amazing correspondence with the Biblical tradition about the seat of king Og of Bashan, "one of the survivors of the Rephaim, who lived in Ashtarot and Edrei" (Josh 12:4)."

[11] The non-canonical book of Enoch supports this same interpretation: "Enoch 6:6 And they were in all two hundred [sons of God]; who descended in the days of Jared on the summit of Mount Hermon, and they called it Mount Hermon, because they had sworn and bound themselves by mutual imprecations upon it."

Sheol

Sheol was the Hebrew word for the underworld.[12] Though the Bible doesn't contain any narratives of experiences in Sheol, it was nevertheless described as the abode of the dead that was below the earth. Sheol was sometimes used interchangeably with Abaddon as the place of destruction of the body (Proverbs 15:11; 27:20),[13] and the grave as a reference to the state of being dead and buried in the earth (Psalm 88:11; Isaiah 14:9-11). But it was also considered to be *physically* located beneath the earth.

When the sons of Korah were swallowed up by the earth for their rebellion against God, Numbers chapter 16 says that "they went down alive into Sheol, and the earth closed over them, and they perished from the midst of the assembly" (v. 33). People would not "fall alive" into death or the grave and then perish if Sheol wasn't a location. But they would die after they fell down into a location (Sheol) and the earth closed over them in that order.

The divine being (*elohim*), known as the departed spirit of Samuel, "came up out of the earth" for the witch of Endor's necromancy with Saul (1 Samuel 28:13). This wasn't a reference to a body coming out of a grave, but a spirit of the dead coming from the underworld beneath the earth.

When Isaiah writes about Sheol in Isaiah 14, he combines the notion of the physical location of the dead body in the earth (v. 11) with the location beneath the earth of the spirits of the dead (v. 9). It's really a both/and proposition.

> Isaiah 14:9, 11:
> Sheol beneath is stirred up to meet you when you come; it rouses the shades to greet you…Your pomp is brought down to Sheol.

Here is a list of some verses that speak of Sheol geographically as an underworld habitation for spirits in contrast with heaven as an overworld habitation for spirits.

> Amos 9:2:
> "If they dig into Sheol, from there shall my hand take them; if they climb up to heaven, from there I will bring them down.

---

12 "Sheol," *DDD*, p 768.

13 "Abaddon," *DDD*, p 1.

> Job 11:8 :
> It is higher than heaven—what can you do? Deeper than Sheol—what can you know?
>
> Psalm 139:8:
> If I ascend to heaven, you are there! If I make my bed in Sheol, you are there!
>
> Isaiah 7:11:
> Ask a sign of the LORD your God; let it be deep as Sheol or high as heaven."

These are not mere references to the body in the grave but to locations of the spiritual soul as well. Sheol and heaven are a dichotomous totality of geographical opposites. As the above verses attest, they are shown in the Bible to be opposing locations. Sheol is a combined term that describes both the grave for the body and the underworld location of the departed souls of the dead.

In the New Testament, the word Hades is used for the underworld, which was the Greek equivalent of Sheol.[14] Jesus himself used the term Hades as the location of damned spirits in contrast with heaven as the location of redeemed spirits when he talked of Capernaum at the judgment, "And you, Capernaum, will you be exalted to heaven? You will be brought down to Hades" (Matthew 11:23).

Hades/Sheol was also the location of *all* departed spirits in his parable of Lazarus and the rich man in Hades (Luke 16:19-31).

In the novel *Jezebel: Harlot Queen of Israel*, I tell the story of Anat going into Sheol to find her brother Baal, held hostage by Mot in his city of Death. There is no detailed depiction of Sheol in the Old Testament, and while the picture of the Greek Hades is commonly used in fiction, I chose instead to use the only Jewish picture of the underworld that I could find because it would be the closest Hebrew understanding to the Bible. Granted, it isn't canonical but only an imaginative construction of a spiritual reality.

Though 1 Enoch is not Scripture, I have argued elsewhere for the high regard that the New Testament gives the ancient text as a source for some of its own theological concepts and language.[15] The revered ancient Jewish book consists of several "books" that recount an expanded version of the Genesis 6 story of the Watchers and Nephilim giants as well as visions the prophet Enoch

---

[14] "Hades," *DDD*, p 382.

[15] See the chapter "The Book of Enoch: Scripture, Heresy, or What?" in *When Giants Were Upon the Earth: The Watchers, Nephilim and the Cosmic War of the Seed* (Los Angeles: Embedded Pictures, 2014).

allegedly experienced. In these visions, angels take Enoch around the earth, up into the heights of heaven, and down into the depths of Hades (which are actually arrived at by going to the "ends of the earth" rather than descending down into the earth). Unfortunately, these visions are obscure, overlapping, and at times contradictory, so scholars have disagreed over their interpretation as well as their actual cosmic geography. I have attempted to use my own reading of the text and to integrate it with several of these scholarly viewpoints that can be found analyzed in the book *A Study of the Geography of 1 Enoch 17-19* by Kelley Coblentz Bautch.[16] Imagination is required!

Since Enoch's "map" is cosmic, it includes Sheol/Hades as well as the heavens and the earth. But some scholars have argued that Enoch's entire journey is to the realm of the dead.[17] So I decided to use the ancient Near Eastern (and Jewish) notion of "on earth as it is in heaven" (Matthew 6:10) or "as above, so below," to apply to the underworld as well. In this way, the geography of Hades is a reflection of the sacred geography of the earth above ("sacred geography" means that it doesn't so much follow physical geography as it does theological meaning).

Since the underworld was believed by the Jews to be under the earth[18] and accessed by the waters of the Abyss,[19] which was the source of the waters above,[20] I have those waters work as a kind of sky in the dome of the underworld (though not in all places). The mountains below rise up from Hades to the earth above. So Mount Zion in Hades rises up and penetrates the ceiling of Hades and becomes Mount Zion on earth above them. This fulfills the ancient Near Eastern notion of the cosmic mountains being an *axis mundi*, a connection between the heavens, the earth and the underworld.[21]

The circle of Hades matches the circle of the earth above it and likewise has an ocean/river (the Great Sea or Abyss) at its outer reaches that extends beyond the "Four Winds" or "Four Corners" of the earth where the pillars of

---

[16]Kelley Coblentz Bautch, *A Study of the Geography of 1 Enoch 17-19: No One Has Seen What I Have Seen*, (Leiden, Netherlands: Brill, 2003).

[17] Glasson, T. Francis. Greek Influence in Jewish Eschatology. London: S.P.C.K., 1961, 8-11; Nickelsburg, *Jewish Literature between the Bible and the Mishnah*, (Philadelphia: Fortress Press, 1981) 54–55; 66, n. 26; also *1 Enoch*, 280; James C. VanderKam, *Enoch and the Growth of an Apocalyptic Tradition*. CBQMS 16. Washington, D.C.: Catholic Biblical Association of America, 1984.

[18] Amos 9:2.

[19] Ps. 136:6; Job 41:34 LXX.

[20] Wayne Horowitz, *Mesopotamian Cosmic Geography*, (Winona Lake; IN: Eisenbrauns, 1998), 334-348.

[21] Richard J. Clifford, *The Cosmic Mountain in Canaan and the Old Testament* (Wipf & Stock Pub, 2010). Also, Isa. 14:13-15.

the earth support the heavens and the earth (1 Enoch 17:5; Proverbs 8:27, 29; 1 Samuel 2:8; Mark 13:27).[22]

In this conceptual map, Jerusalem, or Mount Zion, is at the center of the earth, and has "the accursed valley" (Gehenna) right next to it (Ezekiel 5:5, 38:12; 1 Enoch 26:1-2; 27:2).

North from that center resides Mount Hermon, the "rock" (mountain) upon which Jesus said God would build his new kingdom church.[23] This mountain is described as "reaching to the heavens" and as being the celestial storehouse of the luminaries and storms (1 Enoch 17:3). Many rivers flow from it, including a river of fire and a river of "living waters" (17:4-8), and it is guarded by fiery beings who take human shape (17:1). This "source of the waters" is a reflection of the cosmic Mountain of Eden and its source of living waters (Ezekiel 28:13-14).[24]

In the south are seven mountains of precious stones arranged in a perpendicular layout. The central mountain burns with fire day and night and is called the "throne of God," where God will come down at the final judgment. These elements suggest it is Mount Sinai (1 Enoch 24-25).

In the west are "wintery winds" and the "great darkness," where another mountain hosts "hollow places" for the souls of all the dead. The righteous are separated from the sinners, much like the chasm separates the righteous in Abraham's Bosom from the sinners in the parable of Lazarus. (Luke 16:19-26; 1 Enoch 17:6; 22:1-14).

In the east are "great beasts and birds" at the ends of the earth (1 Enoch 33:1). Tartarus is further "beyond the edge of the earth," where the earth meets to uphold the vault of heaven (1 Enoch 18:10).[25] This is where the angels who sinned in Genesis 6 were kept imprisoned in gloomy darkness (2 Peter 2:4; 1 Peter 3:18-20). They were in deep pits or chasms that are like fiery pillars. (1 Enoch 18:10-16).

There is much more detail that can be quite confusing to follow, so I have included an illustrated map with some of the major elements adapted from Bautch and my own reading of 1Enoch.

---

22 See also Isa. 40:22; Zech. 9:10; Job 38:4.

23 Matt. 16:18.

24 Bautch, *A Study of the Geography of 1 Enoch,* 64-69.

25 George W. E. Nickelsburg, *1 Enoch: A Commentary on the Book of 1 Enoch, ed. Klaus Baltzer, Hermeneia—a Critical and Historical Commentary on the Bible* (Minneapolis, MN: Fortress, 2001), 286.

Enoch's Cosmic Geography of Sheol, the Underworld
(adapted from 1Enoch 17-19 & Kelley Coblentz Bautch,
A Study of the Geography of 1 Enoch 17-19: "No One Has Seen What I Have Seen")

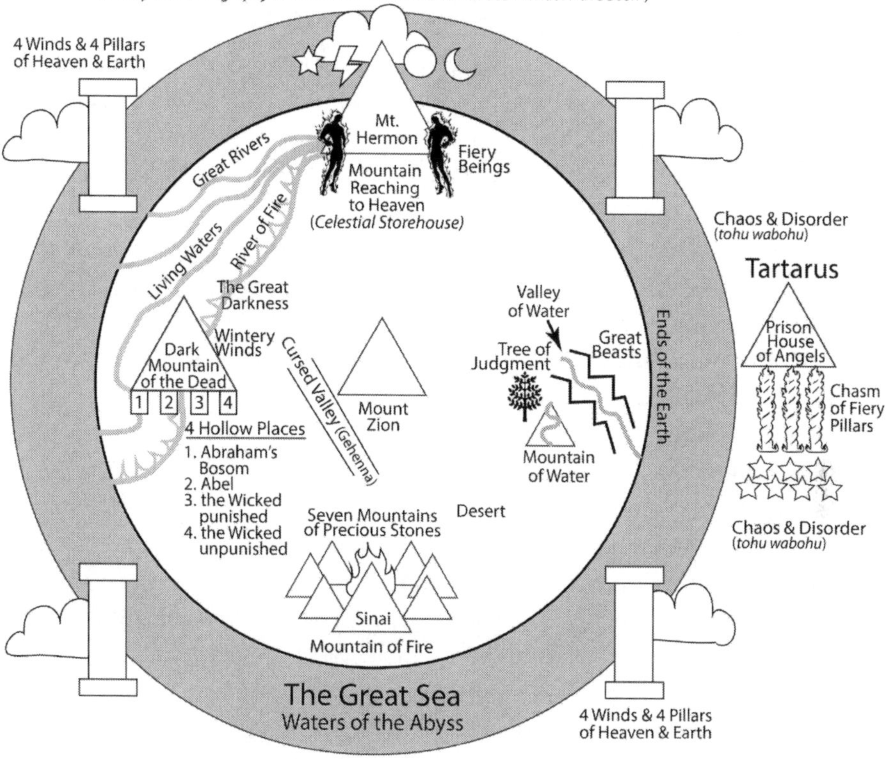

Cosmic Mountains

In the novel *Jezebel: Harlot Queen of Israel*, several mountains become significant locations of divinity and play heavily into the spiritual storyline. They incarnate the notion of a cosmic mountain, or holy mountain, a location where heaven and earth are connected, where deities reside in temples or tents, and where the source waters of life often pour forth. This symbolic imagery has been carried through from the two series *Chronicles of the Nephilim* and *Chronicles of the Apocalypse* (affiliate links) because it is a key feature of the ancient worldview of cosmic geography.

The confrontation between Elijah and Jezebel's prophets of Baal takes place on Mount Carmel, a holy mountain that Baalists had taken as booty from Israel earlier in history. They had torn down an altar of Yahweh that was originally there and replaced it with an altar to Baal. Yahweh took it back with fire from heaven.

Baal has his own cosmic Mount Saphon in the north where, according to the Baal epic, he built his palace after achieving priority among the gods. This actual mountain is in Syria, 180 miles north of Tyre.

Mount Hermon is known as the location where the Watchers fell to earth before the Flood, and it remained the location of their divine council or assembly of rebels to that day. In its foothills was the infamous "Gates of Hades" in the cave of Panias that led into the Abyss. Yes, those "Gates of Hades" that Jesus referred to.

When Elijah became bereft and lost his way spiritually, he journeyed to Mount Sinai, the holy mountain of Yahweh, where the Torah was delivered amidst the divine council of heavenly host. Jerusalem, the location of Yahweh's temple, is referred to as Mount Zion, the new holy mountain that ultimately replaced Sinai as Yahweh's abode.

Biblical scholar Richard Clifford explains the concept of holy mountains or cosmic mountains playing an important role in the religious thought of the ancient Near East, including Israel: "In this view, heaven and earth united were seen as a mountain. The base of the mountain was the earth and the peak was the top of the heavens. Thus the mountain was the central axis of the universe and was the connecting point between the different spheres."[26]

The connections run deep between Canaanite and Israelite cosmic mountains. In Ugaritic mythology, the high god El lived in a tent on his holy mountain and counseled with his heavenly host, the seventy Sons of God.[27] At Sinai, Yahweh dwelt in a tent (tabernacle) at the foot of his holy mountain, where he counseled with his heavenly host and gave his decrees to the people (Deuteronomy 33:1-2; Psalm 68:15-17). In Hebrew, one of God's names is El Shaddai, whose translation most likely means "God of the mountain."[28] By the time of Solomon's temple, the new location for Yahweh's dwelling, Jerusalem, had become designated Mount Zion, the holy mountain "in the heights of the north" (Psalm 48:1-2). I'll explain what "heights of the north" (*sapon*) means below. But for now, notice that this new holy mountain of Zion is poetically linked to Eden, described as "the holy mountain" in Ezekiel 28:13-16. God's presence is linked to mountains from Eden to Sinai to Zion, just as pagan deities claimed mountains as their own.

---

[26] Richard J. Clifford, *The Cosmic Mountain in Canaan and the Old Testament* (Wipf & Stock Pub, 2010),190.

[27] Clifford, *The Cosmic Mountain,* 124-125. Seventy Sons of Asherah: page 61.

[28] Gordon J. Wenham, "The Religion of the Patriarchs," A.R. Millard & D.J. Wiseman, eds., *Essays on the Patriarchal Narratives.* Leicester: IVP, 1980, pp.157-188.

In fact, one could say that the Bible records a battle of cosmic mountains between Yahweh and others like Baal. Certain scriptures point toward God taking over the enemy's mountain as his own and building his city of victory upon it.

One element of Baal's reign was his mountain abode of Mount Saphon (various spellings include Zaphon, Sapan, Sapon). A plethora of Ugaritic texts link Baal with his "divine mountain, Saphon/Sapan."[29] He is said to be buried there[30] in his sanctuary[31] on the mountain of victory.[32]

In Isaiah 14:13, Isaiah mocks the arrogance of the king of Babylon by likening him to another mythological figure, Athtar, who sought to take Baal's throne and failed "on the mountain of assembly on the summit of Zaphon [Sapan]."[33]

In the Bible, this Mount Zaphon of Baal is subverted by Israel's holy Mount Zion.

> Psalm 48:1–2:
> Great is the LORD and greatly to be praised in the city of our God! His holy mountain, beautiful in elevation, is the joy of all the earth, Mount Zion, in the far north [*zaphon*], the city of the great King.

In this scripture the holy Mount Zion is described as being in "the far north," the very location of Baal's Mount Saphon (Zaphon), but not in fact the actual location of Israel's Mount Zion. So "the far north" is a theological, not a geographical designation of Zion replacing Saphon as the divine mountain par excellence.[34]

But God's battle over mountains is far from complete. He also speaks about Mount Hermon, known as "mountain of Bashan," as being a target for conquering. The region of Bashan was translated as "place of the serpent," the area where Og of Bashan ruled, the last of the Rephaim, those warriors

---

29 KTU 1.101:1-9; 1.100:9; 1.3:3:29.

30 KTU 1.6:1:15-18.

31 KTU 1.3:3:30.

32 KTU 1.101:1-4.

33 Michael Heiser, "The Mythological Provenance of Isaiah 14:12-15: A Reconsideration of the Ugaritic Material" Liberty University https://digitalcommons.liberty.edu/cgi/viewcontent.cgi?referer=&httpsredir=1&article=1279&context=lts_fac_pubs

34 H. Niehr, "Zaphon", in *Dictionary of Deities and Demons in the Bible*, ed. Karel van der Toorn, Bob Becking and Pieter W. van der Horst, 2nd extensively rev. ed., 929 (Leiden; Boston; Köln; Grand Rapids, MI; Cambridge: Brill; Eerdmans, 1999). Also see Job 26:7; 37:22; Ezek. 1:4 where the word "north" is used as a spiritual reference, more allusion to the divine mountain Saphon of Canaanite belief.

connected to the underworld.[35] Mount Hermon of Bashan was the location where the Watchers came to earth and made their evil covenant in their diabolical divine assembly.

The origin story of the Watchers is partially revealed in Genesis 6:1-4, where the angelic Sons of God came to earth before the Flood. They mated with humans in violation of God's heavenly and earthly divide. This is one of the reasons why God sent the Flood and imprisoned those beings in Tartarus (2 Peter 2:4-5; Jude 6).

> Genesis 6:1–3
> When man began to multiply on the face of the land and daughters were born to them, the sons of God saw that the daughters of man were attractive. And they took as their wives any they chose.

I've given extensive biblical and historical evidence for this supernatural angelic incursion and its evil results in my book *When Giants Were Upon the Earth (affiliate link)*, so I will save room here. What I want to point out is that Genesis doesn't tell us *where* these Sons of God (aka Watchers) came down to earth. But there is an ancient book that does. This is the writings of 1 Enoch, a non-canonical Jewish text that expands on Genesis 6.

I also argued in my *Giants* book that 1 Enoch is not Scripture, but it was quoted and paraphrased in the New Testament books of 1 John, Jude, 2 Peter, and others,[36] so it certainly deserves the respect that the historic Christian church had given it until the modern era.

In it, we read of the Genesis 6 "sons of God," called "sons of heaven" in 1 Enoch, making a covenant with one another to come to earth and "choose wives for themselves from among the daughters of men" to beget children, just like Genesis 6 says. Here's how it happens.

> 1 Enoch 6:3-6:
> And Semyaz, being their leader, said unto them, "I fear that perhaps you will not consent that this deed should be done, and I alone will become (responsible) for this great sin." But they all responded to him, "Let us all swear an oath and bind everyone among us by a curse not to abandon this suggestion but to do the deed." Then they all swore together and bound

[35] Michael S. Heiser, *The Unseen Realm: Recovering the Supernatural Worldview of the Bible, First Edition* (Bellingham, WA: Lexham Press, 2015), 200.

[36] See the chapter "The Book of Enoch: Scripture, Heresy, or What?" in Brian Godawa, *When Giants Were Upon the Earth: The Watchers, Nephilim and the Cosmic War of the Seed* (Los Angeles: Embedded Pictures, 2014), 24-37.

> one another by (the curse). And they were altogether two hundred; and they descended into ʾArdos, which is the summit of Hermon. And they called the mount Armon, for they swore and bound one another by a curse.[37]

1 Enoch is called the Book of the Watchers, and these "angels" in this passage are elsewhere called "Watchers of heaven who have abandoned the high heaven, the holy eternal place, and have defiled themselves with women" (1 Enoch 12:4).[38] Of course there are many aspects to discuss about this story. But for our purposes here, notice that these fallen Watchers swear an oath of covenant in their assembly on the mountain, like a diabolical inversion of Yahweh's sworn covenant with Israel on Mount Sinai. Hermon became their "mount of assembly," from which they invaded the earth (1 Enoch 13:7).

An enigmatic Greek inscription from the third century A.D. found at the peak of Mount Hermon coincides quite eerily with this Watcher oath. It reads, "According to the command of the greatest and holy God, those who take an oath proceed from here."[39]

From primeval days, Mount Hermon was Ground Zero, the headquarters of rebellion against Yahweh, the original evil cosmic mountain. And that mountain was located in Bashan, "land of the serpent," residence of the last of the Rephaim monsters who defied Yahweh as well. That cosmic mountain of Bashan, known as Mount Hermon, would become the symbolic mountain of power that Yahweh would ultimately defeat and own. He said so in Psalm 68.

> Psalm 68:15–22:
> O mountain of God, mountain of Bashan;
> O many-peaked mountain, mountain of Bashan!

---

[37] James H. Charlesworth, *The Old Testament Pseudepigrapha,* vol. 1 (New York; London: Yale University Press, 1983), 15.

[38] See also 1 Enoch 10:9, 15; 13:10; 14:1-3; chapters 15 and 16.

[39] George W. E. Nickelsburg, *1 Enoch: A Commentary on the Book of 1 Enoch*, ed. Klaus Baltzer, *Hermeneia—a Critical and Historical Commentary on the Bible* (Minneapolis, MN: Fortress, 2001), 247.

"In addition to the oath, which is reminiscent of the oath of the watchers in 1 Enoch 6:6, the title "the greatest and holy God" closely parallels one of 1 Enoch's favorite divine titles, "the Great Holy One," often rendered into Greek as "the Great and Holy One" (see comm. on 1:3c–4). The similarities might reflect cultic activity that was somehow informed by traditions from 1 Enoch...

"Two final attestations concerning the sacred character of Hermon occur in the church fathers. In the Onomasticon, Eusebius says of the mountain that "it is honored as sacred by the gentiles." Interpreting this, Jerome states, "At its peak is a noted temple that is reverenced by the Gentiles from the region of Paneas and Lebanon."

Nickelsburg, *1 Enoch,* 247.

Why do you look with hatred, O many-peaked mountain,
at the mount that God desired for his abode,
yes, where the LORD will dwell forever?
The chariots of God are twice ten thousand,
thousands upon thousands;
the Lord is among them; Sinai is now in the sanctuary.
You ascended on high,
leading a host of captives in your train
and receiving gifts among men,
even among the rebellious, that the LORD God may dwell there…
But God will strike the heads of his enemies...
The Lord said, "I will bring them back from Bashan,
I will bring them back from the depths of the sea."

In this psalm, God takes ownership of Bashan with his heavenly host of warriors, but then replaces it and refers to Mount Sinai (soon to be Zion). It isn't that God is making Bashan his mountain literally, but conquering its divinities and theologically replacing it with his new cosmic mountain elsewhere.

In verse 18, Yahweh leads captives in triumphal procession and receives tribute from them as spoils of war (v. 18). Paul quoted this very verse to be a reference to Christ's ascension and his victory over the spiritual powers.

> Ephesians 4:8–10:
> Therefore it says, "When he ascended on high he led a host of captives, and he gave gifts to men."
> (In saying "he ascended," what does it mean but that he had also descended into the lower regions, the earth? He who descended is the one who also ascended far above all the heavens, that he might fill all things.)

Yahweh will own and live where once the rebellious ruled (v. 18). He will strike his enemies' heads and bring them all out from the sea of chaos, that wilderness where Leviathan symbolically reigns.

This battle of cosmic mountains is the foundation that finally gives meaning to the famous passage about Jesus building his Church upon a "rock" in Matthew 16.

> Matthew 16:18:
> And I tell you, you are Peter, and on this rock I will build my church, and the gates of Hades shall not prevail against it.

Ironically, both Roman Catholics and Protestants are wrong when they interpret this passage. Roman Catholics think that Jesus is referring to Peter as the first pope, as though he was making a word play with Peter meaning "stone" like a "rock." But of course it would be complete and utter nonsense, not to mention blasphemy, for Jesus, the Son of God, sinless God in the flesh, to build his glorious kingdom Church upon a sinful human being rather than upon himself as sinless high priest and savior of that Church.

But Protestants are equally wrong to argue that the "rock" is Peter's confession of Christ's Sonship, for the location where they were standing when Jesus uttered those words was at a sacred place literally called "The Gates of Hades" believed to lead down to the Abyss.[40]

The rock Jesus was referring to was Mount Hermon, in whose foothills they were standing. Jesus was fulfilling the promise of Psalm 68 noted above that Yahweh would conquer the cosmic mountain of Bashan, Mount Hermon, the mountain that was God's rival, the cosmic mountain that represented spiritual rebellion. By creating his Church, the spiritual Mount Zion and its heavenly Jerusalem (Hebrews 12:22), Jesus was then building his victorious kingdom upon the spiritual ruins of that wretched, rebellious "rock" before which they were standing.

With his resurrection and ascension, Jesus as Messiah took back Mount Hermon and was installed as "king upon Zion, God's holy mountain" (Psalm 2:6). Read more detailed exposition of that theological victory of Christ at the Gates of Hades in my book *When Giants Were Upon the Earth (affiliate link).*

---

[40] *Wars of the Jews* 1:405, Flavius Josephus and William Whiston, The Works of Josephus: Complete and Unabridged (Peabody: Hendrickson, 1987).

Chapter 5: Cultic Practice

High Places

When the Israelites first entered the Promised Land to dispossess the Canaanites, Yahweh told them to destroy the altars where the pagans worshipped their gods "on the high mountains and on the hills and under every green tree" (Deuteronomy 12:2-6). This phrase would become a meme for what was called "high places" (Hebrew: *bamah*; plural: *bamot*).[1] The Israelites were told to tear down the altars and chop down and dash into pieces the images of the gods that Canaanites worshipped.

Archaeological digs have uncovered some of these high places throughout the land. They were usually locations of cultic sacrifice that were elevated, either naturally on a hill or artificially on large open-air stone platforms with stairs. Some had large sacred pillars called *massebot* in Hebrew (to be discussed below), asherim poles, and other images of gods. Some were simple sanctuaries. Others were entire complexes of worship that included a courtyard and a dining hall for sacred meals (1 Samuel 9:25) as well as various side rooms, not unlike the temple complex in Jerusalem.[2]

Upon first entering the Land of Canaan, the Israelites were told to create their own high places to worship Yahweh with simple earth or unhewn stone rather than the large platforms that typified Canaanite worship (Exodus 20:24-26). Israel was to be different. Before the temple was built, Yahweh approved of the high places created exclusively for him. David worshipped Yahweh with a priesthood at the high place in Gibeon according to God's own commands.

---

[1] 1 Kings. 14:23; 2 Kings. 16:4; 17:10; Jer. 3:6.

[2] Philip J. King, Lawrence E. Stager, *Life in Biblical Israel* (Louisville, KY: Westminster John Knox Press, 2001), 320.

> 1 Chronicles 16:39–40:
> And [David] left Zadok the priest and his brothers the priests before the tabernacle of the LORD in the high place that was at Gibeon to offer burnt offerings to the LORD on the altar of burnt offering regularly morning and evening, to do all that is written in the Law of the LORD that he commanded Israel.

Solomon too served Yahweh at the main high place (out of many) in Gibeon. But once the king built the temple of Yahweh in Jerusalem, the high places were no longer legitimate locations to worship Yahweh (1 Kings 3:2-4). All worship was to be centralized in the single house of God in Jerusalem.

But the king and his people both failed to obey this command of God. Solomon himself built high places to the gods Molech and Chemosh just outside the walls of Jerusalem (1 Kings 11:7). When the kingdom split after Solomon, Jeroboam placed two golden calves in both Dan and Bethel in high place complexes (1 Kings 12:31).

The high places in both Israel and Judah were never destroyed until the time of King Hezekiah in the eighth century (2 Kings 18:4), *over two hundred years after Solomon's temple was built.* Two hundred years of widespread usage of forbidden high places. And even then, many high places were left in Judah until King Josiah's more thorough reforms seventy five years later. Josiah was the one credited with the most significant elimination of idolatry in Judah and Israel. He destroyed the high places outside Jerusalem along with all their constituent elements of altars, asherim, and sacred pillars, as well as the abominable Tophet of Molech in the Valley of Hinnom and the unholy vessels of idol worship in Yahweh's temple (2 Kings 23).

The Scripture sings praise of Josiah.

> 2 Kings 23:25:
> Before [Josiah] there was no king like him, who turned to the LORD with all his heart and with all his soul and with all his might, according to all the Law of Moses, nor did any like him arise after him.

Yet in spite of this momentary righteousness of Josiah, *all the next four kings of Judah* "did evil in the sight of the Lord," bringing a return to the abominable worship of Canaanite gods and polluting Yahweh's house in Jerusalem that had previously been cleansed (2 Chronicles 36:14).

The ancient Jews simply wouldn't give up their high places and addiction to the spiritual infidelity of worshipping other gods.

Standing Stones

We've already discussed the wooden poles called asherim previously. These were ubiquitous images related to the goddess Asherah that were closely linked with altars of both Baal and Yahweh at high places throughout Israel and Judah.

Another common element of the high place were sacred pillars, or *massebot* (singular: *massebah*). These were standing stone slabs from a few feet to ten feet tall that stood upright. Though pillars like this, also called *stela*, were used for various purposes such as boundary markers and victory memorials, Canaanites also erected such stela as markers for the presence of deified ancestors.[3] In the Old Testament, the term *massebah,* when used for cultic purposes, was nearly always a reference to standing stones "erected to commemorate the appearance or presence of a deity."[4]

Archaeologist Ziony Zevit describes the language related to these standing stones or pillars. They were "made from stone" (Genesis 22:18; 31:13; Exodus 31:45) and were "constructed" (Exodus 24:4; 1 Kings 14:23), "placed" (Genesis 28:18), "raised high" (Genesis 31:45), "stood up" (Leviticus 26:1; Deuteronomy 16:22), "set erect" (Genesis 35:14; 20; 2 Kings 17:10), and "artificially dressed" (Hosea 10:2).[5]

Some of these stone slabs have been found in several excavations of Israelite cities from this time period (Arad, Lachish, Tirzah, and Hazor). Five standing stones were uncovered surrounding a stone altar in the outer gate plaza of the Israelite city of Dan.[6] Standing stones could also be found in city gates. One such massebah was unearthed from the gate of the Jewish city

---

3 CTA 17:1:26–30:
so that he may beget a son in his house,
a scion in the midst of his palace.
He shall set up the stela of his ancestral god,
in the sanctuary the cippus of his kinsman;

N. Wyatt, *Religious Texts from Ugarit, 2nd ed., Biblical Seminar, 53* (London; New York: Sheffield Academic Press, 2002), 255–256.

4 William G. Dever, *Did God Have a Wife?: Archaeology and Folk Religion in Ancient Israel* (Grand Rapids, MI: Eerdmans Publishing, 2005), 99. "(Gen. 28:18; Exod. 24:4; Josh. 24:26–27). They are often said to be associated with a *bāmāh*, or "high place" (1 Kings 14:23; 2 Kings 18:4; 23:13–14), or a temple (2 Kings 3:2); or located near an "idol" (Lev. 26:1; Deut. 7:5; 12:3; Mic. 5:13)." William G. Dever, *The Lives of Ordinary People in Ancient Israel: Where Archaeology and the Bible Intersect* (Grand Rapids, MI; Cambridge, U.K.: William B. Eerdmans Publishing Company, 2012), 290.

5 Ziony Zevit, *The Religions of Ancient Israel: A Synthesis of Parallactic Approaches* (London, Continuum, 2001), 259.

6 William G. Dever, *The Lives of Ordinary People in Ancient Israel: Where Archaeology and the Bible Intersect* (Grand Rapids, MI; Cambridge, U.K.: William B. Eerdmans Publishing Company, 2012), 273-275.

Bethsaida. It contains an engraved image representation of a bull-headed icon of Baal.

In the Bible, Solomon was reported to have constructed sacred pillars for Baal and possibly Molech and Astarte (2 Kings 23:13-14) in the high places of Jerusalem. King Ahab of Israel is reported to have set up a pillar of Baal in the temple in Samaria (2 Kings 3:2; 10:27), as described in the novel *Jezebel: Harlot Queen of Israel.*

Zevit explains the rhetorical connection of *massebot* standing stones with the sacred tree and high place.

> Finally, there are the blanket statements about *massebot* "on every high hill and under every green tree," an expression that is often taken as a rhetorical idiom signifying "everywhere." However, as noted above in the discussion of peak sanctuaries, it most likely refers to locations of two different types of cult places. One Tyrian coin illustrates two side-by-side *massebot* under a single leafy tree while a second illustrates two *massebot* flanking a leafy tree whose branches overhang each of them.

The Bible provides no explicit details regarding the cultic rituals involved with the standing stones. But based on the Jacob narrative at Bethel, Zevit speculates that there was an intentional and silent setting up of the stone, an anointing with oil, followed by a performance declaration of promises and obligations. This ritual most likely established a bond between the person and the deity, whose power allegedly indwelt the stone, as Jacob called the stone itself the "house of God" (Gen 28:18-22; 31:13). This is not equating the deity with the image, but rather the belief that the presence of the deity was within and yet separate from the stone. "Both physically and metaphysically, they represented, expressed, and guaranteed a continuous, immanent presence."[7]

The fact that Yahweh prohibited images of himself (Exod 20:4-5), yet spoke positively of pillars for Yahweh (Isaiah19:19) while condemning pagan pillars to other gods (Exod 23:24; 34:13), suggests that pillars for Yahweh didn't have images on them, but rather represented Yahweh's presence in the abstract as a boundary marker or memorial.

Once the house of God was completed in Jerusalem from the time of Solomon onward, it would seem even properly crafted pillars for Yahweh were no longer acceptable since Yahweh claimed his house was on Mount Zion alone.

---

[7] Zevit, *The Religions of Ancient Israel,* 260-261.

Psalm 132:13:
For the LORD has chosen Zion; he has desired it for his dwelling place.

Psalm 87:2:
The LORD loves the gates of Zion more than all the dwelling places of Jacob.

Masks

I describe the use of masks in a Tyrian ritual of Astarte worship in *Jezebel: Harlot Queen of Israel*. This wasn't an element of creative license. It was based upon a fascinating discovery of the use of masks in religious ritual on the island of Cyprus, a Phoenician colony like Tyre. As it happens, the temple of Astarte in Kition was the most dominant on the island and provided a plethora of mask artifacts for consideration.

Scholar Erin Averett examined the masks, which consisted of both animal and human faces: "Bull, lion, horse, stag, also monsters, cattle skulls."[8] She concluded several purposes for them. Some were used as magical devices ("apotropaic ") in graves to scare away the spirits. But they were also used by royal and priestly elite in libation ceremonies as well as "religious rituals designed to showcase their privileged access to the divine realm, legitimizing their sacred authority."[9] The context and types of Cypriot masks seem to reflect the patterns of masked initiation rites into secret societies of restricted membership.

One possible interpretation of an inscription found on a limestone tablet from Kition may indicate temple ministers wore animal costumes in the cult of Astarte.[10]

Though the precise nature of their usage is unclear, Averett concludes that these religious masks …

> … play a social role by identifying maskers with high profile ritual performances. Thus, individuals or groups became associated with divinities as attendant figures in rituals, which in turn provided these maskers with divine protection and the power and characteristics of the deity…

---

[8] Erin Walcek Averett, "Masks and Ritual Performance on the Island of Cyprus," *American Journal of Archaeology* , Vol. 119, No. 1 (January 2015), 12.

[9] Averett, "Masks and Ritual," 12.

[10] Averett, "Masks and Ritual," 21.

> masks thus become visual manifestations of rituals that affirm existing power structures. As multimedia public events, religious ceremonies established and confirmed social structures through the use of monumental architecture, sacred space, and symbolic objects.

Qedeshim

One of the cultic functionaries in high places and temples that appears throughout the novel *Jezebel* is the *qedeshim*, a Hebrew word somewhat ambiguous and undetermined in meaning, though some Bible translations render it as male or female cult prostitutes (male: *qedesh*; female: *qedesha*). The word "cult" means used in sacred service or worship of a deity.

In the Bible, it isn't entirely clear exactly what the responsibilities of the qedeshim are. But some things can be surmised from the few passages where the term appears. Its first occurrence is in Genesis 32 where Judah has sexual relations with his daughter-in-law Tamar, who is disguised as a prostitute or *zonah* (v. 15). When he returns to pay her with a pledge (v. 18), he asks, "Where is the cult prostitute (*qedesha*)?" Two words used of the same woman having paid sex with Judah. So what's the difference? Deuteronomy spells it out.

> Deuteronomy 23:17–18:
> None of the daughters of Israel shall be a cult prostitute [*qedesha*], and none of the sons of Israel shall be a cult prostitute [*qedesh*]. You shall not bring the fee of a prostitute [*zonah*] or the wages of a dog into the house of the LORD your God in payment for any vow, for both of these are an abomination to the LORD your God.

From these two passages, there seems to be a difference between a normal prostitute (*zonah*) and a cultic prostitute (*qedesha*), where the qedesha is tied directly to the temple and the zonah is most likely not. Another passage in Hosea affirms this separation of secular and sacred prostitution when the prophet declares, "for the men themselves go aside with prostitutes (*zonah*) and sacrifice with cult prostitutes (*qedeshot*)" (Hosea 4:14), again delineating secular from sacred prostitution. Amos described sacred prostitution that occurred "beside altars on garments taken in pledge" also connected to temples (Amos 2:7-8).

During the time period of my novel in the ninth century, there were special rooms set aside for male prostitutes in the Jerusalem temple (2 Kings 23:7). Shocking, but true. The priesthood of the holy temple of Yahweh in Jerusalem had prostitution within its walls for much of its existence.

But what exactly were the temple duties of qedeshim? The Bible is not explicit. Karel van der Toorn has argued that it was a common custom of Israelite women to make good on unpaid vows to God by means of prostitution for the temple. A citizen would go to the temple or high place, engage the services of the qedeshim, whose wages would then go into the temple treasury as payment for the Israelite's vow.[11] Though this sacred prostitution is prohibited by Yahweh in the Torah at Sinai (Deuteronomy 23:17-18), it clearly went on with impunity for hundreds of years in the temple of Jerusalem and on "every high hill and under every green tree."[12]

Ugaritic literature describes qedeshim like those in Tyre with a bit more detail. Since the story of Ahab and Jezebel describes the cross-fertilization of Israel with Canaanite customs, it wouldn't be inappropriate to assume parallels in purpose between the two cultures. In Tyre, the qedeshim included non-priestly personnel of the temple dedicated to the deity who performed menial tasks in the temple as well as sexual activities. The Israelites most likely engaged their qedeshim in like manner.[13] Raphael Patai explains the possible functions of qedeshim:

> The function of the qedeshim had something to do with the fertility cult centering in the figure of the mother-goddess Asherah. Possibly, their services were made use of by childless women who visited the sanctuary in order to become pregnant. Such pilgrimages to holy places for the purpose of removing the curse of barrenness have remained an important feature of popular religion down to the present day among Moslems, Jews, and Christians alike in all parts of the Middle East. The qedeshim may have also functioned in rites of imitative magic in the fertility cult, whose purpose was to ensure fruitfulness in nature, the coming of the autumn rains, the growth of the crops, the multiplication of domestic animals, etc. Fertility goddesses had male attendants or priests in ancient Near Eastern religions, and in the case of the qedeshim in the Jerusalem Temple, one of their tasks seems to have been to supervise the work of the

---

[11] "The phenomenon of women—and, occasionally, men—prostituting themselves in order to obtain the money to fulfill their vows was known and to some extent accepted in broad layers of the Israelite society. Until the Deuteronomic reform, it seems to have been tolerated by the official religion."

Karel Van Der Toorn, "Female Prostitution in Payment of Vows in Ancient Israel," *Journal of Biblical Literature* 108 (1989): 201.

[12] See: Isaiah57:5; Jeremiah 2:20; 3:6-9; and 1 Kings 14:24; 15:12; 22:46; 2 Kings 23:7; Job 36:14; Hosea 4:14.

[13] Karel van der Toorn, "Prostitution: Cultic Prostitution," ed. David Noel Freedman, *The Anchor Yale Bible Dictionary* (New York: Doubleday, 1992), 511.

women weaving linens for Asherah, which, therefore, was done in the chambers of the qedeshim.[14]

Sacred Marriage

A religious sexual ritual that shows up in *Jezebel: Harlot Queen of Israel* is Sacred Marriage. The religious rite has its origins thousands of years earlier in ancient Sumer. It was called "heiros-gamos" in Greek, and it usually occurred at the New Year's celebration. In it, the king would "marry" the goddess of fertility Inanna (later, Ishtar) in a ritual ceremony wherein he would consummate the marriage by having sexual intercourse with a priestess of Inanna as surrogate.[15] This was a cultic drama that performed the mythical love-song cycle of Inanna marrying a human king, Dumuzi.[16]

The idea was that ritual enacted underlying mythology. Since Inanna was the goddess of fertility and fecundity, Douglas Frayne explains the central purpose of the Sacred Marriage rite "was to promote fertility in the land. The rationale of the ceremony was that, by a kind of sympathetic act involving the sexual union of the king, playing the role of the *en*, with a woman, generally referred to simply as Inanna, the crops would come up abundantly and both the animal and human populations would have the desire and fertility to ensure that they would multiply."[17]

As Ugaritic scholar Mark Smith defines it, Sacred Marriage was either "between a deity and a human (ritually enacted with sexual relations)" or "between two deities (imitated by sexual relations between corresponding humans)."[18]

But did the Sacred Marriage continue unchanged for millennia into the time period of the Jezebel story in the ninth century B.C.? Some scholars argue that though there were changes over time, it remained in literature of the time

---

[14] Raphael Patai, *The Hebrew Goddess Third Enlarged Edition* (Detroit MI: Wayne State University Press, 1967,1978, 1990), 299, footnote 59. See also: John Day, "Canaan, Religion of," ed. David Noel Freedman, The *Anchor Yale Bible Dictionary* (New York: Doubleday, 1992), 835.

[15] Samuel Noah Kramer, *The Sacred Marriage Rite: Aspects of Faith Myth and Ritual in Ancient Sumer* (Bloomington, IN: Indiana Unversity Press, 1969), 18.

[16] Pirjo Lapinkivi, "The Sumerian Sacred Marriage and Its Aftermath in Later Sources," in Martti Nissinen and Risto Uro, eds., *Sacred Marriages: The Divine-Human Sexual Metaphor from Sumer to Early Christianity* (Winona Lake, IN: Eisenbrauns, 2008), 8.

[17] Douglas R. Frayne, "Notes on the Sacred Marriage Rite" (review of Samuel Noah Kramer, *Le Mariage sacré à Sumer et à Babylone* [rev. ed. by Jean Bottéro; Paris: Berg, 1983], *Bibliotheca Orientalis* 42 (1985), 6.

[18] Mark S. Smith, "Sacred Marriage in the Ugaritic Texts? The Case of KTU/CAT 1.23 (Rituals and Myths of the Goodly Gods)" in Martti Nissinen and Risto Uro, eds., *Sacred Marriages: The Divine-Human Sexual Metaphor from Sumer to Early Christianity* (Winona Lake, IN: Eisenbrauns, 2008), 96.

period such as the Baal epic (KTU 1.23). In this famous text called "The Gracious Gods: A Sacred Marriage Liturgy," the high god El is described as having sexual relations with the goddesses Asherah and Anat in connection with a ritual marriage feast consisting of human royal and priestly elites. I used this actual text in the novel when Ahab and Jezebel consummate their marriage at the high place in Samaria. A high priestess then takes the place of Asherah as Jezebel is the "Womb."

> Let me invoke the gracious gods,
> Let them give a feast to those of high rank,
> in the wilderness of the end of the world.
> Greetings, king, greetings, queen, priests and qedeshim,
> El enticed his two wives,
> Asherah and goddess Womb.[19]
> Lo, this maid bows down, lo, this one rises up,
> This one shouts, "Daddy! Daddy!"
> And this one shouts, "Mother! Mother!"
> The organ of El grows long as the sea,
> Yea, the organ of El as the flood.
> The organ of El is long as the sea,
> Yea, the organ of El as the flood.[20]

Though this text is hotly debated, some scholars such as Nicolas Wyatt contend that the myth is enacted through cultic drama in the human players of king and priestess.[21] This is not unlike the Babylonian myth of the Enuma Elish being recited and enacted at various points during the New Year Akitu festival in Mesopotamia.

Pirjo Lapinkivi compared similar Sacred Marriage texts over five thousand years from ancient Uruk to modern India, including ancient Israel, and he concluded there was a pattern of two different traditions.

> Either we have a human bridegroom uniting with a goddess in order to bring blessings to the world and to himself, or a human bride (= human soul) who seeks union with a divine bridegroom. In the first case, the blessings can also be obtained indirectly—two deities uniting in order to bring blessings to the king (human) and the land. In the latter case,

---

[19] Adapted from: "KTU 1.23: The Gracious Gods: A Sacred Marriage Liturgy" in N. Wyatt, *Religious Texts from Ugarit, 2nd ed., Biblical Seminar, 53* (London; New York: Sheffield Academic Press, 2002), 325–326.

[20] Richard M. Davidson, *Flame of Yahweh: Sexuality in the Old Testament* (Peabody, MA: Hendrickson Publishers, 2007), 94.

[21] N. Wyatt, *Religious Texts from Ugarit, 2nd ed., Biblical Seminar, 53* (London; New York: Sheffield Academic Press, 2002), 324.

> the bride is impure at first (a prostitute) but through the necessary preparations attains purity and is ready for union with the divine. The union is often co-celebrated by other people (cult personnel, scholars, or the general public), in which case the observers and devotees identify themselves with the bride uniting with the divine bridegroom.

Others disagree. But for the novel, I explored the possibilities of what this might have looked like adapted by Israel from her pagan influencers. I also drew from the ancient manuscript *The Installation of the Storm God's High Priestess* in Emar as a Sacred Marriage text enacted by Jezebel's own installation as high priestess in Tyre.[22]

Family Shrines

While doing research for the novel, one of the surprises I discovered was the idea that many ancient Jews had family shrines, rooms in their homes dedicated to religious cultic practices. Archaeologist William Dever has pointed out that previously archaeologists were preoccupied with public rather than domestic architecture, which resulted in a dearth of evidence for household shrines—until recently.

Excavations of private domiciles in a dozen Israelite cities such as Samaria, Hazor, Megiddo, Beersheba, and others from the 12th to the 7th centuries B.C. have uncovered such shrines used by single families or larger family compounds. They seem to be used for private worship as needed, and women appear to have played a significant role in their operation. The depiction of these family shrines in *Jezebel: Harlot Queen of Israel* was based on these artifacts.

Dever lists the artifacts found in these shrines containing some or all:

> (1) Standing stones [*massebot*]
> (2) Altars, some "horned"
> (3) Stone tables and basins
> (4) Offering stands
> (5) Benches
> (6) Jewelry
> (7) Ceramic vessels, many "exotic"

---

[22] Douglas Frayne argues that the high priestess, at her installation, would have sex with the king as a ritual impersonating the divine pair. Douglas R. Frayne, "Notes on the Sacred Marriage Rite" (review of Samuel Noah Kramer, *Le Mariage sacré à Sumer et à Babylone* [rev. ed. by Jean Bottéro; Paris: Berg, 1983], *Bibliotheca Orientalis* 42 (1985), 5–22.

(8) Animal bones and food remains
(9) Astragali (sheep and goat knucklebones)
(10) Terra cotta female figurines[23]

The last item on the list above, terra cotta female figurines, has proven to be enigmatic, hotly debated, and highly significant in understanding the folk religion of Israelite households. Three thousand of these clay figurines from the 12th to 6th centuries B.C. have been unearthed throughout Palestine. They average six inches tall, are all female with large pronounced breasts, and instead of feet, they have a pillar base, like a tree trunk. These figurines fall into two categories: those that have the female holding her breasts up and those that have the female clutching a disc-like shape in her hand.[24]

Most scholars consider these figurines to be representations of Asherah or Astarte for several key reasons. First, the females are nude with accentuated breasts, a most common way that the fertility goddess was depicted in Canaan as opposed to ordinary women. Secondly, the disc some of the goddesses are clutching to their chests bears perfect resemblance to the breadcakes that Israelites were condemned for baking for the "Queen of Heaven" (Jeremiah 7:18; 44:19).[25] Thirdly, these figurines also perfectly fit the description of *teraphim*, or household gods, that Jacob's wife Rachel had carried with her and hid under her camel's saddle when they fled Laban's household (Genesis 31:33-35). In the time of Judges, the priest Micah had both carved images and *teraphim* in his home that were portable just like these figurines (Judges 17:5; 18:17-20).[26]

Dever concludes that these terracotta figurines must be images of Asherah that were appropriated by Israelites from the Canaanite goddess. The blatant sexuality of the Canaanite imagery of Asherah was restrained and redirected to a more chaste version of Asherah as the Great Mother patron goddess of Israelite mothers.[27]

> In the Iron Age, the principal female deity was not Astarte, but Asherah. Nevertheless, these figurines are not Barbie-

---

23 William G. Dever, *Did God Have a Wife?: Archaeology and Folk Religion in Ancient Israel* (Grand Rapids, MI: Eerdmans Publishing, 2005), 117-118.

24 Dever, *The Lives of Ordinary People*, 278.

25 Dever, *Did God Have a Wife?,* 176-180.

26 One strange exception to this small portable size was the case where David's wife Michal used what must have been a life-sized teraphim to lay in a bed to impersonate David sleeping. But one wonders how she could have possibly moved some so heavy as a life-sized sculpture, unless it was made of light material rather than clay or metal or stone See 1 Samuel 9:13-16.

27 Dever, *Did God Have a Wife?,* 187.

> like dolls. They clearly have to do with reproduction: the desire of their users to be able to safely conceive, bear children, and lactate. These are in effect "prayers in clay": talismans to aid women in having children, nursing them, and rearing them through childhood.[28]

Judean tombs of these periods have also included items used for divination and "magic," including dice and sheep/goat knuckles used for casting lots, amulets, and other good luck charms considered "apotropaic" devices used to ward off evil. "Among the most conspicuous apotropaic devices in late Judean tombs are Egyptian-style glazed Bes figurines and Eye-of-Horus amulets, whose function as popular good-luck charms throughout the Levant is well known."[29]

The Eye of Horus was known as an Egyptian symbol of protection and health. Bes was an ugly Egyptian dwarf deity with a lion face, bowed legs, and sometimes depicted with an enormous phallus.[30] Though Bes was not worshipped per se, his image could be found on vessels, household items, and amulets as a means of protecting children and pregnant mothers in their childbirth.[31]

The folk religion of many Israelites included household shrines that were more like their Canaanite neighbors' religion than has previously been assumed.

Cult of the Dead

In his dissertation "Cults of the Dead in Ancient Israel and Ugarit," Theodore Joseph Lewis defines cults of the dead as "those acts directed toward the deceased functioning either to placate the dead or to secure favors from them."[32] Such acts would include mediumship and necromancy (communicating with the dead), food offerings, libations, prayers, and various

---

[28] Dever, *The Lives of Ordinary People*, 279-280.

[29] William G. Dever, *The Lives of Ordinary People in Ancient Israel: Where Archaeology and the Bible Intersect* (Grand Rapids, MI; Cambridge, U.K.: William B. Eerdmans Publishing Company, 2012), 271–273.

[30] H. te Velde, "Bes," ed. Karel van der Toorn, Bob Becking, and Pieter W. van der Horst, *Dictionary of Deities and Demons in the Bible* (Leiden; Boston; Köln; Grand Rapids, MI; Cambridge: Brill; Eerdmans, 1999), 173.

[31] "Found in Jerusalem's City of David: The Egyptian God Bes": https://www.haaretz.com/archaeology/MAGAZINE-found-in-jerusalem-s-city-of-david-egyptian-god-bes-1.7042407

[32] Theodore Joseph Lewis, *Cults of the Dead in Ancient Israel and Ugarit*, dissertation (Cambridge, MA: Harvard University, 1986), 282.

behaviors such as body modifications and self-lacerations—all activities in which the Old Testament indicated Israelites were guilty of engaging.

The following are activities that Yahweh had forbidden to the Israelites because they were part of the Canaanite abominable cult of the dead:

Cutting and shaving one's self to be heard by the dead (Deuteronomy 14:1)
Divination, conjuring, consulting spirits (Deuteronomy 18:9; Isaiah 8:19-20)
oracles from the deceased (Deuteronomy 18:9)
Food offerings to the dead (Deuteronomy 26:14)
Passing children through the fire (2 Kings 21:6)
Libations (drink offerings) and other offerings (Isaiah 57:6)
Overnight grave vigils and eating pork (Isaiah 65:4)
Cutting the body, shaving, tattoos (Leviticus 19:26-32)
Necromancy and mediums (Leviticus 20:6, 27)
Marzeah feast: eating sacrifices for the dead (Psalm 106:28)

All of these forbidden elements are portrayed in the novel, being performed by Israelites. God had commanded them not to participate in these specific Canaanite practices in order to keep them from idolatry. One could say these commands were given before the Israelites encountered the practices in Canaan. And that they therefore do not indicate that the Israelites were actually doing them. Fair enough for those commands given *before* entering the Land. But a closer examination of the texts *after* Israel was already living in the Land indicate the need to reiterate the commands precisely because Israelites were engaging in these taboo practices in significant numbers. Some passages even explicitly tell us so.

Before entering Canaan, we are told that the Israelites yoked themselves to the Baal of Peor. They ate sacrifices for the dead long after Yahweh had commanded them not to (Psalm 106:28). This was most likely a reference to the marzeah feast, which we will address later.

By the time of King Saul, Israel must have been full of necromancers because Saul had to go to great effort to "expel the mediums and the necromancers out of the land" (1 Samuel 28:3).

Absalom erected a pillar (*massebah*) in his own memory (2 Samuel 18:18), similar to the Canaanite setting up of pillars to invoke the names of their divine ancestors (CTA 17.1.27).[33]

King Manasseh of Judah, who reigned from 697 B.C. to 643, was condemned for burning his son in fire sacrifice, practicing fortune-telling, interpreting omens, and consulting the dead through mediums and necromancers (2 Kings 21:6). He reigned for fifty-five years doing this.

After Manasseh, Josiah got rid of the necromancers and mediums that had been flourishing in Judah for God knows how long. The indication in the text is that Saul's cutting off of the necromancers was only temporary in effect while Josiah's was a more thorough elimination. Which means necromancy had continued throughout the Land for those several hundred years.[34]

Two hundred years before Josiah, consulting the dead was so popular that the prophet Isaiah mocked its well-known rituals as "chirping and muttering." It was a common belief in the Near East that the dead spoke in birdlike whispers.[35] Noted Assyriologist Amar Annus explains that in the Ugaritic literature the spirits of the dead took the form of birds. "The *rpum* [Rephaim] are described as fluttering; they are startled like birds. Apparently they were believed to come like birds to the holy place to enter the company of the gods."[36]

The following biblical condemnations and mockery of necromancy now make sense in that occultic worldview context.

> Isaiah 8:19:
> And when they say to you, "Inquire of the mediums and the necromancers who chirp and mutter," should not a people inquire of their God? Should they inquire of the dead on behalf of the living?
>
> Isaiah 29:4 (NET):
> [Jerusalem] will fall; while lying on the ground you will speak; from the dust where you lie, your words will be heard. Your voice will sound like a spirit speaking from the

---

33 Lewis, *Cults of the Dead,* 196-197.

34 Lewis, *Cults of the Dead,* 206.

35 "So in the Akkadian "Descent of Ishtar" (obv. 10, ANET, p. 107) and the Gilgamesh Epic (VII, iv, 38, 39; ANET, p. 87), as well as the Aeneid vi.492.3; the Iliad xxiii.101; and Horace Satires I.i.viii.40." John N. Oswalt, *The Book of Isaiah, Chapters 1–39, The New International Commentary on the Old Testament* (Grand Rapids, MI: Wm. B. Eerdmans Publishing Co., 1986).

36 Amar Annus, "Are There Greek Rephaim?: On the Etymology of Greek Meropes and Titanes," Ugarit Forschungen 31 (1999), 15; Quoting Klaas Spronk, *Beatific Afterlife in Ancient Near East*, 1986: 167.

> underworld; from the dust you will chirp as if muttering an incantation.

In the second passage, Jerusalem is described as a city of the dead (necropolis) lying fallen in the ground, another indictment that they will become like the chirping muttering dead with whom they consult in place of their creator.[37]

Isaiah then condemns Israelites for more of their idolatry, which includes, "sitting among the tombs and keeping watch all night long" (Isaiah 65:4 NET). Most commentators have seen this as a reference to incubation rituals of all night vigils at tombs waiting for an oracle from the dead,[38] another common activity of the cult of the dead.

What did necromancy in this time period look like in the ancient Near East? The Hebrew word for a necromancer was "Ob." Cognate languages with Hebrew suggest the term *ob* was connected to …

> … a pit dug in the ground, which served as a means of access between infernal spirits of gods or deceased persons and the upper world. Among the Hittites, rituals were carried out which involved the opening up of such pits in places selected by oracle, the lowering of offerings into the pits, and the luring up of spirits out of the pit to eat the sacrifices and drink the blood libations and show their favor and superior knowledge to the sacrificers.
>
> Among the offerings lowered in the pit were foodstuffs, often including a black sacrificial animal (a hog or a dog), silver objects such as a model of a human ear (symbolizing the practitioner's desire to hear from the underworld), and a ladder or staircase (to encourage the spirit to ascend).[39]

Again, the reader will recognize much of these elements as portrayed in the novel *Jezebel*. But now let's turn to one of the strongest elements of the cult of the dead: the marzeah feast.

---

37 Lewis, *Cults of the Dead,* 229.

38 Lewis, *Cults of the Dead,* 244-245.

39 John H. Walton, Zondervan Illustrated Bible Backgrounds Commentary (Old Testament): Joshua, Judges, Ruth, 1 & 2 Samuel, vol. 2 (Grand Rapids, MI: Zondervan, 2009), 382.

Marzeah Feast

One element of the cult of the dead discovered in the Ugaritic culture with corresponding echoes in the Old Testament was the *marzeah* feast, a banquet for the dead.

In Canaan and Syria, archaeological digs have uncovered special buildings outside of towns, sometimes near cemeteries, where an association of persons called "men of the marzeah" would meet for funerary meals for the dead. There is evidence of rituals performed at these locations and that deities were included in the liturgy, specifically Asherah. [40]

Ugaritic texts confirm these locations as "houses of marzeah." They were often near vineyards because the men who had special membership in the religious guild would drink wine in excess during these marzeah banquets as they celebrated the passing on of their dead.[41] Marzeah is now considered to have been a well-known institution in Ugarit and most likely throughout Syria and Canaan.

Ugaritic scholar Mark Smith lists four elements that characterized the marzeah. First, it was a private association, often of members from the royal or upper class. Second, it met in a private domicile, usually the home of one of its members. Third, there was a leader of the marzeah called the "chief." Fourth, the marzeah had a divine patron, usually El, the high god.[42]

This last element of divine involvement is rooted in the possible origin of the marzeah found in the Baal epic. In the text, labeled El's Divine Feast, El invites the gods to a banquet at his house, called *marzeah* (or *marzih*). Asherah and Anat are there among others. El is described as drinking wine until he is pathetically drunk and falls on his own excrement and urine "as one dead." Asherah and Anat then go out hunting and return with an unknown cure for El's hangover.[43]

---

[40] Manfred Bietak, "Temple or 'Bêt Marzeah'?," in *Symbiosis, Symbolism, and the Power of the Past: Canaan, Ancient Israel, and Their Neighbors from the Late Bronze Age through Roman Palaestina*, ed. William G. Dever and Seymour Gitin (Winona Lake, IN: Eisenbrauns, 2003), 165.

Also, Loren R. Fisher, *The Claremont Ras Shamra Tablets, Analecta Orientalia, 48* (Roma: Pontificium Institutum Biblicum, 1971), 46

[41] Loren R. Fisher, *The Claremont Ras Shamra Tablets, Analecta Orientalia, 48* (Roma: Pontificium Institutum Biblicum, 1971), 45.

[42] Mark S. Smith, *The Ugaritic Baal Cycle: Introduction with Text, Translation and Commentary of KTU 1.1-1.2, vol. 1* (Leiden; New York; Köln: E.J. Brill, 1994), 142.

[43] El's Divine Feast CAT 1.114, Translated by Theodore J. Lewis in Mark S. Smith and Simon B. Parker, *Ugaritic Narrative Poetry, vol. 9, Writings from the Ancient World* (Atlanta, GA: Scholars Press, 1997), 193.

As is common in the ancient Near East, the principle of "as above, so below" applies to the marzeah. Humans have their counterpart of a human feast on earth that is based upon and indeed reflects the divine feast in the heavens. As scholar Loren Fisher explains, "El's *marzih* is a projection of the human community standing under his patronage. Presumably El's experience in his *marzih* mirrors that of his worshippers in theirs.[44]

The marzeah was mirrored in Hebrew culture as well. The biblical evidence shows a Jewish identification with the cult of the dead that is more than mere analogy.

The prophet Amos had his ministry during King Jehoram's reign in Israel just before Jehu killed the king in the storyline of *Jezebel: Harlot Queen of Israel*. Amos gives a prophecy of Israel and Judah's ultimate exile based on their pride of entitlement and careless indulgence in apostasy. He uses the description of a marzeah banquet of celebration to condemn Israel.

> Amos 6:4–7:
> Woe to those who lie on beds of ivory
> and stretch themselves out on their couches,
> and eat lambs from the flock
> and calves from the midst of the stall,
> who sing idle songs to the sound of the harp
> and like David invent for themselves instruments of music,
> who drink wine in bowls
> and anoint themselves with the finest oils,
> but are not grieved over the ruin of Joseph!
> Therefore they shall now be the first of those who go into exile, and the revelry [*marzeah*] of those who stretch themselves out shall pass away.

The notion of marzeah feasts was so well known in Israel that God used it as a metaphor to communicate a prophecy. Israelites were like fools celebrating the legacy of the dead without realizing their own deaths were hanging over their heads. We see four of the typical Ugaritic elements of the marzeah here: eating, heavy drinking, anointing with oil, and grieving. But there is a fifth aspect included, that of laying on luxurious "beds of ivory." Ivory was a known commodity of Tyre brought to Samaria in abundance by

---

[44] Loren R. Fisher, *The Claremont Ras Shamra Tablets, Analecta Orientalia, 48* (Roma: Pontificium Institutum Biblicum, 1971), 45.

the Phoenicians in order to upgrade the wealth status of the king's palaces (1 Kings 22:39; Amos 3:15).

While there is no mention of the Rephaim in this Amos passage, the cult of the dead does show up in a prophecy by Jeremiah that also uses assumed familiarity with the marzeah ritual within Israel.

> Jeremiah 16:5–8:
> For thus says the LORD: Do not enter the house of mourning [*house of marzeah*], or go to lament or grieve for them, for I have taken away my peace from this people, my steadfast love and mercy, declares the LORD. Both great and small shall die in this land. They shall not be buried, and no one shall lament for them or cut himself or make himself bald for them. No one shall break bread for the mourner, to comfort him for the dead, nor shall anyone give him the cup of consolation to drink for his father or his mother. You shall not go into the house of feasting to sit with them, to eat and drink.

Jeremiah references the house of marzeah as an analogy for the death about to come upon Judah at the Babylonian exile. We read of the marzeah mourning as well as the feast of eating and drinking for consolation. But this isn't merely a generic mourning ceremony. It is the Ugaritic cult of the dead that also includes the cutting of flesh and beard that is part of the necromantic ritual of calling up the dead. This was the ritual that Anat was said to have done to herself as part of calling Baal back from the dead. It was also the same activity of cutting that the prophets of Baal did on Mount Carmel to try to call Baal back from his absence in the underworld during the drought.

This isn't to say that Yahweh approved of cult of the dead rituals. But it certainly shows that Jews were well-acquainted with such activities and were most likely engaged in them as well. Otherwise it wouldn't make sense for Yahweh to use alien liturgy against the Jews as judgment if they weren't performing that liturgy themselves. Analogies and metaphors as judgment only work if they reflect the audience's own lived experience.

The passage mentioned earlier in Psalm 106:28 about Israelites eating sacrifices for the dead at Baal-Peor during the time of Moses shows the Israelites engaging in marzeah feasts. Though the word isn't used in the biblical text, later Jewish Targums reveal that ancient Jews understood the incident at Baal-Peor to be a marzeah banquet of the dead in which the Israelites were participating.

> The MT of Numbers 25:2 reads "and they (the daughters of the Moabites) invited the people to the sacrifices for their gods and the people ate and bowed down before their gods." Targum Pseudo-Jonathan adds "and the people ate in their *mrzhn*." Similarly Sifre Numbers 131 reads "afterwards they (the Moabites and Ammonites) returned to make for them *mrzbm*, and they (the women) invited them and they ate."[45]

The connection of the marzeah to the Baal-Peor incident by rabbinic sources also included the argument that marzeah feasts involved sacral sexual orgies.[46] The apostasy of the Israelites at Baal-Peor consisted not only of worshipping Baal, but of "whoring with the daughters of Moab" (Numbers 25:1), a sexual nuance that contextually involves more than metaphorically going after foreign gods. The Israelites were drawn to Baal through the sexual temptation of the women. Physical fornication led to spiritual fornication.

Marvin Pope has concluded, "The biblical and rabbinic correlation of the marzeah with both mourning and licentious pagan revelry may seem incongruous and even contradictory from our puritan and Victorian perspective, but not from the viewpoint of a fertility religion which recognized life and death as integral natural process and confronted death with the assertion and reaffirmation of life."[47]

The Israelites were intimately familiar with the marzeah practice of eating a banquet as a means of calling up the dead. They did it themselves. But there is another element of the marzeah that adds an even deeper element of the cult of the dead: the participation of the Rephaim. We will look at those fascinating creatures next.

Rephaim

A small corpus of tablets from the excavated Ugaritic port city of Ras Shamra are sometimes called the Rephaim Texts because of their references to the Rephaim. One of them, *A Royal Funerary Liturgy*, describes a marzeah banquet on earth that gives the order of service for the funeral of a dead king. Wyatt explains that the ritual described is the invocation of the late king's divinized royal ancestors, now called Rephaim, as part of the coronation ritual

---

45 Lewis, *Cults of the Dead,* 146.

46 Marvin Pope, "A Divine Banquet at Ugarit," *The Use of the Old Testament in the New and Other Essays: Studies in Honor of William Franklin Stinespring* (Durham, NC: Duke University Press, 1972), 190-191.

47 Pope, "A Divine Banquet at Ugarit," 193.

for the new king. They were calling upon the spirits of dead warrior rulers to empower the new sovereign. It was a royal cult of the dead.[48]

In the liturgy, the Rephaim are summoned from the underworld to gather in "assembly" called "Assembly of the Didanu," which had its origins in a legendary contingent of Amorite warriors.[49] In another text, the Rephaim are sometimes translated as "netherworld shades,"[50] or "spirits like the ancient dead,"[51] sometimes as "saviors of the underworld," "eternal ones"[52] or "eternal royal princes" with armed forces.[53] They arrive on royal warrior chariots and feast for seven days.

The overall image of the Rephaim banquet is one of military action and procession. As Brian Doak concludes in his dissertation on the Rephaim,

> the rp'um [Rephaim] were indeed once thought to be heroic warriors of old, and that these figures played an important role in funerary ritual as markers of monarchic legitimation and heroic identification… dead military heroes of a period thought to be in the distant past are invoked at local cult shrines, food and drink are offered, and the hero acts in some way—perhaps by guaranteeing fertility of land or empire, or some other status of legitimation—to benefit the supplicant.[54]

---

48 Dennis Pardee and Theodore J. Lewis, *Ritual and Cult at Ugarit, vol. 10, Writings from the Ancient World* (Atlanta, GA: Society of Biblical Literature, 2002), 87.

49 Brian Schmidt, *Israel's Beneficent Dead: Ancestor Cult and Necromancy in Ancient Israelite Religion and Tradition*, Dissertation (Oxford, England, The University of Oxford, 1991), 131.

50 KTU 1.15:3:10–19. Dennis Pardee and Theodore J. Lewis, *Ritual and Cult at Ugarit, vol. 10, Writings from the Ancient World* (Atlanta, GA: Society of Biblical Literature, 2002), 87.

51 Brian Doak, *The Last of the Rephaim: Conquest and Cataclysm in the Heroic Ages of Ancient Israel,* dissertation (Cambridge: MA, Harvard University, 2011), 249.

52 For example:
KTU 1.161:1–14
You are invoked, O saviours of the underworld,
you are summoned, O assembly of Didanu.
Invoked is Ulkan the saviour;
invoked is Taruman the saviour.
invoked is Sidan-and-Radan;
invoked is the eternal one, Thar.
They have been invoked, the ancient saviours.
You are invoked, O saviours of the underworld,

N. Wyatt, *Religious Texts from Ugarit, 2nd ed., Biblical Seminar, 53* (London; New York: Sheffield Academic Press, 2002), 432–434. See also,

53 CAT 1.22.9-10. Mark S. Smith and Simon B. Parker, *Ugaritic Narrative Poetry, vol. 9, Writings from the Ancient World* (Atlanta, GA: Scholars Press, 1997), 203.

54 Brian Doak, *The Last of the Rephaim: Conquest and Cataclysm in the Heroic Ages of Ancient Israel,* dissertation (Cambridge: MA, Harvard University, 2011), 250.

As it happens, the Rephaim are important to the biblical writers, and they appear in the Bible in one of two distinct contexts. The first is that of a race of giants in Canaan called Rephaim by the Hebrews.

> Deuteronomy 2:10–1:
> (The Emim formerly lived there [Moab], a people great and many, and tall as the Anakim. Like the Anakim they are also counted as Rephaim, but the Moabites call them Emim.
>
> Deuteronomy 2:20–21:
> (It is also counted as a land of Rephaim. Rephaim formerly lived there—but the Ammonites call them Zamzummim—a people great and many, and tall as the Anakim…

I want to draw a couple things from this introduction to the Rephaim of Canaan through Israelite eyes. First, *Rephaim* seems to be a generic description of a kind of people that are called by different names in different dialects or areas. Rephaim are called Emim in Moab. They are called Anakim in Canaan and Zamzummim in Amon. So despite the fact that Anakim, Emimn and Zamzummim were all names of people in different locations, they seemed to be interchangeable terms for a generic kind of people called Rephaim. So what kind of people were they?

The text says the Rephaim were giants, mighty warriors ("great") who were "tall as the Anakim." That height was not merely a metaphor for power but a literal reference to real physical stature. When the spies came back from Canaan, they reported the Anakim to be those who "came from the Nephilim" (Numbers 32:33). *Nephilim* in Aramaic and Hebrew literally means "giants."[55] So the Anakim/Rephaim were giants from the stock of the ancient Nephilim. I explain the Nephilim and the importance of giants to the biblical storyline in my book *When Giants Were Upon the Earth (affiliate link)*.

Some still argue that the Bible is using size as a metaphor for greatness. But the distinction between greatness and physical size is made in Deuteronomy 1:28 and 2:21 where the Anakim/Rephaim are described as both "greater and taller than we." Yes, the Rephaim were a great people, but they were also physically tall. Hyperliteralists go too far when they claim giants twenty and thirty feet tall based on the obvious hyperbole of Amos poetically

---

[55] Michael Heiser explains the meaning of Nephilim best here:
https://www.godawa.com/chronicles_of_the_nephilim/Articles_By_Others/Heiser-Nephilim.pdf
And here: http://michaelsheiser.com/TheNakedBible/2013/03/thoughts-nephilim-answering-criticism/

describing the Amorite Rephaim "whose height was like the height of the cedars and who were as strong as the oaks" (Amos 2:9).

Rephaim were not the ridiculous monsters of sci-fi or fantasy, rising to the height of buildings or trees. The biblical evidence indicates their size to be from seven to nine feet tall. Goliath was at most nine-and-a-half feet tall. Some legitimate biblical scholarship suggests he may have only been six-and-a-half-feet tall.[56] Because the average height of an ancient Hebrew male at this time was about 5 feet, 5 inches, that would still make Goliath a giant compared to the average man. The word "giant" simply means "unusually tall."

Goliath's brother Lahmi was as tall as Goliath because he was described as carrying a spear as large as Goliath's (1 Chronicles 20:5). Lahmi was also called a "son of Rapha," the singular word for Rephaim, that may indicate a deity behind the name and a warrior cult devoted to that deity.[57] Some English translations use the phrase "descendent of the giants" in its place.

Other descendents of the giants or "sons of Rapha" are described as being of great stature and carrying weapons that only huge men could wield.

> 2 Samuel 21:16–22
> And Ishbi-benob, one of the descendants of the giants [sons of Rapha], whose spear weighed [over seven and a half pounds] of bronze, and who was armed with a new sword, thought to kill David…After this there was again war with the Philistines at Gob. Then Sibbecai the Hushathite struck down Saph, who was one of the descendants of the giants [sons of Rapha]. And there was again war with the Philistines at Gob, and Elhanan the son of Jaare-oregim, the Bethlehemite, struck down Goliath the Gittite, the shaft of whose spear was like a weaver's beam. And there was again war at Gath, where there was a man of great stature, who had six fingers on each hand, and six toes on each foot, twenty-four in number, and he also was descended from the giants [a son of Rapha]. And when he taunted Israel, Jonathan the son of Shimei, David's brother, struck him down. These four were descended from the giants in Gath.[58]

---

[56] Michael Heiser, "Clash of the Manuscripts: Goliath & the Hebrew Text of the Old Testament" *Bible Study Magazine Online*. http://www.biblestudymagazine.com/extras-1/2014/10/31/clash-of-the-manuscripts-goliath-the-hebrew-text-of-the-old-testament

[57] Sometimes translated as "descendant of the giants." Conrad E. L'Heureux "The yelîdê hārāpā': A Cultic Association of Warriors," *Bulletin of the American Schools of Oriental Research*, No. 221,(Feb., 1976), pp. 83-85.

[58] See also: 1 Chronicles 20:4-8.

The only other one of these "sons of Rapha" in the Bible whose actual physical height is given is an unnamed Egyptian who was seven-and-a-half feet tall (5 cubits) and carried a spear as large as Goliath's.

> 1 Chronicles 11:23
> And [Benaiah] struck down an Egyptian, a man of great stature, five cubits tall [7 1/2 feet]. The Egyptian had in his hand a spear like a weaver's beam.

A few extrabiblical sources add some more context to the size of Canaanite giants. The pseudepigraphal *Book of Jubilees*, when speaking of Og's kingdom of Rephaim, measures the giants from the size of 10 feet to 15 feet tall.

> Jubilees 29:9:
> But before they used to call the land of Gilead the land of the Rephaim; for it was the land of the Rephaim, and the Rephaim were born (there), giants whose height was ten, nine, eight down to seven cubits [10 1/2 feet to 15 feet tall].

An ancient cubit was approximately one-and-a-half-feet long. One thirteenth-century B.C. Egyptian papyrus describes Bedouin nomads (Anakim) in Canaan as being "four or five cubits (7 to 9 feet) from their nose to their foot and have fierce faces."[59]

So one context of Rephaim in the Bible is clans of very large warriors. The key to proper understanding of the word "giants" lies in realizing that our modern English notion of "giant" carries with it a bias toward our fantasies and myths of impossibly tall monsters as big as buildings. In ancient Israel, very tall people, six and a half feet and above, were considered giants, and an entire people of warrior giants had significant meaning because they represented the Rephaim warriors from the underworld on earth.

One of the most well-known biblical enemy kings of Israel was also a Rephaim giant who had a strong connection to the underworld. His name was Og of Bashan, "last of the Rephaim" who was conquered by Joshua before taking the Promised Land. Here is what the Bible says of him.

> Deuteronomy 3:11:
> For only Og the king of Bashan was left of the remnant of the Rephaim. Behold, his bed was a bed of iron…Nine

---

[59] Edward Frank Wente and Edmund S. Meltzer, *vol. 1, Letters from Ancient Egypt, Writings from the Ancient World, 108* (Atlanta, GA: Scholars Press, 1990).

> cubits was its length, and four cubits its breadth. [14 feet long by 6 feet wide]

If the size of his "iron bed" (a possible euphemism for sarcophagus) 14 feet long, was an indication of his height, he would have been about nine to eleven feet tall. But there is a good scholarly argument that the bed is a literary reference to the god Marduk, whose "bed" relic in Babylon had the exact same measurements and was considered "a battle trophy and significant symbol of power…By analogizing Og's bed alongside the bed of a major deity, the author likens Og to a god and bolsters his status as a superhuman warrior. The iron material of Og's bed further emphasizes the fearsomeness of this enemy defeated by Yhwh."[60]

And that fearsomeness was connected with the underworld both before and after Og's death. Og is described in the Bible as living in Ashtaroth and Edrei and "ruling over Mount Hermon and all Bashan" (Joshua 12:4-5). As we described earlier, Mount Hermon was a diabolical cosmic mountain, considered ground zero for the incursion of the Watchers before the Flood. Their progeny were the Nephilim, or giants (aka *Rephaim*). We also discussed that region of Bashan as being translated as "place of the serpent" and abode of the dead. In agreement with this biblical notion, Ugaritic texts also refer to Og with the divine Rephaim and describe a Rephaim "king of eternity" who resided at Ashtaroth and Edrei, exactly like the biblical Og.[61]

In my novel, I combined this connection of Rephaim and the underworld with the other biblical oddity of a necromancer calling up Saul's spirit from Sheol. This was the kind of stuff going on in that ancient world of ninth century Israel, despite it being forbidden by Yahweh (Deuteronomy 18:10-12). The result is depicted in the marzeah feast of Ahab's death in the novel. Frighteningly and biblically possible.

But there is a problem. King David wiped out the Canaanite Rephaim giants in his days. After David, the Bible talks no more of giants on the earth. And that is why in my novel of Jezebel I don't have clans of earthly giants as I do in my series Chronicles of the Nephilim. There may be individual stragglers, but not a clan of them with any real growth of numbers.

But after the time of David, the Bible does refer to the Rephaim *in the underworld*. Rather than affirming the Canaanite notion of them as power-

---

60 Maria Lindquist, "King Og's Iron Bed," *Catholic Biblical Quarterly* 73 (2011), 480-481.

61 *KTU* 1.108:1–3. See "Bashan," *DDD*, p 161-162 and Scott Noegel, "Aegean Ogygos of Boeotia and the Biblical Og of Bashan," *Zeitschrift fuř die alttestamentliche Wissenschaft*, 110 no 3 1998, 416.

giving underworld rulers, the biblical authors mock those Rephaim as being powerless and weak. It's as if the Israelites were dispossessing the Rephaim in both life and afterlife, conquering them both on earth and under the earth.

The Hebrew word *Rephaim* is translated as "shades" or "the dead" in the few biblical cases when it is used in reference to the underworld of Sheol. While it could be interpreted as a generic reference to the souls or spirits of all dead people, there are a couple places that point to the Ugaritic notion of divinized warrior kings.

In Proverbs 21, the phrase "assembly of Rephaim" is used in a way that seems to echo the Rephaim "assembly of Didanu," referenced earlier in the Rephaim Texts of Ugarit.

> Proverbs 21:16:
> One who wanders from the way of good sense
> will rest in the assembly of the dead [Rephaim].

But Isaiah 14 is where the notion of mocking the Rephaim as dead divinized warrior kings comes to the foreground. The prophet is writing a condemnation of the king of Babylon. In verses 12-16, Isaiah likens that king to the Ugaritic god Athtar who sought to take the throne of Baal as the Most High god but failed.[62] As the Baal epic told the story, Athtar's feet couldn't reach the floor because he was too small to replace Baal's kingship. So Isaiah condemns the king of Babylon, using Athtar as a model, for seeking to become divinized, to "ascend to heaven above the stars of God" (v. 12) to "make himself like the Most High" God (v. 14). "But you are brought down to Sheol," writes Isaiah, "to the far reaches of the pit" (v. 15).

In Canaan, such kings when dead would join the assembly of the Didanu in the underworld as Rephaim, divinized warrior kings. But Isaiah mocks this belief. And he explicitly uses the Baal epic as his reference point.

> Isaiah 14:9–11:
> Sheol beneath is stirred up
> to meet you when you come;
> it rouses the shades [Rephaim] to greet you,
> all who were leaders of the earth;
> it raises from their thrones
> all who were kings of the nations.
> All of them will answer
> and say to you:

---

[62] Michael Heiser, "The Mythological Provenance of Isaiah 14:12-15: A Reconsideration of the Ugaritic Material" Digital Commons Online https://digitalcommons.liberty.edu/cgi/viewcontent.cgi?article=1279&context=lts_fac_pubs

> You too have become as weak as we!
> You have become like us!'
> Your pomp is brought down to Sheol,
> the sound of your harps;
> maggots are laid as a bed beneath you,
> and worms are your covers.

To Yahweh, all the pomp and circumstance about mighty Rephaim ancestral kings assembling in Sheol with the ability to confer blessing, prosperity, and legitimation is so much nonsense. For they are not mighty at all. They are weak, impotent, laying in the bed of maggots and worms, unable to do anything, much less "rising" from the underworld to grant favor or power upon the living. To Isaiah, the cult of the dead Rephaim is a fraud.

So despite the fact that the folk religion of Israelites and Judahites was often deeply infected with the corruption of Canaanite practices like marzeah feasts and the cult of the dead, Yahweh and his prophets did not affirm such appropriation of paganism. They mocked it.

Child Sacrifice

Jezebel: Harlot Queen of Israel is a story about the effect of pagan Baal worship upon Israel because of King Ahab's marriage to the Tyrian princess Jezebel. One of the most serious aspects of that idolatrous religion was human sacrifice of children. Thus, the novel seeks to accurately capture what that monstrous ritual may have involved based on historical and biblical sources.

Human sacrifice is mentioned in the very first introduction of Ahab in 1 Kings 16, linking the abominable practice in some way to Ahab's influence.

> 1 Kings 16:34:
> In [Ahab's] days Hiel of Bethel built Jericho. He laid its foundation at the cost of Abiram his firstborn, and set up its gates at the cost of his youngest son Segub.

Though some believe this to be a simple reference to the builder's sons dying as a result of the reconstruction project, the language makes more sense as a reference to a common form of child sacrifice called "foundation sacrifice." As commentator DeVries notes, in this particular ritual, "the children named were probably infants, dead or alive, placed in jars and inserted into the masonry, propitiating the gods and warding off evil."[63]

[63] Simon J. DeVries, *1 Kings, 2nd ed, vol. 12, Word Biblical Commentary* (Dallas: Word, Inc, 2003), 205.

Another reference to child sacrifice is in the story of Mesha the king of Moab sacrificing his son as a ritual way of warding off his enemies in battle. His enemies were the alliance of Israel, Judah and Edom in the ninth century B.C. Though this is not Israel or Judah performing the child sacrifice, it marks the reality of the activity during the same time period as Jezebel and Ahab.

> 2 Kings 3:26–27:
> When the king of Moab saw that the battle was going against him… he took his oldest son who was to reign in his place and offered him for a burnt offering on the wall. And there came great wrath against Israel. And they withdrew from him and returned to their own land.

Notice that the Israelites considered child sacrifice to a foreign god to be efficacious against them such that they withdrew. Whether or not it was truly efficacious, the ancient Hebrews certainly believed it was. They believed in the power of child sacrifice, evil though it was.

Texts from thirteenth century Ugarit were published in 1978 that detailed this exact same ritual of child sacrifice as part of Canaanite laws of holy war.

> If an enemy force attacks your [city-]gates,
> An aggressor, your walls;
> You shall lift up your eyes to Baal [and pray]:
> "O Baal:
> Drive away the [enemy] force from our gates,
> The aggressor from our walls.
> We shall sacrifice a bull [to you], O Baal,
> A votive-pledge we shall fulfill [viz.]:
> A firstborn,
> Baal, we shall sacrifice,
> A child [an off spring?]
> we shall fulfill [as votive-pledge].
> A 'tenth' [of all our wealth] we shall tithe [you],
> To the temple of Baal we shall go up,
> In the footpaths of the House-of-Baal we shall walk."
> Then shall Baal hearken to your prayers,
> He shall drive the [enemy] force from your gates,
> The aggressor from your walls.[64]

---

[64] Alan F Segal, *Sinning in the Hebrew Bible: How the Worst Stories Speak for Its Truth* (Columbia University Press, 2012), 192.

Though the time period of this text is centuries before Jezebel's day, it illustrates the exact same ritual scenario that was performed in Canaanite cities until that day and after. And it was performed unto Baal.

> Deuteronomy 12:31:
> You shall not worship the LORD your God in that [Canaanite] way…for they even burn their sons and their daughters in the fire to their gods.

Child sacrifice was one of the abominable behaviors of Canaanites that was repeatedly condemned by Yahweh (Deuteronomy 12:31).[65] It was sometimes referred to directly as "burning their sons and daughters in the fire" (Deuteronomy 12:31)[66] or "passing them through the fire" (Deuteronomy 18:10 NASB),[67] and sometimes indirectly as "shedding innocent blood" (2 Kings 21:16).[68] Those innocent victims are described as food eaten by the gods (Ezekiel 23:37-39).

Unfortunately, Israelites were guilty of breaking this command of God almost immediately upon entering the Promised Land.

> Psalm 106:38:
> [Israelites] poured out innocent blood,
> the blood of their sons and daughters,
> whom they sacrificed to the idols of Canaan,
> and the land was polluted with blood.

Judah was guilty of child sacrifice from the days of Solomon up to the Babylonian exile:

> Jeremiah 19:5:
> [Judahites] have built the high places of Baal to burn their sons in the fire as burnt offerings to Baal, which I did not command or decree, nor did it come into my mind—

After Solomon's kingdom split, Israel too was guilty of child sacrifice that led to their Assyrian exile.

---

65 See also: Leviticus18:21; 20:2-5.

66 See also 2Kings 17:17; Jeremiah7:31; 19:5; Ezek 16:20-21; 20:31.

67 See also NASB95: 2Kings 16:3; 17:17; 21:6; 23:10; 2 Chron 33:6; Jeremiah32:35; Ezek 16:21; 20:26, 32; 23:37.

68 See also: 2 Kings 24:4; Isaiah59:7; Jeremiah22:3; 26:15; Psalm 106:38.

> 2 Kings 17:17–18:
> And [Israel] burned their sons and their daughters as offerings and used divination and omens and sold themselves to do evil in the sight of the LORD, provoking him to anger. Therefore the LORD was very angry with Israel and removed them out of his sight.

Molech and his Tophet in the Valley of Hinnom in Jerusalem is the one most connected to child sacrifice in the Old Testament.[69] But he is not the only recipient of such offerings. Baal was sometimes connected with Molech as a separate but related deity. He is spoken of as being present in Molech's accursed Valley of Hinnom.

> Jeremiah 32:35:
> They built the high places of Baal in the Valley of the Son of Hinnom, to offer up their sons and daughters to Molech.[70]

Baal here could be a reference to the Canaanite deity by that name or a generic reference to "the lord" (the *baal*) of the valley area. But elsewhere, high places are linked to Baal's fertility cult, while the valley is linked to Molech's underworld cult, two distinct locations of two distinct deities. Nevertheless, an interwoven connection of the two gods and their cults is expressed in Isaiah 57.[71]

> Isaiah 57:5-9:
> …you who burn with lust among the oaks,
> under every green tree, [Baal fertility cult]
> who slaughter your children in the valleys,
> under the clefts of the rocks…[Molech Tophet cult]
> On a high and lofty mountain [high places of Baal]
> you have set your bed,
> and there you went up to offer sacrifice. [to Baal]
> You journeyed to the king with oil [Molech]
> and multiplied your perfumes;
> you sent your envoys far off,
> and sent down even to Sheol. [valley of Molech]

---

69 See Leviticus18:21; 20:2-4; 1 Kings 11:7; 2 Kings 23:10; Jeremiah32:35.

70 See also Jeremiah19:5.

71 About Molech and Baal as separate deities see John Day, *Molech: A God Of Human Sacrifice In The Old Testament* (New York, NY: Cambridge University Press, 1989), 34-36.

The Tophet (also called Topheth) was the altar upon which children were burned in sacrifice to the deity. Everywhere the word appears in the Old Testament, it is always used in connection with the Valley of Hinnom and therefore with Molech as well.

The Valley of Hinnom, where Molech's Tophet of sacrifice was located, became "Gehenna" (a derivative of the Hebrew), a metaphor for hell or final judgment in the Second Temple and New Testament times.[72] It is a common misunderstanding to caricature Gehenna as a garbage dump. There is no textual or archaeological evidence that it was such a thing. But it was a place of evil that was judged with fire and destruction.

In Jeremiah 7 and 19, the prophet predicts judgment upon Judah because of her worship of other gods, including child sacrifice on the Tophet in the Valley of Hinnom. He prophesies that the Babylonians will come and bring great destruction upon Jerusalem. There will be so many dead lying on the ground that the name of the valley will be changed from the Valley of the Sons of Hinnom to the Valley of Slaughter.

> Jeremiah 7:32–33:
> … for they will bury in Topheth, because there is no room elsewhere. And the dead bodies of this people will be food for the birds of the air, and for the beasts of the earth, and none will frighten them away.

> Jeremiah 19:12–13:
> Thus will I do to this place, declares the LORD, and to its inhabitants, making this city like Topheth. The houses of Jerusalem and the houses of the kings of Judah—all the houses on whose roofs offerings have been offered to all the host of heaven, and drink offerings have been poured out to other gods—shall be defiled like the place of Topheth.

Yahweh says that he will turn Jerusalem itself into a Tophet of burning destruction like a sacrifice to him because of their use of the Tophet and worship of the host of heaven. This was what indeed happened when Babylon destroyed Jerusalem in 586 B.C. And thus Gehenna (the Valley of Slaughter) became the symbol of God's judgment upon those who violated his commands.

---

[72] See: 2 Esdras 7:36; 2 Baruch 59:10, 85:13; Mark 9:43, 45, 47. See Day, *Molech,* 52.

Recent critical scholarship has tried to argue that Yahweh himself actually commanded and accepted human sacrifice from Israelites and only later did post-exilic agenda-driven authors write propaganda into the Bible to try to discredit this "once-acceptable sacrifice." This is an attempt to reduce Hebrew Yahwism down to evolving Canaanite religion rather than revelation from heaven. They suggest several key passages to support this contention: 1) Yahweh's command to Abraham to sacrifice his son (Genesis 22), 2) Jephthah's vow to sacrifice his own daughter (Judges 11:29-40), and 3) Yahweh's explicit statement that he had previously commanded human sacrifice in Ezekiel 20:25.

Yahweh's command to Abraham is one of the most debated passages in the Bible. That command was clearly and contextually a testing of Abraham's faith that Yahweh didn't intend for Abraham to perform. Such hypotheticals of testing are more reflective of a contrast with the Canaanite culture than an accommodation of it. Would Abraham be willing to do what he thought was wrong if Yahweh commanded it? Abraham was supposed to trust Yahweh's righteousness and not lean on his own fallible fallen human understanding. That is a test of trust, not the validation of an evil.

Jephthah's vow has also been debated for centuries about whether or not it even referred to human sacrifice rather than a life of religious celibacy (Judges11:30). But at the end of the day, the text gives no moral judgment of Jephthah's behavior from God's perspective. Yahweh is not shown to approve of it any more than he is shown to condemn it. An argument from silence is not an argument for anything. The story merely describes what happened. Jephthah's performance of his vow thus remains to be judged by scriptural passages that do make moral judgments on human sacrifice as evil.

Ezekiel's recording of Yahweh's strange statement about statutes and human sacrifice is surely the most difficult of the passages to address. In it, Yahweh is referencing the disobedience of Israel toward him in the wilderness.

> Ezekiel 20:25–26:
> Moreover, I gave them statutes that were not good and rules
> by which they could not have life, and I defiled them
> through their very gifts in their offering up all their firstborn,
> that I might devastate them. I did it that they might know
> that I am the LORD.

It sounds as if God is saying that his laws of Torah were not good and that he deliberately defiled the people by telling them to sacrifice their children. And then he gets even more strange to suggest that this was done so that they might know that he was Yahweh. It is one list of confusing contradictions against everything else written of God's Law in the Old Testament.

The context of the passage solves the problem of misinterpretation. It wouldn't make sense that Yahweh here would say the opposite of everything he has said throughout the Old Testament about his Law. In fact, it wouldn't make sense to contradict what was previously said in *this very same chapter* of Exodus 20: that his statutes were good (v.12), that they would give life (v.11), that idols defiled them (v.7, 18), and that human sacrifice was forbidden (v.28-29, 31). Yahweh said very clearly that regarding child sacrifice, "I did not command it, nor did it come into my mind" (Jeremiah 7:31).

Context is everything. And the context of the passage is about Israel being given over to pagan control as punishment for her disobedience. The verses before Ezekiel 20:25-26 reiterates Yahweh's warning that he would "scatter them among the nations and disperse them through the countries" (20:23-24). Yahweh gave them up to the godless nations around them whose gods they chose to worship.

Well, those gods had their own statutes and rules that violated Yahweh's law. So the best translation of v. 25 is not God "gave them those statutes," but rather as the NKJV translates, God "gave them up" to those evil laws and rules. This is what is meant by "withholding his hand" from Israel in v. 22. This is also what is meant by Paul in Romans 1 where God "gave up" the pagans to their depravity to be judged by it (Romans 1:24, 26, 28). So God gave up the Israelites to the godless nations with their godless statutes and culture that Israel was seeking after. Yahweh's goal was that Israel would suffer from her bad choices and return to Yahweh.

The attempt to attribute child sacrifice to the Bible as if it were originally a normal part of Yahweh worship has no textual support from Scripture. The fact that many Israelites engaged in human sacrifice is simply proof of what the Bible says that they were spiritually unfaithful to Yahweh for so long that he sent them into exile precisely for sins such as child sacrifice.

The obvious connection that child sacrifice has with the modern practice of abortion is not hard to catch, and thus the parallels between Jezebel's day and our own are instructive. Phrases like "sacrificing children in temples of Molech" or "on the altars of convenience" are used by pro-lifers of abortion clinics because the willing murder of one's own offspring in order to bring benefit to a person's life or to escape personal suffering is exactly what the motivation was behind child sacrifices of the ancient world. In the same way that the ancient world pleaded with the gods through child sacrifice to save them from the suffering of diseases, famine, or wars, so today's culture pleads to Molech through abortion to "save" women from the suffering of poverty, "oppressed status," or gender wars.

True believers in child sacrifice who were mothers of that ancient time considered it difficult but necessary to sacrifice their babies, just as true believers in abortion today will admit the difficulty of their act while demanding it a necessary right to sacrifice their babies. "Safe, legal, and rare" has resulted in a universal sacrament.

In the end, there is just no legitimate moral argument for murdering innocent children. And as in ancient Israel, the child sacrifice of abortion marks the beginning of the end of a civilization by the judgment of God.

Outside the Bible, child sacrifice in Phoenician culture (like that of Tyre's) has a significant presence in both textual and archaeological evidence. Among the most ancient texts that reference it are the following that wrote about the city of Carthage in North Africa, a settlement of Phoenicians.

Fourth-century BC Greek author Kleitarchos [paraphrased]:
"Kleitarchos says that out of reverence for Kronos [the Greek equivalent of Ba'al Hammon], the Phoenicians, and especially the Carthaginians, whenever they seek to obtain some great favor, vow one of their children, burning it as a sacrifice to the deity if they are especially eager to gain success. There stands in their midst a bronze statue of Kronos [Baal], its hands extended over a bronze brazier, the flames of which engulf the child. When the flames fall upon the body, the limbs contract and the open mouth seems almost to be laughing, until the contracted (body) slips quietly into the brazier. Thus it is that the "grin' is known as "sardonic laughter," since they die laughing."[73]

First-century BC Greek historian Diodorus Siculus:
"In their zeal to make amends for their omission to sacrifice the noblest children, they selected two hundred of the noblest children and sacrificed them publicly; and others who were under suspicion sacrificed themselves voluntarily, in a number not less than three hundred. There was in their city a bronze image of Cronus, extending its hands, palms up and sloping toward the

---

[73] Kleitarchos, *Scholia to Plato's Republic*, 337A: Quoted in Paul G. Mosca, *Child Sacrifice in Canaanite and Israelite Religion: A study in Mulk*, PhD Thesis, (Cambridge, MA, Harvard University, 1975), 22.

ground, so that each of the children when placed thereupon rolled down and fell into a sort of gaping pit filled with fire."[74]

Second-century AD Greek author Plutarch:
"No, but with full knowledge and understanding they themselves offered up their own children, and those who had no children would buy little ones from poor people and cut their throats as if they were so many lambs or young birds; meanwhile the mother stood by without a tear or moan; but should she utter a single moan or let fall a single tear, she had to forfeit the money, and her child was sacrificed nevertheless; and the whole area before the statue was filled with a loud noise of flutes and drums [so that] the cries of wailing should not reach the ears of the people."[75]

Though these texts speak of Phoenician child sacrifice in locations geographically removed from Canaan, they actually confirm religious and cultural connection to Jezebel's Tyre. The city of Carthage was founded by Dido of Tyre shortly after Jezebel's death.[76] As Henry Smith explains, "The evidence indicates that the Phoenicians brought this barbaric practice to Carthage from Canaan, and therefore, evidence of child sacrifice at Carthage provides evidential support for the historicity of the biblical accounts which mention such sacrifices."[77]

Critical scholars have recently sought to discredit or diminish the descriptions of Phoenician child sacrifice in both biblical and classical historians by complaining of prejudice in the authors who describe the sacrifices. In other words, biblical prophets used poetic hyperbole against polytheists, and Greek and Roman authors wrote propaganda about their enemies, such as Carthage, in order to paint them as barbarians and to justify their own barbarity.[78]

But this doesn't really fit the facts. First, because authors of different eras and vastly different cultures all wrote about the child sacrifice of Carthage. That is the definition of legally sound corroborating eyewitnesses.

---

[74] Diodorus Siculus, *The Library of History, Book 20*, 14:4-7, *Loeb Classical Library*, 1954, 153. Quoted in Lawrence E. Stager and Samuel R. Wolff, "Child Sacrifice at Carthage: Religious Rite or Population Control?" Biblical Archaeology Review 10,1 (1984), 14.
https://www.academia.edu/2298111/Child_Sacrifice_at_Carthage_Religious_Rite_or_Population_Control_Biblical_Archaeology_Review_10_1_1984_30-51_with_Lawrence_E_Stager

[75] Plutarch, *On Superstition, Loeb Classical Library*, 1928, 2:495. Quoted in Smith, Jr., "Canaanite Child Sacrifice," 98.

[76] Stager and Wolff, "Child Sacrifice at Carthage, 6.

[77] Henry B. Smith, Jr., "Canaanite Child Sacrifice, Abortion, and the Bible," *The Journal of Ministry and Theology*, 93.

[78] Smith, Jr., "Canaanite Child Sacrifice, 93.

Secondly, both Greeks and Romans practiced infant exposure, leaving unwanted infants to die of exposure to natural elements. So they didn't condemn the killing of infants—because they practiced it. Their interest was not moral but theological.[79]

Thirdly, the archaeological evidence confirms that both biblical and classical authors knew what they were talking about. Such physical evidence of child sacrifice has been found in Phoenician colonies all over the western Mediterranean. The most famous of sites is the Tophet at Carthage, North Africa, already referenced above.

Lawrence Stager and Sam Wolff, archaeologists who had excavated the site described it this way:

> The Carthaginian Tophet is the largest of these Phoenician sites and indeed is the largest cemetery of sacrificed humans ever discovered. Child sacrifice took place there almost continuously for a period of nearly 600 years...we nevertheless estimate the size of the Carthaginian Tophet during the fourth and probably the third centuries B.C. to be, at the minimum, between 54,000 and 64,000 square feet. Using the density of urns in our excavated area as a standard, we estimate that as many as 20,000 urns may have been deposited there between 400 and 200 B.C.[80]

The excavation site involves several levels that cover time periods from 800 B.C. to about 146 B.C. Earlier dates are below the water level and not accessible. Each level consists of urns that contain the charred bones of children, both boys and girls, from newborn to three-years old, mixed in with charred bones of goats and sheep. These burnt sacrifices were made to Tanit and Baal-Hammon, the patron goddess and god of Carthage. Tanit is the equivalent of Astarte in Canaan. Some say Baal-Hammon is the equivalent of the high god El. But in Canaan Astarte was the consort, not of El, but of Baal, the "Most High." So Baal-Hammon is most likely the equivalent of the Canaanite Baal-Hadad.

Critical scholars have recently constructed revisionist theories to describe the Carthage Tophet as not being a location of child sacrifice but a cemetery for children who died of natural causes. Stager, Wolff, and Greene debunk this

---

79 Smith, Jr., "Canaanite Child Sacrifice, 99-100.

80 Stager and Wolff, "Child Sacrifice at Carthage, 2.

skepticism by explaining several aspects that mitigate such revisionary speculation.[81]

First, the natural mortality rate of children at this time doesn't match the unnaturally high mortality rate of children in the Tophet, thus indicating deliberate infanticide rather than natural causes.[82]

Secondly, none of the remains of the infants show pathological condition of disease.[83]

Thirdly, naturally expired infants are usually ritually buried in foundations of homes or near the adults of the family, not in a separate cemetery.

Fourthly, some of the inscriptions on stela above the urns describe sacrificial vows to a deity never seen in normal funerary stela.

Finally, burial urns of charred animal bones that are sacrificial substitutions are found interspersed with the children's urns, something that would only make sense in terms of sacrificial rites. There were no pet cemeteries, and animal sacrificial substitution for humans was common though not universal. Some children were still sacrificed.[84]

Some have suggested that animal substitution evolved out of human sacrifice, but the later levels of Carthage show an increase in human sacrifice in later years, not a decrease, thus disproving the evolutionary theory.[85]

Child sacrifice was integrated into the Phoenician culture and the Israelite and Judahite cultures in a deep an affecting way. The biblical, historical, and archaeological evidence is consistent with each other.

•••••

If you liked this book, then please help me out by writing a positive review of it on Amazon here. That is one of the best ways to say thank you to me as an author. It really does help my sales and status. Thanks!
– Brian Godawa

---

[81] These reasons were all drawn from several sources: A debate over child sacrifice: https://phoenicia.org/childsacrifice.html; Brien K. Garnand – Lawrence E. Stager – Joseph A. Greene, "Infants as Offerings: Palaeodemographic Patterns and Tophet Burial," *Studi Epigrafici e Linguistici* 29-30, 2012-13: 193-222; Lawrence E. Stager and Samuel R. Wolff, "Child Sacrifice at Carthage: Religious Rite or Population Control?" Biblical Archaeology Review 10,1 (1984).

[82] Garnand, Stager and. Greene, "Infants as Offerings, 193-222.

[83] https://phoenicia.org/childsacrifice.html

[84] Stager and Wolff, "Child Sacrifice at Carthage, 11.

[85] Stager and Wolff, "Child Sacrifice at Carthage, 13.

The Spiritual World of Ancient China and the Bible

Biblical Background to the Novel *Qin: Dragon Emperor of China*

By Brian Godawa

The Spiritual World of Ancient China and the Bible: Biblical Background to the Novel Qin: Dragon Emperor of China
1st Edition

Warrior Poet Publishing
www.warriorpoetpublishing.com

ISBN: 978-1-942858-56-0 (paperback)
ISBN: 978-1-942858-57-7 (ebook)

Scripture quotations taken from *The Holy Bible: English Standard Version.* Wheaton: Standard Bible Society, 2001.

Get the Novel That is Based on the Biblical Research of This Booklet You are Reading.

2 Epic Storytellers. A Clash of Ancient Civilizations.

A novel of the first Chinese emperor, the Great Wall of China, spiritual warfare, dragons, and the tower of Babel from the Bible.

https://godawa.com/get-qin/

(*affiliate link*)

Chapter 1:
The Spiritual World of the Bible

The Gods of the Nations

I explained in the Note to the Reader at the beginning of the novel *Qin: Dragon Emperor of China*, that it is a part of the *Chronicles of the Watchers* series whose books all share what biblical scholar Michael S. Heiser has coined "the Deuteronomy 32 worldview."[1]

I employ this biblical worldview or "divine council" motif as a fantasy element to tell the supernatural side of the story of the first emperor of China. The basic premise is that there is a world of spiritual principalities and powers whose territories are linked to earthly rulers under their authority.

Deuteronomy 32 tells the story of Israel and how she had come to be God's chosen nation. Moses begins by glorifying God and then telling Israel to "remember the days of old"…

> Deuteronomy 32:8–9
> When the Most High gave to the nations their inheritance,
> when he divided mankind,
> he fixed the borders of the peoples
> according to the number of the sons of God.
> But the Lord's portion is his people,
> Jacob his allotted heritage.

The context of this passage is the Tower of Babel incident in Genesis 11 when mankind was divided and nations first created. Rebellious humanity sought divinity in unified rebellion, so God separated them by confusing their tongues, which divided them into the seventy nations (of Gentiles) described in Genesis 10. Their ownership of those bordered lands would be the "inheritance" of those peoples.

---

[1] Michael S. Heiser, *The Unseen Realm: Recovering the Supernatural Worldview of the Bible*, First Edition (Bellingham, WA: Lexham Press, 2015), 113–114.

But inheritance works in heaven as it is on earth. For the people of Jacob (Israel) would become Yahweh's allotted inheritance, and the other seventy Gentile nations were the allotted inheritance of the *Sons of God.*

For more detailed biblical support and explanation, I recommend reading my booklet, *Psalm 82: The Divine Council of the Gods, the Judgment of the Watchers and the Inheritance of the Nations* (affiliate link). It is the foundation of all three of my novel series, *Chronicles of the Nephilim, Chronicles of the Watchers* and *Chronicles of the Apocalypse.*

So, who were these Sons of God who ruled over the Gentile nations (Psa 82:1-8)? Some believe they were human rulers, others argue for their identities as supernatural principalities and powers. I am in the second camp.

The phrase "Sons of God" is a technical term that means divine beings from God's heavenly throne court (Job 1:6; 38:7) and they are referred to with many different titles. They are sometimes called "heavenly host" (Isa 24:21-22[2]), sometimes called "holy ones" (Deut 33:2-3[3]), sometimes called "the divine council" (Psa 82:1[4]), sometimes called "Watchers" (Daniel 4:13, 17, 23) and sometimes called "gods" or *elohim* in the Hebrew (Deut 32: 17, 43; Psa 82:1; 58:1-2).

Yes, you read that last one correctly. God's Word calls these beings *gods*.

But fear not. That isn't polytheism. The word "god" in this sense is a synonym for "heavenly being" or "divine being" whose realm is that of the spiritual. It does not mean uncreated beings that are all-powerful and all-knowing. Yahweh alone is that God. Yahweh is the God of gods (Deut 10:17; Psa 136:2). He created the other *elohim* ("gods"). These "gods" are created angelic beings who are most precisely referred to as Sons of God.

The narrative is this: before the Flood, some of these heavenly Sons of God rebelled against Yahweh and left their divine dwelling to come to earth (Jude 6), where they violated Yahweh's holy separation and mated with human women (Gen 6:1-4). This was not a racial separation, but a spiritual one. Their corrupt hybrid seed were called "nephilim" (giants), and their effect on humanity included such corruption and violence on the earth that Yahweh sent the Flood to wipe everyone out and start over again with Noah.[5]

Unfortunately, after the Flood, humanity once again united in evil while building the Tower of Babel, a symbol of idolatrous worship of false gods. So,

---

[2] See also Deut 4:19 with Deut 32:8-9; 1 King 22:19-23.

[3] See also Psa 89:5-7; Heb 2:2.

[4] See also Psa 89:5-7.

[5] For more biblical details on Noah and the Nephilim of Genesis 6, see my book, *When Giants Were Upon the Earth: The Watchers, the Nephilim, and the Biblical Cosmic War of the Seed* (Embedded Pictures Publishing, 2014).

Yahweh confused their tongues and divided them into the seventy nations. Since man would not stop worshipping false gods, the living God gave them over to their lusts (Rom 1:24, 26, 28) and placed them under the authority of the fallen Sons of God that they worshipped. Fallen spiritual rulers for fallen humanity (Psa 82:1-7). It's as if God said to humanity, "Okay, if you refuse to stop worshipping false gods, then I will give you over to them and see how you like them ruling over you."

Deuteronomy 32 hints at a spiritual reality behind the false gods of the nations, calling them "demons" (Deut 32:17; also Psa 106:37-38). The Apostle Paul later ascribes demonic reality to false gods as well (1 Cor 10:20; 8:4-6). The New Testament continues this ancient notion that spiritual principalities and powers lay behind earthly powers (Eph 6:12; 3:10). The two were inextricably linked in historic events. As Jesus indicated, whatever happened in heaven, also happened on earth (Matt 6:10). Earthly kingdoms in conflict are intimately connected to heavenly powers in conflict.[6]

When earthly rulers battle on earth, the Bible describes the host of heaven battling with them in spiritual unity. In Daniel 10, hostilities between Greece and Persia is accompanied by the battle of heavenly Watchers over those nations (described as spiritual "princes").

> Daniel 10:13, 20-21
> The prince of the kingdom of Persia withstood me twenty-one days, but Michael, one of the chief princes, came to help me, for I was left there with the kings of Persia." …Then he said, "Do you know why I have come to you? But now I will return to fight against the prince of Persia; and when I go out, behold, the prince of Greece will come. But I will tell you what is inscribed in the book of truth: there is none who contends by my side against these except Michael, your prince.

When Sisera fought with Israel, the earthly kings and heavenly authorities (stars or host of heaven) are described interchangeably in unity.[7]

---

[6] Dan 10:12-13, 20-21; 2Kgs 6:17; Judges 5:19-20.

[7] See also 2 Kings 6:15-17 where Elisha's servant has his spiritual eyes opened to see the myriad of heavenly warriors surrounding Israel preparing to battle Syria.

Judges 5:19–20
"The kings came, they fought; then fought the kings of Canaan…From heaven the stars fought, from their courses they fought against Sisera.

When God punishes earthly rulers, he punishes them along with the heavenly rulers ("host of heaven") above and behind them.

Isaiah 24:21–22
On that day the LORD will punish the host of heaven, in heaven, and the kings of the earth, on the earth. They will be gathered together as prisoners in a pit; they will be shut up in a prison, and after many days they will be punished.[8]

This notion of territorial archons or spiritual rulers is Biblical and carries over into intertestamental literature such as the Book of Enoch and others.[9] It is one of the foundational storylines of this series, Chronicles of the Watchers, as well as Chronicles of the Nephilim and Chronicles of the Apocalypse.

In the Bible, the term "Watchers" only appears in Daniel 4, where a Watcher, also called a "holy one," came down from heaven to proclaim to Daniel the "decree of the Watchers" that Nebuchadnezzar would go mad like a beast (Dan 4:13-17, 23). Though the Watchers of Daniel 4 are not specifically equated with the "princes" over the kingdoms of the nations in Daniel 10, they are considered by ancient Jews to be synonymous. The Watchers over the nations were the princes or principalities of those nations.

Two examples of how the ancient Jews interpreted Deuteronomy 32:8-9 illustrate this notion of territorial principalities watching over nations:

Jubilees 15:31-32
(There are) many nations and many people, and they all belong to him, but over all of them he caused spirits to rule so that they might lead them astray from following him. But over Israel he did not cause any angel or spirit to rule because he alone is their ruler and he will protect them.

---

[8] Interestingly, this passage of Isaiah is not clear about what judgment in history it is referring to. But the language earlier in the text is similar to the Flood when it says, "For the windows of heaven are opened, and the foundations of the earth tremble. 19 The earth is utterly broken, the earth is split apart, the earth is violently shaken. 20 The earth staggers like a drunken man; it sways like a hut; its transgression lies heavy upon it, and it falls, and will not rise again." So this may be another passage that uses a Flood reference tied in with the Watchers and their punishment.

[9] 1 En. 89:59, 62-63; 67; Jubilees 15:31-32; Targum Jonathan Deut. 32, Sect. LIII; 3Enoch 48C:9, DSS War Scroll 1Q33 Col. xvii:7, Targum Jonathan, Genesis 11, Section II.

> Targum Jonathan, Deuteronomy 32, Section LIII
> When the Most High made allotment of the world unto the nations which proceeded from the sons of Noach [Noah], in the separation of the writings and languages of the children of men at the time of the division, He cast the lot among the seventy angels, the princes of the nations with whom is the revelation to oversee the city.[10]

But it is the book of 1 Enoch that uses the term "Watchers" most commonly of these territorial princes (or angels or spirits or holy ones). The Sons of God of Genesis 6 are called Watchers all throughout 1 Enoch.[11] And those Sons of God are described in the Old Testament as Yahweh's heavenly host that surround him in his divine council.

Job describes the Sons of God as divine beings who were heavenly host present at the creation (Job 38:4-7), and who gathered around Yahweh, along with the satan, to council with him and perform his decrees (Job 1:6-7; 2:1-6). 1 Kings 22:19-23 depicts these same "host of heaven" as spirits surrounding Yahweh who do his bidding. Psalm 82 and 89 describe the assembly of heavenly host as his "divine council" of "gods," "holy ones," and "Sons of the Most High" (82:6).

All these terms are used synonymously for the divine beings of God's heavenly host, the Sons of God to whom Deuteronomy 32:8 declared were allotted the nations for an inheritance to watch over (territorial powers).

So the Bible says that there is demonic reality to false gods. But since those Sons of God who were territorial authorities over the nations were spiritually fallen Watchers, that makes them demonic or evil in essence. So what if they are the actual demonic beings behind the false gods of the ancient world? What if the fallen Sons of God were masquerading as the gods of the nations in order to keep humanity enslaved in idolatry to their authority? That would affirm the Biblical stories of earthly events with heavenly events occurring in synchronization.

That is the biblical premise of the *Chronicles of the Watchers*. The pagan gods, like Yu Huang and the Three Pure Ones in the novel *Qin*, are actually

---

[10] See also 1 Enoch 89:59; 90:25, 3Enoch 48C:9, DSS War Scroll 1Q33 Col. xvii:7, Targum Jonathan, Genesis 11, Section II; Philo, On the Posterity of Cain and His Exile 25.89; Concerning Noah's Work as a Planter 14.59; On the Migration of Abraham 36.202; 1 Clement 29; Origen, First Principles 1.5.1. Thanks to Don Enevoldsen for some of these passages. Walter Wink footnotes a plenitude of texts about the 70 angel "gods" over the 70 nations in the Targums in Walter Wink. *Naming the Powers: The Language of Power in the New Testament* (The Powers : Volume One) (Kindle Locations 2235-2242). Kindle Edition.

[11] 1 Enoch 10:9, 15; 12:2-6; 13:10; 14:1-3; 15:9; 16:1-2.

fallen Sons of God, Watchers of the nations, crafting false identities and narratives as gods of the nations that are connected and reflected in the earthly events of human history and its rulers. For a detailed biblical defense of this interpretation see my booklet, *Psalm 82: The Divine Council of the Gods, the Judgment of the Watchers and the Inheritance of the Nations.* (affiliate link)

Leviathan

Leviathan is a crucial character in the Chronicles universe. He shows up in Chronicles of the Nephilim, Chronicles of the Apocalypse, as well as Chronicles of the Watchers. He is drawn from the ancient Near Eastern worldview that permeates the Bible.

Contrary to what some hyper-literalists may think, Leviathan is not a real world sea dinosaur or even an extinct sea monster, it is a spiritual image that was used by ancient Near Eastern religions to symbolize the chaos of the cosmos that their god fought to bring about his rule and order. The Babylonians called it Tiamat, the Canaanites called it Lotan, the Ugaritic translation for "Leviathan." Hebrews called it Leviathan and sometimes Rahab.[12]

The battle of divinity to create order out of chaos is called "chaoskampf" by theologians.[13] In Mesopotamian religion, Marduk defeated Tiamat the sea dragon and split her in half to create the heavens and earth that symbolized the establishment of Babylonian world power.[14] The Canaanite Baal defeated the Sea (Yam), River (Nahar) and Leviathan (Lotan) in order to become the Most High ruler of the Canaanite pantheon.[15]

So, Yahweh is depicted as defeating Leviathan to establish his covenantal order with Israel at Sinai.

> Psalm 74:13–17
> You divided the sea by your might;
> you broke the heads of the sea monsters on the waters.

---

[12] Leviathan: Job 3:8; 41; Psa 74:13-14; Psa 104:26; Isa 27:1. Leviathan is said to dwell in the Abyss in Job 41:24 (LXX). "[Leviathan] regards the netherworld [Tartauros] of the deep [Abyss] like a prisoner. He regards the deep [Abyss] as a walk." Job 41:34, Tan, Randall, David A. deSilva, and Logos Bible Software. The Lexham Greek-English Interlinear Septuagint. Logos Bible Software, 2009.

For Rahab, see: Isa 51:9; Job 9:13; 26:12-13; Ps 87:4; Psalm 89:9-10.

[13] For Chaoskampf in the Bible, see: Psalm 89:9-10; Isaiah 51:9-10; Job 26:12-13. Psalms 18, 29, 24, 29, 65, 74, 77, 89, 93, and 104. Also, Exodus 15, Job 9, 26, 38, and Isaiah 51:14-16; 2 Samuel 22.

[14] *Enuma Elish*, Tablet IV, lines 104-105, 137-138, 144.

[15] See KTU 1.3:3.38-41.

You crushed the heads of Leviathan;
you gave him as food for the creatures of the wilderness.
You split open springs and brooks;
you dried up ever-flowing streams.
Yours is the day, yours also the night;
you have established the heavenly lights and the sun.
You have fixed all the boundaries of the earth;
you have made summer and winter.

In the Psalm above, the Red Sea deliverance of the Israelites ("dividing the sea") was the metaphor of God taking them out of the chaos of pagan Egypt. As in other ancient religions, Yahweh is depicted as defeating the sea, which also represented chaos to land dwellers. And Leviathan is in that sea as its instrument of power. But Yahweh crushes the heads of the sea dragon of chaos, and the creatures of the desert feast on his body. This banquet of eating the flesh of Leviathan symbolizes Yahweh's victory and is a common theme that appears in both biblical and extrabiblical Jewish poetry.[16]

The book of Revelation describes the victory of Christ over his enemies in chapter 19 as the "great supper of God" where the birds of prey eat the flesh of his defeated foes (19:17). While Leviathan is not included in this Revelation passage, it is the same kind of nature banquet motif as described in Psalm 74: creatures feasting on the flesh of the enemies of God. The "banquet of flesh" was a common way of symbolizing deliverance from and victory over one's enemies.

And Leviathan does show up in Revelation as the seven-headed sea dragon who is the satanic enemy of chaos against God's people.[17] Once again, the sea dragon's defeat is symbolically linked to God establishing a new order, namely the new covenant kingdom of God in Christ's blood (Rev 12:9-11).

But did the monster grow some new heads in Psalm 74? Not necessarily. If one looks closely at the fourteenth verse, even in the Hebrew, it says that Leviathan has multiple *heads*, plural, not *head*, singular (Yahweh "crushed the *heads* of Leviathan"). And it is no coincidence that the Leviathan of the Canaanite Baal epic has seven heads.[18]

But the last component of Psalm 74 is the creation language that reminds the reader of Genesis 1. Yahweh separates day and night, establishes the

---

16 For 2nd Temple examples of the feast of Leviathan and Behemoth, see 4Ezra 6:47-52; 2Apoc. Bar. 29:4; 1 Enoch 60: 7-9, 24.

17 See Rev 12:3-13:4; 16:13-16; 20:2-3.

18 KTU 1.5:1:30

heavenly host and makes the seasons (v. 15-17). This is not some unconnected jump back to the creation of the universe, it is another cosmic metaphor of the covenant in terms of a "heaven and earth." Right after Yahweh delivers them through the sea, he brings them to Sinai, where he establishes his covenant order. The Mosaic covenant was a spiritual cosmos, a heaven and earth of God's operations with his people. Yahweh delivers his people, destroys the dragon of chaos with victory and creates his covenantal order with Israel, a new "cosmos."

Hyper-literalist assumptions may cause distress in the believer who thinks this would mean that the Red Sea deliverance was "just a myth" or a spiritual symbol that didn't really happen in history. But this is simply a misunderstanding of the nature of ancient storytelling. Everything is not all "literal" or all "symbolic." It is very common for biblical writers to describe historic events with poetic or symbolic flair. So the Red Sea deliverance connected to the Sinai covenant was an historic event, but it had spiritual ramifications that were so important they had to be described using symbolic terms of Leviathan and creation.

Leviathan cannot be a literal physical creature, because it is destroyed and eaten here in Psalm 74, yet it is described by Isaiah as being alive again then slain *in the future* at another victory of God, namely, the coming of Messiah (Isa 27:6, 9). Leviathan is a spiritual symbol of the chaos that battles against order through history.

> Isaiah 27:1
> In that day the LORD with his hard and great and strong sword will punish Leviathan the fleeing serpent, Leviathan the twisting serpent, and he will slay the dragon that is in the sea.

But this *chaoskampf* in the Bible is not the same as pagan versions of it, where there is a dualist equivalence between the combatants, and either one might win. For example, Genesis 1 depicts Leviathan very differently for its theological purpose. We read of God's Spirit hovering over the dark "face of the deep" (v. 2), which is "without form and void," or "an unfilled wasteland" (Hebrew: *tohu wa-bohu*), an expression of that chaos that the sea tends to represent to the ancient world. The Hebrew word behind "deep" is *tehom*, which scholars argue is a linguistic connection to that sea dragon Tiamat. But in this context, there is no *chaoskampf* battle depicted. God simply speaks and order is established through the separation of things.

And then when a dragon appears, it is simply one of many sea creatures that God created to swarm in the sea.

Genesis 1:21
So God created the great sea creatures [*tannim*] and every living creature that moves, with which the waters swarm... And God saw that it was good.

The Hebrew word for "sea creatures" (*tannim*) is a word that is translated elsewhere as *dragon*.[19] Though Leviathan is not used here, the intent of the chapter is to demythologize the elements of the natural world that pagan cultures had divinized, including not only the sun, moon and stars, but the sea (chaos) and the dragons that resided there.

So, the imagery of *chaoskampf*, sea and dragon, are used poetically in some Bible passages to communicate the notion of God's creation of order out of chaos, but in other passages, those mythopoeic symbols are tamed with ease and without a dualistic struggle because they are after all symbols in the service of their creator.[20] Leviathan has no chance of winning in the Bible as he does in pagan mythology. All things are subject to the sovereign control of Yahweh, even chaos and evil.

See my book, *When Giants Were Upon the Earth* (affiliate link) for more on the theological meaning of Leviathan and its interaction with other fantastical motifs in the Bible.

---

19 Isaiah 51:9. "Serpent, dragon, sea-monster" Francis Brown, Samuel Rolles Driver, and Charles Augustus Briggs, *Enhanced Brown-Driver-Briggs Hebrew and English Lexicon* (Oxford: Clarendon Press, 1977), 1072.

20 In Job 41, God's questions to Job about being able to make Leviathan a servant or "play with him as with a bird" are obvious implications that God does so with Leviathan as a domesticated pet. See also Psalm 104:26. See also "sea creatures" (tannim: dragons) Psalm 148:7; Psalm 74:13; Isa 51:9.

Chapter 2:
The Characters

The Story First

Many of my readers like to learn about the biblical and historical research behind my novels after they have read them. The fact behind the fiction. It helps bring context and explains some of the "stranger things" of the novels to those who are intellectually and spiritually curious. This booklet is a presentation of the research behind my novel, *Qin: Dragon Emperor of China.* But the truth is that the material in this book is so fascinating that it can be read on its own by those who hunger as I do to uncover the biblical background to history.

The novel begins in 220 B.C. in the Babylonian region of the Seleucid empire. The Greek kingdom of Antiochus the Great is crumbling with the winds of revolt. And in the midst of it all, mysterious mercenaries from the Far East slip into Babylon and kidnap a magus from the temple. Magi are the masters of both magic and science, but Antiochus doesn't know why they were chosen as hostages.

So the king sends his bastard son and disgraced warrior Antiochus the Younger into the mysterious land of the Far East with two goals: find the magus and capture a mythical creature that will give the Greek king absolute power: a dragon.

Antiochus the Younger travels to that distant land, ruled by its first emperor, Qin Shi Huang di ("Cheen Shir Hwong Dee"). The Greek warrior discovers a world of both wonder and danger. A contrast and comparison of cultures. A clash of civilizations. Antiochus falls in love with one of the emperor's concubines and he discovers the spiritual truth behind the mythological dragon that protects that world.

What's worse, the emperor is seeking the elixir of immortality. He has forced his own alchemists and scientists to find it before the emperor dies so he can obtain eternal life and rule forever. And he will sacrifice anything and anyone to achieve his goal.

As Antiochus negotiates the treacherous politics of his presence in the land of Qin (spelled in the novel as "Ch'in" from where we get "China"), he also discovers there is a spiritual past to China that the emperor has suppressed. And that past goes back to the infamous Tower of Babel in Genesis 11, where God confused the tongues of the nations in order to stop mankind from the pursuit of divinity. The concubine has spiritual ties to that heritage and the emperor wants her eliminated.

Antiochus and the concubine find themselves on the run to the Great Wall of China where a revolt of slaves breaks out just as barbarians are at the gates of the wall, trying to break in. Unfortunately, the dragon is empowering the emperor's armed forces and Antiochus and the concubine have only one chance to defeat the darkness. They must fight their way to the ancient Altar of Heaven to rekindle the lost power of Shang Di, the true creator God of China's past.

A unique aspect of the novel is the depiction of the spiritual world. The novel pulls back the curtain of the unseen realm. It depicts the "spiritual principalities and powers" that reign behind pagan Gentile nations and how they have influence on the course of history. The gods of ancient China are not mere myths without bite. They are actually demonic powers that are real and have their own agenda.

Thus the god Yu Huang, the supreme head of the Chinese pantheon of gods, seeks to maintain his power over the emperor and his land much like human mobsters might maneuver for power over their regions in a city under their control.

Though this is obviously fantastic and speculative, the principle of spiritual warfare is biblical. There were spiritual entities of power ruling over Gentile nations as depicted in Deuteronomy 32:8-10 and Psalm 82 (explained in chapter 1). The storyline of these spiritual powers is intended to reflect the mythology of pagans and how it reflects spiritual reality within a biblical worldview.

And that is the basic storyline of the novel *Qin: Dragon Emperor of China.* Historical fantasy based on spiritual fact. Now, enjoy learning about the historical and biblical research behind it all…

Xeneotas (Antiochus the Younger)

The protagonist of the novel is a Greek warrior general, Xeneotas, the secret bastard son of Antiochus III of Seleucia, known as Antiochus the Great. Xeneotas is a fictional character based very loosely on a real general of Seleucia of similar name. His family status is creative license.

Historically, General Xeneotas fought against the rebel Molon who launched his forces against the capital city named Seleucia on the Tigris River in 221 B.C. Xeneotas foolishly pursued Molon into an ambush and was killed in that battle, which resulted in the temporary loss of Babylonia for King Antiochus. It would take a year for the king to defeat Molon and quell the rebellion.[1]

In the novel, I make Xeneotas fail that battle in Babylon by the same trick of Molon, but instead of dying, Xeneotas survives and is sent off into the Far East on a secret journey from which he will not return. So his presumed death fits the "space between" the facts, fictional though it may be.

And Xeneotas' fictional bastard status in the novel is not without historical precedent. Most kings, including Antiochus III had concubines and other wives. So making Xeneotas the first-born son of a beloved concubine would justify him claiming the name of Antiochus the Younger, should he win his father's approval. Historically, there were many Antiochuses in the family line. Making The Younger's personal journey one that was lost to history along with his identity, again makes it at least conceivable if not actually historical.

Xeneotas' father Antiochus the Great as well as his military general Hermias, and their political struggles are based on true events.

The Magi

The Babylonian magi in the novel are also fictional characters, but drawn from the historical tradition of the prophet Daniel's influence on Babylonia four hundred years earlier. "According to Herodotus, [magi] were members of a Persian priestly caste who specialized in astrology, interpretation of dreams, and magic."[2]

During the time of the Babylonian captivity of Judah, the young Hebrew prisoner Daniel had been able to accurately interpret the troubling dreams of King Nebuchadnezzar when the "wise men" of the royal court could not. Those wise men included "magicians, enchanters, sorcerers and Chaldeans" (Dan 2:2, 10). The Greek word used to translate "magician" in the Septuagint (LXX) was "magi."

---

[1] Michael Taylor. *Antiochus the Great.* Pen and Sword. Kindle Edition. Location 654 of 4228.

[2] W. W. Buehler, "Wise Men (NT)," ed. Geoffrey W. Bromiley, *The International Standard Bible Encyclopedia, Revised* (Wm. B. Eerdmans, 1979–1988), 1084.

Daniel had made such an impression upon the king that he placed the Hebrew lad in power over those wise men, as well as over all of Babylon.

> Daniel 2:47–48
> The king answered and said to Daniel, "Truly, your God is God of gods and Lord of kings, and a revealer of mysteries, for you have been able to reveal this mystery." Then the king gave Daniel high honors and many great gifts, and made him ruler over the whole province of Babylon and chief prefect over all the wise men of Babylon.

Daniel went on to also impress Nebuchadnezzar's successors, King Belshazzar, and Darius the Mede. In short, the humble Hebrew prophet had achieved so much influence over his pagan captors' own magicians, enchanters, sorcerers and Chaldeans, that by the first century of the Roman Empire, Babylonian wise men ("magi") from the East had come searching for the Messiah based on their astrological teachings. They clearly got that information from Daniel.

This is not to say that the Babylonian system was fully Yahwist or that the magi of the Nativity story of Jesus were Jewish converts. But at least we can say that Daniel's teaching of the coming Messiah lasted for 600 years within the Babylonian magi tradition.

And therein lies the connection with the magi of the novel *Qin: Dragon Emperor of China*. They too are looking for that Danielic Messiah, an apparent reflection of the Chinese search for the one who would unify all under heaven.

The dominant text of the Babylonian magi that shows up in the novel is the *Enuma Anu Enlil*, an astrological text for interpreting the omens of celestial movements. The astrology of the ancient Near East is not the same as today. Though the Babylonians did develop their understanding of the Zodiac as influencing life on earth, it was not so simple as the modern horoscope in the newspaper. It was a commonplace tradition in the ancient Near East that the stars were gods, and that the divine embraced the whole of what we would now call "nature."[3] Therefore the effect of the heavens upon earthly destinies could be divined through understanding celestial mechanics. But it was first understood that astrology related to collective entities, political powers, nations and royalty. Only after 500 B.C. did it begin to be applied to individual lives of the lesser classes.[4]

---

[3] Francesca Rochberg, *In the Path of the Moon: Babylonian Celestial Divination and Its Legacy* (Netherlands: Koninklijke Brill NV, 2010), 22.

[4] Rochberg, *In the Path of the Moon*, 189.

The names of the magi in the novel are Balthazar, Melchior and Gaspar. The astute reader will recognize those names as the names of the three magi (or "wise men") in church tradition who visited the child Jesus in Bethlehem. Though the biblical text does not say there were three magi nor does it give their names, western tradition has suggested there were three because of the three gifts brought: gold, frankincense and myrrh (Matthew 2:11).

An even more astute reader will notice that those magi are 600 years before Christ, rendering them impossible candidates for a visit to young Jesus. Hopefully, the reader has already read the novel for the explanation of that historical anomaly. If you haven't, I won't ruin it for you by revealing the answer here.

Ch'in Shih Huang Di

The emperor's name is pronounced in English as "Cheen Shure Hwong Dee." This character in the novel *Qin: Dragon Emperor of China* was based upon the historical first emperor of China, the first to unify seven warring kingdoms under one ruler. The spelling used in the novel is from the older Wade-Giles translation of Chinese (Ch'in Shih Huang Di). I did this because it would be easier to read in English, and because it also hints at the origin of the name for China as the land of Ch'in (Qin). The more common spelling today would be Qin Shi Huang Di.

Before the Qin empire, the land which we now call "China" was divided into seven kingdoms and was named by her inhabitants *Tianxia*, meaning "under heaven."[5] Like most ancient civilizations, the Chinese considered their land to be the center of the earth, or as they put it, *Zhong Guo*, the "Central Nation." We now translate that as "Middle Kingdom."[6]

The actual inspiration for empire came from the previous four hundred years of Chinese internicene warfare of kingdoms called The Warring States period. Seven major states (kingdoms) fought for dominance of the region until the Qin state achieved final conquest and united the seven kingdoms under one ruler, the emperor. That emperor was Qin Shi Huang Di.

The emperor's historical origins have a rumor of suspicion behind them that is hinted at in the novel. Before he became emperor, his name was Ying Zheng. He was ostensibly the son of Yiren, the king of Qin. The queen, Ying

---

[5] Denis Twitchett and John K. Fairbank, eds., *The Cambridge History of China: Volume 1: The China and Han Empires, 221 B.C. — A.D. 220* (Cambridge University Press, 1999), 20.

[6] Dr. Thong, *Faith Of Our Fathers*, Kindle edition, Location 236 of 344.

Zheng's mother, was also the secret lover of a merchant advisor to the king named Lu Buwei. There is significant historical evidence that points to Ying Zheng as the illegitimate son of the queen and Lu Buwei.[7]

When Zheng became the first (*shi*) emperor, he used his family name Qin and added the old Eastern term for supreme rulers, *Huang Di*. Thus he became Qin shi Huang Di, the first supreme ruler of the house of Qin ruling over all under heaven. But adding that "Di," would prove to be a deliberate claim to divinity.

The will of God (Di) in the choice of government was called "The Mandate of Heaven" because the word "heaven" was often used as a stand-in for God himself. The Mandate would be similar to what the West called "the divine right of kings." The emperor's authority was derived from God, so the emperor was called "Son of Heaven." If the emperor did not fulfill the divine mandate, he would be punished by heaven.[8]

But China scholar John Man explains that the word "Di" in the emperor's name was a term of highest supernatural power. "Huang Di, often translated as August Emperor, thus declaring himself imperial ruler, god, sage and ancestor all in one."[9] Like all tyrants of the world, the first Chinese emperor set a standard of divinity in the office that would continue for centuries.

Huang Di would become known for his peculiar pursuit of eternal life to maintain that divine status. He had ordered his magicians and scholars to create the elixir of immortality through alchemy, and he had sent explorers to find the mythical Isle of Immortals to bring back the elixir should they find it.

It was believed at the time by Daoists that certain metals and elements like gold, mercury ("quicksilver"), arsenic and others, if ingested in small amounts would lengthen life.[10] So, while waiting for his magicians to achieve their alchemic ambitions, the emperor had a regular diet of mercury and arsenic baked into small cakes for easy consumption. As described in the novel, one of the procedures of creating the elixir attempted by the Chinese "supernatural scholars" was that of turning a red crystal, cinnabar, into mercury. Metal poisoning is now widely considered to be the cause of the emperor's perpetual sickness and ultimate insanity.

In the novel, Huang Di's descent into bad health and madness was drawn from a sixth century's record of observations of the effects of such metal

---

[7] Jonathan Clements, *The First Emperor of China* (Albert Bridge Books, 2006, 2015), 45.

[8] Dr. Thong, *Faith Of Our Fathers*, Kindle edition, Location 240 and 244 of 344.

[9] John Man, *The Terra Cotta Army: China's First Emperor and the Birth of a Nation* (Cambridge, MA: Da Capo Press, 2008), 74.

[10] Man, *Terra Cotta Army*, 102.

poisoning, where the very ill effects themselves were ironically considered "evidence" of the purging of sickness:

> After taking an elixir, if your face and body itch as though insects were crawling over them, if your hands and feet swell dropsically, if you cannot stand the smell of food and bring it up after you have eaten it, if you feel as though you were going to be sick most of the time, if you experience weakness in your four limbs, if you have to go often to the latrine, or if your head or stomach violently ache – do not be alarmed or disturbed. All these effects are merely proofs that the elixir you are taking is successfully dispelling your latent disorders.[11]

Huang Di's pursuit of immortality also included a search for the mythical Isle of Immortals. In the novel he sends a Chinese "wise man" Xu Fu to find the magical Isle based on the explorer's reports. This is based on historical fact. Xu Fu had told Huang Di about the Isle and about three spirit mountains where the immortals lived: Penglai, Fangzhang, and Yingzhou. But when pressed to find it, Xu Fu claimed that it was impossible for normal men to go there. Only wizards, or pure boys or maidens could approach it. He was then allowed to bring with him 1000 virgin boys and girls to find the Isle and bring back the elixir of immortality.[12] God only knows what Xu Fu really did to those innocent youth.

As in the novel, so in real life, Xu Fu returned and made an excuse for his inability to get to the Isle: It was guarded by large sea monsters. So the emperor took his counselor, Li Ssu and his youngest son, Huhai, and went off to kill the Great Fish with a large crossbow. By now, the emperor's madness had taken him over on his impossible quest. He shot some fish in the sea and died on the road back to his palace.[13]

The novel covers this incident but adds a fantasy element of fighting the sea dragon Leviathan. The story retains the historical facts out of it: Huang Di dies on that trip, and Li Ssu and Huhai return with the intent to take the throne for Huhai. The fantasy genre becomes a way to picture the spiritual reality of what is going on in the earthly realm.

In fact, this was a common goal of mine as I wrote the story. All the fantasy elements were added in a way that would not contradict what

---

[11] Man, *Terra Cotta Army*, 102.

[12] Sima Qian, (2011-02-10). *Records of the Grand Historian: Qin Dynasty* (p. 49). Columbia University Press. Kindle Edition.

[13] Clements, *The First Emperor*, 156.

happened historically, but rather support the facts with mythopoeic spirituality.

Miscellaneous Factoids

Many of the activities of the emperor described in the novel *Qin: Dragon Emperor of China* are rooted in historical facts. He is depicted as unifying all of China in terms of government, measurement systems, money and travel. He is responsible for completing the "Great Wall" of China, referred to as the "Long Wall" or "Long Cemetery" by his people. He did entomb the bodies of laborers into the Wall as the novel indicated.[14] He also burned all the books of previous history and philosophy, such as the Chinese *Classics*. He wanted to erase the traditional wisdom of Confucius and others and replace it with Legalism, a new Machiavellian political philosophy that rejected tradition and family legacy for power. He also murdered 450 of his "scholars" because of their disagreement with this revolutionary policy.[15]

One curious artifact of history that makes it into the novel is the existence of gigantic warrior statues cast by the emperor as spiritual guardians of his realm. Ancient Chinese historian Sima Qin writes, "According to some reports, these colossal figures, which each weighed the equivalent of nearly twenty-nine English tons, represented twelve giants wearing "barbarian" garb who appeared at Lintao in Gansu... The statues were said to have survived until the close of the Eastern Han."[16] Is this evidence of Nephilim? Not for historical purposes, but for fantasy fictional purposes, yes indeed. Though recent archeological discoveries do indicate that giants are not entirely absent from ancient Chinese history.[17]

As a side note, though the characters and political issues of generals Meng Tian, Fan Zhao, scholar Xu Fu, counselor Li Ssu, and the imperial sons Huhai and Fusu are based on historical facts, the characters of the concubine Mei Li and the warrior Wu Shu are fictional.

---

[14] Clements, *The First Emperor of China* (Kindle Locations 1903-1907). Kindle Edition.

[15] Dr. Thong, *Faith Of Our Fathers*, Kindle edition, Location 292-293 of 344.

On the burning of scholars: Sima Qian, *Records of the Grand Historian: Qin Dynasty,* (Columbia University Press, 2011), Kindle Edition, 55.

[16] Sima Qian, *Records of the Grand Historian: Qin Dynasty,* (Columbia University Press, 2011), Kindle Edition, footnote 77, page 245.

[17] For giants discovery see: https://www.smithsonianmag.com/smart-news/graveyard-giants-found-china-180963976/

Chapter 3: The Spiritual World of China

Tower of Babel and the Tomb of Qin

In the novel *Qin: Dragon Emperor of China*, reference is made to Chinese oracle bones that record contact between King Cyrus of Persia and the Chinese in the sixth century B.C., four hundred years before the Qin dynasty. This is based on real modern discoveries of cuneiform clay cylinders about Cyrus the Great and his conquest of Babylon that match those found on Chinese oracle bones in China.[1] The ancient Babylonians most likely had interaction with the ancient Chinese.

But there is also biblical evidence of that connection. As explained in Chapter 1, the Tower of Babel incident in Genesis 11 is a foundational narrative to the Deuteronomy 32 worldview, or as I call it, "the Watcher paradigm" that guides the Chronicles of the Watchers series along with its sister series, Chronicles of the Nephilim and Chronicles of the Apocalypse.

This paradigm understands the fallen biblical Watchers over the nations to be identical or connected to the gods of the Gentile nations. And these gods were allotted the various nations as their "inheritance" of ownership. Every Gentile nation territory was under the authority of the demonic false gods that they worshipped.

By way of review, the Tower of Babel was a ziggurat step pyramid that was built as a "stairway to heaven" for the gods to come down and meet with priests in the temple at the top of the pyramid. The word for Babylon in Akkadian is *babil-ani*, which means "gate of the gods."[2] This temple tower symbolized a "cosmic mountain," and its basic pyramidal structure is apparent

---

1 See http://zoroastrianheritage.blogspot.com/2013/03/cyrus-edict-chinese-cuneiform-bones.html

2 Anne Habermehl, "Where in the World Is the Tower of Babel?", *Answers Research Journal 4* (2011):30. https://assets.answersingenesis.org/doc/articles/pdf-versions/Tower_Babel.pdf

in most ancient civilizations across the globe, from Mesopotamia to Egypt to India to South America.[3]

One theory that explains this uniformity of structure across geographically and culturally diverse civilizations is that the original unified people at Babel were split up by God at the Confusion of Tongues incident and brought with them their knowledge of such sacred architecture. The biblical word "Babel" is a polemical mockery of the Akkadian name of Babylon that turns the "gate of gods" into "confusion."

One of those separated seventy nations from Babel would end up settling in the territory we now call China. Modern Chinese researcher Dr. Thong, Chan Kei writes,

> I have now come to the studied conclusion that the ancient Chinese were one of the many original nations dispersed after the confusion of languages at the Tower of Babel, described in Genesis 11 of the Bible. Some among these dispersed nations were alienated from God, while others wanted to follow His way. Like the Pilgrims who went to America to preserve the purity of their religious beliefs, the people group that went on to found the Chinese civilization was, I believe, a God-fearing race that desired to worship God appropriately.[4]

Another researcher of this issue, C.H. Kang concludes the same Babel origin of China at the Great Dispersion, concluding that because of China's geographical isolation, it was cut off from the outside influence of the west and thus remained relatively undisturbed for 2000 years. This isolation meant that it retained a stronger connection to its Babel origins (and therefore Yahweh) than did the other nations.[5]

I bring up this information about ziggurats because the tomb of the Chinese emperor Qin Shi Huang Di is in the shape of a ziggurat. Though it currently resides beneath an unexcavated dirt mound called Mount Li located in the Shaanxi province of China, artistic renderings of the tomb indicate its pyramid shape.[6]

---

[3] See: https://www.touropia.com/step-pyramids-of-the-world/

[4] Dr. Thong, Chan Kei, *Faith Of Our Fathers: Finding God In Ancient China* (Singapore: Cru Asia Limited, 2018), Kindle edition, Location 24 of 344.

[5] C.H. Kang, *The Discovery of Genesis: how the Truths of Genesis Were Found Hidden in the Chinese Language* (St. Louis, MO: Concordia House, 1979), 2-3.

[6] See the artistic rendering of the tomb: https://www.uchinavisa.com/qin-shi-huang.html

Though the tomb has never been opened, descriptions of the interior by Chinese historians and the like conjure rivers of mercury and a sky ceiling of gems as stars over the floor created as a map of the world.[7] The novel *Qin* depicts these historical elements as well as the famous army of thousands of terra cotta soldiers created as guardians in the afterlife.[8] It was also a fact that the emperor's concubines as well as the designers of the tomb were sealed in alive in the structure after the emperor was buried in it.[9]

So, who were the gods this temple tower mausoleum of Qin was servicing? Let's find out.

The Dragon

The dragon is a well-known symbol of ancient Chinese history and mythology. Whereas the western tradition of dragons is of a fire breathing dinosaur-like behemoth, the Chinese dragon is born of water and is long and snake-like with small legs. These opposing images reflect a much deeper difference of spiritual understanding.

As classicist scholar M.W. de Visser explains, the dragon appears in the oldest of Chinese literature, the *I Ching,* a divination text that dates back to the second millennium B.C. The dragon is a positive image of power.

> [It] symbolizes those among men who are fullest of Light, namely great men, and its appearance is considered to be an omen of their coming, i.e. of their birth. In the first place the greatest and fullest of Yang among them all, the Emperor, is, of course, symbolized by the dragon. He is, indeed, the representative of Imperial power.[10]

From the Zhou dynasty onward (1122-249 B.C.) the dragon was used exclusively of rulers.[11] Visser reveals that the emperor Qin Shi Huang Di applied it specifically to himself, and even described him employing winged dragons in his battle with rebels, much like the fantasy battle at the Great Wall in the *Qin* novel.

---

[7] Sima Qian, *Records of the Grand Historian: Qin Dynasty,* (Columbia University Press, 2011), Kindle Edition, footnote 77, page 64.

[8] Clara Moskowitz, "The Secret Tomb of China's 1st Emperor: Will We Ever See Inside?" https://www.livescience.com/22454-ancient-chinese-tomb-terracotta-warriors.html

[9] Jonathan Clements, *The First Emperor of China* (Kindle Locations 2901-2903). Kindle Edition.

[10] Marinus Willem de Visser, *The Dragon in China and Japan* (Ithica, NY; Cornell University Library, 1913), 38.

[11] Dr. Thong, *Faith Of Our Fathers*, Kindle edition, Location 200 of 344.

Qin Shi Huang Di was referred to as the "Ancestral Dragon" in the ancient Chinese *Historical Records* by Sima Qian.[12] Qin was one of the first emperors to set himself up as a personification of the dragon, and he is considered the first to introduce dragon worship into the Chinese culture.[13]

In ancient Chinese literature, the dragon is a heavenly creature that symbolizes personal power, the origin of earthly creatures and wisdom.[14] The Chinese *Classics* compiled by Confucius describe the dragon as a god of thunder, clouds and rain, essentially a storm god.[15]

In the Bible, the dragon is clearly understood to be a negative image. As explained in the section on Leviathan, the sea dragon is a symbol of chaos that battles against the Creator's natural and covenantal order (Psalm 74). The Serpent of the Garden is cursed for his deception and lies (Genesis 3:14). His "seed" or offspring are prophesied to be at war with the messianic "seed of Eve," biting the heel that crushes his head (Genesis 3:15). This poetic prediction of the coming Messiah runs through the entire Bible as a picture of Satan's people trying to destroy God's people. And that serpent becomes linked to Satan as the seven-headed sea dragon of chaos in the final dissolution of the Old Covenant, a dragon who also seeks to kill Christians (Revelation 12:4-6).

> Revelation 12:9
> And the great dragon was thrown down, that ancient serpent, who is called the devil and Satan, the deceiver of the whole world…

This contrast of interpretation comes to play in the novel as the biblical reality of the satanic Watchers is unveiled behind the earthly Chinese dragons.

One other tangent related to dragons in the story of *Qin: Dragon Emperor of China* was the red herring thrown out by the emperor to discourage the protagonist's pursuit of a dragon. Huang Di shows Antiochus a graveyard of "dragon bones" to argue that dragons are long dead and therefore only a legend in the present. The revelation to the modern reader, if not the protagonist

---

12 Dr. Thong, *Faith Of Our Fathers*, Kindle edition, Location 280 of 344.
Visser, *The Dragon in China*, 122.

13 Dr. Thong, *Faith Of Our Fathers*, Kindle edition, Location 290 of 344.

14 Visser, *The Dragon in China*, 62-65.

15 Visser, *The Dragon in China*, 109-115.

himself, is that the dragons are actually misinterpreted dinosaur bones. This was not my creative imagination. It is based on a strongly supported theory by Adrienne Mayor in her book, *The First Fossil Hunters: Dinosaurs, Mammoths, and Myth in Greek and Roman Times*. She argues that modern paleontology with its discovery and categorization of dinosaur bones is a relatively recent discipline of the 18th and 19th centuries. Until that time, most people did not know about the "terrible lizards."

But our ancient ancestors did. They just didn't realize it. Occasionally, explorers or scholars would stumble across dinosaur bones in their explorations or travels, but didn't know what they were. So they called them dragons, griffons, giants and other mythological beings. Mayor examines dozens of examples of classical Greek and Roman writers' descriptions of mythical monsters that fit the pictures of dinosaur remains.

She writes that the Chinese too found dinosaur fossils and called them dragons. "It is generally believed that the earliest written descriptions of "dragon" bones appeared in a Chinese chronicle of the second century B.C. During the digging of a canal in north-central China, "dragon bones were found and therefore the canal was named Dragon-Head Waterway."[16]

There could not be two more opposite pictures than the ancient Eastern and Western symbols of the dragon. But rather than casting Chinese dragon imagery as inherently satanic, it actually reveals a much deeper nuanced picture of a civilization that had once maintained biblical roots, but fell with the introduction of the dragon and its false gods. So let's take a look at that primeval religion of the land of ancient Tianxia (China).

Shang Di

Until the first emperor of Qin, ancient China actually worshipped a single creator God whose name was Shang Di (or Di or Tian). As Dr. Thong explains, "'Shang' means 'above' or 'supreme' and 'Di' means 'Lord,' 'emperor' or 'God.'" So Shang Di would mean "emperor of heaven" or "the sovereign above all rulers."[17] The use of "Di" in the emperor Qin Shi Huang Di's name therefore indicates his claim to divine status.

---

16 Adrienne Mayor, *The First Fossil Hunters: Dinosaurs, Mammoths, and Myth in Greek and Roman Times*, (Princeton University Press), Kindle Edition. (Kindle Locations 1220-1223).

17 Dr. Thong, *Faith Of Our Fathers*, Kindle edition, Location 96 of 344.

Shang Di's attributes matched those of the biblical Yahweh. He was considered by the ancient Chinese to be fatherly, sovereign, eternal, immutable, all-powerful, all-knowing, ever-present, infinite, holy, loving, grace-filled, compassionate and just—just like Yahweh of the Old Testament.[18] This may not sound as significant to our western minds that are saturated in the Judeo-Christian understanding of God's attributes. But in the ancient world, those traits stood out from the common notions of a pantheon of capricious deities with limited agency and contentious motivations squabbling for power.

Like Hebrew religion and unlike all other religions, Shang Di was considered to be a father in the eyes of ancient Chinese religion. Also like Hebrew religion and unlike all other religions, visual images of Shang Di were forbidden. There are no pictures of him in Chinese history.[19] This would make the Hebrews and the Chinese the only peoples of that time who prohibited images of the Creator. Every other nation was awash in images of their gods.

Lines from a song of the Border Sacrifice (explained below), called "Song of Central Peace," reads like a Chinese translation of Yahweh creating the heavens and earth of Genesis 1.

> Of old in the beginning, there was the great chaos, without
> form and dark.
> The five planets had not begun to revolve, more the two
> lights to shine.
> In the midst of it there existed neither form nor sound.
> You, O Spiritual Sovereign, came forth in your sovereignty,
> and first did separate the impure from the pure.
> You made heaven; You made earth; You made man. All
> things became alive with reproducing power.[20]

In the sixteenth century, Jesuit priest Matteo Ricci became the first Western advisor to Emperor Wan Li and established mission bases in China that resulted in the conversion of thousands of Chinese to Christ. To this day, he remains one of the rare western foreigners still highly respected in Chinese history because of his love and accurate understanding of the Chinese culture. He wrote in his book, *The True Meaning*, "Having leafed through a great

---

18 Dr. Thong, *Faith Of Our Fathers*, Kindle edition, Location 102-118 of 344.

19 Dr. Thong, *Faith Of Our Fathers*, Kindle edition, Location 100 of 344.

http://allthechildrenoflight.wordpress.com/2013/02/03/the-creator-god-in-ancient-china-genesis-hidden-in-the-chinese-language/

20 Dr. Thong, *Faith Of Our Fathers*, Kindle edition, Location 286-288 of 344.

number of ancient books, it is quite clear to me that the Sovereign on High [Bible] and Lord of Heaven [China] are different only in name."[21]

Border Sacrifice

The system of worship of Shang Di was also similar to Old Testament worship. Before the Qin empire, the various kings would perform animal sacrifices to Shang Di that they called "border sacrifices," consisting of a burnt sacrifice of a bull, without blemish, by the sovereign on an "altar of heaven."[22] Some of this annual ceremony shows up in the storyline of *Qin: Dragon Emperor of China.* It was originally performed on Mount Tai in coastal Shandong by previous rulers which is why it was called "border sacrifice."[23] The ritual had lasted through the entire previous eighteen dynasties of China's history, going back 4000 years.[24]

Dr. Thong describes the details of the ceremony from ancient sources to show its similarity to the biblical ceremony engaged in by the Levitical priests of Old Testament Israel. The notion of blood covenant, of substitutionary sacrifice of an animal without blemish reflects the Old Testament sacrificial imagery of Messiah, ultimately fulfilled in the New Covenant of Jesus Christ.[25]

The Altar of Heaven was not a temple, because Shang Di does not dwell in temples built with hands. It was an altar, and it would be built wherever the capital city was for the ruler. The famous Temple of Heaven (more accurately, "Altar of Heaven") in modern day Beijing is an imperial altar first built during the reign of Cheng Zhong (1295-1307) and rebuilt during the Ming dynasty of 1402-1424. It is the largest altar in the world for the worship of God as the ancient Chinese understood him. There are no idols or statues inside it.

But that's not all. The Chinese understanding of Shang Di was also quite similar to the Deuteronomy 32 worldview or Watcher paradigm of Psalm 82 that was explained earlier from the Bible.

Let's take a closer look at that paradigm.

---

21 http://allthechildrenoflight.wordpress.com/2013/02/03/the-creator-god-in-ancient-china-genesis-hidden-in-the-chinese-language/

22 John Ross, *The Original Religion of China*, (New York, NY: Eaton and Mains, 1909), 50.

23 Dr. Thong, *Faith Of Our Fathers*, Kindle edition, Location 128 of 344.

24 James Legge, *The Chinese Classics* (Vol. III), pp. 33–34, The Shoo King: Canon of Shun, Taipei, Southern Materials Centre Inc., 1983.

25 Dr. Thong, *Faith Of Our Fathers*, Kindle edition, Location 130-162 of 344.

The Lesser Deities

In the Nineteenth Century, Missionary John Ross wrote about the original religion of China as being quite similar to the biblical picture of a divine council of heavenly host called "gods" (*elohim*), that surrounds Yahweh's heavenly throne and do his bidding (Psalm 82). The ancient Chinese spiritual worldview also contained a divine council whose spiritual host were called "shen." Ross explains the primeval Chinese picture thus:

> There is one Supreme Being over all in heaven and on earth, the Ruler alike of gods and men. The inferior deities exist, not as the rivals of God but as faithful ministers of His. God has deputed to each of the inferior deities his own particular sphere of influence and of work. In his own sphere this deity exercises supreme jurisdiction over man, but under God… the references to the "host" of inferior deities clearly indicate not only that these deities were inferior, but that they were entirely subordinate. Yet they were superior to man, whom, in carrying out the will of God, they could protect, reward, or punish, according to his deeds.[26]

Compare this to Psalm 82, and 1 Kings 22 and the similarities are startlingly obvious.

> Psalm 82:1–8
> God has taken his place in the divine council;
>   in the midst of the gods he holds judgment:
> "How long will you judge unjustly
>   and show partiality to the wicked? *Selah*
> Give justice to the weak and the fatherless;
>   maintain the right of the afflicted and the destitute.
> Rescue the weak and the needy;
>   deliver them from the hand of the wicked."

A re-reading of Ross' description of the Chinese divine council above illustrates that it could be applied in its entirety to the divine council of Psalm 82. A supreme creator with inferior "gods" as faithful subordinate ministers carrying out his will in specific spheres or territories.

---

26 Ross, *The Original Religion of China,* 144-145.

William Boone, another missionary of the nineteenth century, made it even more clear that a prayer at the Border Sacrifice contained the divine council understanding of the Bible:

> There is a special point, however, in the prayer, to which I wish to call attention—the distinction made between Shang-Te, and all the *shin*, or, as I translate the word, *spirits*. They are His guards or attendants. Just as Jehovah came from Paran with holy myriads, (Deut 32:2)—as He revealed Himself on Sinai among thousands of angels, (Ps. 68:17) — so do the Chinese believe that when Shang-Te descends to receive their worship offered by the Emperor, He comes attended by ten thousands of spirits. He is not one of them, though He is "a spirit."[27]

And these *shen* or spirits were also called "bright ones," much like the "shining ones" of Yahweh's heavenly host.[28] Divine beings are often described as shining with brilliance and glory in both the Old Testament (Ex 34:29; Ezek 1:4–7, 27–28; Dan 10:6) as well as the New Testament (Matt 28:3; Luke 24:4).

What could account for this amazing similarity without precedent? Some researchers argue that the Chinese had migrated from Babel and were cut off from other nations, maintaining a less corrupt understanding of their Creator than the other Gentile nations that had devolved into idol worship.[29]

But the Zhou dynasty of 1100 B.C. changed all that. Shang Di became removed, distant with the declaration of Prince Wu, "Heaven is the universal Father, and Earth the universal Mother." It was a switch from an "intelligent, active, personal, moral and all-powerful Agent" to a materialistic dualism of "heaven and earth."[30]

Taoism, Confucism and Buddhism developed out of this change and by the third century B.C., Emperor Qin rejected the worship of Shang Di outright, and outlawed the ancient religion of the supreme Creator. The altars of heaven

---

[27] James Legge, DD, *The Notions of the Chinese Concerning God and Spirits With and Examination of the Defense of an Essay, The Proper Rendering of the Words Elohim and Theos into the Chinese Language by William J. Boone* (Hong Kong: The London Missionary Society, 1852), 24-25.

[28] Ross, *The Original Religion of China,* 172.

[29] Ross, *The Original Religion of China,* 144-145.

[30] Ross, *The Original Religion of China,* 63-64, 71.

were abandoned, as depicted in the novel, and he instituted sacrifices to the pantheon of lesser deities along with his idolatrous despotism.[31]

The Sovereign emperor was supposed to rule as vice regent to God, the highest authority on earth called "the Son of Heaven." He was to carry out the "Mandate of Heaven," that is, Shang Di's decrees of justice. But now, the emperor had become a god.[32]

The Dragon had bitten the heel of Shang Di in China.

At least until Messiah came to crush his head.

---

[31] http://allthechildrenoflight.wordpress.com/2013/02/03/the-creator-god-in-ancient-china-genesis-hidden-in-the-chinese-language/

James Legge, DD, *The Notions of the Chinese Concerning God and Spirits With and Examination of the Defense of an Essay, The Proper Rendering of the Words Elohim and Theos into the Chinese Language by William J. Boone* (Hong Kong: The London Missionary Society, 1852), 55.

Dr. Thong, *Faith Of Our Fathers,* Kindle Edition location 130 of 344.

[32] Ross, *The Original Religion of China,* 128.

Chapter 4: The Gospel in Chinese

Words as Pictures

Chinese is one of the oldest known languages dating back to at least 2700 B.C. Like other ancient languages, its written form was originally pictographic rather than alphabetic. That means the words were like little pictures of what was being written about. But unlike other languages, Chinese retains some of its graphic history even today.

Here is an example of modern Chinese words along with their ancient precursors that researcher Dr. Thong, Chan Kei has used to illustrate the graphic nature of the language. Notice how the modern version on the left still maintains an iconic element of their origin on the right.[1]

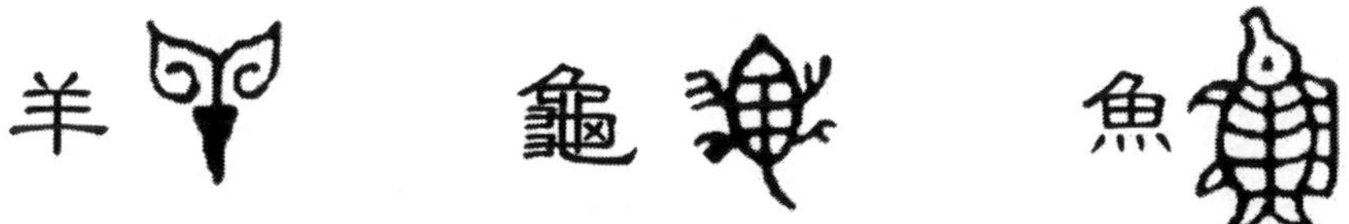

Sheep Turtle Fish

Though the language has evolved through the millennia, and has become more symbolic, Chinese characters still carry embedded within them the stories and meanings of their original pictures.

As Dr Thong explains, pictographs are combined to create ideographs or ideograms, which are still graphic, but a bit more abstract or conceptual. Thus, a picture of a mouth over a tree would mean "wooden mouth" which is a colloquialism that refers to someone who is slow-witted or struck speechless. A single tree is a tree. Two trees would denote a group such as a grove. And three trees in a pictograph would represent a large gathering of trees such as a forest.[2]

---

[1] Dr. Thong, *Faith Of Our Fathers,* Kindle Edition location 64 of 344.

[2] Dr. Thong, *Faith Of Our Fathers,* Kindle Edition location 66 of 344.

Dr. Thong then chronicles many examples of words and phrases that he argues are reflections of biblical influence on the Chinese language. That is, they show concepts that are unique to the biblical worldview that seem to indicate a common origin. I recommend buying his book to learn the fascinating depth of this spiritual connection between China and the Bible. The book is Faith of Our Fathers: Finding God in Ancient China.

Another book from which I drew writing examples of this exchange of biblical ideas was The Discovery of Genesis by C.H. Kang. In my novel, all my examples of explanation of Chinese ideograms are real, drawn from this book. I use some of the following examples that reflect the ancient stories of Genesis:

"Tempter"

Kang breaks out the various visual elements of the word for "tempter" to show the story from the Garden of Eden. I have reproduced my own image of his breakdown here:

Kang explains, "the devil is placed under the cover of protecting trees. The devil waited for Eve in the forbidden tree, which was located in the middle of the garden next to the tree of life—hence the two trees. Furthermore, he was under cover, being hidden in the tree and also camouflaged as a serpent."[3]

The Chinese word for boat tells the story of Noah's ark.

---

[3] C.H. Kang, *The Discovery of Genesis: how the Truths of Genesis Were Found Hidden in the Chinese Language* (St. Louis, MO: Concordia House, 1979), 4.

船

"Boat"

舟	+	八	+	口	=	船
vessel		eight		mouths		boat

Kang explains the ideogram for "boat": "There are three elements pictured: a vessel, eight, and mouth, meaning "people." The word for boat, then, tells the story of this first great ark which, in spite of the years of warning and pleading by Noah to his compatriots, had just eight passengers."[4]

The story of the Tower of Babel from the Bible also finds its way into the Chinese word for "tower."

塔

"Tower"

人	+	一	+	口	=	合	+	艹	=	荅	+	土	=	塔
mankind		one		mouth [speech]		united		grass		undertake		clay [brick]		tower

Kang explains the Babel story embedded in the word,

> On the left side of the figure, artistically accommodating itself to the slope of the tower is the radical dirt, clay, of which the bricks were made. They had boasted, "'Come, let us make bricks, and burn them thoroughly.' And they had brick for stone, and bitumen for mortar" (Genesis 11:3). Then they united, joined together in their rebellion against God. The Chinese placed upon the pinnacle of the tower the sign of Adam's curse , recognizing the folly of this venture.

---

[4] Kang, *The Discovery of Genesis*, 95.

> (It would be unlikely that weeds would grow on top of a brick tower!) One other aspect of the character might also have importance. They were originally all of one speech: [men]; [one]; [speech]. Adding the grass on the top, means to undertake. The Chinese themselves built no towers or pagodas until the Buddhist era. This character for tower must surely, therefore, refer to the Tower of Babel.[5]

Because of the technical nature of the linguistics involved, I will refrain from any more examples, lest I become guilty of plagiarism for copying too many large portions of Kang's text. I recommend getting the book to explore the issue more in depth: The Discovery of Genesis: how the Truths of Genesis Were Found Hidden in the Chinese Language by C.H. Kang.

Conclusion

I hope this booklet of research notes was enlightening for those who have read the novel *Qin: Dragon Emperor of China.* It is not exhaustive and is more a compendium of notes for the background of the novel than an attempt to make a sustained argument for the issues brought up in the text. If you want more, please check the footnotes for books and online articles that go into further detail.

If you have not read the novel *Qin* yet, you can get it here at Amazon (affiliate link) in ebook, paperback or audiobook.

•••••

If you liked this book, then please help me out by writing a positive review of it on Amazon here. That is one of the best ways to say thank you to me as an author. It really does help my sales and status. Thanks!
– Brian Godawa

[5] Kang, *The Discovery of Genesis,* 106.

More Books by Brian Godawa

See www.Godawa.com for more information on other books by Brian Godawa. Check out his novel series below:

Chronicles of the Nephilim

Chronicles of the Nephilim is a saga that charts the rise and fall of the Nephilim giants of Genesis 6 and their place in the evil plans of the fallen angelic Sons of God called, "The Watchers." The story starts in the days of Enoch and continues on through the Bible until the arrival of the Messiah, Jesus. The prelude to Chronicles of the Apocalypse. ChroniclesOfTheNephilim.com. (affiliate link)

Chronicles of the Apocalypse

Chronicles of the Apocalypse is an origin story of the most controversial book of the Bible: Revelation. An historical conspiracy thriller trilogy in first century Rome set against the backdrop of explosive spiritual warfare of Satan and his demonic Watchers. ChroniclesOfTheApocalypse.com. (affiliate link)

Chronicles of the Watchers

Chronicles of the Watchers is a series that charts the influence of spiritual principalities and powers over the course of human history. The kingdoms of man in service to the gods of the nations at war. Completely based on ancient historical and mythological research. ChroniclesOfTheWatchers.com. (affiliate link)

Great Offers By Brian Godawa

Get More Biblical Imagination

Sign up Online For The Godawa Chronicles

www.Godawa.com

Updates and Freebies
of the Books of Brian Godawa

Special Discounts,

Weird Bible Facts!

About the Author

Brian Godawa is the screenwriter for the award-winning feature film, *To End All Wars*, starring Kiefer Sutherland. It was awarded the Commander in Chief Medal of Service, Honor and Pride by the Veterans of Foreign Wars, won the first Heartland Film Festival by storm, and showcased the Cannes Film Festival Cinema for Peace.

He previously adapted to film the best-selling supernatural thriller novel *The Visitation* by author Frank Peretti for Ralph Winter (*X-Men, Wolverine*), and wrote and directed *Wall of Separation*, a PBS documentary, and *Lines That Divide*, a documentary on stem cell research.

Mr. Godawa's scripts have won multiple awards in respected screenplay competitions, and his articles on movies and philosophy have been published around the world. He has traveled around the United States teaching on movies, worldviews, and culture to colleges, churches and community groups.

His popular book *Hollywood Worldviews: Watching Films with Wisdom and Discernment* (InterVarsity Press) is used as a textbook in schools around the country. In the Top 10 of Biblical Fiction on Amazon, his first novel series, *Chronicles of the Nephilim*, is an imaginative retelling of Biblical stories of the Nephilim giants, the secret plan of the fallen Watchers, and the War of the Seed of the Serpent with the Seed of Eve. The sequel series, *Chronicles of the Apocalypse*, tells the story of the apostle John's book of Revelation, and *Chronicles of the Watchers* recounts true history through the Watcher paradigm.

Find out more about his other books, lecture tapes and DVDs for sale at his website, www.godawa.com.

Made in the USA
Middletown, DE
02 June 2024

55159778R00230